BOOTSTRAP *to* BILLIONS™

Proven Rules from Entrepreneurs who Built Great Companies from Scratch™

Dileep Rao, Ph.D.

Adjunct Professor

Carlson School of Management, University of Minnesota

Founder: uEntrepreneurs.com

To my parents
For guiding

To my wife
For advising

To my children
For inspiring

To the business giants profiled in the book
For sharing

To entrepreneurs everywhere
For dreaming

Table of Contents

Foreword

Some wise sage once said: "Executives can be undertakers, caretakers or risk takers." As I see it, undertakers bury the dead, caretakers bury the living and risk takers bury themselves.

By not adapting and exploiting opportunities as the world changes, caretakers think they are minimizing risks even as they fall behind competitors and send their corporations spiraling to their doom. As W. Edwards Deming said, "You don't have to change. Survival is not mandatory."

Risk takers bury themselves because the key to success is not taking risks but exploiting opportunities while minimizing risks. Venture capitalist Tom Perkins said that the "key to Kleiner Perkins's success was determining a venture's risk, then attempting to eliminate it."

From a total of more than 23 million businesses in the United States, only about 0.07 percent (15,100, according to 2002 statistics) have annual sales exceeding $100 million. This book profiles entrepreneurs who have achieved this singular feat (or reached at least $100 million in valuation) from scratch. They exploited opportunities, identified and satisfied market needs, out-executed the industry, out-managed, outsold and out-marketed their competitors, and have just done better in each area that counted.

How did they do this? Having financed and worked with hundreds of entrepreneurs, and based on these profiles, I have learned that there are some common principles to success. But each entrepreneur finds his or her own way based on the nature of the industry, the markets, the financial and economic conditions, and the strengths and weaknesses they discover they have as they face their own situation. This series highlights the accomplishments of a group of remarkable entrepreneurs who built great companies and created wealth, jobs, and economic prosperity.

Above all, this book is part of an ongoing quest to help future entrepreneurs learn from the highly successful, and to find their own way to reach their goals. A highly respected entrepreneur I knew called Joe Francis (who started the Cost Cutters hair salon chain) used to paraphrase Eleanor Roosevelt by saying that it is wiser (and cheaper) to learn from others' mistakes than your own. I hope the lessons I have distilled from the profiles reduces the cost of your success.

Good luck and may most of your dreams come true.

INTRODUCTION

Entrepreneurs are the cornerstone of a free enterprise system. Without them, large corporations or government-related enterprises would run society – potentially leading to ossification and decay.

But entrepreneurs face a daunting hurdle – the risk of failure. Faced with this risk, most finally accept jobs in large corporations or government. Fortunately, enough brave souls tackle this risk head-on and start ventures. Some fail, some succeed, and a few succeed brilliantly. This book is about entrepreneurs who achieved this last, brilliant level that many of us can only dream of, and about the lessons from their unique stories.

Finding the Most Successful Entrepreneurs

The goal of this book is to help those reading it to learn success from the outstandingly successful. The men and women profiled in this book came from a select group of Minnesota entrepreneurs who built $100 million+ businesses (sales and/or valuation) from scratch. I found 36 and interviewed 28. The many who did share their stories built great companies, including the world's largest medical-device company, the world's largest consumer-electronics retailer, the world's largest health-care management company, and many more giants in their field. They all have great lessons to teach.

When Financiers Are Hazardous to Your Wealth

Venture capitalists often think that there are only two categories of ventures – those who qualify for venture capital (VC) and small businesses. This book highlights a third category. While a few of the 28 entrepreneurs interviewed here did use VC, most of them started from scratch, developed unique capital-efficient business, financial, and financing strategies, built great teams and led their companies to dominance in their fields without venture capital.

Based on my decades as a financier, I had assumed that entrepreneurs needed VC to build big companies. This book shows that this assumption is not true. About 80 percent of them did not use VC, did not give up control and kept most of the wealth they created. One of the most important lessons they teach is that it is possible to create wealth without venture capital. And perhaps many of these entrepreneurs were able to keep the wealth they created because they did not have to share it with venture capitalists or with the new executive team they bring to the venture. *Sometimes, financiers can be hazardous to your wealth.*

The lessons from the profiles can be broadly categorized into four groups:

Business Strategies: As the world changes, entrepreneurs make new fortunes, or lose old ones, in existing or emerging industries. Even if the industries and technologies are new, the old rules nearly always still apply. You still have to satisfy customer needs better than competitors and do so at a price that will give you a reasonable profit and allow growth. The profiles show how these entrepreneurs used unique business strategies to find their opportunity, selected the right customer segment to give them a competitive advantage, and maintained their advantage until they dominated their fields.

Financial Strategies: Financial lessons include both financing the business and managing the finances of the business. In addition to developing unique business strategies to get a competitive edge, many of these entrepreneurs showed remarkable expertise in how they defined their financial metrics, managed their company to meet the financial goals they had set, and found the right financing for the business. *They trained themselves to understand the numbers affecting their business.* Many of them knew that they would not qualify for venture capital - even if they wanted it. And most did not want it, because they would have to give up control. By finding unique combinations of financial and financing strategies, these entrepreneurs kept control of the business and kept most of the wealth they created.

Leadership: Creating and growing a $100 million business requires exemplary performance from a strong, focused team. The entrepreneurs needed to find the right people to help them lead their venture. This task can be daunting even with resources. Without money to pay market rates, it takes on whole new dimensions. The entrepreneurs did find these team members, however, and coalesced with them into excellent teams that dominated their market segment.

Personal Development: Rather than following the VC model of changing leaders at stages, these entrepreneurs had to grow with their companies. This meant that the entrepreneurs had to improve their management and leadership skills as the business grew, and the demands on their skills changed. But they rose to the challenge, developed new skills, including delegation, and never stopped learning. *The humility to acknowledge the need for personal learning and growth, and the dedication to seek this knowledge, are the two factors that stand out*.

I hope you get as much from reading these profiles as I have from writing them.

Horst Rechelbacher
Aveda

MINNEAPOLIS, MINN

Find your bliss to build a $300 million aesthetics business

Summary: If you had not demonstrated academic gifts by the age of 12, teachers in the Austrian school system in the 1950s asked you to become an apprentice and learn a trade. Horst Rechelbacher, who admits to being an indifferent student, had an eye for art, drawing, painting, and a passion for aesthetics, and he became an apprentice hair stylist at a salon across the narrow street from his house. He also worked at the adjacent deli after school before he started work in the evenings in the hair salon. On weekends he accompanied his herbalist mother to the mountains to pick herbs. Pursuing his passion for beauty and customer service, combined with his fear of losing, Horst became a champion hair stylist in Europe by the age of 14 and was asked to style hair for the leading cosmetics companies and magazines in Europe.

He came to the United States for a magazine photo shoot and ended up in a car crash and a hospital in the Midwest. To pay his bills, he started working as a hair stylist in a Minneapolis salon. He was so successful as a stylist that a banker-customer encouraged him to take over a bankrupt shop with a $4,000 loan, and he opened his first salon. To create the leading hair-styling salon in the city, he started training his hairdressers to replicate his skills at hair dressing. When he found that other salons were stealing his employees, he decided to start a school to train hair stylists and make a profit from training. Being dissatisfied with the products he was using, he developed a line of products based on his herbal skills and started selling those in the school. In the process, he developed a new way of selling his products and services to quality-conscious consumers. By the time he sold Aveda to Estee Lauder for $300 million, he had revolutionized his industry. This is how he did it.

Before the Startup

1. **The early years**. Horst's mother was an herbalist who made and sold

herbal remedies from a store. Horst, being the youngest in the family, accompanied her on these weekend trips to the mountains to collect herbs. During these visits, his mother taught him about various herbs and their uses, and the benefits they offered to his mother's customers. He also learned about how to help people and make them feel better using the various herbs. His mother's highest priority was to keep her customers happy. She sold only those treatments that were good for her customers and improved their health. Horst learned at an early age that *when customers are happy, they come back and they tell their friends*. With increased demand, he could charge more and increase profits. He applied these same customer-service principles to hair styling. He also applied his expertise and belief in natural remedies to reduce the number of chemicals in his products.

Lesson: From his mother, Horst learned that *products have to perform at or better than expectations*. That results in satisfied and happy customers. Unhappy customers do not return, and they often spread a negative message about the business.

2. **The apprentice**. Horst did not have much interest in academic learning. When his teachers asked him to become an apprentice, he decided to pursue his passion for hair styling because he found that hair styling combined all his interests – in art, drawing, painting and presentation — to which he was instinctively drawn. The fact that he lived across the street from a hair stylist did not hurt. From the narrow Austrian streets, he could easily look into the windows of the hair salon and found that he enjoyed watching stylists create new styles. He looked at hair styling and makeup as sculpture and painting on a live person (as opposed to canvas) to create art. He jumped wholeheartedly into learning about hair styling. He had already started cutting hair at the age of 10, and it came naturally to him. In Austria in the post-war years, times were tough and everyone had to work. He continuously watched his supervisor to improve his techniques. According to Horst, being an apprentice was like being a slave – the first to come and the last to leave, and the wages were pitiful. To make more money, he started cutting hair on the side on Sundays. The Austrian apprentice system involved three years of apprenticeship, during which a student worked under the teacher and went to school one day per week to learn about managing a small business, including studying such subjects as marketing, accounting, and finance. After graduating, apprentices spent three years in the work force and then had to take a master's exam before being able to open a business.

Lesson: While the American system encourages everyone to attend college, it may not always be the best system for some who are motivated differently. Whatever path you take, learn ALL aspects of the business so you have a well-rounded background.

3. **The deli**. Horst had some free time between his classes and the hair-styling job. He filled it by working at the deli that was adjacent to the salon. Horst's job was

to fill the showcase with new items in the cooler and to make the showcase look attractive. Horst found that *sales increased when the showcase presentation was more attractive.* This taught him the importance of presentation in the retail business and taught him skills that would later help him when he decided to set up his own retail store.

Lesson: *Understand how and why people buy.* From each of his jobs, Horst learned skills that were complementary and that would make him a well-rounded entrepreneur. When you find your passion, working long hours is a pleasure.

4. **The competitor.** In addition to fear of deprivation, another key motivator for Horst was recognition. Since he seemed to have a natural flair for hair styling, he started entering contests. He compares these beauty contests to the Olympics. To win, one had to excel in many different aspects such as hair styling for the day, evening, fantasy, sophisticated events, and so on. *He would study the champions and learn to imitate their skills and techniques by continuous practice and working long hours. Then he would look at ways to improve on their techniques* and styles by adding his originality and creativity. While friends went to the beach in the summer, Horst was studying hair styling. He worked with a master who taught him the classic way of hair styling in a special school on Mondays and Thursdays. The master would evaluate Horst's work and technique, and Horst looked forward to the feedback and the personal growth.

Lesson: ***Always study winners.*** Learn from the best, but find ways to improve. Practice, practice, practice - there is no substitute for hard work. Seek out the best and learn from them. Great teachers like to teach talented, dedicated students. So seek them out. Look at criticisms as ways to improve yourself. There is plenty of time to feel sorry for yourself after you become successful and retire and start counting waves in the Bahamas or Hawaii or Tahiti or ....

5. **Make customers happy.** Use the senses. Horst found that he liked to make people happy, which is perhaps the best definition of customer service. In her herbal business, his mother nurtured people to good health and tried to make them happy, and Horst absorbed this instinctively. ***Horst learned that he did excellent work when he did not do the styles for himself but for the customers.*** He found that they were the ultimate teachers and that *people could tell you what they liked after they saw it, felt it, touched it, heard it, or smelled it* (using the senses for selling). If he did something for himself without his customers' approval, his problems and complaints increased. So he would show them photos and experiment with various styles, hair lengths, colors, and so on that he was thinking of and obtained their feedback to find out what they liked, and did not like, before actually cutting and styling their hair. Within two years, at the age of 14, he was winning hair-styling competitions in Austria and Europe, and he expanded his repertoire on the weekends to do paid seminars as well.

Lesson: *Get feedback. Innovation is a continuous feedback loop.* Improve your strengths and learn to enhance your weaknesses. Find ways to get your customers to tell you what they like. You start to excel, and develop happier customers, when you implement what you learned from them.

6. "Secret" formula to higher prices. Although Austria at that time was a hierarchical, class-oriented society with a bureaucratic attitude, Horst found that bureaucrats could not regulate customer demand. As his skills and customer service improved, his list of clients mushroomed. He loved to have people waiting to have him style their hair. The more customers he had, the happier he was, and the higher the price he charged. Horst learned early that high customer demand was the best way to increase prices, margins, and profits. According to Horst, there are two ways to price:

a. **Me-too**: This is when you compete in the mid-class or mass class. According to Horst, the me-too, mid-class is "always a weird place to be," and in the salon business, these are the salons with the least amount of business and the lowest profitability. The mass class is selling a lot for low prices, which requires low costs and is more suitable to the large corporations at the bottom of the pyramid.
b. **How-to**: This is when you create something that the customer "has not seen." According to Horst, ***create newness by "reinventing the past in the moment***." This means that you *understand and improve upon the past to find what the market wants today* and then give your products or services value by talking about it (effective public relations, where Horst has been a master). This will help you reach the top of the pyramid, where you are likely to be more profitable due to higher customer satisfaction.

Lesson: New ventures started by entrepreneurs without an inheritance have a tougher road if they have no competitive advantage. Find, develop, and nurture yours.

7. The fruits of winning competitions. Horst liked to win because he was then in high demand by large beauty-product companies who hired him to demonstrate and sell their products, and by magazine editors who wanted to show photos of his latest styles. When Horst started winning competitions, he became recognized for his skills and talent and was invited by beauty-industry corporations and magazine editors to develop styles for movies and magazines in Europe and the United States, and he started to become famous for his work. He did not get arrogant with his fame but more fearful that he may lose it. According to Horst, he has always been driven by fear due to growing up during the war and post-war years, and this time it was fear that he would lose his fame. His new work and increased recognition provided access and exposure to some of the top photographers in Europe and the United States. He used his increased fame, networks, and access to learn new skills such as photography. He observed, learned and imitated the techniques of the great fashion and hair photographers of the day, and started to make innovations of his own. This helped him to become an accomplished photographer. He started to develop new hair creations and to take his own photographs, which he used to further promote his skills and enhance his reputation.

Lesson: Love what you do. Always learn new skills and never rest on your laurels. Strive to be as good as the best, and then become better. Winning at age 14 was a great confidence booster for Horst.

From Startup to Profits

8. **The first salon**. As previously noted, Horst was in an auto accident in the Midwest on one of his trips to the United States. To repay his hospital bills, he got a job in a salon in downtown Minneapolis. He became instantly successful with his attention to innovation and creativity, and especially to customer happiness. His initial clients were rich Jewish women in Minneapolis. The Jewish community in Minneapolis was a close-knit group, and they talked to each other. Soon, with this word-of-mouth marketing, Horst had all the clients he needed and more. After three months, in a salon of nine hairdressers, he had two assistants and was earning more money than the others. He had an average of 35 clients per day while the others had six to seven. One of his clients was a banker. She knew of another hair salon that had failed and its equipment was available for a reasonable price. She was also willing to lend Horst $4,000 to buy the equipment and start his salon. All the other hairdressers at the initial salon wanted to come with Horst, since he was teaching them how to style hair. With the $4,000 loan, Horst bought the equipment and started his salon. Within three months, his was the busiest salon in Minneapolis. Even though his heart was in the glamorous cities of San Francisco and New York, his destiny was in Minneapolis.

Lesson: You never know when the fruits of your preparation start to appear. But when they do show up, make sure you start to harvest them. *Word-of-mouth (also called viral marketing by the mavens who develop hip buzzwords for previously simple concepts) is a great marketing tool, but it only seems to work for exceptional people, products, and services.*

9. **Second salon**. As his reputation and client list grew, Horst opened a second salon in St. Paul. Life became chaotic between two salons. He did not have good systems, and the trained hairdressers at the Minneapolis salon wanted a higher share of their revenues – 65 percent, compared to the 50 percent that Horst was paying them. They all ganged up on him and threatened to quit. Based on his accountant's advice, Horst decided to sell the salon to them to reduce his headaches and focused instead on his St. Paul salon. Simultaneously, other hair-dressing salons in the area started to steal his trained hairdressers. The other salon operators did not have the skills to train hairdressers, and they found that Horst's salon was a great training ground. Horst did the natural thing: He opened a training school.

Lesson: Find the right strategy that builds on your competitive advantage. Rather than training hair stylists for his competitors, Horst made money from the training and laid for the foundation for an industry giant.

10. Training school and finding the first students. To start his training school, Horst needed money. With the help of an investor who was also his client, Horst decided to open his training school at a building that looked like a "castle" near downtown Minneapolis. Since the castle already had an office next door that had been operated by a dentist, it had the water connections Horst needed. Horst added mirrors, upgraded the facilities and built a spa. After the renovation, Horst sent a letter to all the salon operators in a five-state area, and especially in the Twin Cities, telling them that they had benefitted significantly by hiring his trained hairdressers. Now he was going to help them even more by opening his school, and he was committed to training excellent hair stylists for their salons. He wanted them to send him referrals. His initial break-even level was 35. He got 45 students in his first class.

Lesson: Find the unmet need and satisfy it. Horst decided that there was a large unmet need among hairdressers and hair salons for training – especially due to his own experience in losing the trained hair stylists. He decided to fill this need and marketed through the same intermediaries that were previously his competitors but now were in the best position to send him referrals. He did not have to spend money on expensive advertising and promotion to get students.

11. School takes off. During the first six weeks of the school, the students were not permitted to work on customers. This is when Horst gave them basic training. In addition, similar to what he learned in his apprenticeship in Austria, Horst taught them how to build their business and to manage it. To open a successful salon, they needed hairdressing skills and practice in sound business methods. He wanted them to succeed as hair stylists since he wanted happy customers. It would also enhance his own reputation to have successful stylists around the region and the country who would promote him and his school. He taught them not just how to make their clients look great, but how to become attractive themselves. He instructed in basic grooming techniques and showed students how they could use their skills, and his products and handouts to help their customers and build a successful practice. After six weeks when the students could work on customers, Horst was instantly booked because he had promoted his school to his clients, their network, and to the press. This was the start of his next growth phase.

Lesson: Opening a new business is a difficult task. Make sure that you turn your constraints into advantages as Horst did when he promoted the school before it was ready to open, thus creating demand for the students' services. Make sure you have thought of all the requirements for success.

12. Become a PR whiz. Horst has always had a talent for getting publicity for his businesses and himself, especially in the press. He knew that the press is always seeking news about innovations that are useful to their readers. He was able to generate a lot of "buzz" for his spa, hair-training school, and products in the local and national press. Once when he developed a line of products based on some plants from the Amazon, he received lots of favorable publicity by taking a trip to the Amazon. Horst's rule was to "pre-tell" the press, then tell them with a splashy event, and then follow-up with materials and photos.

> **Lesson**: Buzz never hurts. Build relations with the press. Understand your target market and know how to reach them, whether it is in print, TV, e-marketing, etc. Also, be excellent at what you do so there is a story to tell.

13. Make hair stylists into profitable entrepreneurs. As part of his apprenticeship training in Austria, Horst had to learn how to manage a small business. Obviously, Horst learned this better than most. To make sure that his students were successful and happy with their relationship with him, Horst not only trained them in hair design but he also offered business seminars to teach them how to manage their own operations. He focused on customer happiness as a requirement for profits.

> **Lesson**: In the beauty business, consumers usually bought based on the recommendations of the hair stylists. Hair stylists would recommend Horst's products if they were happy with him and his line, and if they were successful. It was in Horst's best interests to make sure they succeeded. Also, that is how he was taught, so he was passing on this knowledge and philosophy to the next generation.

14. Natural products. Since hair salons also sold products to their clients, Horst wanted to include products that fit with his salon. However, he found that none of the other products satisfied his needs due to the large proportion of synthesized chemicals they contained. He wanted to minimize the use of these chemicals in the products he carried. Based on his childhood background of picking herbs with his mother, Horst decided to develop his own line of products based on herbs and other natural ingredients. His mother came over from Austria to help him develop his products. Horst had also done product testing for chemists, and he knew the formulas of the various products he had tested. He used his knowledge of competing products to develop his own line. His first line of hair shampoos looked like brown goop. When Horst put it on a towel and showed it to the first client, she did not like it since it was brown and her hair was blonde. Horst decided to customize his line of shampoos in colors specially designed for blondes, brunettes, redheads, and so on. According to Horst, he was the first person to sell color-specific shampoos, and he used the merchandising skills he had learned when he worked at the bakery in Austria to merchandise his products. He learned how to design the bottles and display the merchandise in the store to encourage sales. His accountant did not like his expansion to the product line due to the investment in inventory and the lower return on investment. Horst discarded his advice since he saw the product line as a natural expansion that allowed him to expand his brand around the country. He called the first line "Horst." It was an instant success. Horst had a local beauty-products company make his products to avoid the investment needed.

Lesson: Don't just blindly copy your competitors or the industry or listen to your accountants all the time. Often they don't understand what you want to accomplish, and they don't know what you are able to achieve. They are trained to evaluate historical numbers and may not be able to forecast the potential value of what you can achieve. *Understand your mission and develop your strategy consistent with the mission.* Horst wanted to be unique and help his customers look great and feel great. He did not think too many chemicals was the answer. So he developed his own differentiated line and promoted it. This helped him increase his revenues and margins, and helped with his mission and positioning. He kept his investment in fixed assets to a minimum by contracting with a manufacturer who supplied him with the products he needed.

15. Competitive response. His competitors did not copy him immediately because they were waiting to see how his line performed before investing in their own product lines. Horst had the market to himself for a few years. In his third year, one of his advisers contacted a major beauty products company that offered Horst $10 million for his company. Horst was ecstatic. He went to see his spiritual adviser and told him about it. The adviser's response was, "That is great and I am proud of you, but what are you going to do now, die?" Horst accepted this as a lesson that his mission was not done because he had not fulfilled its promise. He rejected the offer. His business adviser was angry, since he lost a potential commission.

Lesson: Understand your mission and your passion. Horst realized that the potential was huge and that the timing was not right, and he did not want to sell out for a low price. His confidence was ultimately rewarded.

16. Fly with the eagles. To be among the leaders of American hair styling, Horst commuted to New York on weekends to do hair shows and to freelance for photo shoots. Keeping himself in front of key fashion leaders helped him to remain at the top of his industry, and continued to build his reputation, especially among his peers, industry leaders, and magazine editors. Horst had become a good photographer by observing, assisting, imitating, and improving upon the techniques of the leading photography masters of his day. He took photos of his creations and sent them to magazine editors and journalists to build his reputation. Horst continuously added to his impressive résumé by developing skills in new areas. After building his skills in photography, he studied makeup, which he terms "portraits on real people." Horst always thought he was a good aesthete, but he wanted to become the total aesthete with leading-edge skills and tastes in all areas related to hair and beauty.

Lesson: *To fly with the eagles, never stop growing.* Become skilled in all aspects related to your work.

17. Product expansion. As his school and his initial line of shampoo took off, Horst decided to add a line of aromatics made from essential oils from plants, roots, flowers, and the like. Many of the active components came from India, where Horst's spiritual adviser lived. Horst had visited India frequently to see him, and to get a degree in Ayurvedic medicine, which is a traditional Hindu system of medicine. He developed product lines from bitter almonds, jojoba oils (used by Native Americans) and the 175 oils in the Ayurvedic pharmacopeia. To encapsulate the name of the new line of beauty products, Horst wanted a name that reflected on the Indian heritage of his line, and he also found that "Horst" was not a strong brand name, since other hair stylists with whom he competed nationally did not want to sell a line that promoted his name. He renamed the expanded line to "Aveda" as an adaption of Ayurveda. This line made him immensely successful.

Lesson: Horst was naturally inclined toward natural products based on his mother's profession. He then added to his knowledge from some of the leading experts in the world to develop his line and promoted it with his natural flair. Learn from the best to be the best.

18. First store in Manhattan. Now that he had a full line of products that could fill a store, Horst wanted his first store to be in Manhattan, because that was the best market in the world, and also because he wanted to compete with the best. Horst had a competent manager who led the Minneapolis operation, which allowed him to focus on the new store. Horst's first store in New York was on Madison Avenue, across the street from his key competitor, the Body Shop. His store was small enough (2,400 square feet) that he was not scared of the rent, and if it didn't succeed, its failure would not damage the rest of the business. When the store opened, Horst was there every day to make sure that customers were happy. The store was such a success that sales reached $4,000 per square foot in the first year, which was much higher than expectations. To capitalize on the success, he opened a second store in Soho, which was such an immediate success that people had to take a number to get in the store when it first opened. He had a product showroom on the main floor and hair stylists on another floor. His first year's sales from the Soho store were $4 million, with 70 percent from his product line. His cash flow was so strong that he could grow at his desired pace without external financing.

Lesson: *To compete with the best, get into the same arena.* Don't be afraid of the competition, especially when you know you are ready. But don't take unneeded risks. Horst knew that the small store would not destroy his business if it failed.

From Profits to the Moon

19. Less is more. Build an exclusive distribution system. When Horst started selling beauty products on a national level, he found that distributors were selling many competing products and they did not adequately point out the uniqueness of

Horst's products. As Horst puts it, "I did not want to be #36, the last one they sold." He took his best sales people from his own organization and helped them become his exclusive distributors so he could control the entire sales and distribution function to ensure that they targeted the right markets and followed the right strategies and practices. In essence, he started a new kind of distribution system to sell to the top of the pyramid. Horst believed that "less is more," i.e., he did not want to be all things to all people. He wanted to focus on the high-end customers who truly valued him and were willing to pay more, and keep them totally happy. He increased his share in his target salons from 5 percent of retail sales to 30 percent of retail sales through product design, training, and offering services designed specially to help them improve their business. Horst did not worry about growth. He worried about the customer experience and made sure that his exclusive distributors worried about the same thing. They became very successful and made him even more so. According to Horst, he was the only person in the salon industry who had a training center and a mass-distribution infrastructure (exclusive sales and distribution channels he controlled).

Lesson: ***Don't settle for being #36***. Design your sales and distribution system to reach your goals, and keep it consistent with your products, services, and philosophy. Help your associates fly higher and achieve their own goals. They can be your best ambassadors.

20. Innovate everywhere. Allow your allies to grow. Since he had developed a channel of exclusive distributors, he was able to help them grow, while helping his own growth, by giving them an opportunity to open beauty schools and stores, which they wanted to do, especially after the success of his own school and stores. Horst learned this strategy from observing a vertically integrated Ayurvedic business in India that had its own channel of retail stores, in effect giving it a monopoly over the distribution. Having seen the success of Horst's own stores in Manhattan, his distributors were clamoring to get in on the action. Horst trained them to get into retail and asked them to open stores in locations with the best visibility to his target market in each major metro area. By the time he sold the business to Estee Lauder, Horst had developed 15 beauty schools and about 250 stores. He only owned two of the schools himself (in Minneapolis and New York) and three of the stores.

Lesson: Design the sales and distribution strategy that best fits your business. Horst not only learned product development in India but also observed how businesses were organized. He copied the strategies that fit his vision and made them work.

21. Copy from the best. The stores themselves were designed very attractively to be his "billboards." He did not believe in regular billboards, since he wanted to appeal to all his customers' senses – to touch, feel, smell and see his products. Horst learned this strategy from Indian sari and carpet merchants who would strongly encourage their customers to touch and feel the fabrics. With more senses at work, the customers were hooked. Similarly, by getting customers inside the store, Horst hooked them with the senses. According to Horst, he was a pioneer in integrating product development, manufacturing, warehousing, distribution, and retail in the beauty industry.

Lesson: The sincerest flattery is imitation. Horst was always observing and picking the best strategies that fit his business vision and strategy. Since he believed in using all the senses to sell, the store as billboard made more sense to him. Find your unique high-return, market-appropriate strategy rather than blindly listening to ad agencies or marketing gurus.

22. Track the numbers and the pulse. Horst liked to know how his operations were doing, so he developed a system of reports that allowed him to monitor each operation. He monitored the sales numbers each day and the income statements each week. He hired and trained his managers to look at the numbers as a way to determine how the business was doing. Horst is dyslexic, so he had to "feel and live" the numbers. The impact did not come to him immediately, but as he thought about it, he would realize which businesses were strong and which were weakening. He calls this *"self-observation" which is an observation of "you and what you are interconnected with."* Each evening after meditation, he would look at himself as a performer, and study causes and effects. *If a business was starting to show problems, he would go there and work with the managers and employees to show them how he wanted them to do it correctly until the operation improved and was better than before.* Horst looks at each crisis as an opportunity, not just to fix the operation but to recalibrate it with customers and their needs, and to stay the leader.

Lesson: The business is an organization and an organism made up of people working with each other and with customers. Track the frequency of the business (whether it is in touch with the market) by examining the numbers and interpreting them to understand how the business is doing and identify strengths and weaknesses before they cause major problems.

23. Build a team. Horst knew that in the beauty industry, attractive people sell more. So he looked for attractive persons, but he also observed how they interacted with others, and how secure they were. He also encouraged them to do a self-introspection to make them more realistic and grounded and to adjust to the "frequency" of the business, i.e., the customers and their "happiness." He and the team set the goals together, and he wanted the team to "be in front of the goals." He monitored key numbers every day or every week as warranted to make sure that the team and the individuals were performing toward the goals.

Lesson: Each business needs a team that works well together to achieve the goals of the business. Understand what the business needs to succeed. In the beauty business, beautiful people sell more. What type of team do your customers want to see? Find them, train them, and lead them. But monitor them to catch small problems before they become big.

Prologue: Aveda and Intelligent Nutrients

24. Horst's next venture. With his passion in natural products, Horst's new venture sells organic aromatics, foods, beauty products, and the like. Horst formed a partnership with a major operator of beauty salons who provided the money and the management, while Horst developed the product line. The partnership has not lived up to Horst's expectations because, he says, they are not going where the "ducks are grazing." According to Horst, he may have to accept his "karma" and return to run this company.

Lesson: Partnerships do not always live up to everyone's expectations. Form them with care and take action when you can. And understand your partners' real strengths and weaknesses.

Rules for Entrepreneurs from Horst of Aveda

- **Fear can be a great self-motivator if you channel it well.** Due to Horst's background of growing up during and after the Second World War, fear of losing what he had was always a big factor in his life. He has found excellent ways of channeling this fear to achieve great successes.
- **Break even within three years**. According to Horst, in the first year, develop and perfect your products. In the second year, learn and perfect your sales and distribution. In the third year, sell, ship, and make money. However, if you can condense this time frame, you could break even faster and lose less money.
- **Try to be authentic with your practice**. Do what is right and be the best. Success will come.
- **Know your numbers**. Track the business every day. If the numbers are not there, somebody is "out to lunch." Raise the flag.
- **A business is like a body and is governed by its own frequency.** *Make sure it is in tune with the market.*
- **Price high when you start** (actually Horst did this all the time and not just at the start). There are two ways to earn shelf space – you can earn it or you can buy it. When you don't have the money to buy it, you need to earn it.
- **Others may not be as talented**. Not everyone is talented. That is why you need to evaluate people before giving them more responsibility.
- **Public relations is critical.** When dealing with consumer markets, public relations is key. It offers credibility and exposure at low cost. However, *journalists only cover you if you are unique and at the leading edge of the industry since journalists love winners*. Learn to get there.

Richard Schulze
Best Buy Co. Inc.

MINNEAPOLIS, MINN

Building the World's Largest Consumer Electronics Retailer

Summary: At the age of 11, Dick Schulze started delivering newspapers in St. Paul, Minn. Using tips from his newspaper route, he bought the first car any sophomore student had at his high school and paid for his own insurance, while paying his dad a small amount as his share of the expenses. His dad was teaching him accountability (and, as a father, maybe trying to get a teenager to postpone the start of his driving). After graduating from high school, he joined the Air National Guard. After his full-time training, Schulze became a sales representative for consumer-electronics companies, including Sony, Sherwood and others. As a representative for these companies, Schulze helped retailers to market their products and learned first-hand how to sell consumer electronics – on someone else's dime. After five years, he realized that a manufacturer could replace these representatives at any time. To control his own destiny, he decided to start his own consumer-electronics store. He borrowed against his house and opened his first store next to some college campuses in St. Paul. From that one store, Dick Schulze created a juggernaut that is today's Best Buy, with about 1,000 stores throughout the world. His initial "aspirational" goal was $1 billion in sales. With the right retail model (the third model in Best Buy's evolution), Best Buy blew past this goal and kept on growing. Current annual revenues exceed $43 billion, with a market value of nearly $12 billion as of Dec. 31, 2008. In the process of becoming the world's largest consumer-electronics company, Best Buy eliminated nearly 5,000 of its competitors, including many global household names. This is how he did it.

Preparing for Success

1. **The paper route**. Schulze started his business career as a youth with a newspaper route serving 126 houses in a 3.5-block area of St. Paul, Minn., and delivering 126 papers in the morning and evening. In the course of four years, he

developed relationships with his customers, learned to be accountable, and realized what it means to offer good service—good service meant higher tips—and to be accountable. When he was 15, Schulze decided to raise enough income from his paper route to be able to buy a car. To earn higher tips during Christmas, he decided to place the papers in the front door (you will appreciate how important this is to customers when the temperature in St. Paul dips below 20 to 30 degrees below zero). The strategy worked. He got $300 in tips (big money for a 15-year-old, especially in the early 1950s) and Schulze became the proud owner of a 1950 Pontiac. He was the first in his class to get a car. He got his driver's license and paid for his own insurance. And in addition to paying for his auto expenses, his dad made him pay $20 per month as his share of the household expenses. Schulze's dad believed in discipline and accountability, and he wanted to be sure that Schulze was a good role model for his siblings.

Lesson: Discipline, accountability, goals, self-reliance, and actions to reach your goal never go out of fashion if you want to accomplish great things. *Set reasonable growth goals (i.e., the next step), plan how to get there and act.*

2. **Lessons from high school years**. Schulze graduated with a unique public high school class in terms of accomplishments. Although he is the superstar of his class, one of his classmates rose to the position of CEO of a Fortune 1000 corporation, and another started and built a venture with sales in the hundreds of millions, becoming a household name in the food industry. Schulze credits these successes to his teachers and their commitment to each student. At the end of each class they summarized the lessons and evaluated how much each student understood. If the teachers thought that any student did not "get it," they would know it and help them. This meant more work for them after school. He incorporated these lessons into Best Buy. The new Best Buy headquarters building has more meeting rooms than offices so that teams can meet to address common issues together. Each meeting room has an electronic whiteboard to note ideas generated by the discussions. The facilitator has to summarize outcomes based on the discussion (just like his teachers concluding the lesson), and list the next steps to make sure that the meetings are productive.

Lesson: Schulze learned the importance of helping employees be productive. So he *insisted that each meeting be productive and end with concrete outcomes, goals, and plans.* Don't meet just to meet.

3. **Air National Guard to inclusive management**. When Schulze graduated from high school, he was eligible for the draft and the Vietnam war. So he joined the Minnesota Air National Guard, expecting three months of basic training, and he looked at it as a reinforcement of the discipline, accountability, and responsibility that his dad had instilled in him. But the three months of basic training extended to six and Schulze never made it to the University (where he had been admitted) since the term had already started. He found basic training easy due to the lessons

from his childhood, but it was not as easy for most of the others. He also developed an appreciation for his teammates' contributions to their joint assignments, and started to appreciate the value of teamwork. He noted that teams composed of individuals who were affected by the team's decision arrived at better solutions and ended up with enhanced results than if the leaders had made solitary decisions. So at Best Buy, he incorporated the use of involving people from all affected areas to make joint decisions to get better input, to take advantage of opportunities, and to prevent avoidable problems. As an example, if something needs changing on the store's floor, those affected, including merchandisers, sales, advertising, and so on, meet to make sure all perspectives are heard. Those affected have the opportunity to offer immediate feedback.

Lesson: Schulze learned that he could improve decisions by adding people from different backgrounds, especially if the decision affected them. *Adding people with different backgrounds can improve the quality of the decision and improve the probability of finding a "richer way to solve problems" especially if they are affected by the decisions. Think upfront together to reduce mistakes later.*

4. Sound of sound vs. the business of sound. Since his dad was a sales rep in the industrial side of the electronics industry, Schulze decided to get into the same business but on the consumer side. Getting more involved with his dad in the electronics business fascinated the young Schulze and he got hooked. He was representing leading consumer electronics companies such as Sony at the dawn of the consumer-electronics age. Schulze found that he was fascinated by the constant stream of new products that enhanced the consumer experience. As a sales rep, Schulze worked with retailers in the Twin Cities and learned the nuts and bolts of the consumer-electronics retail business. He learned what it takes to succeed in retail, including how various offers and pricing affect consumers, how to train and compensate the sales personnel, how to merchandise and set up the floor displays, and how competitors priced their products. This experience as a sales rep taught him more about how and why the retailers' business succeeded than the retailers learned themselves. He was more excited when his retailer-customers did well than when he got his own commission check. In essence, he learned that he thoroughly enjoyed the consumer-electronics business and how to succeed in it without risking his own money. He also learned that many of the retailers were electronic hobbyists but not sophisticated retailers. After five years as a rep, he lost some of his product lines, and he realized that manufacturers could fire him even if he met all expectations. He wanted to control his own destiny and, concluding that he needed to stop being a rep, he went into retail. He ended up competing with some of his old customers. They did not like it.

Lesson: *You are more likely to grow and succeed if you control your own destiny and if you know more about your business and how to succeed in your industry than your competitors do.* Schulze still listens to his sales reps for new ideas since they are in touch with others in the industry. But he makes sure that he knows more about the business than they do. Ask yourself why you are really in business. If you are not in it to excel at the business side and to dominate, you may not belong. What did Schulze learn? He learned how to help the customer put together the best package easily and effectively, to offer more features and to allow consumers to evaluate components with a simple, easily understood floor demonstration so that they could spend less money getting the right sound for them. *Make it simple for customers to understand what they need to know to buy. The other retailers loved the sound of sound. Schulze loved the business of sound.*

5. **Controlling your own destiny**. By the time Schulze decided to take more control of his business life, he was in an enviable position. He knew his competitors, their business advantages and disadvantages, personal strengths and weaknesses, types of customer segments they served, advertising, marketing and pricing strategies, and other details. Obviously, one does not ask a sales representative to sign a non-compete agreement, so Schulze had a significant advantage over the typical entrepreneur. He knew that one of his competitors served professionals, others served the commercial market, and another was in failing health. Only one retailer served the college-student market, and he was not in good financial condition. Since he knew that young male college students and consumers were an attractive market and were not being adequately served, he decided to target them. So he decided to open his first store, which was 2,000 square feet in size, near a number of colleges in St. Paul. To start his first store, Schulze borrowed $9,000 by mortgaging his house. He showed a profit from the first year. Due to his strong retailing skills and experience, and knowledge of this market, Schulze never had a loss year until the mid-late 1970s when legislation changed the market. From this beginning his Sound of Music stores took off till he dominated the Upper Midwest market.

Lesson: Learn all aspects of the business, especially how to better satisfy the customer and make money. Everything starts with customers, and Schulze learned how to segment them, understand their needs and how to sell to them, and how to run a profitable business. Most important, he knew his competition and how to win against them.

6. **Initial spurt**. Schulze started his first Sound of Music store in August of 1966. By December he bought two more stores and converted them to Sound of Music stores. One of the stores was owned by the retailer who was in failing health and the other by the one in poor financial condition. He financed both stores using vendor financing. He even used this type of financing to pay off bank debt on one of the stores he purchased. For both purchases, he paid $1 plus assuming the existing debt. Why did he buy these stores? The price was right and he wanted to have a store near the University of Minnesota's main campus in Minneapolis as the base to build the Sound of Music chain. At this stage, his business plan was more "aspirational" than researched. He started with the level of profit he wanted and determined how

much he had to sell and how big a store he needed. *He monitored his performance regularly to make sure that he reached his goals.* He grew with this business model to eight company-owned stores and three franchisees.

> **Lesson**: Know your market and be ready to take advantage of opportunities when they present themselves, especially if they are consistent with your strategy. You don't always "control the agenda," but be ready to seize opportunities.

7. **Franchise vs. Corporate**. As Sound of Music grew, Schulze added company stores and three franchisees. Each of the stores was being run as an island, and the store managers did not communicate with each other. They did not share their successes or failures so others in the company did not know what worked and what did not. This meant that the stores made the same mistakes and did not take advantage of profitable breakthroughs. Schulze wanted more open communications, so he insisted that all managers share successful (and not so successful) initiatives across the company. Everyone was expected to share information about what worked well and what did not. However, the franchisees thought that their own markets were unique and wanted to adjust their strategies, products, and pricing. This meant that Schulze could not make commitments to vendors about marketing plans and volumes to obtain attractive pricing and terms. He apologized to his vendors and terminated the franchise relationships.

> **Lesson**: Know your goals and who can help you achieve them. Schulze could encourage sharing among his managers and insist on a common strategy. Also, his vendors were willing to help so long as he reached mutually agreed-upon targets, but he realized that he could not force his franchisees to follow his plan. His franchisees who were supposed to accept his direction were not doing so. *Be willing to cut what is not working.* That frees you up to do what is.

8. **Financing growth with trust... the lubricant of business**. Schulze did not obtain key financing from bankers (except for seasonal inventory needs) or investors since he did not want to be controlled by them and knew that they could cause severe problems "if covenants were not met." In addition to the equity from his house, Schulze used his vendors to finance the business, and especially the inventory. He knew them since he had worked for them, and they knew that he always lived up to his promises. *He never promised what he could not deliver.* Due to his strong connections with the vendors and their knowledge of his capabilities, he was able to secure financing from them for all of his stores. The key to this financing strategy was to sell inventory before he had to pay for it. He got 30-60-90 day terms from his vendors and therefore focused on the right kinds and levels of inventory to accurately forecast and increase the number of turns. He monitored sales and adjusted inventory regularly on a store-by-store basis. Although the store and company managers sometimes became careless as inventory and product lines grew, with vendor financing as the key to their growth, they knew they needed to monitor sales frequently and in detail if they were to maintain these relationships.

This included hiring Accenture in 1984 to develop the right information systems at great cost to the company.

Lesson: *Vendors can be an attractive source of financing* since their cost of financing is already factored into the selling price. But they need to know that you can perform and pay them as you promised, and not use their cash for your lifestyle or to pay for your losses. So remember to promise only what you can deliver, and deliver what you promise. Also, know your numbers. Keep a close watch over your performance. Those who provide resources expect a return on their investment. Lose this trust and you lose your resources.

From Sound of Music to Best Buy

9. **When the trends keep marching on**. In the mid-1970s, the consumer-electronics industry changed. The federal ban on transshipment of consumer-electronics products was lifted and the practice became widespread. This meant that consumers could buy electronics goods across state lines from mail-order vendors who had low overhead and lower prices. Schulze was caught with high overhead and high sales, general, and administrative costs. His gross margins dropped from 35 percent to 14-17 percent of sales and his SG&A (sales, general, and administrative) overhead was at 25 percent. This led to small losses in the first year (after the ban was lifted) and continued at higher levels for two more. His stores were too small to offer competitive prices, variety, and service. He had to reinvent the business. Based on customer feedback and analysis of his competitors' strategies, he decided to expand to a much wider array of consumer electronics lines to compete with mail-order companies that could offer a large variety with low prices. This meant Schulze needed larger stores where he could get high sales levels with low overhead to match the mail-order companies. He expected his competitive edge to be the personal advice that his sales staff could offer and the immediate availability of the product. Schulze got this idea for the larger warehouse-type stores from others in retailing. He noted that the fastest-growing companies such as Wal-Mart, Sam's club and Costco had this advantage. In addition, a company called Circuit City had already started selling consumer electronics in this new format. So Schulze decided to adopt this same strategy and build a superstore model.

Lesson: ***When the world changes under your feet, adjust to the new reality or perish***. As W. Edwards Deming put it a long time ago, "survival is not mandatory."

10. **More trust... A pool to finance growth**. While he now knew which strategy he wanted to take, he did not have the financial strength to pursue it. So he decided to leverage his relationship with his vendors to the hilt. He told them candidly that he had lost money in the past three years, and all of his retained earnings had been wiped out. He pointed out to them that he could expand his demographic reach with

the larger format, expand his volumes and offer competitive selections and pricing. Suppliers would be paid based on the pooling concept. Schulze did not want his sales personnel to recommend products to customers that were not right for them just because he had to pay a particular vendor. Pooling was the most equitable solution. This meant that all the money collected from sales would be paid to vendors on a shared, equitable basis - and NOT on the basis of a particular vendor's product sales. Why did vendors accept such a radical strategy? The risk was reasonable and the potential was great. They did not want to be left out if Schulze's strategy worked. And they trusted Schulze.

Lesson: *It is amazing what is possible if you can be trusted to live up to your word. Reputation matters.* Without trust, your customers will not buy from you (well, maybe once). Your vendors will not work with you (well, maybe once). Your financiers will not finance you (well, maybe once). You also need to be innovative to come up with a solution that is profitable and fair to all. Keep searching and ask others for ideas.

11. New superstore format. The first Best Buy store launched with 50,000 square feet of selling space with a combined showroom-backroom concept and all products on display. The location also featured technical service and had to have maximum exposure. He chose an affordable location that had excellent visibility across the Minnesota River valley in the southern suburbs of Minneapolis. He also found the right color for his signage and Sunday inserts—black on a yellow background. According to Schulze, red is worst and blue is next. The new superstore's first year sales were $13 million, which was more than all the Sound of Music stores combined. His SG&A dropped from 25 percent of sales to under 12 while his local competitors were still stuck in the mid to high 20s. Why didn't all competitors follow? His competitors kept waiting for Schulze to fall flat on his face, and they stubbornly kept thinking that the old retail model would still win. They thought that Schulze would not be able to compete against Wal-Mart and that their own models were superior - all the way to bankruptcy.

Lesson: See what works. Copy what is appropriate for you. In MBA-speak, be a "fast follower." ***Test to find the formula. Then grow as fast as you can.***

Growing with Best Buy to Greatness

12. Grow with excellent people. In addition to adjusting his business model to the new trends, Schulze also needed to find and promote the right people to grow fast and profitably. Initially, Schulze hired experienced sales people from within the industry to build a base within the company. He focused on the floor (of the store) and selected the best sales personnel with the skills, passion, energy, and motivation to become managers. His key criterion was whether they could produce successful outcomes, and think first about the business and then about themselves.

Some of the stars from the early years included Brad Anderson (from the floor to former CEO) and Brian Dunn (salesman to new CEO). Schulze believed in base-pay scales that were at the high-end of the range. As he puts it, "why else would they stay with an undercapitalized company? People are the beginning, middle and end of successful outcomes." And he believed in paying bonuses of 30 to 100 percent of salary for individual and store performance. One example is that of a young man from North Dakota who worked part-time as a cashier at a Best Buy store while going to college. When he graduated and was seeking a full-time job and could not find a suitable one, he was invited to become a full-time "operations manager" while waiting to find a "real job." One year later he was promoted to merchandising manager, then sales manager and then a store manager in Chicago making over $100,000 per year and managing more than 130 employees. This was within five years of joining the company. With Best Buy opening 50 new stores per year, Schulze needed all the good young people he could find to become managers and grow with the company. He identified future stars and placed them on the fast track based on their performance—NOT based on their pedigree or whether they went to Harvard.

Lesson: ***Schulze learned that when customer interaction is paramount for business success, competent and motivated sales people who are happy with the company can lead to exemplary performance. Find them and promote them. Meritocracies excel. Bureaucracies fail.*** As Schulze puts it, his competitors focused on the business model, while he focused on his company's culture and people. His competitors could not steal Best Buy's culture.

13. Picking the right growth stars. While realizing that creating the right culture was important, identifying the right people was even more so. To grow the business, Schulze needed to be able to pick potential stars and to make sure they continued to grow in their skills and responsibilities. Schulze learned that an employee's first 30 days on the retail floor were crucial. Employees who were new to the company brought fresh thinking and often found a better way to do the job. So he started evaluating how employees did in the first 30 days and considered the ideas they generated. He acted on these ideas when they seemed reasonable so the individual employees knew that they were important and valued. Schulze thinks that the worst strategy is to thank them and do nothing. If you do that twice, employees will not offer new ideas. And Schulze knew that new ideas that could increase sales were the lifeblood of his business.

Lesson: Pay attention to your customers and to those who deal with the customers. Identify smart, motivated sales personnel, pick them early in their career, and make sure that you ***acknowledge and promote the best ones***.

14. Encourage employee risk-taking. To help Best Buy's employees grow to their full potential, Schulze encouraged his employees to grow and maybe make a few mistakes. He believes that mistakes are a part of learning, especially when you are trying new directions. But he wants his employees to analyze these new directions with the people who will be affected, and not to make decisions in a vacuum. New strategies are first applied locally and replicated across the company if they are successful. If the strategy does not work, it is considered as part of the learning of the company.

Lesson: We all make mistakes. The key is to think through new directions with affected people who can bring unique viewpoints based on their area of expertise, and to know what to expect and to keep losses to a minimum if the effort does not work. ***Think, test, replicate, or cut***.

15. Changing with the times. As the company grew, Schulze found that Best Buy was alone in the superstore format in the Upper Midwest, with annual sales exceeding $500 million. He found no obstacles to growth as he ploughed over his competitors. He had positioned himself well for the post-Fair Trade (when transshipment came in force) era. But now his new competitors were the giants of the industry, such as Circuit City and Highland Superstores, and giant retailers like Sears and Montgomery Ward. They were moving into Best Buy's markets, including St. Louis, and threatening to move into Best Buy's strongholds, including Minneapolis and Milwaukee. The competitors were copying Best Buy's advertising and branded products. This meant that Best Buy had to better position itself with the consumer. To counter this threat, Schulze conducted focus groups and developed the Concept II store. When he examined other retailers such as Sam's Club, he found that they were all pick-up-and-take with no hassles. It looked more like a warehouse and the display was termed a "mass market display" with the actual boxes on the showroom floor. There was no pickup dock. Consumers just picked up the box from the showroom floor. Some vendors did not like the format and refused to sell their products to Best Buy. Perhaps the most important innovation of Concept II store was the elimination of sales commissions. Schulze learned that with the warehouse-showroom concept, consumers could pick the right products with a lot less help and did not need high-value sales people. So he eliminated sales commissions and put his sales people on a base. But Schulze still kept the bonus for storewide and companywide performance. This helped to convince customers that they would not be subject to high-pressure sales but the bonus rewarded great store performance. Many commissioned sales people left, but the new format succeeded.

Lesson: Change is a constant. Just because a strategy took you to your current status does not mean that it will keep you there or take you to the next level. *Constantly track the market and changes. Then stay one step ahead.*

16. Be invisible when you are testing. Schulze wanted to introduce the new concept at a location that would not be easy for competitors or the industry to spot and analyze. So he picked Rockford, Ill., to develop the first store. Why Rockford? According to Schulze, "it was off the radar" of most people in the industry (apologies to the Rockford Chamber of Commerce). He could disrupt his model without his competitors and vendors knowing about it. And he repeated the test in a few other

Tier III cities. According to Schulze, Wal-Mart, Circuit City and Highland Appliance thought Best Buy was a pimple and did not bother to track his changes. This gave him some breathing time to examine the new concept's performance, and its strengths and weaknesses so he could improve it before introducing it to the national market. By the time competitors caught on, Best Buy had already learned enough from this experiment to stay ahead of them. Over the next few years, Best Buy marched across the nation to become the largest consumer electronics retailer in the United States. Incidentally, one of the duties of every Best Buy employee is to watch everything that is happening in the industry, including competitors, customers, and vendors.

> **Lesson: *Test. Test smart*.** Just because you have an idea that you think is great does not mean it is. Only real tests will prove that. And this is true for even a $500-million company. It is often easier for a new company to test a concept without the rest of the industry knowing about it immediately. Best Buy had to find a location where it could keep the experiment "under wraps" until they were ready to announce it.

Post Script

17. Change never stops. It looks as if the trends are changing again, and Schulze can see storm clouds. Best Buy is now competing against even tougher competitors, such as Wal-Mart and Costco, and it is growing globally. This means, as Schulze puts it, that Best Buy stores in the United Kingdom may be different from stores in Spain or Germany. So Best Buy needs to learn from and be open to each unique culture. This means that stores need to share what they have learned across borders, and also across similar stores, such as stores in mega-metro areas like New York and Shanghai, and get ready for tomorrow's trends: mobility and connectivity. Service is also making a comeback for consumers and businesses in the areas of computers, networks, and convergence (of computers and TV). The key, as Schulze sees it, is to be competitive on prices and to be trusted to sell customized services with higher margins and ongoing growth.

> **Lesson**: Trends always change. You need to track them and adjust ahead of the competition. Seek always to reduce costs and increase value. Enjoy the process because the journey is never over.

Rules for Entrepreneurs from Dick Schulze of Best Buy

- **Feel the trends and know how to profit.** The world is always changing. Stay ahead or fail.

- **You can never know enough about your customers.** Find all you can about your customers and how to keep them happier than your competitors can.
- **Develop meaningful competitive advantages.** Base them on improving the customers' shopping experiences, including offering information, service, experience, pricing, products, accessories, warranties, and comfort.
- **Constantly improve how you connect with customers.** Promotion is always key for a consumer company such as Best Buy. However, with newspapers becoming less important, Best Buy needs to find new ways of connecting.
- **Appreciate the value of teamwork and respect others.** Honor what your team does. Good teams should outperform individuals and bad teams.
- **Learn to tap the potential of each team member to solve tough problems.** Schulze knows that he can multiply the number of ideas to solve tough problems by a factor of 2 to 3 by involving team members with different backgrounds.
- **Value people.** Empower them to reach their potential and reward them. They will in turn help the company reach its own potential.
- **Build the culture you want.** For great performance, build openness, honesty, respect, and fun. Recognize good work and contributions.
- **Good leaders reward all members.** People need to know that their contributions are valued. A good leader will give credit to others.
- **Be humble.** You don't have all the answers.
- **Never stop learning.** There are always new worlds to explore.

Guy Schoenecker
BI

MINNEAPOLIS, MINN

Building a $500 million giant in business improvement

Summary: Guy Schoenecker was raised in the small town of Eden Valley, Minn. His parents were in the plumbing, heating, and wiring business. After World War II, they had to be creative to survive in a small community, so they expanded their services by studying mortuary science and eventually opened and operated three funeral homes. As a teenager, Schoenecker helped his parents with their businesses and grew and sold vegetables on the side. He learned the importance of customer service in that small town, where "everyone knows everyone." After high school, he enrolled at, and duly graduated from, the College of St. Thomas and went on to receive his law degree from the University of Minnesota Law School. To pay his way through school, Schoenecker built a thriving business selling diamonds and furniture to veterans returning to campus after World War II. After graduating, Schoenecker built on the success of his businesses, with the founding of his company Business Builders. From there he built a $500 million giant. This is how he did it.

Before the Startup

1. The early years. Schoenecker grew up in a small town where his parents provided services for the town. This included businesses in plumbing, heating, wiring, and appliances. His dad believed in customer service and did not want any customers dissatisfied. With this philosophy, they survived through tough economic times. After World War II, they saw a need and started a mortuary. Both his parents went to school and became morticians. His dad went to the University of Minnesota to become a mortician, and his mom followed to support the family business. After they graduated, his dad became the mortician, and his mom acted as the grief counselor. As was their habit even when they managed the other businesses, his parents believed in totally serving their market. When their neighbors were sick, his mom made food and took it to them. When they needed help, his parents provided support. In those days, funerals were held in the deceased's home, and his dad had to go to the home and remove the body as soon as possible for preparation. Schoenecker was recruited by his dad to help him in the business, including doing tasks such as lifting the casket and serving as a handyman. They helped families of all denominations in a 50-mile radius, so they got along with all the faiths and went to every church dinner in the area. The funeral business is a 24/7 business and Schoenecker had to help out when needed. When he was not working for his dad, he was a truck farmer. He got up at 4:30 A.M. and started gardening at 5 A.M. to grow vegetables on one acre of land. Most truck farmers would sell vegetables off the back of the truck (hence the name). But instead of just finding a crossroads to sell the produce, Schoenecker organized a regular business around his one-acre plot. He contacted restaurants in the vicinity and asked if they would be interested in his fresh vegetables. They were. He ended up getting practically the same prices as regular truck farmers, but did not have to waste many hours waiting for customers. At his parents' suggestion, he also saved all of his profits from truck farming in a college account. Times were tough. Schoenecker learned how to be thrifty and make a dollar go far.

Lesson: Schoenecker learned the meaning of customer service in an entrepreneurial family. This meant serving potential customers when they needed help to build goodwill (and their "brand" as marketers would call it), and making sure customers were happy with their service. Schoenecker also liked to grow vegetables. So he made a profit from his passion. *By finding new segments and unmet needs, he made the highest profit in the least time. The ingredient in shortest supply is time. Use it wisely.*

From Startup to Profits

2. College and business. After finishing high school, Schoenecker entered the University of St. Thomas. World War II had just ended and the GIs were coming back. They had girlfriends and wanted to get back to normality. Schoenecker's dad had a friend who owned a large business importing rough diamonds from South Africa. He had them polished and finished in Minneapolis, and then sold them around the United States. Schoenecker's roommate wanted a diamond for his girlfriend. Schoenecker called his dad to see if he could buy the diamond with his dad's credit and sell it to his roommate. His dad always paid on time and never defaulted on any payment, so his credit was strong. Schoenecker took his friend to buy the diamond and got a good price. The lights went on in Schoenecker's head, and he realized that he could sell diamonds to others, especially to GIs returning from the war. There were millions of GIs who were being released from the armed forces and his timing could not be better to sell diamonds.

Lesson: The time to get into selling diamonds is when couples want to get married. *Track trends to produce great ideas for your business.*

3. Making every sales dollar count. Since the GIs were entering college under the GI bill, Schoenecker decided to focus on this market to pay his way through college. He spread the word to all the colleges in the area by placing ads in school newspapers. But ads cost money, and Schoenecker was looking for more cost-effective and direct ways to build his business. In talking with his barber, he realized that barbers were the information center of the neighborhood, and they knew what was happening in customers' lives (they were the Facebook and Craigslist of the pre-Internet era). He started calling on area barbers and beauty shop operators to let them know that he was able to offer quality diamonds for a lower price, and offered them a commission. He also joined various clubs to spread the word. He contacted fraternal clubs at his college and at the University of Minnesota, and informed them of his service. Schoenecker would always ask his customers how they heard of him and he found that his most productive sales strategy was word-of-mouth. Satisfied customers told others. Schoenecker used what he had learned about customer service from his parents and applied it to his new business so that his customers would spread the word. After his business started to grow, he stopped advertising. Not only was advertising less efficient than his network, but Schoenecker found that ad customers were more cautious.

Lesson: Schoenecker learned three key elements of all businesses: sales, gross margins, and expenses. He had to generate sales and do it cost-effectively. His biggest expense was the cost to realize sales. He also had to generate reasonable gross margins to generate a profit. This meant he had to negotiate a fair price that would bring customers to him and allow him to make a profit. At the same time, he had to keep his expenses low and controlled.

4. Pricing and quality. The keys to selling the diamonds were price and quality. Customers wanted to be assured that the diamonds were of good quality. Schoenecker suggested to them that they could take their diamond to J. B. Hudson's (the major jeweler in town) to have it appraised, and they could return the stone if they were dissatisfied. Once Schoenecker brought the customer to the store, the importer's sales people would take over, explain all the facets and reinforce the quality of the diamonds. Schoenecker knew the importer well and knew that they could be trusted. The diamond importer would bill Schoenecker's dad for the diamond, and every two weeks Schoenecker would pay his dad. The discounts were 2 percent 10, net 30 and Schoenecker's dad kept the discount. The importer would give a 60 percent discount off the suggested retail price to Schoenecker, but would quote a price at a discount of 40 percent to the customer. Schoecker's profit was the balance. He made a profit of $16,000 in his first year and $26,000 in the second.

Lesson: Understand the key facets behind any sale, i.e., why people buy and what are their fears (or risks) about buying from you. ***Make it attractive to buy from you by adding value and reducing risks***.

5. Moving on to law school. After finishing his undergraduate studies at the College of St. Thomas, Schoenecker was not sure about his career, so he decided to enroll at the University of Minnesota Law School. While in law school, he continued to build his diamond business. Many of his diamond customers asked him if he had connections to furniture manufacturers. His father had a furniture store and knew manufacturers, so Schoenecker started building a business relationship with them and got discounts of 50 percent. He gave discounts of 33 percent to his customers. Now he was in diamonds and furniture. He had always thought that it would be enjoyable being a lawyer, and he found that legal studies challenged his left brain. However, as he came close to graduating and selecting a job, he began to realize that, as a lawyer, he could only sell hours. He was used to leveraging his time and resources, as he had done with his network of barbers and beauty shop operators, to multiply his efforts. He wasn't sure which direction to go -- pursue a career in law or continue his path in sales. He went to the chapel at the College of St. Thomas and prayed for guidance. Unfortunately, he did not hear a voice. However, he realized that he had no control over major issues of his life such as birth, life, and death. So why worry about the little stuff? He decided to follow his passion and went full-time into diamonds and furniture.

Lesson: When expanding your business, see if you can sell existing products in additional markets, or sell a wider product line to current markets. *When your customers are asking you for certain products, listen to their needs and be responsive.* Schoenecker prepared himself well with continued education. But ultimately, he decided to pursue his passion.

From Profits to the Moon

6. Expansion and controls. Schoenecker named his business Jewelry Distributors and rented space in the diamond merchants' building to sell diamonds. He continued to talk with barbers, beauty shop operators, and college groups to get names of potential diamond customers. The diamond business fed the furniture business because those who were getting married ended up buying furniture. To sell furniture, he rented space near a major supermarket in a mid-market commercial area (known as the Lake Street area), hired a full-time manager, and opened the store. He wanted to offer immediate delivery to customers, because most of his customers did not have the patience to wait for future delivery. He also changed the name of his business to Business Builders to reflect his wider range of inventory. Now that he was in the business full time and had employees, Schoenecker was determined to manage it with timely and accurate financial statements and sound controls. He hired a well-qualified accountant and a bookkeeper for each business. He knew that the key requirement to build the business was to be able to get credit from his vendors and from bankers. To do this, he needed sound financial information, to know his financial status at all times, and to be able to predict and control cash and cash flow. By adding the bookkeepers and accountant, he made sure that he got timely and accurate financial statements so as to maintain strong controls. He got monthly financial statements, including the income statement, balance sheet, cash flow, and aging of accounts receivables and payables. In the business's second year, he had his financial statements audited to make sure that his comfort level was high.

Lesson: ***Without accurate and timely financial statements, you have no idea where you are heading. It is only a matter of time before you crash***. Learn your numbers and use them to manage your business.

7. Better inventory and pricing. As he got into the business full time, Schoenecker realized that he had to expand his inventory of diamonds and watches and get better pricing so he could pay for the added overhead and increase his margins. He started buying on consignment from a New York polisher who offered better prices and inventory availability. His arrangement was that he would pay for the products immediately when the diamonds were sold. This expanded his inventory, and with better margins, Schoenecker could cover more territory and hire a sales person to reach new markets.

Lesson: Since the New York polisher was able to offer better financial arrangements, Schoenecker was able to expand. ***Negotiate attractive vendor financing and you will reduce the need for financial-institution financing***. Also, you constantly need to stay competitive and grow (if you don't want to get eaten by the large fish). If your current vendors cannot keep you competitive, you may want to consider alternatives. Loyalty has its limits.

8. Expand segments. Schoenecker hired a salesperson from one of the leading companies in the advertising-incentives industry. This salesperson had sold calendars to supermarkets, especially in southern Minnesota. He knew that S&H stamps (these were incentives to consumers similar to airline points today) had expanded to the area and that those who did not utilize the S&H offering were not doing well. One of these supermarket owners from Austin, Minn., was called on by the salesperson. He then approached Schoenecker for help in countering S&H. Schoenecker agreed to design a customer-loyalty program, without knowing all the implications of the new business. He developed a program called "Bonus Bucks" and offered it to the store owner from Austin. The program's centerpiece was a catalog with various merchandise offerings, and it was a success. The store owner's business grew, and he told other supermarket owners, who opted in to this customer-loyalty program.

Lesson: Hire talented fits. The salesperson called on supermarket owners because that was his previous experience. Schoenecker succeeded because he identified a need his customer had and found a way to fill that need to help the customer stay competitive. Satisfied customers are your best source of new business. Make sure you listen and respond to their issues.

9. Match cash inflow to cash outflow, treat vendors like customers, and customers like friends. In the Business Bucks program, Schoenecker developed a catalog and stocked inventory. He included about 500 – 1,200 items in the catalog, including watches, jewelry, sporting equipment, appliances, electronics, etc. He worked directly with factories and negotiated terms of 30 – 90 days. By the time he had to pay his vendors, he had the cash from his customers. He made sure that he kept his word with his vendors and paid them even if he had to forgo his own check – this was one of his father's primary principles. He had no trouble getting credit. *He also managed his inventory to get the maximum possible number of turns so as to improve capital efficiency and reduce the need for external financing from institutions.* He became friends with the Applebaums, one of his supermarket customers, who taught him about buying and selling. With vendors, he learned that he needed to be honest but tough, to treat them with respect like customers, but to continuously seek a better deal by asking, "What if we change this or that? Can we get a better price?" If a customer were dissatisfied, Schoenecker would take action to rectify the situation. For instance, he would get a basket of groceries, take it to the customer, and fix the problem to make things right.

Lesson: It is easier to grow if you retain customers versus finding new customers. *So make sure you treat customers right. And equally important, treat vendors right.* When vendors know they can make a profit from your business, they will want to continue working with you with attractive arrangements. You still have to negotiate to get the best prices.

10. Sales drivers for the furniture side of the business. As the incentives side of the business kept growing, Schoenecker still had the furniture store. Schoenecker did not advertise in the major newspapers because he found that his ads did not draw enough business to pay for the cost of such advertising. He checked with friends who were selling advertising to some large furniture retailers, and found that their ads in the newspapers were "hit and miss," with some ads doing well and others failing. Schoenecker could not afford to gamble, so he focused on a sales driver that worked for him, which was direct mail. He developed a monthly direct mail flyer. This would generate business for the first two weeks of each month, and he would deliver the items in the last two weeks.

Lesson: ***Know the effectiveness of your sales drivers.*** Know the return from each ad and each dollar spent on sales drivers. Cut the poor ones. Focus your resources on the ones that work. Don't advertise or pay ad agencies for image advertising unless you have money to waste. It will cost you a lot of money and the odds are uncertain. Gather competitive intelligence. Check with people who sell to competitors. Sales people are "great gossipers" according to Schoenecker.

11. Hiring and delegating. As Schoenecker expanded his business, he continued to hire more employees. He put all the businesses in one building and renamed the company Business Incentives (BI) to avoid trademark issues on his previous name of Business Builders. To recruit key employees, he hired people he knew. These were mainly people with whom he went to school, and he knew them and their character. His key was whether he could trust them with responsibility. But before he gave them a lot of responsibility, he wanted to be sure that they would do a good job. So he learned to delegate. His criteria included:

- Were they people he trusted?
- Did they know the job?
- Did they communicate openly and honestly without bruised feelings?

As the company grew, he would make sure that each new hire would be interviewed by eight people. This included all positions starting with the sales people. In interviewing people, he would ask about themselves and their family, the "small town approach." He thought that testing was important, but he thought there were limits to the validity of testing. He relied on documentation, peer feedback, and his gut. He would then monitor sales people's performance constantly before promoting them to greater responsibility. BI followed a four-step process to make sure that each employee was able to perform to his or her full potential:

- Tell them the expectations for their efforts
- Teach them how to get there
- Measure their performance
- Reward them based on their results.

Lesson: It's nice to work with people you like. *It is even better to work with people who you like and can trust, who are capable and motivated, and who can do the job.* Develop your own methods, but be aware that you could be wrong. So monitor and make adjustments.

12. Continued growth. As the company grew to support the needs of its customers, the name changed again from Business Incentives to BI, The Business Improvement Company. Schoenecker found that certain principles helped to grow with control, which included:

- *Change is constant, so embrace it.* As the customers, markets, and competitors changed, BI had to continue to change to stay in the lead. By listening to customers and their needs, BI was able to add solutions to meet their changing needs, such as media and events, live marketing, and training. To better serve its customers, the company organized its efforts into three segments: sales channel, employees, and consumer markets.
- *Have a clear vision.* To make sure that all the employees and managers were working toward the same goals, Schoenecker developed clear mission and vision statements.
- *Plan well with good data.* Schoenecker and his team developed a strategic plan, with a one- to two-year action plan. According to Schoenecker, plans beyond this time period can be meaningless because the world changes.
- Malcolm Baldridge Quality Award: BI decided to seek the Minnesota Quality Award and the Malcolm Baldridge Quality Award because he found that the

company had talented and creative people who worked in silos around the company. He wanted them to use common tools and work together using company-wide processes. The company received the Minnesota Quality Award in 1994 and the Malcolm Baldridge Quality award was presented to Schoenecker by President Clinton in Washington, D.C. in January of 2000.

The above principles helped the company reach annual sales of $500 million.

Lesson: As you grow and increase the number of employees in the company, coordination and focus toward a common goal and vision becomes increasingly crucial. If you cannot control this and change as needed, you will become a fossil.

Rules for Entrepreneurs from Guy Schoenecker of BI

- **Embrace change**. You can resist change or embrace it. It is natural to resist change, but change is inevitable. By embracing change, you can better cope and succeed. Develop a culture that accepts change. You cannot control death or taxes, but you can control how you deal with change.
- **Integrity.** Make sure you have high integrity with your customers and suppliers, and they with you.
- **Manage people**. Be close to people and treat them as human beings.
- **Be careful of having too many family members in the business**. Schoenecker has one son in the business. Schoenecker believes that most families with multiple members in the same business squabble when the patriarch leaves.
- **Have open communications**. Inform people. Tell your people what is happening with the company. Offer candid feedback and treat them well. The better you treat your people, the better they treat your customers.
- **Communicate but do not lie**. To get people to cooperate, communicate and share as much as you can, but do not lie. There are too many things we don't know. Don't act as if you do.

Stephen G. Shank
Capella Education Company

MINNEAPOLIS, MINN

Building a $1 billion leader in online graduate education

Summary: When Steve Shank was an undergraduate, he wanted to go to law school. But since he was awarded a fellowship, he used it to get a Masters in International Relations and Law. Then he was drafted and joined the military. After his stint in the military, Shank got his degree from Harvard Law School. When he graduated, he and his wife had two kids, and he wanted to avoid the hassle of the East Coast (the final straw was when he had to stand in line at a grocery store at midnight) and moved back to the Midwest where he grew up. He joined Dorsey & Whitney, one of the premier law firms in Minneapolis. But he found out that he was one of the oldest associates, so when he got the offer to become corporate counsel to a major toy manufacturer called Tonka Toys, he grabbed the opportunity. This soon led to him becoming CEO of Tonka at the age of 34. After an ill-timed acquisition, Tonka was sold and Shank had time on his hands. That is when he saw giant waves converge and came up with the concept of an online university for graduate education. This vision has now grown to a $260 million (sales) company with market valuation of about $1 billion. This is how he did it.

Before the Startup

1. **Learn what "not leadership" is.** After graduating from Infantry Officer Candidate School, Steve Shank was sent to Europe as an intelligence officer. For a naïve kid from Iowa, he found this was a broadening intercultural experience. In Europe, the military assigned him to a bureaucratic organization in a giant headquarters that was being run by a four-star general. Shank's duties included "watching over the free world" from the headquarters in Belgium, and he saw top-secret messages. While not working directly for the general, Shank was responsible for a daily intelligence briefing to him. Late one night, Shank saw a message from Washington that four Soviet divisions were on the border of West and East Germany.

[(this was in 1968 when the Soviet Union squelched a freedom movement, called Prague Spring, in what was then Czechoslovakia). When he went to tell the general about this ominous development, the general was asleep and immediately got cranky and told Shank "Son, I told you never to bother me." When Shank persisted on waking the general up, he was told, "This better be good, or it's your butt." Shank decided that this was not leadership but an ego on parade with a lack of respect for others. This taught him what "not leadership" is—i.e., what not to do (Shank points out that military leadership has changed since his experience).

Lesson: Shank learned early that ***to be a good leader, you have to be a decent and real human being, keep your ego in check, treat other people with respect and be clear about the organization's vision and mission***; i.e., what it is about and why. Otherwise, talented employees will leave you and you will be left with the sycophants.

2. **From law firm to toy firm**. After getting his law degree, Shank practiced business and international law at a law firm in Minneapolis for two years. By this time, he was approaching 30, a few years older than his contemporaries. Not being satisfied with the quality of the work challenges, he gladly jumped to Tonka Toys when they asked him to start a legal department. The company, a major toy manufacturer in the western suburbs of Minneapolis, had annual sales of about $100 million and had two totally unrelated businesses, one in toys and the other in hydraulic valves. Shank was general counsel for Tonka Toys for three years when the board terminated the president and asked Shank to become interim CEO while they did an external search. While Shank was the interim CEO, he did not wait for a permanent CEO but addressed the company's problems and started to make progress. Seeing this, the board asked Shank to be the permanent CEO because (Shank thinks) of his perceived leadership in the interim, his military training, his breadth of view and ability to see the various pieces and how they could be integrated.

Lesson: Don't be afraid to leave a secure job for one that challenges you. Shank learned that he preferred to be a doer and manager rather than just being an adviser, as he was in the law firm. Being a general counsel allowed him to manage people and to implement the decisions, which he enjoyed.

3. **Change at Tonka**. As CEO of Tonka, Shank sold off the hydraulic valves business because it was smaller than the toys, it was more cyclical, and as a vendor to original-equipment manufacturers (OEM), the company had more pricing pressure. Tonka was also the highest-cost manufacturer of these valves in the United States and the world, which is not a good position to be in if you are a vendor to OEMs who expect high quality and low cost. Shank thought that the toy business had more potential and that Tonka should concentrate on this one industry.

Lesson: *Focus, focus, focus.* It is difficult to excel in a variety of unrelated industries, even for larger companies that have more resources than most new and growing companies.

4. **Grow the toys line**. To broaden the toy product line, Tonka constantly searched for new toys outside the company, because Shank believed that transformative lines come from the outside. The company could license these toys to take advantage of the company's key strength, which was its sales and distribution channel. Tonka had its share of hits, such as Gobots and Pound Puppies. According to Shank, when you have a hit on your hands, you can get a hint about its potential success early on, and that the disasters are also evident in early tests. The key is to *limit your instincts to narrowing your options, but test to see if the market agrees*, and not to invest heavily until the tests prove positive. Tonka would test new toy lines with kids, especially by competitive-cohort testing, i.e., testing against other toys in a similar genre such as action toys for boys, and so on. When a line shows promise against its cohorts, the toys start flying off the shelves and "money starts falling from the skies." But product life cycles are short in the industry and an efficient supply chain is a key to making money when you have a hit on your hands.

Lesson: Instinct has a role, especially in idea generation and initial selection. To avoid disasters, however, you need to operate on data. Shank used *intuition for idea generation, and tests for final selection and launch.*

5. **Sustaining growth**. Due to the impact of hits on the company's sales and income, the key problem at Tonka was not just achieving growth, but sustaining it. To reduce volatility and broaden the product line, Tonka purchased the Kenner Toys (Star Wars) and Parker Brothers (Monopoly) toy divisions from General Mills. This was a leveraged acquisition, which meant that Tonka borrowed a significant amount to close on the deal. Tonka closed the acquisition on a Friday and intended to complete the bond offering on the following Monday. This was Black Monday (October 19, 1987), the day of the second-largest decline in stock market history. Tonka ended up with rates of 12 and 13 percent, which were higher than they anticipated. In two to three years the debt was strangling the business. Tonka was sold to Hasbro Bros. Shank had to move on to the next phase of his career.

Lesson: Lesson #1: Don't take on too much debt. In Capella, his next business, Shank has secured no debt. Lesson #2: Hedge before you buy, i.e., make sure you have all the details of your financing lined up or make your acquisition conditional upon the financing. Lesson #3: Get back in the game after a loss. Each mistake can lead you to the next, and better, phase if you learn from it. Never repeat mistakes. You will have plenty of opportunities to make new ones. Lesson #4: Pray for luck and avoid major deals two days before a major stock market crash. Lesson #5: Aren't four enough?

From Startup to Profits

6. **Land where the giant waves converge – trends behind Capella**. After ending his stint at Tonka Toys, Shank started searching for new business ideas.

- Wave #1: Being in the toy business, Shank had spent large amounts of time working with major manufacturers in China and South Korea. When he went to Asia to visit his vendors, he started to observe dynamic changes in Asia and the emergence of millions of ambitious, skilled, and hardworking people. He started becoming concerned about the future of America and especially about the U.S. education system and its potentially negative impact on the country's future. He perceived two giant needs, namely educating the "New America," i.e., the new generations of Americans, and improving the education levels of the existing workforce to make it competitive against the Asian juggernaut.

- Wave #2: Shank also noticed that one of the constants in the toy industry was change, and that the rate of change was increasing around the world. This was affecting every industry and company, which meant that professionals and managers would need to continuously learn new things to stay ahead.
- Wave #3: Shank also noticed how computers had started to change the way the world operated. As an example, buyers were using computers to track toy sales in May, and were using these early sales figures to improve their ordering for the Christmas rush. They also used real-time market information to reduce the turnaround time for rejecting or developing new toys. This suggested to Shank that managers would need to constantly improve their knowledge to keep up with the changes brought about by the increasingly computer-dominated business world if they want to maintain their value as executives and managers.
- Wave #4: While at Tonka Toys, Shank also noticed the potential impact of electronics on games and learning, and he had personally witnessed the explosive growth and potential of the video game market, especially with games such as "Where in the world is Carmen San Diego" that were being sold by Tonka. He realized that electronics could be a convenient tool to satisfy ongoing needs for education for adults.
- Wave #5: Those who were better educated earned more than the others, so there was a strong incentive among many to get a college or graduate degree.

The genesis of Capella was at the nexus of these major trends.

Lesson: ***Change happens***. Understand trends and learn how to take advantage. It is much easier growing at a rapid pace when one is at the leading edge of a hot trend than without one. In this case, Shank took advantage of multiple trends, including the need for continuous learning, the growing importance of cheap computer power, and the ubiquity of the Internet. He staked his claim at the confluence.

7. Understand the space. After evaluating the trends, Shank needed to understand his competitors so he could develop the right strategy for Capella. Shank noted that his competitors included regular campus-based, accredited universities, long-distance accredited universities and non-accredited distance-learning companies. According to Shank, regular accredited universities were bureaucratic and not very responsive to market needs. His research of the market showed that that they focused on "what professors want to teach rather than what students want to learn." In distance learning, Shank noticed that there was increasing interest and activity but that most of the competitors were unsophisticated, with a few exceptions. Non-accredited companies that offered distance learning were of poor quality, but they still had a strong demand for their services. This showed Shank that there was a need for long-distance education for working adults. With the growth of the Internet, Shank knew that it would be possible to find a very profitable niche. To separate his company from many of his competitors, Shank decided that he would not compromise on the quality of the education and that accreditation (as proof of this quality) would be mandatory for Capella. Not only would accreditation qualify Capella for academic funding and allow students to obtain student loans, but it would also force Capella to maintain high standards and would assure potential students of a quality education. Based on this analysis, Shank positioned Capella as an accredited, high-quality distance-learning university that would use the increasingly ubiquitous Internet to provide convenience for adult professionals.

Lesson: Understand your competition and their strategies to know how to differentiate your company. Shank emphasized high-quality education to match his campus-based academic competitors and to excel against the non-accredited distance-learning companies, but got an edge by emphasizing the business side, such as convenience, business friendliness, operational efficiency, and customer value.

8. Selecting the right customer segment. At the outset, Shank realized that no one had mastered the use of the Internet for education because of its newness. Capella had to use existing technologies such as snail mail, e-mail, and phones. But Shank knew of the initial Web browser Mosaic and expected someone to develop a better Web browser that would allow the Internet to become a platform for long-distance education. To minimize potential problems, Shank decided to work with students who had already learned how to succeed in education. He wanted students who had developed good learning habits and had successfully obtained a university degree, so he decided that Capella would only offer graduate degrees. This was also smart because the accredited distance-learning company and the 600-pound gorilla in the field, the University of Phoenix, was strong in undergraduate education but not in graduate programs. But focusing on graduate education also meant that the students would demand a higher level of quality and competence from their teachers, so Capella would have to offer a high-quality product to differentiate itself from the others. To build a dominant leader in long-distance education, Shank decided to focus on graduate programs and combine a high-quality, university-like education, with the efficiency of a business, i.e., with commitment to quality, service and respect.

Lesson: *Understand the segment where you can add the most value and how you can* *differentiate yourself from the competition for long-term advantage.* Understand the limitations of the environment and the technology to minimize potential problems and don't let hope be your business plan. Focus on the market segment whose needs you can best satisfy. This can lead to high value added, higher gross margins, and high growth.

9. **Marketing and sales strategies**. Shank knew that he wanted Capella to have a national image and reputation. But Capella had very little money for national image advertising, and the early objective was to learn what worked and what did not. They wanted to generate leads for enrollments and do it cost effectively. While they tried print media such as The New York Times, the results did not meet their expectations. So early on, they tested results from online advertising, including through sites such as AOL. Capella was the early adopter of this advertising strategy in postsecondary education. The strategy worked and improved the nature of the economic model.

Lesson: What works for a new business is not always known. ***Hardly anyone knows what really works until they try alternative sales drivers and evaluate the resulting sales per dollar invested in marketing. Don't rely on experts,*** especially those such as ad agencies that collect their money based on your expenses. Even if they are willing to take their fees based on your results, be cautious because the money they are experimenting with is yours or your investors'.

10. **Start or acquire**. Shank considered buying a higher-education company but did not find any that fit his vision. He wanted to develop a high-quality institution that was at the same level as a regular, campus-based university and not a diploma mill. Having looked at some of the companies, Shank decided that none of them fit his requirements or they were too expensive. The cost and time to reorganize one of his lower-tier competitors was likely to be very high. Also, Minnesota had a high reputation for quality education and due to the growth of Control Data and Plato Learning, there were a number of people in the Twin Cities with skills and experience in this distance learning. At this time, he started working with an investment company who convinced him to start the business from the ground up and custom-design it to fit his vision. Since he decided to build the business from scratch, it could take longer to get accreditation but he would not have the burden of poor reputations and legacies.

Lesson: Sometimes it makes more sense to buy a company and add value to it. At other times, you may want to start a company to fit your goals. Whichever strategy you choose, ***stay true to your vision***.

11. **Teaching long distance**. Teaching, and learning, long distance was not very common when Shank started Capella. So he had to make sure that Capella did a good job of teaching, and his students did a good job of learning. He understood

that there were two paradigms he needed to understand: the first was to know how to teach, and the learning capabilities, via the computer, and second was to know how to teach adult learners. He found a rich lode of research in the area of adult learning and discovered that teaching online was compatible with the way adults learn, which was to emphasize learning by discovery and through experience. The learning needs to be relevant and practice-oriented, i.e., they learn better when they can apply the learning to their jobs. So this was Shank's, and his team's, focus in the development of Capella. To do a great job of teaching at a distance, Capella had to focus on two more points. The first was to pay intense attention to consistency of delivery and content. Capella's philosophy was that high variability among instructors was not good. So the format of the course was developed as a standard template, and faculty developed this with Capella's course designers. This made the course standard from one instructor to another, and course designers paid attention to the rubrics of the course for consistency. The second point to teach well at a distance was to understand that distance learning was more challenging because students were learning on their own. This meant that the faculty has to challenge the learners to support them and understand whether they really learn the concepts. The environment has to be supportive to substitute for the physical proximity of the classroom. The faculty did this by increasing the level of responsiveness, by probing and enhancing the level of interaction. As an example, the learner has to demonstrate a high level of engagement by demonstrating a certain level of activity every week. There was a record of everything that went on and the faculty chair reviewed classroom interactivity for each student and shared it with the faculty member. Capella had the responsibility of defining how interactivity was developed to make the experience and the learning rich for the student and gratifying for the faculty.

> **Lesson**: When you are exploring new territory, as Capella was with long-distance teaching, make sure that you deliver a high-quality product. ***Your reputation will define your worth***. Happy customers will talk, and so will unhappy ones. Word-of-mouth, or viral marketing to you hipsters, can be devastating if you sell bad products or services.

12. Organization structure. Since Shank wanted to build a high-quality educational institution, he could not let the business side of Capella make academic decisions and dictate to, or override, the educational side. Teachers should be able to focus on quality teaching and not worry about fees and revenues. Everyone talks about building a quality product/service but most want to cut corners and not pay the price. In this case, the business side could not dominate the academic side, or else the company could sacrifice quality at the altar of profits.

> **Lesson:** There is no free lunch. If you want quality, there is a price. This is the same as in the newspaper industry, where a newspaper controlled by the sales department will soon be recognized as an ad-based rag sheet.

13. Build a mission-driven organization. Shank sought to *build a culture of service to the adult learner.* This meant that employees had to believe that they were there to make someone's life better and to help the students achieve their potential. Shank had a passion for this vision and he made sure that all his staff had it also. Since Shank wanted to catch any problems before they got in the door, up to 10 executives interviewed key potential employees to ensure the right attitude and fit. With this vision, Shank was able to hire Harold Abel, the former president of the third-largest public university in Michigan, who had the experience to lead a higher education institution and had built its distance-learning component. This meant that he knew the terrain and had credibility with the educational establishment. Shank persuaded him to join Capella as its president with the goal of building the right culture and securing the license and accreditation. After Abel joined Capella, Shank found to his luck that Abel was one of those individuals for whom "no" was not an answer. This is essential in a startup. There are too many obstacles that make it easy to give up.

Lesson: *Know the culture you want to create and make sure you communicate it incessantly to all current and prospective employees.* When a company is young and is significantly ahead of the curve (i.e., of conventional wisdom), it is difficult to hire experienced talent. Shank's philosophy was to ***hire vision, attitude and a fit with culture over self-professed "talent"***.

14. Cheap and conservative. At the start, Shank managed Capella with very few resources. All of the funding came from his personal resources and from an investment group, and he knew that it would have to last him until accreditation if he wanted to minimize dilution. So he ran the company like a good entrepreneur and got an outrageous amount done with limited resources. He spent only on essentials and *took only the risks that he could not avoid*. The philosophy was to lose very little. By 1998, Capella was an accredited university, and could now access federal loans for its students. This enhanced the value of Capella, and it secured funds from NCS, a large corporation that had a strategic interest in the company. However, the strategic fit never played. In 2000, Capella had to become bigger and went on a serious effort to raise external financing. These were the last days of the Internet bubble. Capella wanted to raise $15 million, but the venture capitalists insisted on investing $40 million to $100 million. Capella was now strong enough to select the venture capitalist it wanted (someone who shared its vision) and on its terms. Shank did not want someone who wanted to build Capella and flip it at an inopportune time to the wrong buyer, but wanted someone who was willing to build for the long-term.

Lesson: If you are frugal and use your resources wisely to go the farthest, you could control the funding process and be able to get the attractive terms you want. ***Desperation is not a good funding strategy***. When raising venture capital, understand the stages of a venture and the key milestones that enhance a venture's value. Try to reach those milestones before you run out of money. As the old saying goes, water is more expensive in the middle of the desert than at either end. For more on stages, see *Finance Any Business* ***Intelligently®***™ (www.infinancing.com).

From Profits to the Moon

15. Growth pangs. As Capella grew rapidly, enormous changes took place in the company and the market. Some employees could keep up and others could not. Individuals who took the company from $250,000 to $1,000,000 in revenues are often not the right ones to take it to $100 million. This meant that Shank had to spend significant time and money on training and development to help those who could use the training and could grow to accept more responsibility. Shank believes that if the person knows what he/ she is doing, then Shank will offer a higher level of autonomy and manage by goals and results. If the person or the relationship is new, Shank will start at a lower level of autonomy and spend more time guiding the new team member. For rapid growth, Shank believes in hiring qualified people who have worked in large corporations and in entrepreneurial businesses. *The large corporation usually teaches business sophistication, while the entrepreneurial business usually teaches self-reliance.*

> **Lesson**: To succeed in high-growth companies with the characteristics of both ventures and corporations, it helps to ***have corporate sophistication with entrepreneurial self-reliance and the ability to deliver results***. Venture capitalists have a cliché that the best entrepreneurial leaders are former executives of large corporations (for sophistication) who have failed in their first new venture (large corporations have resources, which does not help self-reliance).

16. Strategic alliances. In the early years, Capella developed a lot of its own technology for distance learning over the Internet. This allowed the company to custom design how it wanted to teach and to make the experience fruitful for its students. However, as it has grown, and as the industry has grown, specialized vendors can now develop and offer Internet solutions that are more sophisticated than the ones that Capella develops. So now, Capella does not develop any new technology but is one of the leading appliers of educational technology over the Internet.

> **Lesson**: Know when to make. Know when to buy. Don't make if others can offer equally viable alternatives at lower cost if you can save your cash and if you are not losing any proprietary advantage.

17. Management via constructive conflict. Shank's goal in Capella is to mold the best of academic and business cultures and get the two sides to respect each other. To avoid conflicts, Shank had to make sure he hired the right people so that both sides never forgot that the key mission was high-quality education with student convenience, and the key culture was mutual respect between business and academics. Since Shank believed that each of the sides brought a unique perspective and viewed a problem differently, he required constructive conflict. *It is acceptable to disagree, but not to disrespect,* and sharp elbows are not tolerated.

Lesson: Disagreements can be productive to generate the best ideas so long as the culture is one of respect. In Capella's case, the successful execution was possible through the use of management via constructive conflict.

Rules for Entrepreneurs from Stephen Shank of Capella Education Company

- **Land where the giant waves converge**. Shank chose to land his company where the giant trends of adult education, computer ubiquity and the Internet would collide to create a great online education company.
- **Go where they aren't**. Since the University of Phoenix was strong in undergraduate education, Shank decided to focus on graduate students. The bonus was that they already had developed good study habits so they could offer a high-quality education when the Internet was still in its infancy.
- **Focus, focus, focus**. Shank focused on graduate students because they had already developed successful learning habits.
- **Find the right financing**. Be cheap to make each dollar go farther to reach your milestones. Desperation is not a good financing strategy.
- **Hire the right people**. Seek attitude over proven talent. This is not the venture capital way, but then again you don't have the venture capital money. And if you got the venture capital money, then you would get the venture capital dilution and the venture capital control. Choose your poison.
- **Build the culture you want**. If you want high educational quality, make sure the academic side is not reporting to sales.

Dan Cohen
CNS/Breathe Right

MINNEAPOLIS, MINN

A $566 million payday from a hunch on a licensed product

Summary: Dan Cohen, the founder and builder of CNS/ Breathe Right®, has opened his latest venture, BodySound, at one of the premier shopping malls in Minneapolis to test his latest product, which is a luxurious combination of home theater and chair that incorporates sound vibration to soothe the body. Why? Because Cohen believes that market research should be real and that the best data is from customers who pay real money. Cohen has always had an independent streak. After finishing his medical studies at Temple Medical School, he came to the University of Minnesota to become a certified neurologist. But he never practiced as a physician or a neurologist. He was more interested in research and developing new products. He started his first company with a colleague with a total investment of $25,000. This company, CNS, morphed into CNS/ Breathe Right, which he sold for over $500 million. This is how he did it.

From Startup to Profits

1. **Initial concept, money, and partner**. After finishing his residency, Cohen found that he needed a lot of money to know more about the "nuts and bolts" of the brain. But he found that nobody would give that much money to a junior investigator. So he teamed up with a colleague who had started practicing as a neurologist, and together they founded a company called CNS. Each invested $12,500 and each owned 50 percent. Cohen thought that he could always go back to becoming a physician if the venture did not succeed. CNS was started to develop a brain-wave monitor so that surgeons could monitor circulation to the brain and detect potential problems that they would otherwise not be aware of.

   Lesson: Cohen and his partner split the equity equally. Often, the partner who jumps into the venture seeks a higher share of equity than the partner who is only an investor. However, sometimes if you want the right partner or if you have few options, you may have to make some sacrifices. Cohen's partner had a diminished influence after the later rounds of financing, and after the brainwave business was abandoned, his participation in the company was limited to a seat on the board of directors.

2. **The initial angel money**. The initial investment of $25,000 was to study unmet needs and develop a demo software package. With this done, Cohen raised $350,000 from friends, family and other physicians to move toward a prototype. Cohen learned that he had no clue who would invest, and there was no way to predict. Those who he thought would invest did not. Others did. He lost all preconceived notions about investors. Those who believed in the mission and in the people, invested. The others did not.

Lesson: At the early stages when there is nothing to prove your viability, the only ones to believe in you are your friends, family and those who know the field. Friends and family believe in you. If they don't, examine your soul. Those who know the field often are aware of the unmet needs. These informed industry leaders (such as the physicians) often have coattails to bring other investors to the fold.

3. **Money from venture capitalists**. After having tapped out his friends, family and industry connections, Cohen needed $3 million from institutional venture capitalists. He raised $500,000 in the first stage and the rest in the second. Cohen found that there was a herd mentality among the VC community. When he found a lead VC, others joined the investment team, but it was difficult till then. Cohen raised a total of $60 million of equity in nine rounds of financing (four is about the average for the successful high-growth venture), of which $35 million came at the end. Cohen found that there are two good times to raise money. One is when you can sell the dream, i.e., at the startup when you can sell the vision, but reality has not yet intruded. The other is after you are successful, when they all want to get in and you can choose the ones that best fit your needs. Cohen also learned that it helps to have different factions backing you to improve valuation. Once, he desperately needed financing and found that the VCs were going to dilute his share with a down round and low prices. Cohen approached a wealthy angel who had already invested in the company in an earlier round and sold him the entire round at a very attractive valuation.

Lesson: Raise money from as many investors as you can without violating the SEC regulations. Although VCs may not like it, since it is in their best interest to keep the number down and keep control in their hands, this may help you get more attractive financing. Only you can protect your own behind. *Keep all your investors informed so that they will consider investing with you in future rounds. Not sharing data because things are not going well is the wrong thing to do when you need to raise money.*

4. **Flawed business case.** The prototype took about two years, and Cohen did the testing of the automated electro-encephalogram (EEG) monitor at the Mayo Clinic. The automated EEG monitor was much easier to read than existing models, and it interpreted data with built-in math software, eliminating the need for a neurologist to read the data, unlike the previous ones. So Cohen hired a sales force to sell it to surgeons and hospitals. However, to his dismay, he found lots of resistance and discovered that the business premise had some flaws. Firstly, simultaneously with the introduction of CNS's EEG monitor, another new unrelated kind of equipment had been introduced to the market. Even though it was not a competitive product, Cohen found that surgeons would not handle two new pieces of equipment at the same time. Secondly, and more damaging, the EEG monitor had a written record that would show every error, which could be used against the surgeons in a lawsuit. Some surgeons asked if the written record could be eliminated from the machine to limit its use in lawsuits. A third problem that reared its ugly head was the growth of HMOs. With the introduction of HMOs, hospital administrators started vetoing purchases. The confluence of all of these problems was a disaster for the young company.

Lesson: First, be lucky. Secondly, study trends to know how they will affect your venture. It may have been difficult to predict the growth of the HMOs and their impact, and the introduction of the other product that would compete for resources and time. However, one key lesson from the above is that ***customers will not buy if they have to make too many changes, especially major ones, to their current habits.*** Additionally, if your product is damaging to the customers' self-interest by creating a potentially damaging trail of evidence, say sayonara to sales. Would you use a product that could be damaging to your self-interests? Your potential customers are no different, much as we would like physicians to live up to their Hippocratic Oath and not let money be the first factor in their decision.

5. **The board of financiers.** Based on feedback from the customers, Cohen shared his conclusion with his board that the product would not succeed. According to Cohen, the financiers did not agree with his conclusion, suggesting that he was a scientist and not a salesperson. So the board hired a seasoned salesperson from a major hospital-supply company. This freed Cohen to look for other opportunities for the technology, so he evaluated the application of the technology to sleep-disorder diagnostics (not therapy). The problem in the industry was the inability to analyze records fast enough and CNS filled the void. Within two years, the company was selling more sleep-disorder diagnostics and the old business died. Cohen claims that the VCs on the board were a "great group of guys" who taught him a lot about business and that he was like a sponge and absorbed their knowledge. But he was closer to the market and able to find unmet needs that the technology could satisfy.

Lesson: Cohen claimed not to know business or sales. *What he did do well, however, was listen to potential customers and see how he could satisfy their unmet* *needs and "eliminate their pain."* When the barriers were high in one area, he adjusted to find another market that needed his technology. Obviously, it would have helped if, before spending large amounts of money and time, CNS were to see if surgeons were amenable to purchase equipment with a potentially damaging record of the operation. But he did the next best thing, which is to find another need where he could apply his solution. Not the ideal way to do things, but when you are trying to keep a business alive, that may be the best solution.

6. **Sleep-disorder products**. Within three years of introduction, sales of the sleep-disorder diagnostic (SDD) products reached $8 million, and the company was hanging around break-even levels. Cohen learned that selling capital equipment was tough because every quarter's sales started at $0, unlike businesses that rely on repeat sales to existing customers. Since CNS was now a public company, having had an initial public offering in the same year as the introduction of the SDD products, the pressure of quarterly sales was hanging heavily on Cohen. Since the equipment was only a diagnostics tool and not therapy to make patients healthier, insurers and the government were questioning payment in this new era of cost containment. In addition, customers were consolidating into buying groups and competitors were consolidating into larger companies. SDD sales growth was starting to slow down.

Lesson: Understand not only the needs of the consumer but also keep track of the broader trends affecting your markets and your industry. Jump on positive and growing trends that can help you, and try to minimize the negative impacts of adverse trends.

7. **Licensing a new product**. Cohen could see the handwriting on the wall with the limited market for SDD equipment, and he was therefore seeking a therapeutic product that could be sold directly to the consumers, since he was tired of trying to sell to hospitals. Although consumer marketing normally requires a lot of investment, he thought that he could succeed if he was clever about the marketing and did not have to market the way others (with lots of money) did. As a physician, he knew that he could get on the radio and obtain free publicity. So Cohen started searching for unique technologies that he could license and promote and scoured data bases and let people know he was a potential licensor. One day an inventor walked in with the nasal strip. When Cohen saw it and tried it, he found that it worked for him. He also felt an immediate instinctive reaction that the strip could be very successful. According to Cohen, the inventor put the strip on the table. When Cohen picked it up, it was as if a movie ran in Cohen's head in which he saw the life of the strip and its eventual success. Cohen says that that vision was a gift that has never happened before or since.

Lesson: Cohen's vision is not something that a third party will understand or can explain. Nor is it repeatable. In some cases, such "sample size of one" surveys can also be dangerous, i.e., the concept that "I like it, so others will like it." In this case it worked out.

8. **Board's reaction**. Cohen licensed the strip exclusively in return for a 50,000-share option and a royalty of 3 percent. He did not pay any cash since he could not spare any but convinced the inventor that this arrangement would be mutually profitable. During the negotiation, Cohen had built an excellent relationship with the inventor. When the inventor's lawyer was being difficult, Cohen suggested that the inventor control his lawyer. Since the inventor trusted Cohen, he did that. They are good friends to this day, and the deal turned out to be a winner for both. The inventor was a brilliant mechanical engineer, so Cohen also hired him as a contractor to get the strip manufactured. However, the board did not have as favorable a reaction. When board members were informed of Cohen's actions, they asked him about his opinion about the potential market. When Cohen mentioned that he thought that the strip had a potential market of about $100 million (based on instinct), they had a meeting without him and the next day two of them came unannounced to meet with Cohen and suggested that he quit as president to pursue the nasal-strip business, since he liked it so much. The board would hire someone else to take over the management of the SDD business. This was done even though Cohen pointed out to the board that he had hired a search firm who had found four excellent prospects from large consumer-products companies who were willing to quit their high-paying jobs to join CNS to market the strip (normally this is the kind of credibility that can convince investors). The implication was that if the strip did not succeed, Cohen would not be working for CNS. Cohen did not agree with this strategy, since he thought that he was the best person to run the entire operation, because in medicine, it is often easier for one M.D. to sell to other physicians. But the board's decision prevailed. Cohen hired someone else. Sales of the SDD equipment dropped from $8 million to $5.5 million.

Lesson: Sometimes it is not easy to convince others when all you are using is your intuition. If Cohen had some valid data, the investors may have been convinced. He did not have the data or the time to get the data. He was willing to go with his gut. Unless you have a proven Midas touch that you know will never fail you, this is not a great strategy in general. Keep in mind that you could pay the price. Instincts can be fallible, and the more instinct you use, the more extinct you are likely to become. Even though he followed his instinct, Cohen was careful not to pay any cash but gave equity and a slice of future revenues. So when you use your instinct, be smarter.

From Profits to Home Run

9. **Get FDA approval**. Since CNS had experience in diagnostics, but not in therapeutics, the company did not know how to get Food & Drug Administration

(FDA) approval and confused the FDA with a complicated test. CNS wasted time and money in this phase. During the time when CNS was doing the tests and getting approval, Cohen went to medical shows and talked to the largest wholesalers and drugstore chains to develop his marketing and public-relations strategy. What he found was that retailers would not carry the product unless consumers wanted it, wholesalers could deliver it, and they were satisfied with the details of the advertising and promotion plan. Wholesalers wanted assurance from retailers that they would carry the product before they would make any commitments. CNS had to prove that consumers would buy.

Lesson: When you don't know something, you may have to do a lot of leg work, especially if you don't have the resources to hire the needed expertise. *But hiring "professional" expertise may not be the best move, since they may suggest the low-risk, "proven" techniques that cost a lot of money that you don't have.*

10. Promotion plan A. While waiting for FDA clearance, Cohen gave free samples of the nasal strip (CNS could give free samples but could not sell them before FDA approval) to stockbrokers in the Twin Cities area. They liked them and gave them to their friends and customers. Then they called back and asked for more strips, which was good. The stock went up.

Lesson: Find innovative ways of promoting your company and product. Know the regulations.

11. Distribution plan. Once the FDA cleared the product for sales, CNS went to Walgreens' headquarters to meet the buyer, who would not agree to carry the strip. CNS then went to regional managers, five of whom took it for their regional stores. Why? Because the regional managers liked it and wanted to prove that headquarters was wrong and also to make their own mark. Because headquarters did not authorize the product, it was put on the counter. It sold like hot cakes and the buyer called from headquarters to buy the product for the entire chain. That's how the nasal strip was approved for national distribution in Walgreens. Once Walgreens approved the product for its stores, CNS went to brokers in Chicago who worked with Walgreens and other regional chains and suggested that they carry the product for their customers. The brokers told CNS that "you already have our best customer." In return, to help CNS, they arranged for CNS to work with other brokers around the country. CNS had its national-distribution network, and it filled up 24,000 stores with its product. This was scary since now they had to move the products off the shelves.

Lesson: Understand that all national chains have multiple buyers at different levels, whether at the national, regional, or local levels. Understand how this works and take advantage.

12. Promotion plan B. Cohen decided not to sell the product directly to consumers, since he wanted mass distribution and did not want to compete against his own channel customers. This meant that he simultaneously had to promote the product, obtain access to stores and develop the channels for distribution. CNS hired a public relations firm that charged by the placement and placed $25,000 on account. The P.R. firm got $250 for each radio interview that it arranged. Each time he was interviewed on the radio, Cohen gave out the 800 number. When consumers called, CNS asked them for the name of their pharmacists. The company then called the pharmacists and asked them for the name of the wholesaler who would deliver it to the pharmacists. Both the pharmacist and the wholesaler now became aware of the product.

> **Lesson**: If you are planning on working through distribution channels, evaluate whether you should, and can, undercut them by selling direct. In some industries, you might lose your channels. In others, you might not get any cooperation. You often have to choose yin or yang.

13. P&G. When Procter & Gamble (P&G) saw the nasal strip in the Walgreens store in Cincinnati, executives called and wanted to sublicense the product. They asked if CNS would share its market research on the product if P&G would offer its own findings. Cohen said he would be glad to do so, but he did not have much research to share. P&G shared its data anyway. When P&G executives learned that CNS had only $10 million to launch the product, they commented that it was a very low figure for launching a new national consumer product and suggested that Cohen license it now rather than lose money. Cohen replied that if the campaign did not work, he was sure the product would be available for a bargain. CNS spent $1.5 million of its $10-million hoard to launch Breathe Right.

> **Lesson**: Faith moves mountains – and nasal strips. ***When you don't have cash, use your brains.*** According to Cohen, "think outside the box." Large companies constantly exhort their employees to think outside the box to improve innovation. However, what is left unsaid is that there is another box outside the first box.

14. Promotion plan C. CNS had a third promotion plan under way. Cohen thought that football players could benefit from the strip and would wear it if informed about the advantages. CNS also had to make sure that reporters did not think it was a bandage. So CNS seeded the media with press kits, and Cohen's wife called about 700 newspaper reporters and told them that it was a really neat product, that they will hear about it, and to file the kit and not throw it away. CNS then sent cases of the strip to all National Football League (NFL) team trainers and called them to inform them of the benefits. The trainer of the Philadelphia Eagles had placed his box on the floor next to his desk and constantly kept tripping over it. After a few kicks to the box, he took it home, tried the strip and liked the benefits. The next day, running back Herschel Walker complained of a cold. Since Walker had a habit of not taking medications, the trainer suggested that he try the strip. That Sunday, Walker scored two touchdowns. The camera got a close-up of his face as he was crossing into the end zone, and the photo showed up in the newspaper. One beat reporter called CNS for facts behind the strip and wrote an article. CNS copied the article and sent posters to all the NFL teams. Wide receiver and future Football Hall of Famer Jerry Rice saw it and used the strip on Monday Night Football. When he scored touchdowns, the strip was the talk of the football world. The Wall Street Journal carried the story. All the journalists who had received the press kit pulled it from their files and wrote hundreds and hundreds of stories. CNS and the nasal strip were featured on newspapers, TV, and radio. Sales jumped from $1.2 million in the fourth quarter of 1994 when Jerry Rice wore the strip to $16 million in the first quarter of 1995. Lightning had struck.

Lesson: See what works and copy it. CNS learned about the value of visual advertising at NFL games from Gatorade. And it never hurts to get your product on Monday Night Football or on the pages of the Wall Street Journal. Come up with a plan that will take you there.

15. The virtual company. Cohen ran CNS/ Breathe Right as a virtual company. Operations were simple and consisted mainly of inventory control. CNS had a manufacturer make the product, and the warehouse shipped the product to customers based on orders. The company had only to feed the promotion machine. CNS had 75 employees before the SDD product was sold and 28 afterwards. Even though Breathe Right accounted for most of the sales, only four employees worked mainly for the nasal strip. The rest worked for SDD and in administration. Breathe Right did, however, benefit from the existing infrastructure (finance, warehouse, and purchasing) that was developed for the SDD products.

Lesson: Keep it simple and focus on your strengths. Control and protect your intellectual property, brand, and competitive advantage.

16. Raise money when it is available, even if you don't need it. In 1996, CNS and its stock were having a great year and the company raised $35 million at $25 per share. When the price fell, CNS bought back 5 million shares at an average price of $3 (it took CNS two to three years to complete this repurchase). Shareholders who stuck with the company did very well.

Lesson: ***When equity is cheap, attractive and available with few strings, raise all the money you can. You never know when you might need it.*** But don't waste money on frivolous projects just because you have it.

17. The next product. After the nasal strip had its peak, CNS decided to launch a chewable fiber supplement called Fiber Choice. The company decided to launch the product despite initial market research that was not favorable about its positioning. The initial positioning was as an alternate to Metamucil. It bombed. They then repositioned it as the "food for people who don't eat enough fiber." Sales took off from $0 to $35 million.

Lesson: Positioning is key. Understand the one benefit that will resonate with customers and keep testing until you find what works. This is especially true in mass-market national campaigns, but it is a valuable strategy for every product and campaign. You need to find the right message. Test before you launch.

18. **Exit**. When GlaxoSmithKline offered $566 million, CNS sold.
    Lesson: When the time is right and the price is great, exit, stage left.

Rules for Entrepreneurs from Dan Cohen of CNS/ Breathe Right

- **Success requires continuous personal improvement**. Cohen had to continuously improve his personal skills and learn what he wanted to do. He looked at his business as his second college and always had a learner's attitude to adjust to new situations and external changes.
- **Damn the roadblocks**. Cohen believes that the key difference between entrepreneurs and professional managers is that when successful entrepreneurs have a belief that something needs to be done, they will improve the solution until it is perfected and they are aware that not all the answers are available at the beginning. Professional management will test. If others don't believe, they will stop.
- **Market research for revolutionary products**. For revolutionary products (or services), market research is not very useful in prediction because customers do not always know what they are evaluating. Test. See what works. Only then, invest to expand. Otherwise, you are gambling.
- **CEO at VC-backed companies**. Cohen found that the venture capitalists he worked with did not appreciate that he had grown with the company and had developed new skills. They treated him based on the skills they had found when they first started working with him. Others judge you based on what you have done, not on what you think you can achieve.
- **You need to believe in your product**. If you don't try, you will not succeed. If you try, you have a chance. When CNS studied Breathe Right, the conclusion from the market research was not to launch it. But when you try, test small.
- **Seek the right screens when licensing**. CNS's record shows that licensing can be a great strategy to find unique products. But develop good screens to find the right ones for you. Cohen's screens were the following: They had to work (no research-stage products); they had to have intellectual property (for competitive advantage); the cost of manufacturing had to be reasonable; and the licensors had to be reasonable (no huge cash demands, both have to win for either to win).

- **Take equity with care.** Once you accept someone else's money, you are obligated to have an exit strategy.
- **Hire good people.** Attitude is the most important ingredient.
- **Find out how people feel about things.** Give people permission to share their fears and/ or excitement. Many beliefs or judgments cannot be quantified or justified, only felt. Intuition can often be just as good as current facts, so do not discount it. Allow people to say how they feel – both bad and good — as an early-warning sign.
- **Be humble.** No one has all the answers. (Notice how this is a constant theme.)
- **When it comes to public relations and promotion, try.** You can "throw" something at the media, but you don't always know what will happen. "If I don't throw it out, then nothing will happen. If I do, then anything can happen. It's all about the possibilities. P.R. is like that: It's about possibilities."
- **Find complementary advisors.** Find those who can fill the gaps. You don't need someone who matches your strengths.
- **For personal development, read a lot.**

Gary Holmes
CSM Corporation

MINNEAPOLIS, MINN

Becoming one of the U.S.'s largest real-estate developers

Summary: Gary Holmes started a business selling light bulbs with a lifetime warranty at the age of 11. By the time he was 16, the business was grossing over $200,000 per year and his mother suggested that he sell it to have a "normal" childhood. However, he had already started buying apartment buildings and sold his light bulb business. After finishing college at the University of Minnesota Business School (later renamed Carlson School of Management) Holmes became a mortgage banker to learn how the "big boys" played the game and to build a network. In about three years, he became the highest-producing mortgage banker in his company. That's when he decided that he had built a foundation and went into his real estate company full-time. Since then, Holmes has developed a real estate and business empire that includes over 111 commercial properties, 22 apartment communities and 37 hotels with annual revenues over $500 million. He also owns manufacturing space and many other businesses. This is how he did it.

From Startup to Light-Bulb Tycoon

1. **Vision at age 11.** At age 11, Holmes was a "normal" kid. That's the year one of the dads in his scout troop who had a garage filled with chrome cleaners donated the bottles to his troop and suggested that they sell it and use the proceeds to pay for summer camp. For each bottle sold, the troop kept part of the proceeds and the kids got the rest. However, when the bottles ran out, the troop was left with nothing to sell. This was the start of Holmes's career. He scanned a number of magazines to find the right franchise or products for sale and came across a light bulb that had a lifetime warranty due to a more durable, high-grade tungsten core, but was more expensive than the competition. Holmes learned that he could sell these everlasting light bulbs by pointing out that GE and Westinghouse built their bulbs to fail in a few months so they could sell replacements, but that the bulbs he was selling had lifetime warranties. These light bulbs were especially useful for sockets that were difficult to

reach, such as those that were very high up. Holmes sold the bulbs himself by going door-to-door (which was more common in those days). He compared this business with a paper route and liked selling bulbs because he could set his own hours (after school), and he could show better results if he worked harder. He learned that you needed great will power to sell since you could always make excuses to avoid going out. No one forced him to do it and held him accountable. When he went to the homes, *some homeowners slammed the door in his face. It bothered him initially, but he learned that people had different personalities and only a few were rude.* Others invited him in, offered him cake and invited all the members of the family to hear him give his sales pitch. Invariably, he sold to such homes. He developed a great big display and memorized the manufacturer's brochure and the pitch. He learned that he had to cut down the pitch to the best three or four bullet points using trial and error to get his customers interested. He only mentioned price near the end of his pitch, since the bulb was four times the price of ordinary bulbs. *If customers were inclined to turn him down, he told them to think about the light bulbs that were tough to replace and to start there. It worked.*

Lesson: Find those who value your product (or service) and when selling, highlight the specific advantages and benefits it offers. Perfect your sales pitch based on the reasons people buy. *Don't let the rude ones get you down.*

2. **Sales network expansion.** Holmes offered these bulbs to the troop as a means of raising money for their troop expenses and for each kid to make some money for their summer camp. He first started with his own troop and then started selling to other troops in Minneapolis. He found that there were different kinds of troops just like there were different kinds of people. When Holmes was forecasting his sales, *he estimated that each kid was good for at least three bulbs, what he called his "lay-down" forecast. Each scout could sell one to his parents, one to at least one neighbor and one to at least one set of grandparents. He also found that there were about two superstars for each 50 kids and he estimated higher sales from these kids.* He went to each troop's meeting every Monday until there were too many troops, and then he went to a few each week. The bulbs did become a hit, since everyone could use them, and Holmes was selling light bulbs to most of the troops in Minneapolis.

Lesson: Multiply your efforts by getting a distribution channel. Once you find a channel, find a product. After Holmes saw that the troop was able to sell chrome cleaners, he started looking for something new to sell when they ran out of the limited supply. He examined magazines before selecting light bulbs. He wanted something that was universally used, carried reasonable margins and was easy to sell. He built his projections based on reality and the fundamentals of how kids could sell the bulbs. He kept detailed records of how many each kid sold and used these to build realistic forecasts.

3. **The Exclusive.** When Holmes's sales improved to the point where he became the largest seller of light bulbs in Minneapolis, he decided that he needed to

protect his "franchise." So he asked the manufacturer for an exclusive for the area. His dad was in sales and he had heard how companies took over territories when sales started increasing so as to keep the sales force "hungry." He did not want that happening to him. With the exclusivity, he maintained his territory and his market, and created value for himself.

Lesson: *Worry about your own backside. Don't assume that others will protect you.*

4. **Expand your market.** After capturing all the scout troops in Minneapolis, Holmes then decided to sell bulbs to the commercial market. The same company had a product line for offices. So each evening after school, Holmes would dress up in his Sunday suit and go downtown to meet buyers for large companies. As closing time drew near, the buyer would come out and see this "kid in a suit" and invite him in even though others may have been waiting longer. When the buyer found out what he was doing, he would invite others to hear the sales pitch. Holmes understood that he was a novelty and took full advantage. Actually, as he now says, he wanted to "freeze himself at that age." And he found that 65 to 70 percent of the buyers bought bulbs from him.

Lesson: Understand your unique competitive advantage and exploit it to the fullest. Find new market segments where your current advantage works for maximum leverage.

5. **Expand your product line.**. When the company came up with a new plumbing product called Durasand, that kept toilets fresh and the water blue, Holmes decided to sell it. What clinched it was the fact that the product was unique and "gimmicky", margins were much better, the inventory more controllable and the repurchase was strong. Whereas he was buying light bulbs for about 50 cents and retailing them for 89 cents (and from this margin he had to pay the troop, the scout and himself), he was able to get much higher margins on Durasand. He was able to buy the product (in quantity) for about 40 cents and the troops resold them for $1.98. In addition, there was only one model of Durasand whereas there were six models of the light bulbs, so this allowed him to cut inventories and get quantity discounts since he was selling more of this one product. The product was also unique (P&G had not yet entered the business) and each average scout still sold the magic number of three. The kids made more money so they were more enthusiastic. By this time, he had established good credit, so he did not need to borrow from the bank to finance his purchases. Now the troops were making "real money." He would also give the best sellers prizes at the end of the season. He trained at least one lead parent in each troop so that he or she could advise the scouts. Holmes showed them how to sell the products and the best sales pitches to use. The troop benefitted and so did Holmes. Each kid had to earn $40 to go to scout camp for two weeks and Holmes helped them do this.

Lesson: *Innovate and adapt constantly with low-risk tests.* Understand your sales channel, especially their strengths and needs. After building your channel, try new products that it can handle. Help channel members profit and continuously adapt to changing markets and opportunities. Seek higher profit margins to avoid becoming stagnant, to reward your associates and to become more profitable. Seek uniqueness to establish a niche.

6. **Find an exit.** When Holmes turned 16, his Mom suggested that he sell his business so he could have a "normal" childhood. By this time, Holmes had about 3,000 kids selling his products in the Twin Cities and had annual sales of around $200,000. So Holmes sold the business and moved to real estate.

Lesson: *Always listen to your mom.*

From Light-Bulb Tycoon to Real Estate Startup

7. **Find the right building.** When he was growing up, Holmes had a friend whose family was in the real estate business. Every time he went to their home, the friend's two older brothers and mother would be discussing real estate on a 24/7 basis. They built and managed apartment buildings, and Holmes found their discussions fascinating because he wanted to invest his earnings from light bulb sales and the proceeds from the sale of his business. So he decided to explore investment alternatives. Because his friend's family was constructing larger apartment buildings, Holmes decided to check out the want ads to find the right building to buy. To do this, he got a writing tablet, the Sunday paper and started calling. He developed a system to note the apartments he wanted to call and the ones he had called. When he called the sellers, he asked them for details about the apartments, such as the size, number of bedrooms, utilities, and the like. He learned to ask more questions as he went along and he thought that no question was too stupid. He asked about issues such as the gross income, operating costs, asking price, size of units, and so on He did not know what income statements or balance sheets looked like – just the facts. He found that some of the sellers had ads for three or four buildings. By the time he was ready to buy his first building, he was very knowledgeable. He had gone to look at the buildings, had an attorney and started a company called Holmes Enterprises. He got a release from his parents and his attorney signed for his company. He bought three buildings in quick succession and ended up selling light bulbs to some of the sellers.

Lesson: Don't be afraid to ask questions, even if you think it makes you look stupid. That is how you protect yourself. People are always willing to take your money and give you poor service or assets if you don't do your homework.

8. **Financing purchases.** Holmes knew that financing was the most important factor in a real estate purchase, and found that most sellers were selling on Contracts for Deed (where they financed the sale themselves with the existing mortgages being "wrapped around" the new financing, which was a common practice at that

time). He could buy the buildings (mainly four-unit or five-unit buildings) for $2,500 to $7,500 down. $7,500 was "too rich for my blood," he said, and the "sweet spot" was $3,500 - 5,000 for 4-6 units. He realized that positive cash flow was the most important criterion before he bought his first unit. All of his units had positive cash flow and Holmes profited from them.

> **Lesson**: Even if you don't know financial statements, you need to know enough to figure out how you will make money and the kinds of risks you are taking. Saying, "I am not a numbers guy" is the first step to problems. Know the right numbers.

9. **Managing units.** *When Holmes evaluated the properties, he found that there were three types of problems with the units* (attributable to the owners). The first was when the landlord offered cheap rent so that renters did not call him and bug him about repairs. The landlord offered a discount on the rent and told the renter to fix his own problems. Secondly, some owners never fixed up the units, even by such simple improvements as painting and other minor cosmetics. To compensate, the landlords kept rents low. A third kind did not know the level of market rents since they had not checked and done their homework.

> **Lesson**: Holmes learned that if he managed the units well, he could get more rent. He became an avid student of market rents to find out levels charged for various kinds of units.

10. **Going to college.** Holmes was interested in avoiding the military draft, so he went to college. According to him, only the accounting classes were useful. He stayed in school and expanded his real estate ownership business. He also bought other businesses during this period, including a garbage-hauling business. However, due to his age, the insurance carrier for his truck sent him notice that it was canceling his insurance since he was too young to be the driver. So he decided to sell the garbage-hauling business. However, he actually sold it between 90 and 120 days later when the business had lost more value and he consequently lost money on the sale.

> **Lesson**: Don't procrastinate. When a business does not look good, sell when there is still value. If buying a business, check with your insurance carriers and other vendors and customers on whether they will work with you and at what cost.

From Real Estate Startup to the Big Leagues

11. **First step to the big leagues.** When Holmes graduated from college at 22, he owned about nine buildings and was managing them himself. This is when he decided that he needed to learn how the "big boys played," i.e., developed and financed bigger jobs than the small apartment buildings he owned. So he got the

only job of his life (working for someone else) as a commercial mortgage banker with one of the larger mortgage bankers in town. His salary was $7,500 per year, but he was expecting over $1 million a year in experience. He "got $2 million worth." He hung in there for a little under three years and developed a great network with lots of contacts. He stayed focused on his job and only bought one building for himself during this time. After he became successful, he negotiated a compensation package that included a percentage of the business he brought in. He had very high sales, and his profits were higher than the entire residential mortgage division. He "put myself in the shoes of the people coming in" to see if he could do the project himself. He learned all the numbers and everything about the projects. The early 1970s were "go-go" years for public companies in Minnesota, and there were many individuals with lots of money from initial public offerings. *He learned all he could about tax shelters and designed tax shelters for these newly minted executives.* He became so good at it that he started designing packages for executives such as Nathan Cummings of Nabisco (General Foods). He was young, knowledgeable and made use of his "novelty." He learned how to put together financial packages for entrepreneurs such as Harold Roitenberg of Modern Merchandising, who was aggressively expanding the LaBelle's catalog stores. He obtained financing for about 65 LaBelle's stores, and these successes expanded his network. When he left his job, he continued to build, finance and lease stores to LaBelle's, and found financing for the stores they bought. He made about $375,000 in his last year with the mortgage bank. They offered him a partnership when he resigned, but Holmes wanted to "select his own partners rather than inherit them".

Lesson: Understand the key trends and growth areas and learn all you can about hot opportunities. Become an expert by reading all you can and asking all the questions you can think of. Get into the industry to take advantage of the new opportunities opening up. If you are looking for connections and a track record, don't worry about the base salary but negotiate a compensation package based on results, especially if you have confidence in yourself. Build a track record and network of success. Then launch yourself.

12. Early years of the venture. After his stint at the mortgage bank, Holmes left at the age of 25 to start developing properties for LaBelle's stores, along with other projects, such as apartments. Since he did not want to create lots of overhead that could jeopardize his new venture, he would work out of his partners' offices rather than adding overhead. His own files were in the trunk of his car. One could say he had portable files before the advent of PCs.

Lesson: When the cash flow is light, make sure your overhead is even lighter. Don't think you have to add overhead and spend money before you have it. Positive cash flow is the elixir of entrepreneurial life.

13. Build a strong base with partners. When he started on his own, Holmes started working with two other real estate experts. One was Leonard Gassparre, who was specializing in building apartments. Gassparre would build the apartments after Holmes put together the package, i.e., the land, plan and financing. They got along very well, and together built about 2,000 units. The other expert was Cy Sheehy of Sheehy Construction, who was the contractor for LaBelle's stores. After the store was constructed, they would sell the store but keep the extra land surrounding it, where they built shopping centers. They still own these properties and Holmes manages all of these units for his partners (who are in their 80s) even today. Holmes had few partners. One was Harold Roitenberg, who was on a bank board and got loans very easily. The other two partners were specialists in their fields and got along well with Holmes. Holmes kept away from social contacts with partners, believing that such relationships did not serve any business purpose.

According to Holmes, Gassparre was a "character" who had lots of cash in certificates of deposit (CDs) earning interest, but he would still borrow money from the banks. He grew up during the depression and held a high value on cash. He would pay his interest payments but was very reluctant to repay the principal, and Holmes had to intervene on behalf of the bank to get Gassparre to repay the principal.

Lesson: Select your partners carefully based on their integrity, specialty and whether their skills complement your own. Do not select them based on social connections.

14. Getting into a kitchen cabinet manufacturer by restarting a bankrupt company. Holmes and Gassparre ended up owning a furniture company by default. They had given a deposit of $5,000 to a small furniture company (with $250,000 in annual sales) for cabinets. The bank foreclosed on the business and took control of the equipment. Gassparre wanted to restart the business. Holmes did not want to diversify, but Gassparre kept badering until "he wore me out". They offered the bank monthly payments on the loans for up to six months if the bank would let them use the equipment to operate the business. Since the bank had nothing to lose (wood-working equipment does not fetch a lot in a bankruptcy auction), it agreed. Gassparre found a great sales person, rented an unused building in the area at low cost, found a good manager and restarted operations. They did not do any homework before the purchase but applied business logic, added a marketing program, got better sales personnel and built a rep organization. They got big booths at national homebuilder shows, which were expensive. They made full use of these booths by getting all their top sales people from around the United States to build relationships with customers. As sales grew, they had to add new factories. They then acquired other kitchen cabinet companies to add new lines and continued to grow the business. They also had a third partner who ran the business. According to Holmes, they were all unique characters and individuals with strong convictions and different perspectives, but they pooled their talents together to reach conclusions and respected each other. They sold the business in about 23 years for $88 million. After a few more acquisitions, the buyer resold the business for over $350 million.

Lesson: Just because others failed at something does not mean that the business is bad. It could be that the operators were bad. When taking over a failing business, you may not have much time to do your due diligence. Don't risk a lot of money until you prove that the business can be managed profitably. Existing financiers may finance you if you can show them how they can avoid losing more money. Find good partners, especially ones who are talented. You need different skills and perspectives to run a successful business. So get what you don't have. And once you decide to get into a business, understand what is needed to dominate the competition. Holmes and his partners would go to trade shows and differentiate themselves due to their ability and image as unique characters, while being as competitive as anyone in the industry. According to Holmes, no one could understand how such different personalities (Holmes, Gassparre and Harold Dokmo, the operations partner) with unique lifestyles and views of life could function well and run the company so successfully. Gassparre was unique and eccentric, Dokmo was 'by the book', and Holmes was the one in the middle who was always trying to find the right way to solve the issue.

15. Diversify your business. Due to his experience in building the LaBelle's stores and because Best Buy was a tenant in one of Holmes' office buildings, Holmes built a significant number of the initial Best Buy stores constructed outside the Twin Cities. However, Holmes did not want to concentrate more on Best Buy due to its shaky finances at that time.

Lesson: Don't be too concentrated. Move beyond one or two customers.

16. People and circumstances change. When the kitchen cabinet company was losing money, all of the partners invested in the company to keep it growing. After it showed a profit, disagreements arose about how to run it. The business was not capital intensive and the business did not need much cash to grow. However, some of the partners needed cash and the others did not. Those who did not need the cash wanted distributions at the end of the year, and they only wanted distributions to pay taxes (since the corporation was an S corporation where the partners had to pay taxes on the business' earnings) whereas the others wanted distributions more frequently and in larger amounts. This resulted in three of the partners (those mentioned earlier) buying the others' interest over the years to ensure that the company was managed for maximum potential.

Lesson: Problems often arise when there is money to distribute rather than during the lean times. Usually some partners have short horizons and want the money now. Others are willing to ride with a winner to generate more profits later. Make sure that you have clear objectives and agreement among the partners to avoid problems.

17. Invested in a bank and got on the board. When Holmes was about 29, he owned a local bar called Bullwinkle's, which was close to a new bank called Riverside Bank, which had been founded by a local banker named David Cleveland.

Cleveland asked Holmes to invest in the bank and sit on the board. Holmes did so and profited from his investment. However, the key benefit derived by Holmes was the advantage of seeing how bankers analyzed deals, examined loans and evaluated borrowers. This added to Holmes's own education.

Lesson: If financing is a key component of your business, understand how financiers think. It can help you obtain better financing packages and make your business stronger.

18. Adding an office. In 1975, when Holmes had already established his business, he decided that he needed to expand from the trunk of his car. So he opened an office and hired a bookkeeper/ receptionist, property-management experts and architects. This was the start of his corporation. The five or six people he hired at this stage helped Holmes with all the tasks that he used to do himself on the weekend, and allowed him to focus on strategic issues and new projects. When Holmes visited new cities to examine sites for LaBelle's, he would question the local brokers about the city, prospects and opportunities. This allowed him to find a number of other attractive projects. He would also buy more property than he needed for LaBelle's. On this excess property, he and his partner would build apartments, shopping centers or hotels.

Lesson: *Don't add overhead before you absolutely need it.* Keep looking for opportunities, especially if you can acquire them as part of synergistic deals that can enhance their value.

19. Financing the expansion. Holmes was expanding at breakneck speed, adding shopping centers, apartments and hotels. Financing was a crucial component. Holmes' three partners (Gassparre, Sheehy and Roitenberg) had substantial net worth and were active in the industry as contractors or investors. They also had good connections, so getting bank financing was a breeze when one of them was his partner. Holmes would find the project, get control of the land, find the best use, design the project, sign up tenants and then approach one of his partners to bring him into the project. Holmes co-invested with the partner. The unique aspect of this arrangement was that, for about 31 years, Holmes never charged his partners for all his efforts and shared in the ownership of the project based on his cash investment in the project itself. He was essentially offering the benefits to his partners of all the time, effort and cost it had taken him to develop the project. They never refused to participate, and this allowed Holmes to expand at a very high rate without having to "waste" time finding partners for equity. And the partners' connections made debt financing easy to get.

Lesson: Don't nickel and dime your partners. Some might say that Holmes should have charged for all his efforts. Maybe; but the question is whether he would be able to develop the number of properties he built and owned if he charged his partners for every task. The partners must have known they got a great deal. They never refused to invest. How much is that trust worth? Holmes still manages the properties for his partners.

In 2006, after about 31 years of not charging his partners for his services in finding and developing projects, Holmes decided to charge his partners for their share of the development costs. One partner objected. He had become used to getting it at no cost. When Holmes pointed out the costs involved in doing all the work and told the partner that they could get third party vendors and pay them for it, the partner relented and started paying for the services.

20. Control when growing. As the number of projects grew, Holmes realized that he needed to develop a system to secure the right types of information about each project. He and his staff grouped the projects by category (apartments, hotels, and so on) and developed unique information spreadsheets for each type by stage: i.e., at construction, leasing, ongoing management, and down the spectrum. This allowed him to compare the various projects and immediately pick up the variances in various revenue and cost categories. The spreadsheets had data that did not have clear uses when first added to the sheet. But each new piece of data added to their knowledge, and invariably he and his staff started finding better ways of analyzing the projects and their own performance. This is opposite of common practice in which managers decide their goals and then collect the data that contributes to reaching them. He started a rolling budget and updated it each month, and would compare each project to this rolling budget and with similar projects. He would examine each project every month to decide whether to keep, improve or sell it. Unlike many entrepreneurs, Holmes did not hesitate to delegate. However, he did keep close tabs on performance to monitor when a mistake occurred. Once, when interest rates were falling, a staff member decided to fix the interest rates on about $300 million of variable-rate debt to save $3,500 per month (in transaction costs) without checking with Holmes. The net cost to Holmes from this debacle was over $1 million.

Lesson: Understand how to manage "by exception" where you delegate the routine items that cannot cause excessive harm, but be aware of the items that can cause severe losses. Train your staff to know when they are making decisions within their domain and which decisions need input from seniors, such as you. While Holmes sometimes paid a high price when staff members made mistakes, he did not hesitate to continue delegating because he was reaping bigger gains from allowing his staff to grow. And he did not fire the manager who did not give clear instructions to the staff member who fixed interest rates. However, he did not make the same mistake twice, and he tried to limit his losses from any mistakes. This also raised the question of how much authority to delegate. No one in Holmes' organization would spend millions for land without approval, but fixing rates in a falling market that would cause the same level of loss was not a decision they had made before. Therefore, Holmes developed a tracking system to monitor all relevant interest rates daily.

21. Keeping staff too long. Holmes notes that his key mistake was not in delegating but in keeping some staff members on too long, especially when the company grew and the staff member did not. As the company grew, this resulted in some staff being in positions that they did not know how to handle. At the same time, they were reluctant to reduce their responsibilities, since that was seen as a demotion.

Lesson: People you work with, and who helped you when the business was young, may become your friends and confidantes. Even though you may feel guilty, let them go or reduce their responsibility if they have not increased their skills to keep pace with your business's growth. You are jeopardizing the health of the entire organization.

22. Management team. How should an entrepreneur build a team as the business grows? If the entrepreneur is in charge and has controlling interest (without an investor dictating strategy), the entrepreneur may get "yes" persons on the team. These sycophants are afraid to disagree with the owner for fear of losing their jobs. Holmes' practice was that no one would have negative consequences for disagreeing with him. *He would tell them that he did not need associates who said "yes" to everything he suggested.* He would tell them that the danger for him was that he could get caught up in an idea and become its champion and lose objectivity. If he did not get accurate critical feedback from his key team members, he could look in the mirror and make all his decisions. He would also save a lot of money. He wanted others to tell him whether his ideas were sound or not. Holmes also wanted to find new team members with the same mission as he had, and people who understood interrelationships between various aspects of the business, so they could see the issues from a strategic perspective.

Lesson: Unless you think you are the greatest entrepreneur in the world and your decisions are never wrong, you don't need team members who agree with you on everything. *If your ego cannot handle your staff telling you that your ideas may sometimes stink, you have more problems than you know. Get a shrink.* Realize that many people may not be as talented as you are in certain areas, but may have more strength in others. Holmes still cannot understand why project analysis is so tough for his staff members, especially when many of them have MBAs.

23. Design unique incentives. To make sure that each department is properly motivated, Holmes has designed a unique incentive system for each department. There are different incentives at the hotel division than the development division or the apartments or shopping-center division. As an example, in the hotel industry, efficiency and cost has to balance with guest satisfaction. Otherwise, staff could cut power to the room to save money.

Lesson: Try to *find the right benchmarks to reward good performance.* Make it appropriate to the business. One size does not fit all.

24. Titles. Holmes found that giving someone a fancy title sometimes went to his or her head. Someone who was an excellent manager would become ineffective when promoted to CEO of a division. As CEO, they thought that their role was to sit in the office and expect others to do the job since they were too important.

Lesson: *While some feel that titles are cheap, not everyone agrees.* Even if you give fancy titles, make sure the person understands the job and the requirements.

25. Exit stage left. Holmes is at the stage in life now when he is concerned about succession. To this end, he has started a family office with people who are experts at portfolio management rather than business management. This office can handle the hiring of the CEO of Holmes' flagship enterprise and 65 other investments in hedge funds, venture capital funds, and the like.

Lesson: Know that you are mortal. If you are not, tell us how you did it.

Rules for Entrepreneurs from Gary Holmes of CSM Corp.

- **Don't become an entrepreneur to become rich**. It may not work. Do it because it is your passion.
- **Nothing replaces hard work and attention to detail**. Don't expect to succeed by being less competitive than your competitors.
- **Seize opportunities**. Holmes saw opportunities and took full advantage of them. He learned how to analyze and followed that up with action. He sees his key strengths as business analysis and implementation.
- **Treat people fairly and they will want to work with you**. He was very fair to great partners, so he never had to waste time trying to find new ones.
- **Train employees but don't keep people in positions that have grown beyond their skills**. People need to grow with the organization or accept that they need to be in less-demanding positions. Without this, you will have incompetence at key levels.
- **Think like the customer**. Make it easy for them to use your services. *Always put yourself in the other person's shoes.*

Kenneth Dahlberg
Dahlberg Electronics

MINNEAPOLIS, MINN

Building two home-run ventures and beating the odds

"I will be the best person I can be all my life"
...Lesson from Ken Dahlberg's teacher in a one-room school in Wisconsin.

Summary: Ken Dahlberg was a triple ace and one of the most successful pilots of the Second World War. At the age of 91, he still flies his own jet. With $1,000 earned from his salary when he was a POW, he built his first fortune by bringing the benefits of the transistor and miniaturization to millions of hard-of-hearing persons with his "Miracle Ear" invention. In retirement, he then started a venture capital fund and found a second venture called Buffalo Wild Wings that he led to a second home run. Most of us find it difficult to create one home run. This is how Ken Dahlberg did it — twice.

From Startup to Profits

1. Becoming an ace pilot. When the Second World War broke out, Dahlberg joined the army as a private. One day, the corporal asked for a volunteer and Dahlberg stepped forward without knowing why he was volunteering. The corporal pointed out that Dahlberg was a leader and that comment influenced Dahlberg profoundly. Then Dahlberg found out that he had volunteered for KP. But that did not diminish Dahlberg's enthusiasm, because the corporal's words about the need to step forward for leadership stuck in Dahlberg's mind. He continued to find ways to move up. He volunteered for cooks and bakers school. What he found was that this training was in the administrative building, and closer to the bulletin board where he found out that the military was looking for aviation cadets for the Army Air Corps. Dahlberg applied, passed the equivalency test and was one of two finalists. He asked for referrals from people he knew when he worked at a restaurant at South Bend, Ind., and had made many connections. Among the references were the coach of the Notre Dame football team and the mayor of South Bend. The officer selecting the winner for the post was a graduate of Notre Dame. Dahlberg was selected for the aviation school for the Army Air Corps, which led to his becoming one of the most successful pilots of the Second World War.

Lesson: Luck helps. But luck seems to come to those with initiative. It would have been very easy for Dahlberg to avoid volunteering in the future after knowing that the first time led to KP duty. That was not the lesson Dahlberg learned. He continued to volunteer and to stand out.

2. **POW and venture capital.** Dahlberg's strategy to secure equity capital is quite unusual, and not highly recommended, including by him. Dahlberg was one of the most successful pilots in the Second World War, shooting down a number of German pilots and earning Purple Hearts, a Distinguished Service Cross and the Silver Star. The first two times he was shot down, he escaped. The third time he was not so lucky, and he ended up serving as a POW for five months. While he was in captivity, he continued to earn his officer's monthly pay of $250 and ended up with $1,250 when he was released. He put down $250 for a car ("one has to have wheels") and used the balance of the $1,000 (plus $2,000 borrowed from the bank) as his seed capital when he started his company three years later.

Lesson: ***According to Dahlberg, capital is what you produce less what you consume***. In Dahlberg's case, consumption was zero due to his circumstances. However, the need to save for future investing is one of the best lessons you can learn if you want the resources to become a successful entrepreneur. Many successful entrepreneurs have saved prodigiously so they have equity when the opportunity shows up. As the cliché goes, don't be caught sleeping when opportunity is knocking on your door.

3. **Keep looking for opportunities.** After leaving the military, Dahlberg joined a local company called Telex as the assistant to the president. In those days, Telex made hearing aids in the form of large headsets. Dahlberg was also the commanding officer of the Minnesota National Air Guard and used many of the head sets Telex was making. He realized that there was a need for a better headset and evaluated the technology to make them. He carved the model of the first one from balsa wood. This was the start of Telex's dominance in the headset industry. Telex is now the largest manufacturer of headsets.

Lesson: ***Continuously monitor advances in technology and the needs for the technology. Apply the technology in areas where you know that a real need exists***. Academic researchers have found that product "wizards" are those who are aware of the leading edge of technology and the unmet needs of the market, and are able to integrate the two into leading-edge products.

4. **The start of Dahlberg Electronics (Miracle Ear).** Dahlberg found that he had more product ideas than Telex was able to incorporate into its slower corporate structure. Like many aggressive entrepreneurs before him, and since then, he left Telex with two of its engineers and started his own company, Dahlberg, Inc., in 1948.

Since he had not signed any non-compete agreements, he was free to leave Telex, even though Telex did not like it. He offered the engineers a share of the profits. As noted earlier, his total capital was $1,000 from his savings and $2,000 borrowed from a bank. He decided to focus on the fields that he knew, i.e., communications and hearing aids. Both products used similar technologies (communications and electronics) and Dahlberg knew both markets. He knew about hearing aids from his days at Telex. From his days in the military, he knew how military hospitals operated. There were 30 patients in each room and everyone played music loudly so that they could hear their own music above the others'. Dahlberg came up with the idea for customized extension speakers with controls. The speaker was placed under the pillow so the soldier alone could hear it, and the controls were on the headrest. To pay for the speakers, since the hospitals had no money and the patients were not going to buy them due to their uncertain length of stay in the hospital, Dahlberg connected payphone-type, coin-operated controls to the speakers. The patients paid 10 cents per hour if they wanted to hear music. Dahlberg sold about 44,000 of these systems.

Lesson: Find a need and fill it. It sounds simple but very few are able to make it happen. Dahlberg was able to do it since he knew the market and the unmet need. He also knew the technology and was able to fit the technology to the market.

A key lesson for politicians. *You can make the non-compete agreement in favor of the corporate employer and tough for employees (potential entrepreneurs) to start new ventures, or you can make it easier for employees to leave and start their own business, as in California. When you make it tough for employees to leave to start their own business, you are in essence stifling entrepreneurship. Don't complain later when you don't have too many new ventures in your state.*

5. **But he also had to find a way to finance the sales.** The hospitals liked Dahlberg's system but could not pay for the equipment. They were willing to sign a five-year lease allowing Dahlberg to implement his system. However, Dahlberg had to find a way to finance the sale since he did not have the money to carry the investment. He went to companies that sold products, such as milk, to hospitals and offered to sell the equipment and transfer the lease to them for $75 per speaker. With an average of about 100 speakers per hospital, the vendor invested $7,500 per hospital. If each patient used the speaker for an average of 12 hours per day, the daily revenues were $1.20 per speaker on an investment of $75. Dahlberg had no trouble finding companies that were willing to buy the equipment and take over the lease. Dahlberg and his brother, Arnold, developed this as a financial strategy. Arnold had a financial education and more financial expertise than Dahlberg and ran the equipment-communications division that sold to the hospitals.

Lesson: When you don't have the money to lease and your customer cannot afford to buy, find a way around the problem. ***Often, you need to innovate not***

only in the product but also in the sales and financing strategies. According to Dahlberg, he had to talk his way through (which means develop and sell innovative strategies) since he did not have much money. "All he had was opportunity and hope." This is similar to most entrepreneurs. Innovate and find a way to solve the problem.

6. **Key people.** To attract key people, Dahlberg offered two Telex engineers an opportunity to share in the upside via profit sharing and stock. According to Dahlberg, this was "the logical thing to do." Using this strategy, he was able to find the key people he needed to complete his management team.

Lesson: Don't hog all the equity and profits. Others have the same dreams that you have and might work harder for the upside from equity. However, make sure they are the right people for the venture. Select the ones you like who have more expertise than you in areas where you are weak.

7. **The need for change.** When TVs came along, Dahlberg used the same strategy to put TVs in hospitals. He placed the TVs on a bracket and connected them to extension speakers (not coin operated). He sold about 40,000 systems to hospitals.

Lesson: As technologies and markets change, evolve with the times. Otherwise you die.

8. **More needs at hospitals.** As Dahlberg and his team served the hospital market, they noticed that nurses were constantly hurrying around the hospital to monitor many patients. Dahlberg had the technology to help ease this problem and came up with the idea of the central departmental station to help the nurses monitor their patients. Simultaneously, Dahlberg's team also noted that physicians were often needed immediately to treat patient emergencies, and this was a problem especially if the physician was on a break, such as for lunch. So they developed a paging system that allowed the nurses to call the physician for emergencies. They "covered the waterfront" for the hospital's internal-communication needs and became the leader in this area.

Lesson: Dahlberg's team constantly monitored changes in communications technology and customer needs in the hospital sector. This allowed them to develop leading-edge products that filled an immediate need and to become the leader, even though there were much larger companies that could have dominated this market.

9. **Hearing aids – the other division.** Dahlberg also found that his technology could be easily used for hearing aids. Due to the transistor, he could eliminate wires and reduce the size of the battery, which miniaturized the hearing aid to fit completely in the ear. He developed a scale model (again with balsa wood) and showed it to some dealers in the industry for feedback. One of them, who was from

Oregon, said that if Dahlberg could build something so small that it would fit in the ear, "it would be a miracle." Dahlberg developed the first in-the-ear hearing aid and called it "Miracle Ear."

Lesson: Understand other uses for your technology so you can make full use of it. Understand the benefits of the technology and the benefits to satisfy customers' unmet needs. Get feedback from key industry practitioners so you are not the only one who thinks it is a great idea. We are often biased in our opinions about ourselves and our ideas.

10. Selling without money. Because Dahlberg now had two products and two markets (hospitals and consumers), he had to find a way to sell both products and do it cheaply. During the course of talking to potential customers, he found that "everyone knew at least 10 people with hearing problems," and they were glad to refer Dahlberg to them. So he would ask for references "with a smile." Dahlberg believed that people would help you if you asked them nicely. He built a distribution system with exclusive distributors (the precursor of today's franchising arrangement) whom he trained in this system. By the time he sold the company to Motorola, the hearing-aid division was the same size as the hospital-communications division.

Lesson: Selling to consumers can be very expensive, primarily due to the cost of advertising and sales, and/or building a distribution system to reach and sell to them. Not having money was a blessing in disguise for Dahlberg because it forced him to find low-cost ways of selling his product. However, many professional investors in new ventures would caution entrepreneurs to avoid multiple businesses, especially when financing is tight and the company is in danger of not dominating any of its markets. Dahlberg was talented enough to succeed in both and exited from them with a handsome profit when the timing was right.

11. Network to find attractive connections. As his company grew, Dahlberg joined the Young Presidents' Organization and became the regional vice-president. At a regional meeting in Chicago, Dahlberg met another YPO leader named Bob Galvin. Galvin's father had developed and built a company called Motorola, based on the car radio. Motorola wanted Dahlberg to use its own TV sets in the hospitals rather than a competitor's. Dahlberg suggested that the one way to be sure that that would happen would be to buy Dahlberg's company. Motorola did and Dahlberg and his brother each ended up with about $2 million of Motorola stock. He lived off this stock for a long time and recently donated the last $750,000 worth to the University of St. Thomas.

Lesson: When somebody with a lot of money and a strategic interest in your company wants something from you, it might be immensely profitable to exit at a very attractive price. And you can often find these people if you network.

Act II: Buying Back and Growing the Hearing-Aid Division

12. Buying back the hearing-aid business. Dahlberg, Inc., was a wholly owned subsidiary of Motorola for five years when Motorola decided to physically integrate the communications portion with Motorola's large communications division in Chicago. According to Dahlberg, Motorola never got its heart and soul into hearing aids, so he bought back the hearing-aid division for $1 million in cash. The division had $3 million in sales when he bought it back.

> **Lesson**: If you can do better than the current owner, consider buying it. Especially, look for poorly managed corporate divisions that don't fit the current CEO's strategic vision and direction.

13. Understand your skills and learning curve to determine your core competence. Dahlberg thought that Motorola squandered a heritage of miniaturization, elegance and design when it neglected the hearing-aid division, because that is what his company specialized in. These strengths could have helped Motorola when it started to compete against Nokia in cell phones, and Dahlberg believes that Motorola could have been the world leader in cell phones if it had shown more interest in hearing aids – and married them with wireless communications to develop cell phones. Motorola made phones for the military. These were big and durable, but not portable. According to Dahlberg, Motorola never examined how miniaturization and design could affect phones (until it was quite late).

> **Lesson**: Track changing markets and technology to integrate needs with technology and find new markets. Motorola did not do this, and this is where Dahlberg excelled. According to Dahlberg, this was due to his growing up on a farm during the Depression and he was "obliged to think while working." What a novel concept.

14. Motivating employees in the hearing-aid business. After buying back the hearing aid business, Dahlberg wanted to eliminate the corporate bureaucratic attitude that had developed. He sold 25 percent of the company to his employees in an employee stock-option plan (ESOP) to give them pride of ownership and a significant stake in the growth of the company, which would get them motivated and working in the company's best interests. He also found excellent employees. One day at church the minister asked if anyone had jobs for two refugees from Vietnam. Dahlberg hired them and found that they had unusual finger dexterity and aptitude to manufacture miniaturized products, such as hearing aids. By the time he sold the business again, he had about 300 refugees from Vietnam working for him in various departments.

> **Lesson**: Find the right people and put them in the right spots so you can get the highest productivity. However, be careful not to stereotype because, not only is it unfair, but you may lose valuable employees with different skills.

15. Understand the issues before expanding. When the business started to grow, Dahlberg opened one plant in rural Wisconsin and another in Arizona. Again, he found good employees at both locations. However, Wisconsin was closer to the main plant in Minneapolis. So Wisconsin benefitted from constant attention from Minneapolis personnel and performed much better than the Arizona plant.

Lesson: Communications and control are important when expanding. Make sure you constantly monitor your progress and take corrective action.

16. Expanding the consumer business to Europe. Dahlberg was aware of how important foreign markets could be for his business. So to expand in Europe, he bought half of the equity in a European company. The entrepreneur who had founded this company had essentially copied Dahlberg's products and designs and showed exemplary skills. This acquisition allowed Dahlberg to significantly expand into Europe.

Lesson: You don't have to expand organically, especially into new markets.

17. Grow with Sears. In the United States, Dahlberg used the Sears stores to grow his business. Since he grew up on a farm, he was aware of the importance of the Sears' network and was comfortable with it. Sears was dabbling in hearing aids and wanted to significantly increase its presence in the industry. Their existing hearing-aid counters in their stores were not doing well because the company did not understand the special needs of this business. So Dahlberg invited the vice-president of Sears on a fishing trip to Canada and sold him on the idea of having Dahlberg take over the stores as a concessionaire. Sears was already doing this in some specialty areas and was ready for it. Dahlberg changed the name of the stores to Miracle Ear from Silvertone to take advantage of Miracle Ear's marketing and brand recognition, and convinced Sears that it was more efficient and effective for marketing. In addition, he changed the name of the parent company from Dahlberg Electronics to Miracle Ear. Why was this alliance successful? Because it was an ideal fit. Dahlberg knew how to sell hearing aids. Sears had the traffic. Sears wanted to promote its own brand but it had failed when it had tried to do so. Since another specialty retailer had succeeded in optical retailing, Sears was open to the same strategy in audio retailing. Dahlberg suggested that Sears do what it did best, and to let him do what he did best.

Lesson: Form strategic alliances with large corporations in areas where they do not have your expertise or technology and you can fill this gap. Make sure that the business is designed to fit the needs of the market rather than designing it to fit the needs of the corporation. Don't be seduced or cowed into agreeing to the demands of the larger company if you think its strategy is not right. If the larger company always knew what it was doing, it would not need you.

18. Second exit from hearing aids. The venture succeeded spectacularly. That's when Bausch & Lomb came calling. Bausch & Lomb was already the "eyes of the world." It wanted to be the "eyes and ears of the world." For $139 million, Dahlberg helped it to meet its goals.

Lesson: When the price is right, take your cash (or stock) and run.

The Second Home Run: Buffalo Wild Wings

Summary: Not many people succeed a second time. Dahlberg did it by following some of his same basic principles.

19. Finding the opportunity. Dahlberg's son-in-law, Jim, skated for Holiday on Ice. One year he and a number of others were caught in a snowstorm in Buffalo, N.Y., at a bar. The bar was snowed in, and the customers could not leave. The owner used up all her food to cater to her "locked-in" customers. The final item she cooked were some chicken wings that were usually considered a throwaway. The wings were cooked with a proprietary recipe and Jim found them to be delicious. So he bought the recipe from the owner and started his own restaurants, called Buffalo Wild Wings (BWW). For a competitive advantage, Jim featured the wings as the main course rather than making them an appetizer, and he added TVs to make it into a sports bar. When Dahlberg met his son-in-law Jim for the first time, Jim owned three bars. Dahlberg liked the concept, and wanted to know how well the bars were doing. Jim pulled out a money clip with about $29. Dahlberg became the chairman of the company, financed the concept's expansion, and brought in a management team and a board, including Sally Smith, who had been CFO of Dahlberg Electronics, to help Jim. When Jim became ill, Dahlberg asked Smith, to become the CEO. Smith needled Dahlberg by saying that CEOs were supposed to be gabby men from marketing (a jab at Dahlberg, who fits the description). Dahlberg retorted that this business was a food business, so it should be ideal for a woman. Smith took the job and built it into a colossus with sales and market cap exceeding $300 million.

> **Lesson**: Find a concept that fits the needs of the target market. This concept was targeted towards younger people who wanted good food, good service and a comfortable hangout. It was also consistent with market trends, which were moving towards finger food, sports bars and value.

20. Manage the growing food business. Six of the top seven executives at BWW are women. According to Dahlberg, the keys to the success of BWW's management are its expertise in retail and the ability to attract, recognize and retain good people. The culture is softer but the company is just as results-oriented as any of his other businesses. In BWW, the field managers are key. They know (or should know) what is happening at the restaurants and should be able to inform management. They need to be the right people and be properly motivated. Dahlberg believes in the old-fashioned, but never out of style, practice of selecting people by "looking them in the eye and seeing who they are." He compares it to U.S. Supreme Court Justice Potter

Stewart's 1964 comment about obscenity – tough to describe, but you "know it when you see it." His criterion for selecting his team is whether he likes them. He finds that it is easier to be truthful and kind with people you like.

Lesson: People are key to every people-oriented business. Know how to find the best ones for your business. Then train them. Motivate them. Keep them. And succeed with them.

Rules for Entrepreneurs from Ken Dahlberg of Dahlberg Electronics (Miracle Ear) and Buffalo Wild Wings

- **Keep your powder dry.** Save so you have the resources to take advantage of opportunities. Always keep your eyes, ears and mind open to unmet needs and technological advances that you can capitalize on.
- **Plan and be prepared.** According to Dahlberg, you get bean soup by planting a bean in the spring, cultivating in the summer and harvesting in the fall. Know what you want, plan for it and take action.
- **Observe, observe, observe... to find new ideas**. Nowadays corporations are spending fortunes on consultants to become more innovative. According to Dahlberg, he got his ideas by keeping his eyes, ears and mind open growing up on the Depression-era farm. To survive, he had to find unmet needs and fill them. According to him, the profitable ideas were as "plain as an ass on a goat." So his solution was to observe what people were doing, where they were frustrated, ask them about it, and find out how to solve it profitably by knowing the technology to develop a unique product.
- **Balance knowledge and action**. According to Dahlberg, all the knowledge in the world is useless if it does not create wealth and enhance the human condition.
- **Get the right lessons**. Some would have become cynical when they got KP duty when they stepped forward to volunteer as a private in the military. Dahlberg saw it as an opening of doors to become a leader.
- **Become a leader**. When Dahlberg was taking an executive program at Harvard Business School, the instructor asked the class to define a leader. Dahlberg wrote that a "leader is one who has followers. You can evaluate a leader by how many followers (s)he has." And that people follow leaders because they like them.
- **Work with people you like and who like you**. Dahlberg maintains that he did not always agree with all of the people he worked with, but he picked only those

he liked. This way, they could disagree, still be friends and accomplish great things together.

- **Really listen to people**. Know what the person is saying but also understand how it affects you and can enhance your mutual objectives. Mesh your collective self-interests. This, in my opinion, is one of the key reasons behind Ken Dahlberg's success.

CRAIG SWANSON
DEFINITY HEALTH

MINNEAPOLIS, MINN

Building a $307 million health-care venture in four years

Summary: Starting with mowing lawns in fifth grade, Swanson graduated to painting houses in junior high, aspiring to paint them like a professional. From there he graduated to full-time construction work in the summer and college at the University of Vermont during the school year. With a degree in economics and political science, he joined the management group of Meredith & Grew, an old-line real estate company in Boston. Soon, he moved to TCF Bank in Minneapolis during the S&L crisis, before joining the MBA program at the University of Minnesota. After graduation, he became a consultant with Deloitte & Touche, where he spotted an opportunity in health care payment. With his colleagues and partners, he started a new venture called Definity Health. After investing nearly a million of their own money, the partners raised $75 million in three rounds of venture capital. Four years later, they sold the business to United Health Group for $307 million. This is how they did it.

Before the Startup

1. **The first venture**. Swanson started his first venture in fifth grade when he made a deal with his dad. His dad let him use the family lawnmower to mow their neighbors' lawns if he also mowed his own. And he had to buy his own gas for the mower. From there, he graduated to stripping and painting houses. He did one over the summer in junior high, and the next year a few of his neighbors asked him to do theirs. So Swanson hired five friends who helped him with the painting and the mowing. He lost some girlfriends along the way because he could not stay up late on Fridays. He had to get up early on Saturday (his wife was one of the girlfriends he lost; but she later changed her mind). This led him to other "real" jobs in high school, and in college he worked as a union construction worker for two years for M.A. Mortenson, a major contractor in the state.

Lesson: Swanson learned early that everything he did was a reflection of who he was as a person. So he learned the right way to paint and became better than most professional painters.

2. **The first job**. Swanson graduated from the University of Vermont (UVM) with a degree in economics and political science. He had originally joined UVM due to its business school, but had found out that he did not like finance as much as some other classes. So he switched. After graduation, he followed the path of least resistance and joined the property-management group of Meredith & Grew, which was an old-line real estate company in Boston. Swanson had experience in real estate and was comfortable managing it. The economy was in poor shape in 1988, and there were few other options. In his new job, Swanson managed commercial real estate, did renovations, and managed the company's work with contractors, a task with which he was very familiar. He stayed there for 18 months. During this time, he renovated two office buildings for the company. One of the buildings was fully occupied at the time of renovation, and Swanson had to shuffle tenants and people as the contractors tore up the windows and the interior. What he realized while doing this was that people complained no matter how smooth their transition was from one space to another. What they were looking for was for someone to appreciate their "pain." Swanson learned to help them in any way he could without offering financial incentives, but pointing out the benefits to them from the renovation.

Lesson: When someone complains, listen to their issues. Repeat their problem back to them. Understand their feelings. Come up with a solution that solves their problem, while being acceptable to you, i.e., without costing you money (if you can).

3. **The S&L crisis**. This was the time of the savings and loan (S&L) crisis when the nation's S&Ls were in deep trouble caused by profligate lending caused, in turn, by loose regulations. Many of them were about to go out of business. He talked about the situation with some professionals in the real estate industry who thought that there was potential in buying distressed assets. He came home to Minnesota during Christmas and after talking with his parents, went door knocking at large local S&Ls. One of the doors he knocked on was that of the Executive V.P. of commercial lending for TCF Bank. He introduced himself and asked if he could join the bank to help solve the bank's real estate problems. Swanson also noted that he planned to go to business school after helping to solve the problems, so he noted that he would not be a long-term cost for the bank. He ended up working for TCF. He spent one year in commercial underwriting to understand lending and TCF loan policies. Then he went into the commercial workout group, which had four people and a $350 million portfolio of properties that had been foreclosed. The workout group was charged with solving the loan problems quickly. If it could not solve it, the property would be taken over. The team had to present the status of all loans to top TCF executives including the CEO. Swanson learned some valuable lessons:

- *Do not sugarcoat or over-promise. "It is what it is."* Swanson thought that the senior executives were smart and entrepreneurial, and it was a challenge to live up to their requirements and expectations.
- Senior executives were likely to get irritated if Swanson had not thought of the key issues regarding each loan.
- Understand, as a team, all the issues surrounding the problem, including the borrower, its prospects, the real estate involved and its alternate uses.

Lesson: *Don't be afraid to knock on doors. All that can happen is that people can say no. Some might say it rudely. Others will be polite. And there might even be a few yes's.* It is also highly educational to be in the middle of a mess and to do turnarounds. Successful turnarounds require knowing all the key issues and how to get them resolved – in limited time.

4. **Moving on**. Near the end of the assignment, Swanson went to the CEO and told him that he had fulfilled his promise and so had TCF. Now he was ready to go back to business school. TCF offered to pay for business school if Swanson stayed on, but one month into this arrangement, Swanson realized that he was not able to do justice to either option. He also realized that he did not want to be a banker forever. He liked solving banking problems. He did not like the calm of everyday lending. He left TCF to become a full-time student.

Lesson: Know yourself. Know where your passions lie.

5. **Analyze turnarounds**. During the summer between the first and the second years of business school, Swanson worked for a company called Marshall Financial, which was part of the Mathiesen Group (MG). MG owned a variety of companies and banks, and it also did turnarounds for companies that were on the edge of bankruptcy in return for equity in the companies. He found the work interesting enough that he continued working for them during the second school year. During this time, he worked on a range of companies, including a welding company and a biomedical company. Out of 10 companies that Swanson worked on, three failed. The rest were turned around or were sold in an orderly process to a strategic buyer. This was a very rewarding training ground for Swanson, since he learned how to do "high-speed, iterative due diligence" by examining all the issues regarding the company, including the market, industry, competitive advantage, employees, management, and other factors that affected the company. Each issue was considered to be a concentric circle, and the process was to stand in the middle of the circles and pick the key factors for each issue by "turning around in the circle." In 24-48 hours, they had to decide whether or not to do the deal. He learned that the key was to understand everyone's bias, and to consequently adjust the information received. Having done the "high-speed due diligence," the next step was to understand the key issues that could affect the future of the company, and to analyze the financial impact of these issues. If the company decided to do it, they would then "run the company as an entrepreneur," i.e., someone with his or her own net worth on the line.

Lesson: If you can get involved in operating turnarounds, you will learn more about how business operates in a short time period than in most other positions.

6. **After graduation**. After graduating with an MBA from the Carlson School of Management (University of Minnesota), Swanson went to Deloitte & Touche to become a consultant. He liked the fact that the company had a variety of projects to work on, and he was interested in seeing new types of projects that he had not worked on before. With this goal, he worked on projects involving mergers & acquisitions for large telecom and health companies such as Kaiser, Blue Cross companies and others. For telecom companies, such as Bell Canada and Sprint, he also worked on value-based management (see lesson below). After four years at D&T, Swanson left to start his new venture.

Lesson: Value-based management was a concept used by his firm to identify and understand the value drivers in any company. They looked at companies from the perspective of an outsider, without the potential biases of an insider who may be too close to the trees. Mastery of value-based management helped Swanson to understand and improve the company's competitive advantage.

From Startup to Profits

7. **The venture**. After leaving D&T, Swanson started the Lemhi Group (LG) with Tony Miller (and a third partner who left the firm in the initial phase). LG was organized to develop a new health insurance concept for American consumers that included incentives to change behavior. Their plan was to offer consulting services to corporations as a bootstrapping revenue generator, while they developed the new service that they wanted to offer. LG was the precursor to Definity Health. Lemhi Group was named after the Lemhi Pass that Lewis and Clark had to traverse on their historic transcontinental journey across America. Until they reached the Lemhi Pass, Lewis and Clark were reasonably comfortable with the amount of knowledge they had about the passage to the Pacific. But the journey beyond the Lemhi Pass in the Rocky Mountains was a blank slate. They had no idea what the future would bring. Based on their consulting in the health industry, Swanson and Miller knew what did and did not work in health care. They reasoned that with the right financial incentives, they could develop a health-payment system, called the Health Reimbursement Account (HRA), that could cut costs. The HRA would combine aspects of the medical savings account with insurance above a defined limit, include consumer tools to inform and select the right type of care, and include the right network of care providers. It took them two years to develop the prototype. During this time they consulted and used the $1.5 million earned from consulting to pay advisers and other associates who helped them build the prototype. Their goal was to understand everything about consumer behavior regarding healthcare.

This included understanding every detail about every competitor, including the people, tools, markets, and clients and an analysis of which clients were likely to switch and which would not. Of the $1.5 million invested by the two principals, $200,000 was used for travel to do the leg work, and $500,000 was for technical expertise to develop the prototypes so that the human resource experts of various potential clients could see what it actually looked like. PriceWaterhouseCoopers (PWC) agreed to consider becoming the first strategic customer. During this time, the principals lived on their savings and liquidated their 401(k) accounts. They used credit cards to borrow additional amounts for expenses. They did not take a salary for two years. The pressure was too high for one of the partners, who left due to incompatibilities.

> **Lesson**: Customers and investors often cannot understand what they are buying if they cannot see it. People cannot see when the suitcase is empty. It often costs money to develop sophisticated prototypes and requires intense dedication. Understand the price to move it to the stage where you can sell. Picking partners is also an important decision. Clarify key issues that can derail partnerships, such as goals, strategies, salaries, level of investment needed, debt, and time spent on the job. Perhaps most importantly, discuss whether the partners can handle the stress involved in a development-stage company.

8. "Boil the ocean." Swanson and his partner spent two years building the prototype of the Definity model so that they could show the actual scaled-down version to potential investors and customers. They also completed a thorough business plan that covered all of the risk factors that could derail the company. They first presented the model to employees and human resource executives of large corporations, and to a few venture capitalists who had expressed interest, knew the industry and would be good partners for Definity. They got very valuable feedback from these sources, including their strengths, weaknesses, and challenges. *Corporate customers expressed interest, and many of their employees agreed to sign on if the service was available, because they noted that the alternative models did not meet their needs.* Based on the positive feedback from these presentations, they were able to raise $23 million in the first round (Series A) of institutional venture capital. As Swanson puts it, Definity tried to "boil the ocean" by capturing an attractive slice of an extremely large market.

> **Lesson**: Find a need and fill it. Based on Definity's analysis of the health consumer (employees) in large companies, they knew that an attractive percentage of employees would sign on if the model was built. The result from the presentation of the prototype was proof of that, and that proof was needed for VCs to jump on board. ***Know that VCs like to see proof of competitive advantage***. The investment to obtain this proof was quite significant. In his second venture, Swanson has decided not try to "boil the ocean" so he could control the venture.

9. Raising venture capital. But before they raised the first round from VCs, Definity went to UnitedHealth Group (UHG) to raise financing with more attractive terms than from VCs. UHG is the 600-pound gorilla in healthcare. Swanson and his partner told UHG that Definity would come up with a new way to pay for health insurance that could help UHG gain a significant advantage and increase its market share. UHG's response was that it would be very interested in considering Definity as an acquisition if Definity succeeded, but that the current stage was too early. So Definity was forced to get financing from the VC funds. Six VC funds were involved in the first round. To negotiate the deal, Definity found that one of the VCs "got it," i.e., he understood the industry and the value proposition that Definity was developing. He became their champion and sold the concept to the others. The board had seven directors, three of whom were VCs, two were Definity's partners, and two were independent directors selected by Swanson and his partner.

Lesson: A few large corporations get involved in early stages of a venture and invest at the research and development stage. In return for this attractive financing, they seek the right of first refusal, which means that they have the right to match the highest offer to buy the company when the investors want to exit (note that some potential buyers may not bid because they may think they are wasting their time by setting a price for someone else, so you may need to protect yourself from this possibility). Others wait until the venture has proved itself in the market, and then they may just acquire it. Obviously, UHG preferred to wait. To select VCs, Swanson *suggests getting a lead VC with a deep understanding of the industry and the business.* According to Swanson, some VCs did not understand the business and were just "financial guys," and this often created unneeded friction.

10. After the first round. After obtaining the first round of financing in March of 2000, Definity built the actual health plan in about seven months. By October, they were enrolling customers. The development period was very short, and this created goodwill with investors. The reason they were able to expedite the construction of their software and the broader plan was that they had been planning the building of the model for two years – while they were working on their business plan. They did not want to lose time and had developed multiple, parallel paths to achieve their goals. The sales cycle in large corporations and organizations was set. Open enrollment was in the fall (October and November), and this meant that they had to sell to the employees in late summer (August and September). If they did not meet this deadline, they would not have customers for a whole year, and the venture could be in jeopardy. They did meet the deadline and started recruiting customers by the fall. They broke even in June 2003, which was about two years after first introduction...right on schedule.

Lesson: When it is do-or-die, you do or you die. ***Having a deadline focuses the mind.*** A good plan also helps. Plan. Do. Monitor. Succeed.

11. Pick the right market segment. For their point of entry into the market, Definity selected large self-insured employers. Definity did not want to carry the risk of selling insurance, and these types of employers have a strong incentive to keep their employees happy and save money. Definity recruited a sales team of benefit consultants and sales personnel who had a significant level of experience working with these types of employers. To focus their efforts, they tried to develop a system of ranking customers based on various factors, but they were never able to formulate a good system to predict the likelihood of customers signing up.

Lesson: ***Your initial market segment should be selected based on a number of factors***, including its unmet needs, how easy it is to reach and sell, your competitive advantage, the risk and costs of switching for the customer, and the potential of dominating the market to prevent someone else from dislodging you from your perch. If you are able to build a dominating position in an attractive segment, a large corporation that wants attractive segment is likely to pay you a significant premium to buy your business, which should make your investors and you very happy.

From Profits to the Moon

12. Three rounds of financing. In all, Definity raised $75 million in three rounds of financing. The first round of $23 million in March 2000 was followed by a second round of $24 million in the fall of 2001. This was a "down" round, which means that the valuation of the venture was below the first round. After 9/11, it became very difficult to raise money. The company was 48 hours away from shutting the door. Due to the initial uniqueness of the product, sales were slower than expected in the first two years but picked up afterwards. This is the classic "hockey stick" sales curve. Entrepreneurs always expect a higher growth of sales than what they are able to achieve. Customers are slow to switch and they often need more information and persuasion, which takes time. For Definity, it took several large employer clients including Medtronic, Textron, and the APWU (American Postal Workers Union) to act as a catalyst. When these employers signed on, it provided a positive signal to the other large organizations, which promptly signed on. The third round of $15 million was in 2003 and it was used to buy a service bureau and a claims shop. Definity had built its own version of claims software internally that an external vendor was managing. Definity used the funds to buy back its portion of their business so as to be totally self-contained.

Lesson: There are a few key lessons here:

- ***Desperation is not a great strategy to raise money.*** Swanson and his partner learned that finance can be complicated and that down rounds are painful.
- ***Sales are nearly always lower than in projections offered to venture capital funds.*** Don't be too optimistic initially because your high sales

projections could cause investors to lose confidence in you, resulting in down rounds.

- ***Lastly, get your bell (lead) cow and then promote that strategic customer to get additional sales.***

13. Sale to UHG. In December 2004 Definity was sold to UHG for $307 million. Swanson was not eager to see the sale go through, but the venture capital investors wanted to exit from their investment and book their profits. The board and investors were concerned about the possibility of new competitors, including UHG itself, copying their model, since the pain of customer loss was getting too high for them. New products were entering the market, and they were reasonably similar to Definity's. The venture was sold.

Lesson: If you take money from investors, you owe them an attractive exit. So decide if that is what you want (before you take their money). And understand the consequences of not seeking venture capital.

Post Script

14. The next venture. Swanson has now started another company called Insignia Health with one other early employee of Definity. Besides them, they have two employees. He has no outside capital and is hoping to build this venture without venture capital. He has bootstrapped the early expenses and found customers who are helping him grow and financed a major portion of the growth. Insignia has about 40 clients ranging from health plans to biopharmaceutical manufacturers. Insignia invests in itself and grows its capabilities as its client list and revenue grows. Swanson is living the lessons he learned from the first venture.

Lesson: Smart entrepreneurs try not to repeat mistakes. They only make new ones.

Rules for Entrepreneurs from Craig Swanson of Definity Health

- **Study your business.** Before seeking money from investors, learn everything about your proposed business. The more you know, the better you will be at presenting details to investors, increasing your credibility and getting the financing.
- **When you raise money from VC funds, you give up your freedom.** If you can limit outside capital, you can control your destiny. Initially, Definity had some limited financing from angels who were fun to work with and gave good feedback. However, the amount of funding needed to get into the market was huge.

- **VCs care about their investment – first and foremost.** They are not concerned about the interests of the entrepreneur unless, of course, they coincide with their own.
- **Trends can carry you far.** It is easier to grow with a trend than without one.
- **Find the right partners.** Make sure they have the same interests, goals, and staying power.
- **Work hard.** Five years ago, Swanson ran across a saying from Thomas Edison: "Most people miss an opportunity because it comes dressed in overalls and looks like work."
- **Corporations don't like to start unique businesses.** Large corporations are better at buying ventures after they have proved their business model than starting a venture from scratch.

Joel Ronning
Digital River Inc.

EDEN PRAIRIE, MINN

Building one of the largest online software vendors

Summary: When Joel Ronning was at the University of Minnesota, he joined the sailing team and became its president. He found that he enjoyed organizing people so much that he started his first venture – a newsletter to connect buyers and sellers of Mercedes-Benz cars in the United States and Canada. In succession, he started a venture to sell personal computer peripherals for the Apple computer, a consulting firm in the software industry and another company to sell computer peripherals for the Apple computer. This taught him that it was more efficient to sell software over the Internet than by including them in disk drives or disks and sending them physically to buyers. From that insight, Ronning has built a company with annual sales of around $400 million and a market cap of nearly $1.3 billion. This is how he did it.

Before the Startup

1. Get involved and learn new skills. As a student at the University of Minnesota, Ronning made a life-changing (in retrospect) decision – he joined the sailing team and became its president. Within a year, he had expanded the number of members from 15 to 225 and the number of boats from three to 45. How did he do this? He asked people for help and organized them into various committees such as membership, sailing, having fun (he calls it entertainment). He delegated authority. He helped people to work together and made it fun. He learned that he had a gift for building groups and getting them to work well together to achieve common goals.

Lesson: Ronning found that the critical factor in getting students to volunteer and contribute was recognition, and thanking them for their contributions. *People like to enjoy the work they are doing and the people they are working with, and when they are recognized for their contributions*. This was one of the keys to Ronning's success.

From Statup to Profits

2. Buying and selling Mercedes-Benz cars. When he was in school, Ronning got a part-time summer job selling car parts. As part of his job, he had to find some of the parts from dealers around the country, and some were hard to find. In the course of this search, Ronning realized that there was no central information source for the demand or supply of used Mercedes-Benz (MB) cars. Having developed computer skills and having an Apple IIe, Ronning started to track the availability of MB cars in the United States and Canada from his dorm room. He would contact dealers to get a list of cars that were available and included them in a newsletter. He then started a brokerage, whereby he would sell cars and arrange to have them shipped. Due to exchange rate advantages, he found that adding Canada to the market was very profitable. He had assistants who organized the mailing, and his friends would fly to cities around the United States and Canada to pick up MB cars and transport them to his buyers. Before long, his annual sales exceeded $1 million and he made over $10,000 in income in good months. The recession of 1981 put an end to this business, as his customers stopped buying expensive cars when interest rates spiked above 20 percent.

Lesson: Find your own strengths and use them to your advantage. Although Ronning did not think of himself as a sales person and did not have high levels of sales skills, he realized the importance of the computer for finding data and to package information. He realized that the right information could be very profitable.

3. Second venture. When the recession of 1981 put an end to his auto business, Ronning got a job as a product manager with Remington Rand managing peripheral products for the Mac computer. When Remington Rand was sold, Ronning was able to get the new owner to let him take the Mac peripheral-products business and do with it as he wished. He formed a company called Mirror Technologies, hired engineers and expanded the line to include other peripheral products. He sold products via local newspaper ads, and to a national market via computer magazine ads. He had two groups of customers, namely consumers and small business. He sold to them directly (from the ads) and indirectly via computer dealerships. He found that direct was better – the cash inflow was much better and more than made up for the increased advertising expenses. When he sold indirectly via dealers, he had problems with payments and returns. The dealers would return the goods after a number of months if they were unable to sell, thus putting the risk of their sales ability (or inability) on Ronning.

Lesson: When opportunity comes your way, grab it. If you have a choice between selling directly to your customers or selling indirectly to consumers via intermediaries, think of the cost, discounts, and hassle (such as the risk of unintended returns) that intermediaries can impose on you. Direct sales are usually preferred, especially at the start of the business, but obviously many have done well with indirect sales and marketing strategies.

4. Mirror's start. When Ronning started Mirror, he invested his savings and raised additional financing from his family and friends. Since he did not come from a wealthy family and did not have many wealthy friends, he borrowed additional funds. His sales quickly grew to an annual rate of $12 million. While at Mirror, Ronning focused strictly on Apple products because he understood Apple. He never did analyze the Microsoft tidal wave to see if he should expand and add Microsoft products. Perhaps if he had, with his skills in direct marketing, he might have started a Dell or a Gateway. Ronning stuck to Apple because he liked its culture and community. Ronning believed that he should like what he did.

Lesson: I cannot argue with passion. That seems to be a common trait among great entrepreneurs. However, I would also suggest that you keep your eyes open for new, hot trends that can affect your business and industry. The Microsoft juggernaut was starting to dominate the PC industry. If a hot trend starts, examine it to see if you can capitalize on it or if it can threaten you. It is much easier to grow with a trend than without the help of one. You may still reject it for other reasons, but at least you would have considered it.

5. Mirror's ship hits the rocks. When Mirror started to grow, Ronning secured financing from angel investors. But he did not develop a good accounting system, so while he thought he was making money with gross margins of 20-30 percent, he was not. His management of accounts receivable was inadequate, and he gave too much credit to poor dealers, ending up with large write-downs. To turn Mirror around, Ronning reduced his sales to dealers and concentrated on direct sales to consumers and got paid immediately via credit cards. This improved his cash flow. He hired a major accounting firm to audit his books and improve the back office. But it was too little, too late and his angels encouraged Ronning to leave by giving him a vastly diminished role in the company.

Lesson: Learn accounting and become a numbers person. ***You cannot run a business without knowing your numbers***. As I noted in another book (*Finance Any Business* ***Intelligently®***/ available at www.infinancing.com), ***managing a business without numbers is like driving a car without being able to see***. Sooner or later, you will crash. So acquire the expertise you need. Ronning learned that he needed operations and control skills. He was already strong in product development and sales.

6. The consultant. After he left Mirror, Ronning spent a year consulting with a friend of his in Silicon Valley. The business developed control and software logic to make different devices work together and was selling software and disk-drive operating systems. Friends don't always make good business partners. However, in this case, Ronning and his friend complemented each other's skills, since the friend did not have a network to generate sales, and they trusted each other. At the consulting firm, Ronning learned how to write software and encryption, in which area he now has a number of patents.

> **Lesson**: Be careful whom you partner with. Good partnerships are like a good marriage. Bad ones are like a marriage from hell. Ronning and his partner trusted and respected each other's skills and expertise.

7. The second time around. About a year and a half after leaving Mirror, Ronning was itching to get back to what he knew best, and that was selling parts for personal computers. So he started Tech Squared with $40,000 of financing from credit cards. This meant, as he puts it, that he "had to make money." Having reflected on his mistakes at Mirror, Ronning wanted to make sure that Tech Squared did not repeat them. His first hire was an accountant and his first capital expenditure was an accounting system. Tech Squared (TS) was set up to compete directly with Mirror (his non-compete agreement ran out after six months) and Ronning had a similar line of products. The front end, i.e., products and direct sales, was instinctive to Ronning. The back end, accounting, finance and controls, was not. So he spent a "tremendous amount of time" studying finance, accounting, and controls, including items such as contract law, cycle times, receivables, etc. As Ronning puts it, he "read anything I could" on the topic. It became "fun" for him to learn about these areas, and excelling at it became a passion. His goal was to avoid any weaknesses that could destroy his company again. Although Ronning does not know how much TS had to do with the eventual demise of Mirror, Ronning ended up buying about $500,000 of hard assets from Mirror for $80,000 when Mirror went out of business. Tech Squared did very well, reaching $48 million of sales within four years. Even the first quarter was profitable, and this time Ronning had accurate financial statements.

> **Lesson**: Ronning believes that the best general managers and entrepreneurs of a business need to respect and understand all aspects of the business and become good at all of them, especially sales. When you are selling, you can understand customer needs. But to build a successful business, all parts have to integrate smoothly and have to be in the best condition. Even the best Indy racing car can lose if its tires are flat. This means that you have to learn how the inside operates and make it hum, or else even the best sales organization will come apart.

8. Tracking the pulse. While at TS, Ronning realized that he had to continuously monitor the company. This meant tracking sales and the sales effectiveness of various magazines and layouts. He would track the leads, prospects, sales, and margins from every ad and every magazine to see what worked and what did not. He would ***track the velocity of sales***, i.e., how a new product performed over six weeks to see if the growth rate increased or not. At the same time, he instituted tremendous control over costs so he knew how the business was doing at all times. All of the sales were credit card sales, which meant that TS received payment before they shipped the products. He located the business near the distributor so that he could pick up the product from the morning's sales in the afternoon, pack them and ship them the same day. This cut his inventory needs. He got 30-day terms from his vendors, but he always paid in 29. He often personally hand-carried the check to the credit managers so that they knew him and knew he was paying them on time. This attention to keeping his vendors' credit managers happy meant that Ronning did not ever have to seek bank financing for his growth from startup to $48 million in annual sales. The initial $40,000 of credit card financing was all he needed.

Lesson: Pay attention to detail. Understand how to improve the effectiveness of your sales drivers. Keep inventories low and collect receivables on time – it is great if you can collect them before shipment. That is one of the advantages of direct marketing to consumers. If you can find consumers who want to buy, you can usually get them to pay before you ship. Keep your creditors informed. Every creditor appreciates a customer who pays on time.

9. The next change. When TS reached an annual sales level of $50 million, Ronning found that it became tough to grow due to market and competitive forces. In the meantime, he saw that they were shipping a lot of blank disk drives across the United States. To increase sales, he started adding software with free trial periods on it. The free benefits expired by usage or with time. He then started experimenting with encryption software on his own and wrote some programs for which he received a number of patents. Since he had strong connections to Fujitsu (he was selling a lot of their equipment), he showed them some of the benefits of the encryption software. His contact at Fujitsu recommended a meeting with senior executives. so Ronning flew to Japan. The CEO saw a strategic fit for the encryption software since Fujitsu could potentially enhance the value of their disk drives, which were a commodity and had low margins. To take advantage of this fit, the CEO decided to invest $600,000 in the new company, called Digital River, for 40 percent of the company. The technology did not work out because they could not find a way to write the software on the disk at a low enough cost. But the investment ended up being worth about $60 million. This alliance started as a research project but ended up becoming an investment bonus. According to Ronning, Fujitsu executives think this is the "best U.S. investment they have ever made." Looking back, Ronning thinks he should have asked for $6 million since it would be a "rounding error" for a company of Fujitsu's size.

Lesson: When seeking alliances with large corporations, make sure you ask for a large amount if you are going to give them exclusivity, and especially if you are dealing with the CEO. Another reason why the alliance worked out was because Ronning never "leaned" on Fujitsu. He made sure that he protected and controlled his technology and he implemented his own business plan without relying on Fujitsu. An alliance such as this one can have significant benefits for a new venture, including an expanded network and terrific credibility.

From Profits to Home-Run

10. Selling software on the Internet. Ronning's vision for Digital River (DR) was to sell software over the Internet using his encryption software. Adding software to a disk drive adds cost since it needs separate equipment and the large disk-drive manufacturers do not want to customize their automated assembly lines. To make the DR model work, Ronning needed to offer high-value products with higher customer close rates. DR spent two years in the research and development phase, developing and filing patents for its software encryption and distribution process. His experience taught him to be very prudent with the cash he received from Fujitsu and with the small amount he was able to raise from angels. He bought a few servers and rented the balance of his needs from TS, which by this time was being managed by a president that Ronning had picked. By the time he was finished with the development and was ready for market, he still had $200,000 left. This was his working capital. He started small with a minimal amount of sales and marketing, and started selling software for his initial clients before investing any money for growth. With Mirror Technologies, Ronning wanted to grow fast, so he obtained funding from angels who de-invited him when he ran into problems. With TS, Ronning had borrowed $40,000 from credit cards, so he had to be cheap. With DR, Ronning was not about to repeat the mistakes of Mirror and was determined to follow his strategy with TS. He kept the growth rate, and his cash needs, low until he had generated sales and had proved the concept.

Lesson: It is tough to raise a lot of money at the early, high-risk stage. If, however, you are able to raise a lot of money at the start, you may have to suffer a high level of dilution or give up control (or both), and there is the risk that you might end up with little to show for all your effort. ***So be frugal and make sure that every dime spent earns the targeted return.***

11. Secret to Digital River's success: Boost revenues for your customers. DR's customers are mainly manufacturers who are very experienced at channel management, i.e., at selling through distributors. DR, and Ronning, developed experience in one-to-one marketing that the manufacturers did not have. DR has been successful because the company has been able to increase customers' revenues by better merchandising, search-engine and site-flow optimization, affiliate management, improving order rates and the re-buyer rate, and better e-mail marketing.

Lesson: Develop your unique skills for your competitive advantage. In addition to his encryption software, Ronning had developed direct marketing skills that he exploited fully in DR.

12. Fail fast. Feed success. Ronning tests everything that is new. With clear objectives and goals, he keeps track of new products and other business strategies to check whether they are going as planned. If not, he changes the test and tries again. He invests more cash only if the tests succeed. He does not get emotionally involved in ideas. As he puts it, "***there are many ideas, some are bad, many are just OK, and a few are meaningful.***" The trick is to test them as cheaply as possible, sift through the things that don't work, and quickly get to the ideas with merit. This means not spending much time on ideas that don't make the grade. *Fail fast*. To decide which new products to pursue, Ronning sifts them using a Strategic Analysis Model that uses the "wisdom of crowds" concept to rank ideas based on potential value, costs, time, and strategic value. Key managers and staff members get together to discuss and rank the ideas. Usually loudmouths dominate. Here loudmouths can talk all the time, but they need to be prepared unless they want to put their feet in their mouth. As Ronning puts it, "if they are brilliant and right (all the time), they can have the floor (all the time)." The problem he has found is to get people to speak up. He encourages the use of sticky notes for anonymity to make sure that all opinions are heard. Then they do a "group sniff test" to see if it makes sense.

Lesson: Get everyone's opinion. Ronning has found that ***the "crowd" does make good decisions so long as everyone gets involved***. So test, test, and test. If it does not work, change and test some more. Instinct is only the first step. Testing to confirm instincts is the next key step. Once you know it makes money, step on the gas and accelerate.

13. Focus on community of employees. To grow, Ronning believes in a tremendous adherence to metrics, i.e., ***how are the numbers working, and also to a super-focus on the community of employees***. The company offers great benefits, but expects equally top-notch performance. The goal is to keep Digital River as a great company that makes money, which is key for shareholders. The culture in the company is one of fun and performance. Ronning has each manager rank all the employees they manage. For promotions, they have to be at the top of the "stack rack" (all on performance and not on popularity with the gang), which is the same as Jack Welch's method at GE. Ronning reads voraciously about topics in which he wants to improve his skills and implements best practices from top companies. At DR, no one wants to be at the bottom of the stack rank for two years. If they are, they self-manage themselves out of the company. The stack ranks are confidential but people at the top are informed about the rankings to make sure employees are happy and to get feedback on how well the company is doing.

Lesson: Good people will come to work for you if they feel challenged, their efforts rewarded and they are recognized. People need to see a culture that emphasizes performance rather than one where "popularity" wins. They should also enjoy the process. Tough jobs can become easier when you are having fun.

14. Building new managers. Ronning believes in promoting talented people, whether the employees come from the inside or came to DR in an acquisition. He works with the managers of the divisions to make sure that they are strong in all aspects of the business. This means that in the early days of a manager's tenure, Ronning expects more detailed business plans, more frequent reporting, and more intense guidance. As Ronning becomes more comfortable with the skills of the division manager, he delegates more authority (although he still keeps track of daily sales and weekly income statements). At this stage, these executives ask Ronning for his input when they want his insights. He has a number of such stars in the company who are managing divisions with annual sales of $60 million, $70 million, and $50 million. They all started managing businesses with about $3 million in sales.

> **Lesson**: *Delegate to build managers with skills, but monitor based on their level of expertise and your comfort level with them.* Know what you want to see at each step of the process and loosen the strings as the manager grows.

15. Rules for acquisitions. Buy for the strategic fit and integrate smoothly. Digital River has made a number of strategic acquisitions to keep its growth at a high pace. When Ronning buys a venture, he makes sure that there is a strong fit with his existing company. A key requirement for any acquisition is that a top executive of DR has to champion the acquisition and make sure that it does not become an orphan with no voice or clout within the company. Most of the acquisitions are structured as earn-outs in which the selling entrepreneur makes about 40-60 percent of his base pay based on the performance of the unit. To ensure success, Ronning makes sure that the entrepreneur is assigned an executive (often the sponsor) from DR who works with the entrepreneur and will help focus on areas where the entrepreneur may not be as strong. If the entrepreneur was a strong product developer, the executive-coach teaches him/her sales and to control the business. This becomes a win-win for both since the entrepreneur not only makes more money but also learns how to become a complete entrepreneur and CEO. Ronning measures good integration with the rest of DR, revenue growth, expense reduction, and controls.

> **Lesson**: Don't buy a unit if you don't know why you are buying it, what you expect from it, how to integrate it and have a champion for it within the company. About two-thirds of corporate acquisitions fail because CEOs buy companies to have more assets under management or to grow sales. Key is to grow revenues, income, margins, and return on equity.

16. When going global, go local. To sell to local customers, Ronning believes that you need employees who understand local culture, the people, language, and the selling culture. Since DR sells to customers globally, they have opened 20 offices around the world, with hundreds of employees in the various offices. These offices can relate well to the local markets and complement the online experience.

> **Lesson**: *People buy more from people whom they like, assuming of course that these people can solve their problems.* Cultural affinity is part of this strategy. So when expanding globally, get local help.

17. Track the pulse. Due to his unpleasant experience with Mirror Technologies and his "learning' at Tech Squared, Ronning rigorously implements an accounting and financial tracking system so that he knows how the company is doing in real time. He gets daily sales figures by 10:30 AM; and weekly run rates, quality reports, and financial results (compared with goals) by Monday at 9 AM. This allows him to schedule meetings with his managers even when he is travelling, since they all have the same information in front of them, and they can discuss problems and opportunities. His daily revenue manager tracks revenues across the entire company, including exchange rates, international interest rates (such as LIBOR), trends, and danger signals. As an example, he knew that his markets were tanking on September 15, 2008, on the same day due to real-time tracking of the steep decline in his sales. Same for September 11, 2001. This allowed him to immediately discuss the situation with his senior managers and cut expenses based on a new plan within weeks. While developing the system may be hard, Ronning has found that implementing it becomes easier with experience.

Lesson: Know where you are and where you are going. Otherwise, as a wise sage once said, "any road will get you there." Not knowing your numbers means that you are relying on divine providence to protect you. I would not count on that.

Rules for Entrepreneurs from Joel Ronning of Digital River

- **Get involved and learn new skills**. Learning how to organize and motivate as president of the sailing team helped Ronning understand his key strength.
- **Get as many new customers as fast as possible**. Then "up-sell" them. Having many customers increases your comfort level.
- **Know your numbers.** Ronning is a prime example of an entrepreneur who paid the price when he did not track his numbers and has benefitted handsomely when he did.
- **Develop your sales skills**. Although Ronning does not consider himself a "dynamic" sales person, he is one of the leading experts at selling directly to consumers using the media. This is one of his competitive advantages.
- **Delegate responsibly**. When delegating, know that managers need to have authority but you need to know that they are capable of handling it. So be close to them initially and allow them more freedom as they mature. But continue tracking their performance.

- **Don't confuse fun and performance.** Many companies have beer parties on Fridays, but performance should be the main criterion. Popularity is not a substitute for performance.
- **People like to buy from people they understand and like.** When selling globally, hire local talent.
- **Control costs. Revenues are only half the game.** The other half is cost control. Otherwise you are "trading dollars" and sometimes at a loss.
- **Ask for more from a corporation in a strategic alliance.** Whatever an entrepreneur asks for is usually a rounding error for large corporations. So don't be afraid to ask for more. If the benefit is strategic, you just might get your money.
- **Never lean on the large corporation.** And never be dependent on a corporate partner; otherwise, you will end up working for them and they will get all the wealth created.
- **Promote based on performance.** Talented people need to know that promotions are based on performance, and not because they know how to play the political game.

TIM DOHERTY
DOHERTY EMPLOYMENT GROUP

MINNEAPOLIS, MINN

Building a $400 million giant in corporate staffing

Summary: Tim Doherty grew up in Minnetonka, Minnesota. When he was a teenager in 1970, his family moved to Litchfield to run an A&W Root Beer stand that his parents had purchased. The drive-in did not do too well, and his parents shut it down after seven years. After finishing his undergraduate degree at the University of Minnesota, Doherty tried his hand at life insurance sales, and then he went to work for Procter & Gamble. When P&G wanted to move him to St. Louis, Doherty decided to quit because his fiancée was studying law in Minneapolis and she did not want to move, because she would have to start all over studying to pass the Missouri bar exam. After searching for many months in mid-1979, he landed a position as a salesperson for a temporary help service. The economy was heading into a recession, however, and the business owner decided to reduce staff. Doherty was out of a job after just four months. Frustrated with the lack of job opportunities due to that economy, he followed his father's suggestion and decided to start his own temp firm with his parents' help. Today, that firm has nearly 10,000 worksite employees and annual revenues of over $400 million. This is how he did it.

Before the Startup

1. **Dad's first business**. When Doherty was 16, his dad bought a root beer stand in Litchfield and moved the family close to the business. Unfortunately, the stand was not successful when he bought it, and it was not successful after he bought it. His dad did not know the fast food business, and he didn't sufficiently check the business before he bought it. He took the word of the sellers that the business was a good one to buy. The sellers had falsified sales receipts and profit data, and they went to court to settle their differences. The lawyers won. In hindsight, it was easy to see the mistakes. However, the silver lining from this episode was that Doherty met his future wife, Valerie, who was a carhop at the drive-in. They became friends, started dating when they were sophomores at different colleges, and got married after she finished law school.

Lesson: *Don't buy a business before you know the business.* Learn the industry and the business before you decide to buy something. Otherwise, you need to be gifted or lucky. Doherty had many bad memories from this episode, but as the old cliché goes, there are always silver linings. He met his future wife.

2. **The first business**. Following in the footsteps of his parents, Doherty decided to start and manage his own food stand, selling pronto pups and root beer at the local county fair when he was 17 years old. His inventory investment included some old barrels and drums, and his time investment included 16-hour days for 12 days in the summer. He built the counters himself and used the drums as counter seats. He started the day at 9:30 a.m. and ended around 1 a.m. He hired his first employee – a part-time helper. The environment was dusty, the hours were long, but he made $850 in the first year selling pronto pups and root beer. In the second year, he decided that he could manage the entire operation and did not hire a part-time helper. His profits exceeded $1,000. The only fly in the ointment was that his friends stopped by the stand and asked him for credit. They ended up not paying.

Lesson: Be careful whom you trust. Doherty learned early on to carefully evaluate whom you extend credit to and how much credit you extend them. And he also learned that help can be expensive. Know when to seek it and when not to.

3. **Managing the fraternity**. Doherty attended the University of Minnesota Business School and joined a fraternity, where he became active in managing its affairs and became its president for 18 months. This episode helped him to understand budgets, and he realized that managing a frat was a lot like managing a hotel. The fraternity house served three meals a day, and he ended up cooking the meals if the cook did not show up. He had to manage volunteers to run the frat, and motivate them to manage it well. He was the final "doer," since there was no one else to rely on if his team or staff were busy. This position taught him valuable interviewing skills. The first two cooks he hired lasted only a month. To prevent having to frequently rehire cooks, he had to determine whether his new hires were likely to last in the position. So he started to examine their job history and tenure, including why they left or were fired. This helped him to hire better staff and reduce turnover.

Lesson: Even volunteer-leadership positions, and maybe especially volunteer positions, teach you a lot about how to lead. When you are in business and you screw up, you lose money. When you are in a volunteer position and you screw up, you lose time. Learn how to do it right to avoid paying a high price.

4. **Selling insurance... not**. After graduation from college, Doherty joined a large agency of a life insurance company to sell life and disability insurance to dental and medical students. He tried this for a year but found it difficult because he had to convince people to buy more insurance than he thought they needed. He moved on to Procter & Gamble (P&G).

Lesson: *Find something you believe in if you want to sell successfully.* If you are not convinced that what you are selling provides a good value, you are unlikely to sell it successfully.

5. Sales reports and controls. At P&G, Doherty was a management trainee and sold Folgers coffee to grocers. His territory was around Minneapolis and central Minnesota, and he was in route sales. He had to track calls and fill in daily reports, including mileage, maintenance, etc. He did not like to write reports every day (is there anyone in sales who likes to fill out reports?), and tried to recreate events for the last three days. When Doherty ended up managing a sales force years later, he remembered his own reluctance to write reports, insisted on getting daily reports from them so he could track and control their activities, and monitored their results or lack of same. To increase sales, P&G consistently came up with new promotions, end-of-aisle displays, and plans to capture additional shelf space. Doherty learned that the only way he could get more shelf space was by convincing the store owner (or manager) of the greater ROI from offering more space to P&G. Until he could prove that the grocer got a higher return by offering more shelf space to P&G, he did not have much success. At this time, coffee prices skyrocketed due to a global imbalance caused by bad weather, and consumers cut back on their purchases of coffee. He had to show grocers the right time to buy. Before prices spiked, he would get on the phone and warn his customers of an impending price hike. Doherty had to convince grocers that they needed to develop a reputation for being the best store for a staple like coffee, and customers would come to buy other more profitable items. When grocers promoted coffee according to P&G's plan, they got more customers and increased their overall sales. At the end of his training, P&G wanted Doherty to transfer to its St. Louis office and become the district manager. But since his fiancée was graduating from law school in Minnesota and they both wanted to live in Minnesota, where she would be eligible to practice law, he resigned from his position. Due to his good relationship with his manager, he was allowed to stay on in his job till he found another one.

Lesson: Use a sales force tracking mechanism like salesforce.com. As an entrepreneur, you need to control your sales personnel, and without a sales tracking software tool, you will not be able to monitor and evaluate their activities, and therefore manage their success. Also, focus on the value you bring to your customer. Doherty was able to succeed only when he solved his customers' problems and added value to their business by showing them how his product was able to increase the grocers' profits.

6. Entry into temporary staffing. After his decision to exit from P&G, Doherty decided that he should focus on local, rather than national, employers. So he found a job as a sales representative at a temporary help service in 1979. But the economy was starting to deteriorate and companies were reducing their workforces. Sales started to fall and the owner of the agency decided to reduce headcount. So Doherty was out of a job about four months after starting in the business.

Lesson: Doherty learned what it is like to be fired, and decided to be more compassionate when he became a decision-maker. In addition he learned to use a cushion of temp workers to staff his own agency so that a part of his overhead was variable, and he could adjust his workforce with minimal disruption when he needed to do so.

From Startup to Profits

7. **What does it take to start an agency**? When he lost his job with the temporary help service, Doherty's father asked him if it was a good time to start his own company, and what it would take to get one going. The industry was young, and Doherty thought it had lots of potential for growth. There were a few national agencies but very few local ones. Doherty started looking at the requirements to start an agency, and decided that the basics were an office, furniture, and phones. The key need was for accounts-receivable financing to pay employees weekly and wait for customers to pay in 30-45 days. So Doherty started doing a business plan to determine his revenue potential and cash needs. He decided that he needed about $50,000 for an internal staff of two to five people and 1,600 billable hours per week, i.e., about 40 billable, hourly temp employees on assignments. Doherty thought it would take six months to reach this number. It took two. And further good news was that Doherty overestimated expenses, so he lost only $2,500 in the first year.

Lesson: Understand the key requirements to get the business started, and especially the number of customers and the level of revenues you need to make the business viable. Then the next crucial question is how soon you can get there? Normally, entrepreneurs are optimistic when seeking financing from investors. But *it pays to be pessimistic when borrowing money, especially if you are offering collateral and/or a personal guarantee.*

8. **Financing the startup**. To finance the startup, Doherty did not have any cash, and neither did anyone else in the family. The key asset the family had was the equity in the house that was owned and occupied by Doherty's parents. The prime rate was around 18 percent, and banks were not eager to lend, but Doherty thought that the business was viable. Why? Because he needed very little to run the business, and he thought that recruiting 40 employees and placing them in jobs was possible. (He never thought that the company would become as large as it has.) He had also done his market research and had talked with many potential customers in the area, and knew that they were interested in the service. "Even the poor economy could be made into an advantage for him because, as his competition was downsizing, he had the opportunity to pursue business with extremely small overhead. He could go on the offensive. Despite the poor economy, the trend toward using temporary help was taking off in the early '80s. Many companies were considering expanding the

use of temporary employees, and due to the recession, many potential employees were seeking work. Recruiting costs were at an all-time low. His competitors were mainly the large national chains such as Manpower and Kelly, and a few local ones. Doherty thought that he could compete with all of them. Doherty's parents got a home- equity loan of $40,000 from Household Finance at an interest rate of 24 percent. He paid off that loan after the first year and then established a line of credit from a bank using the receivables as collateral. His mother was nervous (because of the drive-in experience), but his father had more pull. His dad was a little bit of a gambler. It was the best investment he ever made.

> **Lesson**: Do your homework. Fear should be greatest at the start of the business. However, Doherty knew that there was a market since companies were trying to gain flexibility with their workforce, and reduce the pain and cost of laying people off. He knew he could find people to place and that he could outdo his competitors. But you will always need to have faith in yourself. That is what helps you to take the first crucial step. And know that your family and your parents are often the ones who are likely to help you. That's why they are family.

9. Unmet need - the third shift. To better serve their needs, Doherty asked employers for their major problems. Some would tell him. Many would not. He found out that this was because the executive decision-makers often did not always know the real issues and the real pain. The answer lay with lower-level supervisors who actually experienced the problems and knew the issues. The higher-level managers were trying to drive a hard bargain over costs, while the supervisors needed the right people to do the work. So Doherty started contacting supervisors at the production line or at the supervisory levels before reaching higher up in the corporation. This made his job easier because he already knew the people who had to implement the program and understood their problems when he approached the top-level managers. Some liked the fact that Doherty knew and could solve their pain. Others were irritated that he had talked to other levels in the organization before talking to them (you cannot please everyone). As he talked with more companies, a pattern started developing. Doherty found that his competitors did not adequately serve the needs of the third shift, which were the less glamorous positions in the firm. The larger-company managers liked to have free evenings and nights when the shift supervisors had problems getting help. So Doherty took calls at home in the evenings and nights, and he took his files home with him so he could find employees for these companies whenever they had needs. He got calls till around midnight or 12:30 a.m., and he and his wife (and future business partner) called employees and often woke them up to offer them work. And, with unemployment over 10 percent, the employees were happy to get those calls. Doherty found that the national company executives (his competitors) were oblivious to the third shift. Doherty capitalized on this oversight and grew his business on this unmet need. His office hours became 6 a.m. till 9 p.m., and he would take calls at any time of the night to solve a customer's problem. This focus on the third shift was not a predetermined strategy or the result of market research. He just started getting calls from desperate supervisors who got his name from the yellow pages, and he was perhaps the only temp agency who would answer the phone.

Lesson: ***Find the pain. Solve the pain.*** Develop your strategy around solving the pain. Understand the customers' real pain, not just the one that the customers tell you. Usually the person who is responsible for the implementation knows the pain and the importance of solving it. Their futures are at stake. Managers of the competing national chains did not spend time worrying about the third shift. ***To them, this was personal time. For Doherty, this was opportunity.***

From Profits to the Moon

10. Adjust to customer needs. In the first year, one of Doherty's clients, a meat packer, was working through the Thanksgiving weekend. Doherty wanted to spend time with his family on Thanksgiving and the next day, so he closed down the office and did not answer the phones. On Saturday, he found a nasty message on his answering machine reminding him that his customers were open and had needs. In essence, he fired Doherty over the phone. After that, Doherty always asked about his clients' hours and needs, and made sure that his offices were open and phones were answered whenever their clients' operations were open.

Lesson: If you are a service operation, serve. Your business exists to serve their needs, not the other way around.

11. The breakthrough. Doherty's initial clients were small companies in the food and battery industries. His breakthrough came when he got a million-dollar account with United Mailing. Their business required quick turnaround with their mail processing, and their needs were immediate as well as unpredictable. As such, they embraced the strategy of using temp workers to help with their fluctuating needs. The facility was within five to six blocks of Doherty's office, which also made it convenient to serve them. Initially, Doherty was supplying the bulk of the people on just the third shift, while the client used other vendors for the other shifts. The human resource manager wanted to work with one vendor. Since Doherty had the experience of providing qualified people for the third shift (the largest and the most difficult to serve), he was selected over his larger competitors.

Lesson: Understand your advantage. Then push it. Doherty knew he had the best operation for the third shift, so he used this advantage to gain leverage over his larger national competitors who focused on the more convenient (for them) first and second shifts, while Doherty satisfied all the needs of the customers. And understand how your customers buy and their buying criteria. Doherty did.

12. Presentation vs. Delivery. His next big customer was a giant food company that needed people for all three shifts at their research facility. Since the order was large, corporate decision-makers got involved and asked for a formal proposal. Doherty was not selected. The vendor who was selected boasted to Doherty, "You got outsold, kid." But the company could not deliver on its promises and the client company asked Doherty to help them. Doherty asked why he had lost the sale in the earlier round, and he was shown the competitor's sales materials to compare with his own. Doherty's was simple and plain, while the competitors had lots of razzle-dazzle. It is unfortunate, but in this case it seemed as if the corporate customer was seduced by beautiful graphics rather than looking at the underlying reality of who could best satisfy their needs. Doherty realized that big corporations want impressive-looking sales presentations, and want to buy from others who can sell like they do when they market their products or materials – with a lot of flash. Doherty decided to improve his presentation designs and skills.

Lesson: *Impressions matter.* It is amazing that corporate buyers could be sold based on superficial form rather than substance, but that is how some companies buy. ***So understand not only your competitive advantage, but also how the customer buys.*** It is not enough to have a good product or service. You need to be able to sell it.

13. Develop your competitive advantage. After the above experience, Doherty decided that he needed to differentiate his company more and add competitive advantages. He and his team decided that it would be in the area of using information technology (IT) for presentations and marketing. Doherty had added a computer in 1982 to print paychecks and invoices. The company and the industry had been printing these checks manually. Doherty had gone to the trade association and obtained a software package to do search and retrieval for résumés, and also to print paychecks. When selling to the large corporation, Doherty realized that he was ahead of his competitors in the use of IT for operations, but not for marketing. He rectified that and started doing presentations on his computer. He also brought clients over to his offices to show them how the company did the searches, and asked them to check how their competitors did it. The clients realized that Doherty's presentations had the substance, even if they sometimes lacked the flash. Doherty also placed a full-time person on site at the production facilities of large clients, which was a new practice at the time (but now widely practiced). The idea seemed to make sense. Doherty found that each large client had special needs, and he thought that an onsite manager would be a benefit to ensure that the temp employees worked to standards and that the client was satisfied. The ancillary benefit was that having someone onsite allowed the company to stay in touch with the client to find new business.

Lesson: Don't worry about what you want to sell and how you want to sell it. *Worry about what the customer wants to buy,* the problem they are seeking to solve, and how to convince them that you are the best one to help them.

14. Ride the wave. In two years, Doherty grew the business to about $2 million in revenues, and he had acquired more sophistication in sales and presentation skills. The business continued growing throughout the 1980s till it reached $16 million in sales by 1991. That was when the industry experienced its first slowdown. One of the key reasons for Doherty's growth was that he rode the trend. The industry was growing at a breakneck pace, and Doherty grew along with it. He was well-positioned to be a dominant force in the right industry at the right time.

Lesson: It is far easier to grow in a high-growth industry than to grab market share from competitors in a stagnant industry.

15. How to recruit key people. As the company grew, Doherty started adding people with skills that he did not have. He needed and added a marketing manager and sales support. They worked out very well and helped the company grow. But not all his selections worked out. One of his first key managerial hires did not do well with the company because Doherty followed the "classic" model of emphasizing personality and references. The individual had great references but he did not fit in with the others. Doherty found that he was basing his decision on his instinct, and his belief that everyone wants to succeed. But he realized that not everyone had the same motivation, skills, and experience. Doherty started to use evaluation tools to gauge all three, including determining what people liked to do, what they were good at, and to match their personality with the job. They found that some crave attention and are motivated by recognition, while others want money. They had to understand each, and adjust their handling of each individual to their personality and needs. They tried many tools, found one they liked and stuck with it. This gave Doherty a baseline to compare the scores of those who fit with those who did not, so they could look at the scores as a reasonable indicator of future performance. Doherty found that the single biggest mistake in hiring was when the manager did not check references but delegated that task to the human resources (HR) department. The HR staff often did not get the subtle feedback that the managers picked up, and Doherty found that this issue became even more critical when the position being filled was high up in the organization. When he as the CEO called a reference, he got much better feedback than when a junior-level person called, and especially when he listed what he was looking for and whether the person fit.

Lesson: To grow, you need good people. To find good people, you need to expend the effort to find those who have the right motivation, skills, and experience. And then you need to make sure that you design an environment where they can contribute to their highest capacity. Even talented people sometimes do not fit in. Find the right chemistry and the right talents.

16. "Under-hire" sales experience, "over-hire" motivation. Doherty realized sales were key to the success of his business. Without sales, the rest of the firm would have no reason for being. He tried to hire sales people with a proven sales track record and found that they had very high base-salary expectations that were inconsistent with his organization. So he sought out those who had the potential and the motivation, but maybe not the track record, who were willing to work for a lower base salary. He offered them higher commissions based on results. Although the selections were satisfactory, sometimes he wonders whether he should have hired experienced sales people. Experienced sales persons would show a dramatic improvement in their results if they were going to fit in. Those who were new to the industry took about a year to show results.

> **Lesson**: Understand how to hire sales personnel. They are crucial to your company and your growth. And they are expensive. If they don't perform, your odds of success decrease. Hiring sales personnel is often the most difficult job you will have, because they are usually good at selling themselves, but it takes time before they prove their skills. As an entrepreneur, you may not have the money to hire experience. Track the sales force's efforts and improvement with the appropriate software. Most importantly, understand the difference between eagles and bureaucrats. Eagles soar and you need to reward them with money and recognition. But be careful not to waste money before they prove themselves.

17. Don't push an expansion before its time. The year 1991 saw the second recession to hit the industry since Doherty had started his business, and he began to look for a new growth strategy. He had been keeping track of a new industry trend, which was then called employee leasing, which was being implemented initially in Florida, Texas, and California. He started studying this trend with industry leaders and members of his trade association, and he decided to pursue his new business offering in Minnesota. There were a number of synergies between this new service and his existing temporary staffing service. For example, he was already managing payroll, workers' compensation, unemployment, and benefits for the temporary staff assigned to his clients. Now he would also take care of all these needs and more for his clients' own staff. For many of his smaller clients, this meant a large reduction in paperwork and human resources (HR) administration and resulting overhead. To implement this new strategy, Doherty started a new business, now called Doherty Employer Services, which is an HRO (Human Resource Outsourcing) organization. In addition to hiring a staff of HR and benefits professionals, he hired sales people experienced in selling outsourcing services. His first sales person for the new service had been selling payroll services to similar clients for Ceridian, and calling on CFOs, controllers, and business owners who were also the potential decision makers for employee leasing (now HRO services). But the HR outsourcing service was new in the Twin Cities, so Doherty was the local "missionary." The large companies initiated the outsourcing trend when they began outsourcing their IT departments in the early 1990s, and then having others do their payroll. But Minnesota companies were reluctant to outsource HR. Doherty invested a significant amount of funds on marketing this new service, including the profits and more from the temp-staffing side of the business. The company initially lost a "boatload of money." He got a wake-up call when the bank wanted to move his business to the workout department, which is where companies with less than stellar balance sheets are relegated. Doherty called the head of business banking, whom he had never met before. The banker came to his office and Doherty talked to him very candidly about the reasons for the loss, the mistakes made and how he was going to fix them. Doherty had been trying to sell something for which the market was not ready and spending too much money in the process. Instead of adjusting to the pace of the market, he was spending a lot of money (much of it from the bank) to convince customers to move faster, and they were not doing so. The bank decided not to send the loan to workout, Doherty cut expenses, changed his business marketing philosophy to a more realistic, less costly and less aggressive approach, and soon returned to profitability.

Lesson: Timing is nearly everything. Don't drink wine before its time. Don't try to push a service when the customer is not ready. Many experienced investors think that new products and services grow in the shape of a hockey stick. Sales are slow to ramp up initially, and more money spent on marketing is usually more money down the drain. ***When the market is ready, it takes off***. This is usually called the tipping point. Keep your gunpowder dry till the market is ready and start to invest when it is. And be candid with bankers. They are used to entrepreneurs evading reality. A realistic business plan is often the best way to get them to work with you.

18. The tipping point. The HR outsourcing business took off when Doherty found a client in this business that had to solve a unique problem. A Fortune 500 company based in Minnesota was starting a joint-venture arrangement with another company. The company was expanding into many new markets, and their lawyers did not want the employees of the joint ventures to be corporate employees of the majority partner, which was to be Doherty's client. This turned out to be a natural fit for Doherty, because no one else was offering this service in this market.

Lesson: Thank god for lawyers sometimes. Thank god for luck all the time. It's great to have a lot of one and just the right dose of the other.

19. Working with a spouse. Doherty Employment Group currently consists of Doherty Staffing Solutions (temporary help) and Doherty Employer Services (HRO organization). The company has two partners - Tim Doherty and his wife, Valerie, who joined the company in 1984 when it had sales of about $3.5 million. Valerie Doherty is a lawyer and her skills complement Tim's. Tim's talents are IT, sales and marketing, and Valerie's are in HR, benefits, risk management, and legal. According to Tim, this naturally evolved. Valerie had been helping with the company in its early stages in the 1980s and gravitated to areas where she had expertise. This allowed Tim to focus on his skills and areas of interest.

Lesson: Marry right. If you are going to work with your spouse, make sure that your skills are complementary.

Rules for Entrepreneurs from Tim Doherty of Doherty Employment Group

- **Find the unmet need.** Understand and satisfy your customers' real unmet needs, which may be more important than a lower price.
- **Find complementary people.** As you grow, find people who are smarter than you and more talented in areas that the company needs.
- **Hire right.** Learn interviewing techniques. Test. Test. Test. You need to hire right.
- **Hire the right sales people.** Understand the difference between true sales people and the others. Great sales people have strong egos, and they want commissions with no limits.
- **Know the right time.** Don't drink wine before its time. Don't push a string.
- **Don't try to evade discussing reality with your banker.** It seldom works.
- **Keep track of trends.** Jump when the time is right.

ROBERT KIERLIN
FASTENAL INC.

WINONA, MINN

Building the U.S.'s Largest Fastener Company

The company: In 1967, when Bob Kierlin started Fastenal in Winona (Minn.), it was the smallest of 10,000 fastener (such as nuts and bolts) businesses in the United States. By 1997, it had become the largest. The company became profitable by 1969, reached $100 million in annual sales by 1993 and $1 billion in sales by 2004. Kierlin was the chief executive from startup and still remains chairman. The only equity raised, prior to the initial public offering, was $22,000 at startup from Kierlin and three Winona friends, and an additional $9,000 a year later from a fifth investor who was a friend. From this start, Kierlin has built a company that has a market cap in excess of $5 billion. This is how he did it.

From Startup to Profits

1. Vision at startup. After finishing his MBA, Kierlin spent two years in the Peace Corps and then started to work for IBM. But his dream since high school was to develop a vending machine to sell nuts and bolts. So in 1967, he and three friends raised $22,000 and developed a vending machine to sell fasteners. This vision, which was gestating for many years, produced a product that lasted only a few months. The quantities and sizes demanded by customers were different from the ones in the machine. Kierlin listened to his customers and scrapped the vending-machine strategy. He continued the business in a 1,000 SF store, and hired a store manager while he continued to work at IBM.

Lesson: *Be flexible and humble.* When your initial idea does not work (as it often doesn't in new ventures), talk to your customers and adapt to what the market demands.

2. Strategy for growth. The first store had sales of $18,000 in the first year and was showing promise. So Kierlin started looking for expansion opportunities. Since he was working for IBM in Rochester, he bought a contractor supply house there. This was a mistake. The business had been for sale for about six months, and the good inventory had been sold. What was left was dead stock. This was the last business purchased by the company. All future expansions would be internal.

Lesson: Growth via acquisitions can be a risky strategy especially if you don't know how to buy a business, including its valuation, pricing and financing.

3. Right time to jump in full time. By 1973, the business had grown to $255,000 in sales from three stores. Kierlin decided that the time had come to leave IBM and jump full time into the business. Joining the business meant that he no longer had his IBM salary, and Fastenal had to generate the cash flow to pay him. So he had to be sure that the business could be expanded to pay for the increased overhead.

Lesson: Lay the groundwork, if you can, before you have to leave your corporate job. This way you may not have to seek venture capital when you are ready to jump in.

4. Riding the trends. Prior to the 1960s, fasteners were made by the large integrated steel companies. They saw fasteners as an imposition, something they had to make to sell steel beams, which was their primary product. Their service and pricing were poor. So some fastener buyers persuaded Japanese companies to make fasteners. Fastenal took advantage of the lower prices offered by importers of these fasteners. Its average gross margin grew from 34% to 50%, and this fueled faster growth.

Lesson: Understand trends, study the big picture and take advantage of new situations, including better prices and margins.

5. Expanding with flexibility. Initially Fastenal only had 1,000 SF of space. But to take advantage of the lower Japanese prices, Fastenal needed to buy inventory in bulk. This meant that the company needed storage space. So the company started renting nearly all the available garage space in Winona on short-term leases. The company kept track of the inventory on 3"x5" cards. When a new store opened up and needed inventory, all Kierlin had to do was go around to the garages and ship the inventory to the new store.

Lesson: Be flexible and find the most cost-effective way to solve your problem.

From Profits to the Moon

6. Connecting with the industry. Kierlin's goal was to make Fastenal into the leader of the fastener industry. Since Kierlin and his key team had learned the business themselves, and since they had not gained much from the industry, they did not see the need to share what they had learned with the rest of the industry. They decided that the best strategy for them was to continuously improve on their own, and to rely on their employees for their competitive advantage and industry dominance.

Lesson: When you are ahead of the industry, others will pick your brains to gain advantage at your expense. *Don't boast about what you have learned.*

7. Buy or make. Fastenal wanted to make sure that it could serve the fastener needs of all its customers. To do this, it had to be able to sell the standard items with fast turnaround times (which means Fastenal needed inventory), and at competitive prices. The company also had to offer customized fasteners when customers needed them. However, the small machine shops that made these special fasteners did not have the same sense of urgency or reliability as Fastenal. In some cases, they had not even started manufacturing them by the promised date. So Kierlin decided to manufacture these specialized fasteners internally. This allowed the company to better serve its customers and improve its competitive advantage.

Lesson: Understand why customers are buying (or will buy) from you and serve them on time and without excuses. Be able to control the level of service you offer.

8. Treating employees with respect. Fastenal gave wide latitude to its employees. Store managers picked their inventory, developed their customers, and were judged on results. Machine operators selected their jobs. Open jobs were color-coded in groups by order of delivery date and placed on a board where all the operators could see them. Machine operators who finished a job picked their next job from the highest-priority group without interference from supervisors and the central scheduling department. This gave employees a variety of jobs, minimized boredom and allowed them to maximize their potential.

Lesson: Cut overhead and allow your employees to make decisions they are capable of making within the larger framework, and they will appreciate it. *Treat employees as if they had other job offers.* In any type of market, the best ones will have options.

9. Serving customers. One Friday, a Fastenal manufacturing estimator got a call from his store manager in Indiana. A Ford plant had lost one of its main mixing machines due to a broken part. The machine was made in Europe and used the metric system, and it would be about a week before a replacement part could be obtained from Europe. Could Fastenal make the part any sooner? The estimator found some blanks in Ohio and had Northwest Airlines fly them into La Crosse, Wis., where Fastenal picked them up. The company then machined the fasteners on Friday night, had them heat treated on Saturday and asked the Winona Flying Club to fly them back to Ford. The part was at Ford's plant on Sunday morning, installed by Sunday night and the machine was ready for the Monday-morning shift. Fastenal's cost was $1,700, and Kierlin felt uneasy that Fastenal charged Ford $7,000. But that was only until he received a thank you letter from a Ford executive saying that Fastenal's timely actions had saved Ford about $400,000.

Lesson: Make customers your top priority. Go beyond "reasonable" service, and you will differentiate yourself from your customers.

10. Finding new products. Kierlin found that he was getting ideas for new products from branch managers, and he attributes this as one of the key reasons for the success of Fastenal. Early on, when he expanded into his third store, a local contractor told him that his own performance suffered when he had three houses under construction since he could not be at all three places. Kierlin decided to decentralize decision-making. He found good people, trained them in the company culture and beliefs, set some basic rules of conduct, treated them fairly and challenged them to achieve their potential. Many companies and executives talk about this but don't always develop a structure that does this with trust. Except for quality-control manuals, the other manuals are very thin. Store managers can make their own decisions on ordering, buying, selling and pricing. They are rewarded on their store profitability and return on assets. With each store manager innovating to meet customer needs, the company got many practical and innovative ideas that worked in the field rather than based on business-school marketing theoreticians. To this day, managers only receive about two-thirds of their products from central purchasing. The rest of their purchases are from sources developed by the managers themselves. However, to control "irrational exuberance" in new managers, all large custom-inventory purchases have to be approved by district managers and backed up by dated purchase orders.

Lesson: Find good employees. Give them good training and tell them your expectations. Give them the freedom and challenge them to find their potential. Keep the rules simple. *Delegate and reward based on results. But have basic rules to control risk.*

11. Minimizing hierarchy. Everyone pitched in when needed. When the company moved its headquarters to a new building in Winona, all the employees including the CEO moved the furniture, fixtures and files over a weekend. Senior managers who held class C drivers licenses drove the trucks, since some of their truck drivers had driven over their quota for the week.

Lesson: Don't show off. Don't act superior. Share the load.

12. Opening communications. Fastenal has a policy that anyone can call to talk to anyone else at any time. They do not have to get permission before doing so. Kierlin found that this open-line communication system develops a culture of trust and openness. Open communications went both ways. Every morning starting at 7 A.M., Kierlin would check the sales of the stores for the previous day. Each store that had sales in excess of $5,000 got a phone call from Kierlin and he would congratulate whoever picked up the phone. Many of them were surprised to hear from the CEO, but this spurred them to better performance.

Lesson: Develop "chaotic" communications rather than "silo" communications if you want your co-workers to feel valued. And let them know you appreciate good performance. Money is important as a motivator. Recognition may be equally key.

13. Upgrading and retaining. All of Fastenal's managers are promoted from within, except for its legal staff (for some reason, lawyers don't seem to want to become store-manager trainees). All the officers started as trainees, and the HR director (who is also on the board of directors) started as a receptionist. This created a deep sense of loyalty. To make sure that new and promoted employees live up to their potential, Fastenal started the Fastenal School of Business in Winona to train them (instead of renting hotel rooms, Fastenal bought and maintained an apartment building to reduce costs and improve their employees' stay). To motivate sales employees, Kierlin developed a pay package where the base salary is less than half of the total potential. The balance is based on performance, including store profitability and return on assets.

Lesson: Train your employees and treat them well. Be fair. Believe in your people and give them a chance. Offer incentives in their pay package that motivate them.

14. Sharing the wealth. Kierlin could pick the right time to go public because he had patient investors. This happened in 1987 when the company had 52 stores and $20 million in annual sales. In addition to liquidity for key shareholders, Kierlin also wanted to offer employees an opportunity to share in the company's growth. Therefore, in the IPO, *10% of the 1,000,000 shares (at $9) were reserved for employees*. Some enterprising employees went around and acquired shares allotted to others who were not interested in buying the shares, and became wealthy.

Lesson: Allow your employees to share in the dream.

15. Controlling expenses. Fastenal always believed that executives and employees needed to be frugal when spending corporate money. This applied to all, starting from the top. When they traveled, they were expected to find the most reasonable rooms and means of transportation. Kierlin himself followed this rule, including staying at low-cost motels. He believed in leading by example, not by edict. When buying trucks, Fastenal found that buying used trucks was not wise, since they tended to break down. So Fastenal bought new trucks in large quantities and sold them at retail after using them for a year for practically the same price they paid for the new trucks. This idea came from the field.

Lesson: Don't expect your employees to be frugal if you are not. If your employees come up with an innovative plan that works, implement it and recognize them.

16. Develop your company's key metrics to grow with control. Early on, Kierlin found out that the company could grow without external financing if he stuck to certain metrics. For growth, Fastenal needed to fund inventory and receivables for new stores. They found that there was a relationship between inventory turns, gross margins and growth. *When gross margins were 50%, and inventory turned over three times annually, the company could grow at an annual rate of 30% without external financing.* So each year, they would calculate the average number of stores in the past year, and increase the number of stores by 30%. For any product that had three turns, they expected minimum margins of 50%. For two turns, the margins had to be at least 60% and with 40% margins, they needed four turns. At 30%, they did not stock the inventory but bought it from the manufacturer for direct ship to the customer. The company also set up its management training and growth plans for 30% growth. This meant that they needed to have enough experienced managers who were ready for the new stores, and trained store assistants who could take over the existing stores. One year, Kierlin got enthusiastic and suggested growth of 40%. His managers became even more enthusiastic and tried to get 50%. Chaos ensued. There were insufficient trained store managers, cash flow became tight and customer service deteriorated. Kierlin resolved never to do that again.

Lesson: Know your company, your people, your products and the financial metrics. Ultimately, all roads lead to Rome, i.e., to the financial results. When making changes, make sure you test the impact of the changes on a small scale before engulfing the entire company in potential chaos.

17. Listening to Wall Street analysts. After Fastenal went public, investment analysts constantly questioned Kierlin as to whether Fastenal needed new, experienced leadership to take the company to the next level. One benefit of owning a huge chunk of stock, and not having venture capitalists with even bigger chunks, is that you don't always have to listen to the analysts. Kierlin did not. All he did was reward his stockholders with one of the best performances of any publicly traded stock. A 1996 study of initial public offerings for the previous decade showed that Fastenal ranked second among the best performers. Only Microsoft ranked higher. One dollar invested in Fastenal at the IPO was worth $59 in 1996.

Lesson: Wall Street analysts are not always right even if they call themselves "smart money".

Rules for Entrepreneurs from Bob Kierlin of Fastenal

- **Pursue a common goal and bring out the potential of all employees toward the goal.** Challenge your managers rather than controlling them, and give them the freedom (with some basic financial restrictions) and training to help them reach their potential.
- **Listen more. Speak less.** Build open communications that allow anyone to directly call anyone in the organization without supervisor permission to discuss a company problem.
- **Hire employees who practice empathy.** According to Kierlin, *employees who are likely to leave their carts in the middle of the grocery-store aisle don't have empathy, or even awareness of other people.* Train employees to be aware of how little they know rather than how much they know.
- **Reward achievement.** Employees will work to their full potential if given the chance and if rewarded when working toward a common goal.
- **Build the culture you want.** Develop a great company with extraordinary people who can continue on the path toward greatness even after you have stepped down.

Ray Barton
Great Clips

MINNEAPOLIS, MINN

Building the world's largest salon chain and a great brand

Summary: Ray Barton started working at the age of 8. He learned at a young age that if he wanted things, he had to work for it. He held a variety of jobs, including working at a drug store, delivering papers in the morning and evening, and shoveling snow. In college, he sold cars for a living. After finishing his degree in accounting, he became a CPA, and worked for one of the large accounting firms. As many accountants do, Barton switched to the business side and became a CFO for a Century 21 real estate franchisee. On his own, he became a franchisee for a hair-cutting chain. He lost the hair-cutting store due to some bad decisions, and when the economy went into a tailspin, he lost his job as the CFO of the real estate franchisee. When he was invited into a partnership that was starting a new hair-salon chain, he reentered the industry. He built this business, called Great Clips, into the largest salon brand in the world. This is how he did it.

Before the Startup

1. **The school years... learn what you need and some more**. As early as the third grade, Barton started working at a drug store, delivered morning and evening newspapers, did lawn maintenance and shoveled snow. Barton learned that he got a higher tip when he did a better job. Most people appreciate hard work. He also learned how to get along with others, take directions, and develop discipline. When he was a sophomore, his family moved to a Minneapolis suburb, and he applied for a job at a local grocery store. There were more kids than jobs, so Barton kept reminding the store owner that he was looking for a job. Eventually he got it. Barton's dad was the first in his family to go to college. His parents had a strong belief that education was the road to success, and even though they were not rich, they tried to give their children the best education possible. They sacrificed to get them into Catholic schools. They earned scholarships, and if there was no money for

lunch, Barton and his siblings had to work for it by busing tables, doing the dishes, etc., rather than playing during recess. As he puts it, the experience did not scar any of his family, because the other kids did not make fun of them. The nuns at his school motivated him and the others by pointing out that their potential was unlimited.

Lesson: Your values and character form when you are young. *Hard work and smarts never go out of fashion.*

2. **The college years**. When Barton went to college, he was a solid D+ student. To pay his way through college, Barton sold pots and pans door-to-door. To improve sales, he needed to find additional prospects in his area of south Minneapolis, so he hired four to five friends to work for him. The company promoted those who did well, and Barton was one of them. He realized that, as a sales manager, he had to find good people, which was the toughest part of the job, because not everyone succeeded at sales. To succeed, good salespersons needed to deal with rejection, and not let it bother or discourage them. They needed persistence, follow-through and discipline. He found that when someone followed the prescribed systematic process, they succeeded at selling. He also learned that he needed to keep his ego in check. When he became successful, his ego took over, and he thought that he did not need the system. He thought he could shorten the sales process and make more calls. Sales dropped off the cliff and he went back to the system. Sales improved.

Lesson: When you find a process or strategy that works, follow it. There is a reason why it works. Understand it. But take care to see that there are no major changes in the underlying assumptions or trends that would cause you to change your system.

3. **From pots to cars**. Along with pots and pans, Barton also started selling cars while in college because there was more money in selling new cars. He worked for a Chrysler dealership, and this job allowed him to drive a new car. The manager of the dealership wanted to buy a piece of an island in northern Minnesota, but he did not have enough money for the down payment, so he asked Barton if he wanted to co-invest. Barton, who had saved some of the money he made, did. Years later, his partner wanted to borrow against the land to buy another dealership. Barton asked for his share of the land free and clear. This was fortuitous, because the manager lost his share when the dealership failed. Years later Barton sold the land for about five times what he had paid for it.

Lesson: Save. Invest. *If you don't have to take a risk, don't.* Be lucky.

4. **A rolling stone**. Barton kept switching colleges, and his fourth and fifth colleges were in California. He graduated from San Diego State. While in college, he used a local dealer's license to attend the Los Angeles Auto Auction. Every Tuesday, he would buy a car from the wholesale auctions. He would place ads in the local newspapers and sell the car during the weekend to consumers. The buyer had to pay

cash for it. If the buyer did not have cash, Barton took him to the bank on Monday so that he had enough cash to pay for the next car on Tuesday. This was a profitable system for Barton. He always bought a Volkswagen, because he knew this car, and it was easy to sell in San Diego. He quickly learned how to evaluate cars. One week he did not get a lot of calls from his ads. The one customer who did come offered to buy the car but at a price that gave Barton only $100 profit rather than his regular $150 profit. Barton should have realized from the number of calls that this would be a slow weekend, but he did not. He did not sell the car that weekend, which meant that he did not have the cash for the next car. Hanging on for an additional $50 of profit cost him $150. This episode taught him not to get greedy, but to develop good judgment about when to accept a different price. He paid his way through college selling cars.

Lesson: Barton learned the importance of cash flow. If he did not sell the car, or did not collect cash for the car he did sell, he did not have cash for his next car. And every system has flaws and requires judgment. In hindsight, Barton knew that the slow weekend should have warned him to accept the offer so he would have cash for the following weekend. So understand your assumptions and the reasons why you arrived at your system. Know when to follow the system and when to use your judgment.

5. **The first job**. In his last two years of college, Barton decided to buckle down and study. His major was accounting and he went from being a D student to an A student. He knew that he needed a good job when he graduated and that a D average would not get him one. Upon graduation, he went to work for the CPA firm Alexander Grant & Co., which is now Grant Thornton. He became a CPA and audited firms for five years. He learned the value of professionalism and appearance. He cut his hair from its indifferent college length, and switched from sweats to professional suits and ties. It even made him feel different, and he started to "look like guys downtown and not like the guys on the beach." Barton wanted to fit in based on his appearance, and he decided to differentiate himself through hard work.

Lesson: Adjust to the environment if you want to succeed.

6. **From audits to real estate**. After five years at Grant Thornton, Barton got a job offer to become CFO of the North Central Region franchisee of Century 21. The company awarded and serviced operating franchisees in the region. This was Barton's first exposure to franchising. He learned that for the franchisor to succeed, the franchisees had to make money. While at Century 21, he learned the power of a national brand and an operating system.

Lesson: To be a successful franchisor, you need to develop successful, profitable franchisees. Interestingly, some franchisors have not figured this out.

7. **Hair franchise.** While at Century 21, Barton started looking for a franchise in an industry outside the real estate industry but with similar characteristics. He was seeking an industry where there were no national franchise chains, but with a few that were on their way to becoming them. He wanted to stick to some broad guidelines that he was comfortable with. He noticed that hair-cutting salons were mainly "mom and pop" small businesses, where the owners were not very sophisticated. The salon was not very capital intensive and the returns were attractive. The business was also one that needed strong customer service. So he became a part-time Barbers franchisee and opened a salon in 1981. The Barbers was a regional franchise, and Barton was not given much guidance in store location or size. So he built a big salon with 16 stations without much analysis of the location, the local market, or its needs. Barton borrowed heavily to build a big store, and make a big bang. As he puts it, he made a series of bad decisions. The store did not live up to its expectations. He sold it to the Barbers.

Lesson: Find a good devil's advocate. ***If you think that you have all the answers, or that your investment is risk-free, have someone relentlessly poke holes in your assumptions and instincts – so you understand that you can make mistakes and develop some humility.*** That is one of the reasons kings had clowns. If your best defense is that it is based on your instinct, know that instinct is not infallible. If the risk is high, test it. In any business that depends on customer traffic, location is a paramount factor. In addition, retail space is expensive to rent, so the size of the store is important. Analyze both factors (cost and size), and the market, if you want to succeed in retail.

From Startup to Profits

8. **Starting at Great Clips.** Simultaneously with the closing of the franchised store, interest rates started climbing, severely affecting real estate. Barton lost his job at Century 21. He liked the security of a paycheck, fringes, and perks. Two guys were starting a hair-cutting chain called Great Clips, and asked Barton to join. Barton did not want to be in the hair business again, so he went to work for a small energy company. When that company started having problems, Barton knew he was going to lose that job also. So when the co-founder of Great Clips called again and asked if Barton would be interested, Barton said, "Maybe; let's talk." The company had four salons, three were company-owned and one was a hybrid partnership where an investor funded the operation and the company managed it with a 50-50 split of the ownership. He made a $30,000 investment and got involved in the fall of 1982 as the CEO of the company.

Lesson: Many people start their venture when a crisis hits. They put their dreams for a corporate T-shirt and the fringes on hold. As Barton puts it, "*his major growth happened when he got fired.*" Be open to new opportunities. You never know when the right one shows up.

9. **The partnership from hell.** Great Clips was profitable from the beginning except for one year. However, the problem was that it did not grow to its potential, and did not live up to its plan, which was to expand nationally. Each of the three partners owned a third of the business. As Barton puts it, the partners were sharp and were good guys, but they had differing views of how to build the business. When each saw the business differently, including how to work with and help the franchises, frictions started. Barton wanted a simple, disciplined system without any variations from franchisee to franchisee, whereas the others did not always agree. His partners did not mind granting variances to franchisees. Franchisees started playing off the differences among the partners to get what they wanted and they chose the "right partner" to ask for variances. So one of the partners resigned and some of his shares were split among a number of people. The result was Barton and one partner owning 38 percent each, two others (one of whom was Barton's sister) owning 10 percent each and one owning the rest. The partner with the least shares held the key vote, and ended up making the important decisions. There was no exit since the partners had not decided on a pricing mechanism for exits. They tried to sell to another buyer, but he was not able to secure the funding. So the two key partners decided on a "shotgun" buy-sell agreement, where one decides the price and the other decides whether to buy or to sell. But they could not make this agreement work because neither wanted to offer a price. The disagreements continued. Sales increased but profits were flat. The other partners could not fire Barton, so it was not fun for anyone. So Barton decided that he would be better off without the business and he became open to sell. This was a "freeing moment," and he no longer felt trapped. He hired an investment banker, found a private equity investor and allowed his partners to buy Barton out or to sell. The other partners ended up selling their stock, and Barton and his sister kept their stock. Barton controlled the company along with the private equity company. He wanted a fund that was willing to reinvest all the profits and cash flow back into the company to help its growth, and he wanted the fund to let him have control as long as he performed to expectations. The agreement with the private equity firm was that the firm would have two out of five board seats. If there was any hiccup, they would end up with three seats and be able to fire Barton. The partnership was very productive and profitable for both. They never fired Barton.

Lesson: Some lessons include:

- When you get into a partnership, make sure you have a way to exit. Not every partnership is made in heaven, where all the partners see eye to eye.
- The key to success as a franchise is consistency. Inconsistency among stores dilutes the power of the brand and negates the value of the franchise. Customers appreciate consistency of quality. Fail to deliver that and you weaken your brand.
- When you get too attached to a business, you could lose all perspective. Free yourself.

From Profits to the Moon

10. Focus can beat "first mover" for growth. After the equity issues were settled, Barton focused on Great Clips' growth strategy. He decided to employ a rifle-based strategy rather than a shotgun principle of expanding without a focus. The strategy he and his team decided was to focus on one market at a time, and to develop a strategy to dominate the market to become the biggest hair-cutting chain in the market before considering other markets. Franchisees had to succeed for Great Clips to succeed. This required that they develop a local training center to train hair stylists, and have local support staff to offer assistance to the franchisees to make sure that they did well. There had to be enough units in each market to pay for the investment in the training center and support staff for operational assistance, and the franchisees needed to have the capacity to develop the number of units needed to saturate and dominate. Many other franchisors in the industry expected to successfully grow without a focused srategy, and did not support their franchisees. They crashed.

Lesson: ***Not all first movers win***. Barton did not worry about being the first mover. He just wanted to be the last survivor. Understand the needs of your customers and the strengths of your competitors and focus on dominating each market you enter.

11. Market selection. After starting to grow in the Twin Cities market and making it profitable, Great Clips focused on Des Moines, Iowa, and Omaha, Nebraska, because they were within driving distance of headquarters. The next city was Denver because Barton liked to ski. He does not claim to be scientific in his selection. This was unlike other franchisors that expanded in cities just because there were franchisees who were interested. Barton had to invest in a training center, real estate people and operations help before there were franchisees. And he had to give up potential franchisees in markets he did not target. Barton had just built a training center in Omaha and Des Moines when a potential franchisee from Indiana came to Minneapolis headquarters to talk to Great Clips and a competitor. He wanted to become a Great Clips franchisee, and Barton told him that he would call when they decided to expand to Indiana. Barton also gave him a franchise agreement and the offering document. The franchisee signed the document and sent it in with a check for $10,000. Barton needed the cash for Great Clips, and it would have been very easy to change his mind. But he would not be able to support the franchisee in Indiana, so he returned the check. Barton did not want the franchisee or Great Clips to fail.

Lesson: Decide your strategy and stick to it, unless someone comes and offers riches beyond the dreams of avarice, or unless changes in your assumptions warrant your reversal. Then you can go to the Bahamas and count waves. Otherwise, you will end up confusing your team and fail. When you don't know what you want, any road will get you there, or not.

12. Financing the expansion. Expanding Great Clips required lots of resources. Barton and the fund decided to invest all of the annual profits to finance the expansion into new markets. While this had the impact of reducing annual profits, it also meant that the company was geographically concentrating its expansion costs and had a better ability to control it. Sales and markets were growing at an exponential pace due to improved reach in selected market media, and profits soared when the company reached the targeted level of sales it wanted in each market. The money that would have gone to pay taxes was now going for business expansion, and the company could self-finance its expansion rather than finding equity and diluting ownership. And best of all, when Great Clips expanded to all its targeted markets, it would have the ability to deliver higher profits than if it had scattered its resources. To make this strategy real and minimize potential problems, the franchisees had to do well; otherwise, all of Great Clips' investments would be lost.

Lesson: Put your eggs in one basket and watch the basket. This strategy can have a better chance of succeeding against those who scatter their resources and don't dominate any markets.

13. Sharing the dream. After the problems in the previous partnership, Barton decided he did not want to have any problems with his new partnership. Although there were about 12 shareholders among the senior executive team, the key investor was the private equity fund that had bought into Great Clips when Barton bought his previous partners' share of the business. He looked at the conflicts in the earlier partnership and decided that he needed to over-communicate with the investors. So he talked with his contact at the fund two to three times per week. He made sure there were no surprises, offered information about issues that were affecting the business, asked questions and allowed the contact to ask questions. He told funders exactly what he was thinking, and if there was a disagreement, he bit his lip and went back to work. If there was any bad news, he looked at the worst possibilities, "added three to four new levels of bad possibilities," and presented these to the fund, because Barton wanted them to know the situation that Great Clips could face. There were no conflict drivers as in the previous partnership because both key partners agreed on the long-term vision and agreed on the need to reinvest to achieve their goals. He ran the business conservatively and built trust and confidence between the partners. He bought back their interest in 2007 at a price that gave them a compound annual return of 30 percent.

Lesson: One key to a successful partnership is to promise less and deliver more. Partnerships are a two-way street. Make sure you and your partners have the same goals before you get into a partnership. Then make sure that everyone feels that the relationship is fair and no one is marginalized.

14. Building the world's largest salon brand. By the time Barton bought out the fund's interest in 2008, Great Clips had system-wide sales of $700 million with 2,700 salons and 25,000 team members. How did he get there? His initial partners did not believe they could dominate the industry. From the beginning of the new partnership with the private equity fund, Barton focused on growing and dominating one market at a time. The key ingredients making this explosive growth happen were:

- People: Barton claims that the company got lucky early on in the high-quality of the early franchisees. These franchisees were committed to the same criteria of training and quality. Most important, they wanted both franchisor and franchisee to succeed because they saw the linkages. Barton selected these key franchise leaders and invited them to a special meeting to help franchisees learn how to grow their business.
- Vision and long-term thinking: These franchisees and others who came in their wake did not create problems but solved them and stayed focused on the plan and the selected strategy. At the first annual convention of franchisees in Minneapolis, Barton gave the opening address, listing his goal of 3,000 Great Clips salons by the year 2000. He noted that someone was going to do it, why not them? He repeated the "3000 by 2000" vision in his notes to franchisees. He wrote an "as if" article under The Wall Street Journal banner saying that Great Clips had reached 3,000 units by 1999. When he hung it up at a convention, spontaneously the franchisees and employees signed the "article signifying that they were also committed to this goal. This even changed the way Great Clips thought. The leadership did not have all the details settled, but they moved toward this vision with discipline. The culture of the entire organization (employees, franchisees, and franchisors) became "us vs. them"...them being the competitors. It was powerful and motivating. Great Clips became the largest salon chain in the country by 1999, although falling short of the goal of 3,000 stores. The "3000 by 2000" vision was the "right thought at the right time and the right place."

Lesson: Find a common goal that is both challenging and motivating to unite your organization, and constantly remind them of your joint endeavor. Give meaning, and challenge your team. It will add to your performance.

15. Number of stores per market. To get some rationale behind his thinking, Barton used demographics to calculate the number of potential stores in each market. Based on distances travelled by customers to reach the store, Barton initially estimated that the company could have 28 salons to saturate the Twin Cities market. Currently, Great Clips has 150 stores in the Twin Cities market. The main factor behind the improved performance was that Great Clips ended up as the leader with a much higher market share than expected.

Lesson: It is good to have a rationale and assumptions for growth and marketing expenses. But these initial assumptions will nearly always be wrong. You need them, however, to know when you are going off direction so you can adjust your plan.

16. Need for consistency. Barton realized the need for consistency and discipline, especially in a young franchise system. He and the other franchise salons were trying to change the industry from a "mom and pop" model to one with the consistency of a franchise system. They did not offer appointments, and were open till 9 p.m. on weekdays and all day on the weekends (till 5 p.m.). This was unusual for the industry. In addition, the stylists did not build a clientele for themselves but for the chain. Many tried to change the system and drag them back to the old model. One franchisee, who was also a lawyer, sued Great Clips to be allowed to be flexible and manage the business with his own rules. Great Clips countersued and won. This was a message to all current and potential franchisees that they should stick to the system.

Lesson: There are few secrets in business, and none if more than one person knows of it. You cannot make exceptions in a system without everyone expecting the same. Find what works and stick to it. Consumers expect consistency from the various salons. Allowing each salon to do its own thing would negate the value of the franchise and the brand.

17. Need for open discussions to build the brand. Barton believed in feedback from his franchisees, and he spent a lot of time getting input from them. He tested potentially viable concepts to see what worked and what did not. If something worked, he would expand it to the entire system. If it did not, he ended it. He found that making a decision and expanding it to the entire system before testing it was a major mistake. One of his franchisees came up with an information system that worked. Barton had a vendor buy it from the franchisee, and he expanded it to all the franchisees in the system. A few years later, salon sales flattened. The franchisees blamed the company for poor marketing and for building too many stores. Great Clips got together with the franchisees and decided to hire a consultant to understand the issues. The consultant found that the company and the franchisees had made a simple business very complicated. They were collecting and analyzing 33 pieces of information (most of them "garbage" according to Barton), but very few of them related to customer satisfaction and market dominance. They worked together to rebrand the service and to develop a simple, one-page summary that offered the same answers to common problems. They found that there were only a handful of variables that affected the business. The company and franchisees started focusing on these variables that drove sales. Sales took off. There was peace between Great Clips and the franchisees.

Lesson: ***Listen to get new ideas. Test to see what works. Then expand with the profitable ideas.*** But understand what really makes a business tick. Don't run a business if you have not tested your key assumptions. Sooner or later, more likely sooner, you will pay the price. As Barton puts it, brand happens in the salon, not what is shown on TV.

Rules for Entrepreneurs from Ray Barton of Great Clips

- **Focus on the long-term good.** Barton was willing to sacrifice short-term profits to build the business for the long-term. He notes the example of a restaurant chain in which he was invited to invest. When he performed his due diligence, he found that the entrepreneurs skimmed and did not pay taxes; consequently, the venture failed. Barton did not invest.
- **Get a good board of directors.** Find successful business people who think differently and who are experienced in what you will go through. Find people with complementary skills.
- **Save to invest.** When Barton moved back to the Twin Cities, he saved his money and invested in real estate. When he needed cash for his venture, he sold his real estate.
- **Test before implementing.** Get ideas from everyone. Test to see what works. Implement it across the system.
- **Monitor frequently. Monitor right.** Know the key variables to track the business. Most relate to customer satisfaction, profits, and cash.
- **Your brand is what you deliver.** It is what you do and your customers' experience. Brand is not what you say it is or advertise it to be.
- **Find good partners.** To succeed, you need partners with the same vision who can complement your skills and your efforts.

TOM AUTH
ITI

ST. PAUL, MINN

Building the world's largest wireless security equipment company

Summary: Two entrepreneurs with experience in the security-alarm industry started ITI in 1980. Their goal was to build a wireless security-alarm company after the Federal Communications Commission (FCC) modified regulations that made the development of reliable wireless systems possible. Tom Auth got involved with ITI in 1981 when he invested $25,000 in the company. He was aware that the company was without funds and was still in its infancy so he didn't do much due diligence. Shortly after investing he found that the company had not filed any payroll tax returns and that used up his entire investment. So he took control of the company and raised an additional $300,000 from friends and neighbors. Between 1981 and 1983 he also raised an additional $3 million from Network Security Corporation, a publicly traded alarm installation and monitoring company and from others. From this beginning, Auth built ITI to annual revenues in excess of $120 million and valuation in excess of $350 million. This is how he did it.

Before the Startup

1. **Keep looking for the right opportunities**. Auth got married early, and he and his wife had three kids by the time he was 25, so he needed an income. With his wife teaching and Auth having a couple part-time jobs he went to graduate school. Upon graduation, he took a job as a CPA for one of the top firms in the country. But he was always looking to make more, and while keeping his job as a CPA, looked for and answered ads that offered a meaningful (40-50 percent) jump in salary with the potential of ownership. This search paid off, and he found a company at which he was able to become the Chief Financial Officer and a partner. He was able to buy 6 percent of a business in St. Paul, MN, 16 percent of an affiliated business in Milwaukee, WI, and 25 percent of the real estate used in the businesses. Since Auth and his wife were dedicated savers, he was able to invest $33,000, which was a significant amount for him in those days. Auth negotiated and structured the

acquisition in the Milwaukee business and the real estate, which included borrowing the entire purchase price. To buy the real estate, the companies used tax-exempt, fixed-rate industrial-revenue bonds that had below-market interest rates. In the late 70s, Auth sold his interest in these businesses, but maintained his investment in the real estate. When interest rates spiked up in the early 1980s (with the prime rate reaching 22%), the businesses lost value. However, due to the favorable financing, the real estate became very attractive to another company, which then bought the building for a nice gain due to the assumable low-rate financing.

Lesson: *Be frugal* so you can invest when good opportunities come your way. The key to the first success was the real estate, which benefitted from the low rate and attractive tax laws. As a CPA, Auth knew the benefits of owning real estate with attractive long-term financing, and also gained an appreciation for structuring transactions in the most tax advantageous ways. Every dollar of tax savings is a dollar you don't have to borrow or raise as equity.

2. **Buying a business. Do not overpay. Be tenacious. Maintain credibility with sellers and bankers**. Auth had previously bought and invested in about 10 small companies before investing in ITI. These companies built his net worth and gave him the resources and connections to hang in there with ITI. All of the sellers tried to negotiate a higher price, but Auth never paid more than the value based on his own analysis of what was both viable in the marketplace and a reasonable price to him based on collateral value and cash flow. Auth always spent time analyzing the business he was considering and stayed in touch with the sellers and the bankers. He never exaggerated. He told them his honest view of the situation and explained the reasons. This allowed the seller, financiers and intermediaries to understand Auth's position and rationale, and to trust it more than people they believed were less than entirely honest on the price. One seller did not give him an answer for eight months. And then one Christmas Eve he called and said he was ready to sell and he wanted to sell it to Auth's group and that the terms discussed eight months earlier were ok. For another company, Auth flew down to North Carolina to complete an agreement – only to be told by the seller that he wanted to keep the business after all. He just told the presumed seller, "John, you are a great guy and this was a nice dinner, but you could have told me what you just told me over the phone." About a year later, the same seller called him, after checking out the market, and said he was ready to sell, and Auth bought the company at approximately the same price he originally offered.

Lesson: Know how to value a purchase. Give a comprehensive, detailed proposal showingyou have doneyour homeworkand to build credibility with the seller and the financiers, and do not overpay. Don't fall in love with a company. Understand that you have to be able to buy it for a good price. Asking prices are usually high because merger and acquisitions (M&A) brokers often tell clients that they can get an attractive price, such as seven to eight times earnings before interest, taxes, depreciation and amortization (EBITDA), in order both to be hired and secure a significant fee. They often end up getting a smaller amount, such as four to five times. Don't get seduced into paying a high figure just because the seller or broker claims it is worth more. Build and maintain your reputation. It can be worth more than money. But also be willing to look at the transaction from the seller's perspective and recognize value when it is there.

3. **Structure the transaction to your advantage.** As a CPA, Auth was an expert on tax laws, and he made full use of this knowledge. While he stopped using seller financing later on in his career, in his early years when he did not have much money to invest, he used all the options open to him, including seller financing. In addition, he also used earn-outs (where the seller is paid conditionally based upon certain events happening) when there is strong customer concentration, and pays the earn-out if the customers stayed. He also used tax-favored strategies, such as payment via non-compete agreements. He prefers to purchase assets rather than stock to avoid inheriting the previous company's liabilities and also to be able to amortize intangibles. However he has purchased stock where it was required to get a good deal done and the structure and representations, warrantees and indemnifications to safeguard the buyer were provided by the seller. And he used holdbacks (payments made to the seller if certain conditions are met) to guarantee items such as accounts receivable and inventory. In his later years, he made all-cash offers using internally generated funds and occasionally, bank financing, to avoid seller financing and to get a better purchase price.

Lesson: Know what you are doing. Know what is needed. Learn how to use knowledge to your advantage. (Note to reader: Sometimes it may be advantageous to buy stock rather than assets if the price is discounted, warrantees are strong and you hold back a sufficiently large cushion. Check with your attorney or qualified advisor for ways to secure your investment.)

4. **Keeping dry powder**: One of the companies Auth purchased a couple of years before the ITI venture was a road-construction company with lots of assets. Instead of selling the assets and reducing debt, Auth and his partner tried to run the business with all the acquired assets and high debt levels. The economic climate worsened, interest rates exceeded 20 percent and the business suffered. The deal went from being wonderful to a very tough situation. One day at their lawyer's office, Auth's partner offered his interest to Auth for $50,000 because he did not have the staying power. Auth immediately asked his partner to stay put, went to his bank and borrowed the $50,000 to buy him out. Auth's conservative financial habits allowed him to wind down and liquidate the business in a controlled manner over a five-year period. His net profit from the business was $2 million.

Lesson: Be prepared for all eventualities and be conservative. If your business is highly leveraged, reduce debt during good times when you can get good prices for your assets. Build strength to survive downturns, because they do happen.

From Startup to Profits

5. Check for alligators before you enter the swamp. When he invested in ITI, Auth didn't do enough due diligence, since he was aware that the business was a start-up and had been struggling and needed money. He thought his initial investment would tide the company over until he raised additional funds. After all of his initial investment went to pay the company's unpaid back taxes. Auth immediately had to commit himself fully to ITI, raise more money from others quickly and keep the promising venture going forward while doing that. If he had spent two to three weeks doing his due diligence, he would have discovered these problems and would not have had to scramble or more likely would have negotiated a better equity position before investing.. (On the other hand, he may have stayed away from ITI and lost an opportunity to make a fortune, so the lesson to draw may not always be as clear as you would like.)

Lesson: Do your homework before you get in. It may be too difficult after you are in the swamp and the alligators are nipping at your rear. Because Auth was experienced, had a great track record, and was able to secure financing from others, he succeeded. You may not be so fortunate.

6. Keep the opportunity in mind since the problems can overwhelm you. In addition to the tax and cash-flow issues, ITI also took 4 years to reach profitability, and took far longer than Auth initially expected to make its products reliable and marketable. There were many days when bankruptcy seemed like a good option. According to Auth, "If I had brains, I would have had ITI file for bankruptcy." But since he had already invested in ITI, had raised money from friends, neighbors and family and because he saw the opportunity in wireless security systems, Auth continued his commitment to the company. His friends' investment and the fact that they had placed a bet on him bothered him more than the potential of loss bothered them. They could afford to lose the cash and Auth had explained the risk to them. But they had believed in Auth and in the product. So instead of filing for bankruptcy, he persevered, and saw his $25,000 investment grow to $30 million over the next 20 years. Each of his investors saw his or her $12,000 investment grow to $180,000 by the time of the 1986 public offering. In 1983 during ITI's darkest hours, Auth raised $3 million from Network Security in exchange for 51% of ITI. However when Network Security made this investment, Auth obtained the right to go public to have an alternative exit strategy that could offer a higher valuation for his equity than a controlling shareholder would most likely pay.

Lesson: The road to success is not clear and not smooth. If it were, there would be many more successes. When you are in the middle of the swamp and the alligators are gently nibbling at your behind, the success attributed to you by journalists who write about you later makes it seem like it was easy. Mostly, it is anything but easy. But if you see the potential and believe in it, hang in there to overcome the numerous pitfalls along the way. Raising money from friends and family can often motivate you more than your own money will—you do not want to fail in front of them. All ventures take time: "It takes twice as long and costs twice as much" is a famous but often accurate cliché. So be ready for the long haul. And if you do plan to give up control to any one investor, make sure you protect the value that you plan to create by negotiating a way to exit from the investment (check with a competent securities attorney).

From Profits to the Moon

7. **Timing is everything.** ITI developed its first product and reached $1 million in sales in 1982, and went public in 1986 at a valuation of $28 million, when it had $8 million in revenue and net income of $1.3 million. By 1988, ITI had grown to $28 million in sales when a U.S. subsidiary of Inspectorate International of Switzerland purchased the company in a transaction that valued ITI at $78 million. Auth negotiated to keep seven percent of the new equity for himself and his managers, with an option to sell this equity to the company with a guaranteed minimum return. Not thinking that the equity piece would ever amount to a major payday, Auth was considering resigning as CEO to look for another opportunity. In the fall of 1989 he became aware of a business by the name of Vomela that was for sale. At the time, Vomela was primarily a contract manufacturer for 3M. He purchased Vomela in the spring of 1990 and was again thinking of resigning from ITI when ITI got its biggest order ever from Westinghouse, increasing the size of the company by around 50 percent. Auth stuck around. When the Swiss company decided to sell in 1991, Auth bought the company with new equity partners, an LBO fund from New York. After selling some of their stock in the existing company to the new buyer, Auth and his management team rolled over the balance into a leveraged equity position in the acquiring company and also received significant options in the new company. Over the following years, Auth also got additional options based on performance, and he took a portion of his compensation in equity rather than in cash. The company continued to grow to revenues of $60 million in 1994, and it went public again in November 1994 raising almost $40 million and had a secondary stock offering in May 1995 for $80 million. The LBO fund got five times its investment and still owned 13 percent. Auth did well, too, and continued to lead ITI till 2000, when with annual revenues of $120 million it merged with a competitor to form Interlogix, Inc., in a reverse merger in which ITI was valued at $360 million and in which ITI shareholders received $180 million in cash and a 25% interest in the new combined entity. In 2002, GE bought the combined company. Auth sold his shares in ITI for the last time and left to run Vomela, which he has since grown from $3.8 million in sales when he bought it to $81 million in sales in 2007. Vomela is currently one of the largest designers and manufacturers of specialty graphics in the country.

Lesson: When you believe in a business and in yourself, it pays to get equity, especially if you have negotiated the option to be able to sell it at an attractive price. When the right offer comes around, sell – or buy. When circumstances change, be flexible. Don't fall in love with a business. *In life and business, timing is key.*

8. Putting the right person in the right position and treating superstars with care. After getting involved in managing the company, Auth found that some of the founding members of the management team wanted to retain management control, but Auth thought they were not right for the jobs regardless of their entrepreneurial traits. Auth had to replace key managers with the right people who could perform. Auth got a group of people who were turned on by being part of a high-growth venture, and whose goal was not just making money. This meant that they shared the vision and were willing to share the risk. He offered a low base with stock options or profit sharing. The base reflected the amount that the company could afford to pay in cash. He made key employees equity players.

Lesson: Don't make long-term commitments to new hires because you don't know how they will perform, especially under changing circumstances. Many think they are qualified, but few are able. When someone is delivering, take a risk. Pay more for potential superstars; they are worth the time and effort. But treat superstars with care. Make sure they understand the difference between a sale and a profitable sale. Make sure they respect their fellow employees and that they acknowledge the role the entire organization plays in their success. Manage compensation across the company. Be consistent and have good reasons for your compensation structure. This includes raises and health insurance, which are among the key issues for employees. People will talk about their compensation, and it's ultimately impossible to keep your payroll a secret.

9. Understand the value to the customer when pricing. Dealers who installed security systems made money on the monitoring aspect of the business. Installation was a bottleneck. If the dealers could install more systems, they could monitor more customers, create more recurring revenue and make their business worth more. With wireless, the dealers did not have to run wires through walls and installation was cheaper. This meant that they could install more systems, and monitor more customers. The recurring revenue each new customer provided to the dealer enhanced the dealer's net worth by $1,500. So Auth priced ITI products based on the business model of his customers. He sold the benefits of increased net worth to his customers to get maximum margins for his company and make the business case for wireless. But ITI captured a significant portion of the labor savings that the dealers enjoyed and earned high profits. He wanted to be sure that the value that was created accrued to ITI.

Lesson: Think like your customer. Learn the value that your product has to your customers and sell value if you want to get higher prices and maximum margins. Higher margins allow you to make mistakes and still succeed. And you will make mistakes. Higher prices increase your net worth. So find how to gain competitive advantage and price higher.

10. Controlling costs. At ITI, Auth had his priorities. This meant not hiring expensive sales and marketing people until there was product for them to sell, not renting expensive offices, not wasting money on trade shows when there was nothing to show, and so on. First get high-margin sales by emphasizing the value to the dealers. Then cut manufacturing costs. He invested his money in product development, in manufacturing processes, equipment and in inventory that was critical to get the product done, ready for the market and sold. In retrospect, however, Auth thinks he was too slow in cutting manufacturing costs. Competition grew (which was bound to happen anyway) but his dealers were loyal. Still, his market share did not grow as fast as he had hoped. He thinks he would have had a higher market share if he started controlling and cutting costs sooner to become more efficient, and putting these extra profits into sales and marketing. To improve his cost competitiveness, he moved the operations to Mexico. He did not rush it, since he wanted to keep control of the process. He started with 20 employees in Mexico and grew the number there to 250, while he had more than 800 employees in Minnesota.

Lesson: Focus on getting sales, but also concentrate on reducing and controlling costs. It is easier to grow when you are offering higher value. But control costs. *Money is precious, especially when you don't have it.* In the early stages of the venture, your cost of money can be very expensive, ranging up to about 100 percent a year. Don't spend it on unneeded things or on your ego. Competitors may be afraid to take you on if they don't see obvious weaknesses, such as bloated costs.

11. Use acquisitions judiciously for growth. Auth has always used acquisitions to build his businesses. But the acquisition had to be the right fit and at the right price. In 1996, ITI's largest customer pulled its $40 million account. This would have left a huge hole in the company, but because Auth had built a large cash hoard, he did not have liquidity problems. By coincidence, at an industry conference Auth met the president of a wired security-alarm business that was a great fit for ITI. The wired products allowed ITI to offer a complete line of products and services, and to develop hybrids, which included the best features and benefits of wired and wireless products. The price was reasonable. So he bought it and with that acquisition and growth from other customers filled the huge hole from the loss of the $40-million account.

Lesson: Have cash and be prepared for any eventuality. Buy when the price and the strategy are right.

12. Know when to hold 'em, know when to fold 'em. As Kenny Rogers' song "The Gambler" says, timing is everything. When Auth saw his competitors selling products to extremely marginal customers who could not afford to pay for the security systems, he knew that the market was saturated. He decided to get out. He sold his business and got a great price.

Lesson: Sell all the wine when its time is up.

13. Understand the other side before negotiating. In 1989, Auth sold ITI to a Swiss conglomerate. In 1992, Auth, in partnership with a leveraged buyout (LBO) group, repurchased ITI from the Swiss Company. He thinks he did not negotiate hard enough with the LBO group. He and his executive team received a reasonable equity and option package in the buy-back transaction. In addition, the group received an additional tranche of options that would be in the money after the LBO fund saw capital gains of 50 percent. In retrospect, he thinks he could have secured a better deal if he knew the return that the LBO group was expecting, so he could negotiate a sharing of profits from that point.

Lesson: Understand the other person's point of view if you want to do better in any negotiations. Investors are more open to sharing upside gains after they have met their target returns.

14. Don't gamble with juries. One of the early investors in ITI had loaned $10,000 to the company before the company split its stock 10-for-1 and raised additional financing from other investors. This party later claimed he had acquired stock, (even though it was clearly documented as a loan). A couple of years later he came back and claimed his loan was really an equity investment and that it was made prior to the stock split. On the courthouse steps, a settlement could have been made for $30,000 but Auth and his attorney (this was her first trial) thought ITI had a slam-dunk case and was willing to have the jury settle it. Unfortunately for Auth, the jury believed the opposing lawyer's case rather than Auth's and somehow awarded his opponent over $2 million. The amount was reduced on appeal, but the cost was still far higher than the settlement offer.

Lesson: Get an experienced attorney. If the issue involves securities, get good legal counsel from an experienced securities lawyer. Inexperience will usually cost you more. Settle if the amount is reasonable rather than gambling on juries. You may believe in your own position but others may not agree. Juries usually have no business experience and many times little education and often sympathize with the underdog, especially if the case is complicated and the attorney cannot explain it adequately for them to understand it.

15. Treat rainmakers (professional builders and great sales people) differently from professional managers. The rainmakers are driven to show results, and they need to be compensated accordingly. They are confident in their abilities and want to be paid when they deliver, i.e., in commissions. Pay rainmakers a low base with generous commission programs with no upper limit. Some of the rainmakers at Vomela are paid over $400,000. Unless circumstances require, Auth honors the sales compensation plans put in place when sales personnel were hired. At ITI, he sometimes adjusted programs due to ITI's explosive growth and the fact that sales personnel could not effectively cover their large territories as the product offering and dealer network grew. At Vomela, he maintained the terms at hiring and has made few changes as it was good business. This encourages professional builders to work hard and to achieve more since they know that the "sky is the limit." But don't forget to require profitable sales. With professional managers, Auth pays a higher base and larger bonuses rather than commissions. The bonus is based on both overall company performance and individual performance.

> **Lesson**: ***Keep the rainmakers motivated.*** Do not remove incentives just because the rainmakers may be earning more than a preconceived number you have in your head. When sales people are too comfortable, their motivation may be affected. It is a mistake to structure the compensation at the extremes – too much base or too little. Make sales people feel part of the team. Give them a vision about what the business can become. If they don't buy into the vision, they won't sell well. If they don't sell well, if they are not pulling their weight, let them go. In some cases, Auth was slow to pull the trigger and kept hoping for improvement that never materialized. Be slow to hire and quick to fire. You will know the value of an employee in 30 to 60 days. If a public company, plan to give them equity options in six months, if they are "keepers."

16. Focus on revenues each day of the year. Auth reviewed recurring costs a couple of times annually and did not raise them in the interim unless required to grow sales and profit.

> **Lesson**: Costs are key, especially recurring costs such as base salaries, benefits, rents, and the like. Make sure that you can afford all of the commitments you make. Be careful before committing to adding to recurring costs. Review expenses annually and more frequently to see that they are all still appropriate and necessary for the business. Carefully consider whether costs that aren't related and necessary to create or support sales are necessary. If not, eliminate them. Then devote all your attention to raising revenues and getting sales. That is what makes the company grow.

17. Right strategy for growth. Due to the high cost of installing security alarms, the penetration rate of residential security systems was low when Auth started with ITI. The wireless security alarms that ITI built reduced the time and cost of installation for the dealers, giving the company a competitive edge. Auth took advantage of this benefit and the low penetration rate (of the wireless industry) to grow ITI organically (without acquisitions). With Vomela, Auth faced a mature industry. There were many competitors, and most of them were small, undercapitalized and in need of some management help. Auth decided to buy competitors, especially if he could buy the businesses at the right price. In ten years, he bought six companies with $34 million in annual sales and through growth and acquisitions built Vomela from $3 million in sales to $81 million.

Lesson: *Adjust your strategy to the circumstances.* Evaluate the trends in the market and industry. Pick the best way to grow and succeed.

18. Maintain congruence of interests. Often sales personnel want to lower prices and margins to get the sale and keep competitors out. In such a case, have a frank discussion with the sales personnel and pay a reduced commission as appropriate under the circumstances. This keeps them focused on solving the customers' problems and getting high-margin sales.

Lesson: *Make sure that the pain is shared. It keeps people honest.*

19. Different types of customers and sales people. Some customers and accounts are always up for grabs and getting or maintaining the account requires the sales personnel to understand the latest advances and benefits that the company can offer. This requires higher levels of problem-solving expertise among sales personnel to be able to develop solutions, competitive advantages and presentations. Other customers, such as the buyers for the major chains, know what they want and why, and there is not much you can tell them that they don't know. In these cases, there is not much that you can do that is unique, other than price. The people serving them should be relationship managers.

Lesson: Match your sales personnel to the type of customers.

20. When you know what you are doing, keep control. Auth kept the number of minority shareholders to a minimum. After achieving financial independence, Auth has kept 100% ownership of his operating businesses. There are a lot of complicating factors (buy sell agreements, minority shareholders rights, etc.) that additional shareholders bring to privately held businesses. Auth has tried to create the same incentive as ownership provides by using a Deferred Compensation Program where contributions to key management's deferred compensation accounts go up and down based on the results of the business.

Lesson: Having too many shareholders when you don't need them can require more maintenance and higher costs. Shareholders also want to be able to sell their shares at the highest price that could create liquidity or exit issues. So be careful when you add new shareholders.

21. Select your board for candid feedback. Auth believes that entrepreneurs should be able to have a totally open discussion and get honest feedback from their board of directors. According to Auth, the board should not have too many directors, and they should be people whom the entrepreneur trusts to have a frank, candid and friendly discussion, and they should spend the time to do it right (one to two days per month). They should be experienced at various aspects of venture development and be willing to offer value in return for cash compensation or equity in the venture. Be careful of bringing on people as directors who are doing it to add to their resume without wanting to spend the time to become really engaged and knowledgeable about your business.

Lesson: Find good advisers. Make sure that they are committed and reward them well if they help your venture growth. Manage board meetings to get benefit out of the board rather than spending excessive time on the quality of presentations while the venture itself is suffering. Focus your time on solving the key issues of the day. Don't waste it on developing dazzling presentations of your "brilliant future" when your present is cloudy. Make sure that directors are "policemen" and keep you focused on your planned direction without allowing you to spend money like a drunken sailor on anything that strikes your fancy.

22. Be careful when offering bonuses. Auth believes in bonus programs. He is also very careful when offering bonuses and is clear about the circumstances under which bonuses will be paid. He does this to prevent employees from feeling entitled to bonuses regardless of individual and company performance. Sometimes employees may have spent their bonus before they have earned it. Keep expectations clear and avoid an entitlement attitude.

Lesson: Explain how bonuses are calculated. Let them know the company has to be profitable and the company needs to retain cash to fund growth and to invest in equipment, facilities and to be able to weather difficult times, should they occur. Keep your employees updated so they know how the business is generally doing. Most know by the activity level anyway. Cut back when needed but explain the reasons, and how you plan to turn the company around.

Rules for Entrepreneurs from Tom Auth of ITI and Vomela

- **Know your strengths and make full use of them**. As a CPA, Auth was able to use his accounting and tax expertise to structure financial deals for gain. He used this to build his reputation and net worth.
- **Be frugal and conservative**. Tom Auth was able to make lemonade from lemons when he was able to stay in a venture that was suffering from very high interest rates due to very unusual economic circumstances. His staying power allowed him to liquidate the assets without a fire sale and earn $2 million on a $100,000 investment.
- **Do your homework before firing your guns**. Tom Auth did not do sufficient analysis before investing in what became his most successful investment. If he had, he would have known the true condition and done a better job of getting ready to invest in the venture. As it was, the first few years were not very pleasant, and Auth was very close to shutting the venture down.

- **Hire slowly. Fire quickly**. Not all your employees work out. So be careful when hiring. But when someone is not performing at the levels that were clearly required, don't expect miracle turnarounds in behavior.
- **Find value when pricing**. Auth understood how his products added value and priced them to gain maximum advantage and net worth.
- **Cut costs**. Auth learned that he should have been more diligent in cutting manufacturing costs in order to increase his sales and marketing budgets and gain market share after competition entered the market he had created.
- **Understand the difference between rainmakers and bureaucrats.** Rainmakers love to hunt and kill – and bring in business. Bureaucrats run what is there. Know the difference and reward them accordingly.
- **Develop your strategy based on your situation**. When ITI was able to penetrate the market and grow organically, that is what Auth did. When he needed to plug a hole caused by a major account leaving him, or when he found himself in a mature industry, he did not hesitate to buy competitors and consolidate. However, he bought opportunistically to avoid paying too much.

Lloyd Sigel
Lloyd's Barbeque

ST. PAUL, MINN

Building a national brand in ribs and meats

Summary: Lloyd Sigel started his business career selling roofing and siding with his dad, whom he calls "one of the best salesmen he has ever seen – one who could overcome any objection and get the sale". This was at the age of 13. From there he moved on to painting houses while in high school and selling advertising while in college. When he finished college he took his first professional job with a reduction in pay because he could not find a job that paid him a comparable amount. His first job happened to be in the food industry where Sigel quickly made his mark as a superb salesman. This caught the eye of a food industry entrepreneur who hired Sigel and then made him a partner. This partnership became very productive and Sigel soon found himself buying a nearly bankrupt food company to pursue his passion – to sell pre-cooked ribs to restaurants and food stores. He bought the assets by assuming the liabilities, which is a great way to get into your own business especially if you do not want to invest a lot of cash and you know how to turn the business around. Over the years he built this business into a giant in the food industry and then sold it four times. The last time was to General Mills when sales reached over $100 million. The next time you eat Lloyd's barbeque from a supermarket, know that this is how he did it.

Before the Startup

1. The school years. Sigel started working at the age of 13. His dad was in the business of selling roofing and siding and home remodeling. Sigel learned house painting from his dad's painting foreman and started painting houses on his own while he was in high school. In addition, Sigel started to sell with his dad. According to Sigel, his dad was the "greatest salesperson alive." Sigel claims that he learned all the sales skills he has ever used from his father. At an early age, he learned how to generate sales leads, how to qualify prospects, overcome rejections, and get the order. Many times, Sigel went on sales calls with his dad, but often he was sent to knock on doors himself.

Lesson: Business runs on sales. There are different levels of sales, ranging from door-to-door consumer sales to big-ticket, corporate or government sales. But the key is that without the sale, you don't have a business. And you are always selling yourself. If you are not great at sales, learn how to do it and/or you may need to work with someone who is good at it. Remember that *the world seldom beats a path to your door.*

2. **Leads at the state fair.** The state fair was also a good source of leads and Sigel's dad and uncle had a booth at the fair to generate new leads. They would set up a booth but needed a gimmick to attract attention and get leads. So they got a spotted monkey in a cage and the consumer who guessed the correct number of spots would win a grand prize. One day, his uncle and dad took off for a minor errand leaving Sigel in charge of the booth, and warned him not to open the cage door. Sigel was 14 at the time. In a teenager's brain, a command not to do something gets translated as 'wouldn't it be nice to do it'? So Sigel thought he would open the cage door to hold the monkey. Faster than a speeding bullet (this was super-monkey), the monkey proceeded to move to the highest rafters of the building and stayed there for two days.

Lesson: Monkeys also like freedom. But unlike teenagers, their brains are not on hold. *Listen to your dad, especially about monkeys.*

3. **Ad sales.** When Sigel graduated from high school, he entered the Army for a six-month active duty enlistment followed by a reserve obligation. After the active duty, he began college at the University of Minnesota in the school of journalism. However, college was interrupted for almost a year as he was called from the Army reserve to serve active duty in the Berlin Crisis. Upon returning to the University, he chose to sell advertising for the college newspaper to pay his way through college. He was paid a straight commission and according to Sigel, the "pay was good." However the newspaper did not publish in the summer, and since Sigel could not get something as attractive as his newspaper job, he decided to start a "Crazy Days" event at the shopping complex near the U. Sigel found that the area merchants were open to new ideas to drum up business. Crazy Days involved publishing an advertising insert for the Minnesota Daily and Sigel could charge higher ad rates. While at the newspaper, Sigel also developed a yellow pages section for the student/faculty directory. This was a great summer job and he was rewarded handsomely for his efforts. In fact he earned so much that he had to take a cut in pay when he took his first job after graduating.

Lesson: Find a need and fill it. Sigel knew his market and understood that the local merchants were open to an event to promote their businesses. He also copied the yellow pages concept as a means of generating revenues. If the word "copying" turns you off, try "fast follower" (which is MBA-speak for copying).

4. **The first job.** Upon graduating, Sigel wanted to get into advertising. But there were only a few ad agencies in the Twin Cities and he did not get any job offers there. He did get an offer from the Chicago Tribune to sell classified ads for $70 per week in Chicago, but he could not relocate since his wife had a much better paying job in St. Paul. So he took a job at a meatpacking company called Armour & Company as an "advertising/ marketing specialist." Essentially, this job involved sitting at one of the hundreds of grey desks and collating stacks of paper (this was before the days of collating copiers). At the end of two weeks, Sigel noticed that his paycheck was the same as what it would have been selling ads in Chicago and he was becoming restless since he thought that his talents were not being used. That's when a sales manager, who is a friend to this day, came and said "kid, you are in the wrong department – if you come to sales, I'll give you a raise." The sales manager's office was opposite Sigel's desk and he saw Sigel's dedication even to a dead-end, boring job. Sigel accepted on the spot.

Lesson: Why did Sigel get this offer? If you meet Sigel, you will realize that he is warm, cheerful and open. Managers like cheerful, positive people. *Don't be a grouch even if you are stuck in a crappy job.*

5. **Selling meat.** Sigel knew nothing about meat, except one assumes to eat it and he claims to be a good cook of barbeque ribs. For his training, he was given a thick three-ring binder with prices of all kinds of meats and cuts. Meat companies at that time killed and sold everything to everybody. The days of segmentation and focus had not yet arrived. As the saying went, "meat packers sell everything (about the pig) but the oink." Sales training in those days was limited to studying the price lists and binder for two weeks followed by accompanying an experienced sales person for two weeks. Sigel was initially asked to be a relief salesperson and call on butchers. One butcher asked him for a 30 pound box of "mountain oysters" (which was a euphemism for bull testicles). When Sigel responded that the company did not sell seafood, the butcher told him to "get the hell out of here."

Lesson: You will be tested and you will be thrown out. That is the price you have to pay. Hang in there.

6. **Sales success.** At that time, Armour slaughtered a lot of hogs. Ribs were not a very desirable, high demand part and Armour could not sell all the raw ribs at profitable prices. Armour also had a substantial canned ham business and one of its bright ideas was to sell canned BBQ ribs in a round can. This led to a new idea for a product called "cooked ribs in a tin." The rationale behind this strategy was to combine a lot of unused canning capacity and a lot of unsold ribs so combining the two would lead to a successful product that consumers would buy. However, no one was successful at selling this even though the package was "not bad looking." Sigel calls this the "Just because we want to" system, i.e. because we want to sell something, we will make it and it will sell. Since Sigel was new, he was introduced to the mountains of cases and told that his job was to sell them. When Sigel went to see the butchers

on his route, they all noted that he was the "fifth person from Armour who had tried to sell them this product and that the consumer had not bought the product." So Sigel did some research and realized that the consumer did not understand the product. To remedy this problem, he took about 25 empty tins with labels, built a faux, portable barbeque pit with brick facing, placed the can in the middle on a pole and added a motor to rotate the pole – to convey a rotisserie image of meat that had been cooked. This gave a visual, immediate picture to consumers about the product. It worked. People immediately understood the product and bought it. The inventory was sold and Sigel was promoted to a sales manager.

Lessons: There are two lessons here:

a. Customers will not buy something just because you have excess capacity. *They will buy something they understand and need or want.*

b. *Customers will not waste a lot of time to understand something* and they will not buy if they don't understand the product (or service) and the benefits to them. Communicate the benefits immediately if you want to grab interest. As Sigel puts it, make it "instantly intuitive."

7. **One rung up.** Applebaum's was one of the larger retail chains in the Twin Cities with a significant share of the St. Paul market and a smaller share of the Minneapolis market. Stuart Applebaum (SA) was the meat buyer and he had a reputation of being a tough buyer. The salesperson who was selling to SA had not gone on vacation for 3-4 years since Armour did not want anyone screwing up this account. Since the salesperson was due his vacation, Sigel was asked to take over his route while he was gone (as a sales manager Sigel was now expected to sell to bigger accounts). This was supposed to be a tough assignment. Rather than just doing what meat sales persons did in those days, taking orders without clearly understanding the customers' problems and solving them, Sigel developed a typed, orderly presentation for the Applebaum stores, and presented it to SA on his first visit. According to Sigel, "Stuart was blown away." No one had organized a sales and marketing pitch for him in those "wild, wild days of meat selling." During those few weeks when the regular salesperson was on vacation, Sigel got a significant amount of business and secured his opportunities.

Lesson: Understand not only your customers, but the entire retail process, i.e. the consumers and the competition. Know that you need to be prepared, anticipate objections and understand that the customer nearly always has alternative purchasing options. Put yourself in their shoes and understand their problems. Retailers want to be more competitive and sell more to increase their profits. Suppliers need to offer a better package (than their competitors) to increase retail sales and profits.

8. **The larger chain.** Having proved his skills at Applebaum stores, Sigel was asked to sell to Country Club Markets. Howard Alkire, the owner of Country Club Markets, had a reputation as a tough operator, having taken over defunct grocery

stores and turned them around. He now owned 30-35 stores and salespeople from all food companies called on him. Each was given 1–3 minutes each week. Meat people were on a certain day, produce on another, and so on. Alkire's office was at the top of the steps from the reception area in a wooden loft over a product department. To see him, salespeople had to be on the way up when they heard the previous sales person descend, and meet the other salesman coming down. If you were even a few seconds late, Alkire did not see you that day. Armour had not developed any key business relationships or steady sales with Alkire. He only bought the specials. Sigel was not able to do any better in the first few months. So he decided to find out more about Alkire from his meat managers. He learned that Alkire was an avid hunter and a meat manager suggested to Sigel that Alkire liked shotgun shells. The next time he met Alkire, he had a heavy load of shells. Over the next six months, Alkire became one of Armour's largest customers. Armour was impressed.

Lesson: According to Sigel, Alkire was testing Sigel for tenacity and persistence. He was forcing Sigel to earn his stripes. Alkire was continuously checking with his store managers and meat managers whether Sigel was handling all problems and taking care of the business he was being given. Only when he found that Sigel was handling his end well was he given more business. ***Keep in mind that when the product is a commodity, the difference is you.***

From Startup to Profits

9. **Becoming a partner.** After three years at Armour, Sigel volunteered to manage the company's booth at a weekend food show for restaurant operators. Actually he found out later that none of the other salespeople wanted to work on a weekend. Meat at that time did not attract younger people so most of the sales people were older and not very aggressive. Sigel was still looking to "move up the food chain." Although Sigel did not know about the restaurant business, he wanted to learn and decided to attend. At the food show, another vendor named Neil Feinberg, who owned a local meat processing and distributing company, came up and started chatting with him. Feinberg offered Sigel a job with a jump in pay, which Sigel accepted. Sigel opened new accounts for Feinberg's company, including Applebaums, Target (which was operated by Applebaum) and others. This led to Sigel becoming a minority partner in the Reuben Meat Company, which they sold to International Multifoods in 1972.

Lesson: If you want to stand out, you may have to stand up for more work and higher performance. And continuously expand your network. Networking is not randomly passing out business cards to strangers hoping for business. It is meeting and impressing people with whom you can have a mutually beneficial relationship.

10. Starting Lloyd's. After his contract with International Multifoods IM ran out, Sigel rejoined Feinberg in a business that they still owned together. One day, he received a call from an entrepreneur who was managing a small, failing meat company. The business had one product and one customer and the entrepreneur had not expanded the business. When Sigel went to see the entrepreneur, he found him playing solitaire. It struck Sigel that a person who was failing should have more to do than play solitaire. However, since he had one customer, one product, three employees and equipment with value, Sigel decided to use them as a springboard to embark on his next endeavor – to sell pre-cooked ribs. Sigel offered to assume the liabilities in return for taking over the business. The entrepreneur agreed and Sigel was in his own business.

Lesson: Sigel believes that it is easier to make fire if there is a little spark than nothing, i.e. buying an existing business at the right price, even if it is about to go into bankruptcy, might be better than starting one from scratch.

11. The start of Lloyd's. Since Sigel had to move the company from its rented space, Sigel decided to move it to his own building in Minneapolis. He had rented some of the space to another tenant and he moved the company to the remainder of the space. Originally, Sigel and Feinberg started Lloyd's BBQ as a partnership. Sigel liked manufacturing and branding so he decided to focus on the new company, which he called "Lloyd's" based on Feinberg's suggestion. After the new company was started, with financing connections from Feinberg, the two decided to end the partnership with Sigel taking Lloyd's and Feinberg taking 100% interest in a fresh meat distribution business. Initially, Sigel was wondering whether he had made the right move. One day when he doubted his decision, his wife told him to hang in there and see it through since this was what he wanted to do and he was prepared for it.

Lesson: Pursue your passion. Marry the right spouse. There are no certainties in life.

12. The growth of Lloyd's. To add to the one product and one customer that he bought from the entrepreneur, Sigel started a new line of precooked and raw ribs for restaurants. In the early months, Schwan's (the one customer he got when he purchased the business) kept the business alive. Although Sigel wanted to get into corned beef, pastrami and roast beef, he could not do so due to his non-compete agreement with International Multifoods. That is why he liked ribs – because he knew the product (ribs) and the customers (restaurants) from his previous jobs and he could sell it without violating his non-compete agreement. In the early years, Sigel did all the managing and the selling. He received the ribs and processed them in the morning, and delivered them to customers in the afternoon. This was particularly important because he got seven-day terms from his vendors and he gave seven day terms to his customers. He was able to collect his customers' checks and pay his vendors with a bank line of credit. So he did not need equity financiers to fund his growth. In two years, Sigel's sales reached over $1 million per year from ribs.

Lesson: Expand with your strengths. Also, get a good lawyer who can help you negotiate a fair agreement without very harsh clauses. Find a way to use vendor financing to fuel your growth. This requires a very efficient throughput system so there is minimal, or no, inventory in process. It also requires good collection of receivables so you can pay your payables promptly. Vendors do not like customers who cannot pay. Keep a bank line of credit to fill the gaps and for emergencies. Also, in the meat business, you can minimize the effects of "shrink" by reselling the inventory as soon as possible. As the water in the meat evaporates, meat shrinks. So each day of storage means that your inventory is more expensive. Faster throughput is essential for profits, especially when profits are razor thin.

From Profits to the Moon

13. Space and management expansion. When he reached the $1-2 million sales level, Sigel found that he was running out of space and had to move to larger quarters. So he bought a building in St. Paul based on a contract for deed. Simultaneously with the move, the Applebaum's chain was sold to National Food Company (a larger regional chain from Chicago) and Stuart Applebaum left the family business. Since he was looking for a new opportunity, Sigel offered him a desk at his office and the use of a receptionist. Since the expanded operations required more management, Sigel was hoping that Applebaum would join him in the business. It was also frustrating working alone. Sigel had not had a vacation for 3-5 years. Within a week, Applebaum became interested in the barbeque business and started getting involved in the meat purchasing and helping out with the operations, especially since he was in the office and Sigel was out making sales calls. This is when Sigel offered Applebaum a partnership since they had complementary skills. Applebaum liked the operations and finance side of the business, while Sigel liked product development, branding and selling. They had also developed a strong friendship while Sigel was selling for Armour and for Feinberg, and Applebaum was his customer while working for his family's retail chain. Sigel and Applebaum went to a bank, arranged for an expanded line of credit and the partnership was formed. They had a fantastic and productive partnership. According to Sigel, there was never an argument, only discussions and agreement on a common purpose.

Lesson: Know when you can grow faster with a partner. Then find the right partner who can add skills and interests that are complementary to your own. Sigel knew he needed a partner and had worked with one so he knew what to look for and how to form a mutually profitable relationship. As Sigel says, *50% of a much larger pie is better than 100% of nothing.*

14. Ribs at retail. Since Applebaum knew the retail business, he wanted to sell ribs through retail stores. However, Sigel knew from his Armour days that customers would not buy unless they understood the product immediately. So he pointed out the need for better packaging before introducing it at retail. Jointly they created the package and introduced it in Rainbow Stores, which was the new chain started by Applebaum's family. This was new since no one had sold fully-cooked ribs in transparent packages in retail stores. Lloyd's was the first such product (initially the product was called St. Paul Smoke Company ribs but it was quickly changed to Lloyd's). Selling at retail required a clear package with long shelf life. The mechanical requirements were very challenging. It took a few years to perfect the technology.

> **Lesson**: *Presentation matters.* When introducing a new product, make sure that customers instantly know what it is and the benefits for them. Make your product or service stand out, but be clear about what it is and why they will benefit.

15. Grow with the trends. At that time, the Minneapolis chain called Byerly's was the talk of the retail world for their opulent stores. Pillsbury and others would fly in retail executives from around the country to Minneapolis for a tour of the stores. One of the executives was the meat buyer for Lucky Stores in California (this was rare since meat buyers were normally not included on such junkets). When he returned to California, the meat buyer (who had also visited Rainbow stores) called Sigel and wanted Lloyd's cooked ribs. Sigel flew to California and negotiated a deal for Lucky to carry the ribs. Within two months, Kroger's, which was one of the nation's largest chains, called and wanted to carry the ribs. The Kroger's meat buyer was taking his daughter to San Francisco to drop her off at school and he stopped by Lucky to check the meat shelf. Sigel had jumped on some fast moving trends:

- Women had increasingly started working outside the home and had no time to cook raw meat at home. They, and retailers, were looking for refrigerated, cooked meat (frozen would mean that the meat was not as fresh) that could be taken home and heated.
- Refrigerated space was available in the stores because raw meat sales were declining. But the demand for refrigerated pre-cooked meat was growing. So Sigel did not face much competition for shelf space when he introduced his fully-cooked barbeque ribs.
- In addition to the lack of time, many younger women did not know how to cook raw meat so refrigerated pre-cooked meats that only required heating filled the need.
- Microwaves were becoming "hot." The ribs had to be compatible with microwaves. This presented a problem since the slab of ribs was too long to fit in the microwave. So Sigel, along with the help of a friend and microwave expert, figured out a way to roll the package and secure it with a rubber band. Sigel branded the idea "Microband" and included a specially marked rubber band in each package. They actually received a U.S. patent on the idea.

Lesson: Monitor trends and find out how to exploit them. *It is much easier to grow with a trend than without one.* It pays to be at the right place at the right time with the right product and you can be there if you study the trends and plan for products or services to jump on them. How you get there requires some original thinking and guts to go where others have not gone. Sigel rode the prepared, refrigerated, fresh meat trend all the way to the top.

16. Breaking the sound barrier. The retail food industry has an annual convention in Chicago when all the meat buyers of the country get together to discuss innovations and trends. The meat buyer for Kroger's was to be a keynote speaker on trends and innovations in the retail meat business. He wanted to talk about Lloyd's products. Obviously, Sigel had no objections. This became the hot topic at the convention. When the Kroger's executive started his slide show, the first slide he showed to the country's meat buyers was his entire meat case filled with Lloyd's products. The next day, Lloyd's phones were ringing off the hook. Lloyd's even stopped answering their phones temporarily. Sales took off. They could not produce enough to satisfy demand. Ribs went from being the hard-to-sell meat product to the hot meat product. They expanded rapidly renting meat plants in Fridley (a suburb of Minneapolis), Klemme (Iowa) and Newport (Minnesota). In a few short years, sales grew from about $8 million to in excess of $40 million. It was tough to control four small plants scattered across many miles so Sigel and Applebaum bought a large plant in St. Paul and expanded it, and consolidated all their operations in this 45,000 SF operation.

Lesson: When you are the hot product, take advantage by expanding before competitors jump into the space you created. Your operations and financing need to be in control so that your cash flow and profits don't suffer as you are expanding. *Don't add overhead before it is time.* One of the most difficult decisions in expansion is when to add overhead. The business world is littered with the carcasses of entrepreneurs and executives who added overhead and then found that their sales or competitive advantage faded. The additional overhead destroyed their company. So be very careful before adding overhead, because this increases the risk dynamically. Know that you can sustain your sales and margins to pay for the added overhead.

17. The financial side. Since Sigel and Applebaum had financed the start and growth of Lloyd's with their own equity and with funds borrowed with their personal guarantees they always kept a tight grip on operations and finance. The company had made money from the start except in one year when Sigel lost $100,000 due to increased overhead before sales caught up. So when Lloyd's expanded to four plants, they were concerned about losing control. The main plant was so crowded that they did not always have the necessary space to produce within meat inspection regulations. Another problem was an explosion causing one of the company's two smokehouses that were used to cook ribs to be destroyed. The company lost over 50% of its capacity. Since Lloyd's had business interruption insurance, they were able to get a payment of $200,000. Otherwise, the company would have been bankrupt. When the company was expanding to its new St. Paul plant, they could not afford new equipment so they ended up buying it used. One vendor was Sigel's old employer, Armour, which was closing a plant in San Francisco. Sigel ended up buying Armour's equipment for significantly less than the price for new equipment.

> **Lesson**: Companies can fail during their highest growth periods if they are not under control. Working at maximum capacity is not always easy. Both cash flow and profits are key, especially in a business that is cash-intensive like meat. Make sure your insurance is in order, including business interruption insurance. You never know when disaster will strike. Also, be nice to people when you are on top. You may need their help when you are in trouble.

18. Pricing a revolutionary product. Lloyd's quickly became the largest cooker of ribs in the U.S. Rather than following the industry average of a few cents per pound. Lloyd's was able to obtain much higher margins. At a market share of 95%, there were no strong competitors and Lloyd's was the price leader. Since Lloyd's was a revolutionary product, there were no direct competitors to benchmark against. So Sigel would conduct tests to find out what customers would pay. He knew all the key retailers in the country because he called on them himself. He would ask 3-4 of them to place the packages on the shelves at different price points and would check each day to see the rate of sales. The customers' reactions allowed him to determine the right retail price point and he then worked backwards to determine his selling price after deducting retailers' margins.

> **Lesson**: *Price to value. Cost is the floor.* Find the level of value through actual tests with customers rather than relying on "experts" or your own instinct. Understand the impact of "price elasticity." This means you need to find out how much your sales will increase or decrease with changes in pricing. Many make the assumption that you will sell more at lower prices. Unfortunately, this is not true in all businesses. In some businesses, where perception is key, higher prices can actually result in higher sales. So test it. Don't just make an assumption and put your business at risk.

19. Market research to find the right packaging. Sigel used the same test-based approach to find the right packaging for his product. He did not want to waste money on expensive market research nor did he believe in the "sample size of one" (I like it so everyone will like it) entrepreneurial approach. Sigel would have his artist (a solo practitioner without the overhead of a big agency) prepare about five to six different labels. With these labels, he would prepare actual packages and leave them on the lunchroom table. When employees came to lunch, they would see these packages and Sigel would stand back and observe the ones that were picked first and most. This became his package. It was cost effective and market-based.

> **Lesson**: Do not rely solely on your own intuition. Your instinct may be a good

way to come up with ideas but test those ideas against what the market demands especially if the decision is crucial. To paraphrase Kenny Rogers in the Gambler, "you need to know when to test, and when to go with your gut", especially when you don't have much money and time.

20. Building an organization. Sigel did not hire a second salesperson until sales exceeded many millions. He sold to all the retailers around the country himself. Applebaum took care of the internal operations and financing, and Sigel took care of sales and marketing.

Lesson: The entrepreneur normally has more passion for the venture than others - or they should have - and should be able to sell more. So Sigel was able to channel this passion for his "baby" to generate extraordinary sales. However, also have backup plans . If Sigel was incapacitated, the company would have suffered. It worked out for Sigel, but it may not be worth the risk.

21. The next great product. Since the dependence on barbeque ribs created a vulnerability, Lloyd's began processing other cooked meat products. Most of them were not related to barbeque and Lloyd's was losing its productivity and efficiency. Lloyd's was busy and active. But their profits were in danger of falling. So Sigel and his partner decided to stop making "me-too" products where they had no competitive advantage and focus, exclusively on barbeque branded products where the company had an edge and higher profits. One of their products was chopped pieces of meat with barbeque sauce for sandwiches. They tried many different types of packaging. One package showed a hot sandwich that could be built from the meat pieces in the package. Some customers were confused, thinking that they were getting the bread along with the meat. Other failed versions included an aluminum tray and a tray with film, which did not work since the product did not look very appetizing before it was cooked. Lloyd's invested about $1 million on these alternatives. Sigel went to stores every day trying to find the right packaging solution. One day he went to the dairy case, saw a Shedd's margarine package and got a vision of how he could sell his product with a similar packaging concept. He bought a few packages of Shedd's, emptied the contents, changed the labels to add Lloyd's and it was instantly intuitive to consumers about the contents of the "bucket" because they could visualize what was inside. The product sold like hot cakes and annual sales growth reached 20-25%. Eventually, this product's sales (with beef, chicken and pork in different types of barbeque sauces) exceeded the sales of packaged ribs.

Lesson: Just because you came up with one idea that was great, does not mean that the second is also great. Have clear goals for new products and be disciplined about reaching them. Develop criteria, including minimum levels of sales, growth rates and profits to keep products. If the product does not reach your criteria, shelve it and seek others unless you know how to fix it. Keep trying until the product, package and price are right - when it is instantly intuitive to customers.

22. Selling Lloyd's: Sigel sold Lloyd's four times. The first time was to Bongrain (a French company). He ran it for the French company for five years, but they did not want to fund its growth after buying two other companies. Lloyd's was then sold to a venture capital fund with Sigel retaining a large share for himself. Three years later, they sold it to a leveraged buyout (LBO) fund. Sigel retained his shares. Then in 1991, they sold it to General Mills. Lloyd sold out and helped General Mills manage it for a few years before moving on to other endeavors.

Lesson: Selling is a complicated subject. There are many reasons to keep your business and many to sell. *Sell if the price is right (what is the right price – if it is priced to perfection, it could be right). Sell if you have lost your passion. Sell if the trends are likely to turn against you.* Get good advice on this topic, especially from someone who knows you well and is not afraid to tell you the truth.

Rules for Entrepreneurs from Lloyd Sigel of Lloyd's Barbeque

- **When your customers ask "what's new", they are not asking about your kids.** They are asking what you have that can get new sales, get customers excited, solve a problem and make money for them. If you don't have anything new, they will treat you like a commodity rather than a valued partner.
- **Focus on a limited number of efforts and do it well to succeed even in a very competitive environment.** Don't scatter your energies or your resources.
- **Give stock options to key managers only based on performance and after they prove themselves.** Sigel does not give equity to ANYONE before he knows what they are capable of doing for him. For lower-level employees, provide market-rate salaries and perks, and a bonus when the company does well.
- **Delegate to help people grow and show them that they are important.** They will perform well when they know they can grow. But monitor them closely until they have proven themselves.
- **Sharing performance of all key managers in a monthly round-table meeting will help cull the ones who are failing.** After two or three months of poor managers blaming external circumstances, the others will pounce on them and they will fire themselves.
- **Get into sales early in your career.** "Nothing happens until something is sold" (this is from Curtis Carlson, the founder of Carlson Companies).
- **When hiring key executives, take your spouse with you.** They can help sniff out "phonies."
- **Know who your competitors are and why you are better.** Be creative in discovering your advantages. Be sure you are prepared.

Earl Bakken
Medtronic, Inc.

MINNEAPOLIS, MINN

Founding the electronic medical device industry and enriching lives

Summary: Starting from a young age, Earl Bakken was fascinated with all things electrical, including the wiring, equipment and the porcelain insulators in his home. As a youth, he rigged up numerous electrical devices, such as a phone system to his friend's house, a method to set off Fourth of July fireworks from his attic, and a knife-wielding, cigarette-smoking robot that scared a neighbor's child. In high school, Bakken maintained the school's electrical equipment, such as the public-address system, projectors, and electric scoreboards. After World War II, as an electrical engineering student at the University of Minnesota's Institute of Technology, Bakken would stop by the medical department to visit friends. He would repair their equipment on-site and realized that here was a business opportunity. So, in 1949, he and his brother-in-law started Medtronic to repair medical equipment on-site. But the early days were agonizing and arduous. The venture's highest annual net income in the first decade was $10,400. To grow, they worked with physicians to develop custom-designed equipment for specific treatments. One of them, Dr. C. Walton Lillehei, was working on medical devices for the heart, but these devices stopped during power interruptions and risked patients' lives. So Lillehei asked Bakken if he could develop a device that would work through power failures. Bakken experimented with various options and, in four weeks, came up with a solution based on a circuit in Popular Electronics for an electronic metronome. This pacemaker was attached to a child's heart the next day, heralding the dawn of the modern-day electronic medical device industry. The year was 1957. Initially, as sales grew, so did losses. In 1962, sales were $518,000 and losses grew to $144,000. But the next year sales nearly doubled and profits reached $73,000. The company never looked back. Today, Medtronic is a $14.6 billion (sales) global giant with a $32 billion market valuation (on March 16, 2009). Medtronic has spawned dozens of great companies, created a lasting legacy and enriched millions of lives. This is how Bakken did it.

Before the Start

1. After high school. During the Second World War, Bakken was a radar instructor for the Army Signal Corps in Boca Raton, Fla. At the end of the war, he left the Army to enroll in the bachelor's degree program in electrical engineering at the University of Minnesota's Institute of Technology. To earn some money while in school, a few young engineers and he started a business to produce music records. After producing music by artists such as Slim Jim and the Vagabond Kid, who sang Norwegian folk songs, the company gave up on music and moved on to repairing car radios, and then to making squirrel traps. Bakken moved on.

Lesson: Learn and try new things. But move on if you don't have an abiding passion for what you are doing, such as squirrel traps.

2. Fixing medical equipment. After graduating with an undergraduate degree, Bakken started working toward a master's degree. Since his friends were in the medical department across the street from his classes, Bakken would wander over to visit them and soon started repairing the department's equipment. He was visiting there so frequently that they even gave him his own locker. During this time, he also married Connie Olson, who was his classmate in high school. She had studied to be a medical technologist and was working at Northwestern Hospital in south Minneapolis. When he went to pick up his wife after classes, he got to know the physicians and technical personnel in the medical departments. And he started fixing their equipment, too. The medical technology in hospitals and doctors' offices at that time were mainly diagnostic and not therapeutic. They were based on vacuum tubes and were bulky to move. There were no established firms to service and fix these bulky pieces of equipment, and they were usually hauled out to repair shops or returned to the manufacturers for service. At a family birthday party, Bakken was telling his brother-in-law, Palmer Hermundslie, who was married to his wife's sister, about this business gap. The two decided to start a business to fill this unmet need.

Lesson: Find a need and fill it. This advice is as old as the hills. Perhaps this is because it is true again and again. Keep your eyes *and your mind*, open. And act. Nothing happens until you act.

From Start-up to Take-Off

3. Starting a business. A few days after the party, Hermundslie and Bakken started the new company, called Medtronic, as a partnership to service medical equipment. They did not have a long-term plan, since they viewed it as a short-term opportunity before Bakken started his Ph.D. program at the University. Bakken's long-term dream at the time was to become a researcher at a giant corporation like Honeywell. Bakken and Hermundslie decided to split responsibilities, with

Bakken taking care of the operations, and Hermundslie the business side. Their first office was in a garage that was owned by the Hermundslies. The three-stall garage was cold in the winter and hot in the summer, but its saving grace was that it was rent-free. They operated out of the garage for about 10 years. The first few years were tough and painful, and they relied on Hermundslie's savings and Mrs. Bakken's earnings. Their revenues were meager, and they did not charge enough for their services, which resulted in insufficient profits. To increase sales, they started selling medical equipment to customers throughout the Midwest. In addition to taking care of operations, Bakken also started to sell. But first, he had to get over his shyness. He found that he enjoyed solving people's problems and showing them what could be done with the equipment. This sales effort allowed the company to grow modestly, but the major benefit was that it created a great network of potential customers, including lab technicians, nurses, and physicians who would eventually buy Medtronic's own devices.

Lesson: The startup stage is never easy. If you bootstrap, i.e., start with your own money, life is likely to be tough early on. If you get venture capital, your business is likely to be controlled by others. That is the price you have to pay to build a business. But a key lesson is that you have to do what the business needs, and this could mean that you get out of your comfort zone. *Since selling is key for any new business (there is no business if you don't sell), you need to enjoy selling.* While selling may have a stigma for some, it may be helpful to look at *selling as finding your customers' pain points and solving their problems.* Medtronic did not hesitate to suggest competitors' products if theirs was not the right one for a specific customer. This is selling by building long-term relationships, which is the best kind of selling.

4. New technology. Bakken and Hermundslie noticed that most of the devices other manufacturers were introducing were for monitoring and recording, rather than for therapy. But there were a number of advances in the world outside medicine and the time was ripe for the dramatic transformation of the medical-device industry, although this was not obvious at the time. The introduction of the transistor and advances in materials, such as new types of plastics and synthetic materials, were pushing the frontier of what was possible. Medtronic was starting to incorporate some of these advances and designing medical equipment to satisfy special requests it was getting from physicians and surgeons for specific ailments. The company would satisfy these requests, hoping that it could sell it to other physicians. But few others bought. The partners were also adapting other manufacturers' equipment for new uses. The company had become a job shop and a sales-rep organization in the medical-device industry. In the meantime, they were adding space to their garage and connected the first garage to a second one on the property. They had grown to about seven employees. They were profitable, but not yet burning any tracks. Then they received a request from Dr. C. Walton Lillehei.

Lesson: A lot of lessons in the early years can be summed up as "hang in there and don't quit if that is your passion." You never know if you will create a great corporation, but the key question is whether you are pursuing your dreams. ***Lightning may strike or it may not. The question for you: what is your price for giving up your dreams***?

5. From tick-tock to shock-shock – positioning yourself at the take-off of a giant wave. Dr. Lillehei and his group of young physicians were working at the leading-edge of open-heart surgery at the University of Minnesota. Medtronic would sell customized recording devices for this surgery to the anesthesiologists, and then help them, the surgeons, and the others use these devices. Since Bakken was always available to fix the equipment without the physicians and technicians having to slog through the University bureaucracy, he was always in high demand. This allowed him to build relationships with many of the young residents and interns who were learning open-heart surgery and were close to Bakken's age, giving him a global network of connections that immensely helped Medtronic in later years. But that would be getting ahead of the story. More important, he was the "go-to guy" when Lillehei wanted help with equipment that could help treat "blue babies," i.e., babies with insufficiently oxygenated blood. These babies needed a pacemaker to assist their hearts after surgery and the surgeons were using huge, alternating-current pacemakers that had to be plugged into the power network. They were bulky and uncomfortable for the patients. If the power failed, these pacemakers failed. On October 31, 1957, power failed for three hours. One baby died and Lillehei asked Bakken to come up with a better solution. Bakken did not know it then, but this was the transformation point for Medtronic, when it took the first steps to world prominence in the treatment of humans. Within four weeks, Bakken had come up with the first battery-powered pacemaker. Thus was the electronic pacemaker industry born.

Lesson: As Albert Camus said, *"Great ideas come into the world as gently as doves." They don't announce themselves as great, unless they are financed by Silicon Valley venture capitalists, their PR agents, or journalists breathlessly covering them.* Foresight is not 20-20. So stop waiting for that blockbuster technology. Pursue your passion – if you are willing to pay the price.

6. What is innovation? Innovation often involves the application of a solution from one field to problems in another. To come up with a solution for Lillehei, Bakken first tried to hook up an auto battery to the pacemaker, but it was too unwieldy. Then he remembered a circuit in a Popular Electronics magazine for an electronic metronome. He adapted this circuit for the pacemaker and in four weeks, developed the world's first electronic pacemaker to pace the human heart. He took it to Lillehei, fully expecting the device to be tested on animals for an extended period. Instead the next day, he found that Lillehei had applied it to a child's heart. When asked about the immediacy, Lillehei noted that the labs had tested it on animals, it worked and he did not see any reason not to help a child live with the latest available technology. There was no need for any clinical trials or FDA approval, which today can take about seven years and tens of millions of dollars. More to the point, there was no bureaucracy within Medtronic, which like any other large corporation today, has lots of scientists, technologists, executives, and committees to approve new research strategies. The young venture was "struggling to survive," as Bakken puts it and they "were operating - not by design, but by necessity." Bakken has since codified this principle as "ready, fire, aim."

> **Lesson**: There is a direct, powerful and totally inverse relationship between the fullness of your stomach and the priority of your mind. ***An empty stomach focuses the mind on the right priorities***. It helps you find and satisfy unmet needs that your customers have and for which they will pay. That is how you build successful corporations, which then have the luxury of wallowing in the bureaucracy of committees.

7. NIH - RIP. As with many great technologies, once the initial barrier has been broken and the product proven, many technological improvements start to happen. Witness the growth of the PC and the Internet. Other teams of surgeons and technologists started coming up with new applications and new technologies to add to Bakken's ground-breaking achievement, which the global press heavily promoted. One was from Dr. Samuel Hunter of St. Paul and Medtronic engineer Norman Roth, who jointly developed and applied a new type of electrode for the pacemaker and used it to treat a heart disease called Stokes-Adams that affected older patients. Contrary to the short-term pacing of children from 1957-1959 that Bakken's invention allowed, the Hunter-Roth electrode pacemaker allowed long-term pacing of children and adults to begin in April 1959. This electrode used about 70 percent less electric current, but the battery's capacity was still a drawback to the long, effective life of the pacemaker, especially if it was to be implanted in the body. This is when Medtronic heard about the team of Dr. William Chardack and Wilson Greatbatch, of Buffalo, N.Y., who had developed an implantable pacemaker with a very powerful, advanced battery. The Chardack-Greatbatch implantable pacemaker allowed even longer-term pacing of the heart with greater longevity, more convenience and fewer surgical complications. Medtronic licensed the technology from them on an exclusive basis in return for 10 percent of sales. The key to Medtronic's eventual dominance in the implantable-pacemaker industry was due to these groundbreaking alliances, agreements, and relationships with the leaders of the field such as Lillehei, Hunter, Chardack, and Greatbatch. Medtronic was able to partner with them because Bakken and his team were humble enough to know that others were equally adept at developing great advances, and they kept their eyes open for such leaders and advances. They were eager to help these leaders solve their challenges and market their technologies. They developed fair agreements with them for exclusive licenses based on future royalty payments, especially since they could not pay them in cash or stock. They did not have the arrogance to believe in the "Not Invented Here" syndrome, which is the attitude among some large corporations that products not invented by their own staff cannot be any good.

Lesson: ***Arrogance and hubris are the parents of self-destruction***. Avoid the notion that all the world's greatest minds work at your company. Amazing as it seems, some large companies still delude themselves into that type of thinking. Since they try to recruit the best people they can find, they are under the mistaken impression that all of the "best people" work there. Nothing could be further from the truth, and the humility to know this is key to any successful venture or corporation. To this day, Medtronic tracks advances around the world, forms alliances, and licenses or acquires promising new technologies that can further transform its industry. This is in addition to the world-class labs the company maintains for internal research and development. Bakken's and Hermudslie's early understanding that they needed external technologies to develop the best products was the foundation for this belief. But it is not enough to be open to such advances from the outside. You need to be able to attract these leaders to work with you and without trust, you will not attract them. ***People like to do business with people they like (so they can enjoy their times together), trust (so they don't have to hold on to their wallets) and admire (for their ability to get things done)***.

8. **Land at the confluence of great trends**. Medtronic found itself, although hindsight was clearer, at the confluence of great trends. Society was willing to accept the implanting of man-made technologies to extend and enrich human life. Although some religious leaders questioned this, none were successful in stopping this trend. Technology advanced rapidly in the fields of electronics and integrated circuits, materials, batteries, and other areas to make pacemakers smaller, longer lasting, and more effective. Clinical experience and innovative physicians helped to identify other areas in the human body that could use this new technology. And government, in the form of Medicare, helped a large number of older patients to take advantage of these new technologies, thus dynamically expanding the market. Medtronic was ready for take-off.

Lesson: It is much easier to soar with the trends than against the current. Sometimes you can advance the trends by doing the right things, as Medtronic did by continuing to be the leader in implantable technologies. Sometimes you can surf a great wave, but make sure you put in the effort to stay competitive. Otherwise, hungrier entrepreneurs will grab the wave. It helps to be at the right place at the right time. But you still need the right people with the proper skills and dedication.

9. **Missionary sales**. With the introduction of the pacemaker and Dr. Lillehei's writing and speeches on the topic, Medtronic started to receive worldwide attention and more important, orders. By the end of 1959, two years after the introduction of the pacemaker, global sales of pacemakers had helped the company reach annual sales of about $200,000. The company had to use missionary zeal and every

available and effective means to promote its products. For 10 years, the company used an exclusive distributor to build its business outside the United States. Within the United States, it used sales reps along with the company's own sales force to cover the entire market. In addition, Bakken and Hermundslie were on the road constantly to promote their products, see customers, and attend trade shows. This travel allowed the partners to meet customers one on one, and know their problems and their needs. They realized that technology is not enough. They had to be able to solve customers' problems using their technology. This meant knowing what the customer really wanted, and then exceeding expectations. Since the pacemaker was such a revolutionary technology, customers did not always know what the product was, or what it was capable of doing, so they did not know how their needs could be met. As Bakken puts it, "He or she always knows, however, what wants and needs are going unmet, and this you most often learn one person at a time, face to face, asking questions and listening."

> **Lesson**: Customers never beat a path to your door. Technologists often believe that all they have to do is to build a great product and it will sell itself. Unless you are incredibly lucky, that never happens. You have to seek customers and convince them about how you can solve their unmet needs. If this was true for a game-changing, life-enhancing product like the Medtronic pacemaker, think how much harder you will have to sell. Don't get in the game if you don't want to sell.

10. The right sales driver. As Medtronic started to market the pacemakers, they tried a variety of sales drivers, including some of the ones noted earlier such as distributors, reps, internal sales personnel, and trade shows. However, Bakken and Hermundslie found that it was not easy to convince the conservative medical establishment to use their pacemakers and to treat their patients. Bakken found that physicians would try to avoid them at these meetings. However, when other physicians, including Dr. Lillehei and Dr. Chardack, presented their ground-breaking advances based on using Medtronic pacemakers at surgical conferences, other physicians would listen and start to use their products. They were obviously willing to listen to leaders in their own profession but not to entrepreneurs trying to "sell" them a product.

> **Lesson**: Credibility and trust are the key ingredients in most missionary sales of new, revolutionary products. Every business needs to understand how to sell its products and the company most efficiently. Credibility is always crucial when selling any product, especially one involving human life, and other physicians were the most credible promoters of new medical devices. So find the best sales driver that allows you to get the highest return (in the form of sales and cash flow) on your sales investment in the shortest time. Find it before you go broke.

From Take-off to Home Run

11. Without the right financing. Between 1949 and 1959, financing was primarily through partners' equity, accruals, supplier credit, and other debt. The company was actively searching for a market niche, and for products that could provide the desired growth. With increased sales of its core pacemaker product starting in 1959, Medtronic continued to spend heavily for growth in areas such as sales and marketing, research and development, operations and administration. They expanded from 13 products in 1961 to 21 in1962, and were spending heavily to move into new markets. While sales jumped to $500,000 in 1962 from $180,000 in 1960, they were about to go under because their losses were growing even faster from $16,000 in 1960 to $144,000 in 1962. To fund its growth, Medtronic initially sold $215,000 of convertible debt that was converted to common stock. This is the time when Medtronic went public on the over-the-counter market in what was then a hot Twin Cities market for public offerings. Control Data Corporation had just gone public and had done well, opening the doors for other companies. When Medtronic suffered severe losses in 1960-62 and was close to bankruptcy, it raised $200,000 of equity from private venture capitalists. The company also secured bank debt for financing inventory and accounts receivables. It is important to note that the company's public offering and venture capital happened after it was able to develop a unique, high-potential product that jump-started the company on its high-growth trajectory. However, unlike most ventures, Medtronic had its public offering before it secured venture capital. Most do it the other way around. From 1965, the company had an uninterrupted trend of impressive growth in sales and profits and has been able to finance its needs through retained earnings, stock offerings, accruals, and supplier credit.

> **Lesson**: While top-line growth and new-product introduction is exciting, a sound financing plan is a must if you want to stay in control of your business. During your high-growth phase, debt may not be right for the business because lenders want their loan to be repaid with interest and as scheduled. Negative income and cash flow make them nervous because they know this endangers their loan. A sound financing plan includes the right levels of debt, equity, and development financing based on cash flow so you can pay all bills as they come due. High-growth companies usually need to reinvest operating cash flow back into the business to sustain growth, so there is little, if any cash flow left to repay debt. Therefore, high-growth companies favor equity over debt.

12. The blessings of corporate thinking... for entrepreneurs. To get out of its problems and offer founders, investors and employees a good way out, Medtronic considered a sale of the company to Mallory in addition to considering alternatives such as seeking venture capital. Mallory was a large manufacturer of batteries and the supplier for Medtronic's pacemakers. Since Medtronic had recently sold debt that was convertible to common stock at $1.50 per share, Mallory offered to buy Medtronic shares for $3 per share, subject to its due diligence. While Medtronic was evaluating the offer, Mallory was doing its due diligence on the potential size of the pacemaker industry and they came to the conclusion that the maximum global market for pacemakers would be 10,000 units. Mallory considered this to be a very small market and withdrew its offer. For Medtronic, sales of 10,000 units would be a bonanza. The company hung in there and the rest is history. By the end of the last century, 115,000 pacemakers were sold each year in the United States, and 440,000 were sold around the world.

> **Lesson**: *Bureaucrats want facts. Entrepreneurs need faith.* It is very difficult, if not impossible, to accurately predict the potential market for truly revolutionary technologies and products. Many large, risk-averse corporations and consulting firms have tried to guess and failed. It takes the faith and passion of an entrepreneur to prove this potential.

13. Focus to grow – the transformation of Medtronic. After the turndown by Mallory, Medtronic put together a sound financing plan and a strong board of directors and management team to transition from an entrepreneurial venture to a professionally managed corporation. In addition to a bank loan, Medtronic secured a $200,000 investment from a venture capital company that placed two people on Medtronic's board. These two were experienced business professionals who insisted that Medtronic decide on the kind of company it wanted to become, encapsulate this mission in a written statement, share it with all the employees, and focus the company's scarce resources on products and markets consistent with this mission. After discussion, Medtronic decided to focus on implantable therapeutic technologies (devices) that restored people to meaningful lives. This meant that they would not spend resources in other areas such as diagnostics or laboratory products. In addition to the key requirements of the financiers for Medtronic to develop and write the mission, another of their key requirements was to instill corporate discipline, which meant keeping track of all expenses, knowing the return for each dollar spent, and hiring a comptroller who was charged with controlling Medtronic's costs. *This new mission and plan helped Medtronic to focus, bring order and control while keeping its zeal, and to grow its sales and profits.* Medtronic started to thrive.

> **Lesson**: There comes a time in every entrepreneurial venture when it needs to become more focused and controlled. As the number of employees increases, entrepreneurs start to lose touch with them and the need for control grows. However, without the missionary zeal that entrepreneurial ventures usually have, the transformed entity can suffocate in its own rules. To maintain the initial zeal and to successfully transition to a major corporation, write down your mission and stick to it. You will encounter many temptations to change it or add to it. Do it rarely and with the utmost care and gravity. Changing your mission too frequently can cause confusion, and waste resources and time.

Employees and resource providers may also lose confidence in your leadership abilities. Make sure that the employees know the mission and keep repeating it so that they use it consistently as a compass to guide their actions and decisions even when they are not in constant contact with you or the leadership team. Medtronic thrived in this transition because its founders understood the need for the transition and were able to maintain the mission and zeal while enhancing focus and controls.

14. Innovators with abrasive brilliance. To stay a leader, Medtronic has had to work with people who were intellectually gifted, powerful, and had the responsibility for saving lives. Their intellectual gifts allowed them to develop solutions for complex problems that frustrated peers with lesser capacities. And this often developed an arrogance and pride that would demean others, including many of Medtronic's engineers. Bakken found that Medtronic had to deal with such abrasively brilliant people if the company was to thrive. So he and Medtronic's managers developed a variety of techniques to honor all its employees, connect each one to the sales of the company and to the company's mission. They learned to encourage its innovative culture by creating and maintaining the right atmosphere to hear all ideas. They developed new types of award systems to encourage the free flow of creativity. They listened to the "idea people" even if they were abrasive. Bakken has found that non-linear and erratic conversations often generate brilliant ideas . Terminating the discussion when this happens could stifle creativity.

Lesson: Innovation is difficult because innovators can be abrasive. *Innovation usually sprouts from the minds of brilliant people who see solutions where others see problems, who envision the future while others are focused on the present, who communicate with impatience because their mind is moving faster, and who can be difficult to work with because of their intellectual arrogance*. But their longer-term vision leads to a blind spot regarding the present, so they don't implement well, their reluctance to delegate (because of their high opinion of their capabilities) makes them ineffective managers, and their arrogance can demean others so few want to work with them. But a corporation that wants to lead needs them. So develop a culture to capture this brilliance. Diversity, and diverse opinions, can help.

15. Ready, fire, aim. Medtronic was blessed with dedicated employees who could have made more money elsewhere but selected to work at an under-funded company because they believed in what they were doing. In the early days, Bakken and Hermundslie could know each employee and build a sense of camaraderie as a team. As Medtronic's sales grew to hundreds of millions (and then billions), and the number of employees grew to the hundreds and thousands, Bakken's role changed. He was no longer in constant touch with the engineers. But he still wanted to have an impact on their work. He did not want the growing layers of management to stifle creativity. So he started developing his philosophy of innovation that had led to his own success. He encouraged them to see the "big picture" and to exercise their imaginations to see big possibilities and take risks. He did not want them to always take the safe route and avoid all risks. He wanted them to use their instinct, pursue hunches, and not just rely on "proof" before deciding what to do. He codified this philosophy as "ready, fire, aim."

> **Lesson**: Making too many assumptions without testing them can lead to disaster. But requiring proof before all activity leads to a bureaucracy. The key is to ***develop the judgment to know when to take risks and when not to***.

16. Growing through adversity. All companies have problems. The key is how they deal with them. In the 1970s, Medtronic introduced a new type of pacemaker called the Xytron®. This was the first system to use integrated miniature circuits, and while it had been tested, it failed. This was the first major product failure in Medtronic's history, and the company suffered a blow to its reputation and confidence. Its market share dropped and Bakken, who was now chairman of the board, took it personally. Medtronic expanded its staff and joined forces with experts to solve this problem. But their customers had also changed in their attitudes toward the company. Physicians who had previously been content to accept Medtronic's products and recommendations now wanted to make their own final choice among products, models, and manufacturers. They wanted to pick a customized product for each patient based on their own analysis. Out of this came the notion of "mass customization" for Medtronic. Medtronic was one of the leaders in this wave, and it led to new, ground-breaking products such as Activitrax®, which adjusted the heart rate based on the wearer's level of activity. In 1984, the National Society of Professional Engineers named the cardiac pacemaker one of the 10 outstanding engineering achievements of the second half of the 20th century.

> **Lesson**: *You have two choices when you fail. You can wallow in self-pity or you can learn from your failures and move to higher achievements.* When your product saves lives, choose the latter.

17. Leadership v. management – the need for personal growth. As the company grew, Bakken needed to adjust and grow with the company so that the company could continue to grow. His brother-in-law and partner, Palmer Hermundslie, died in 1970, and Bakken increasingly relied on a number of experts who worked with him over the years. He promoted a trusted executive and board member, Tom Holloran, to the presidency while he assumed the role of chairman. He developed a strong board from among area and national executives, and they helped him select succeeding chief executive officers from within the company or from the outside. Bakken's strength was that he was able to work with all of them and build the company without a clash of egos, at least not one that hurt the company. He got help from his family and friends to look and sound more like a business leader and chief executive. In addition to switching his attire from flannel shirts to three-piece suits, he learned to communicate the company's values, mission, and message by becoming a better public speaker. He developed the practice of meeting with each new employee to share the company story and vision, and to link them "in a common cause." He learned to become a very good ballroom dancer because his employees wanted to have a company dance (not all that you do for the company can be termed a sacrifice because Bakken enjoyed dancing and became a champion dancer). To improve customer relations and stay connected with them on a personal level, Bakken started to keep notes about his customers, their interests, and families. He started to study the differences between good management and great leadership to help him guide his company. He wrote these down in his essay called "Reflections on Leadership" (see below).

Lesson: As a business grows, it will place increasing demands on you and your family. If you don't want to put in the effort, find others who can. Otherwise the business will suffer.

18. Leaving a legacy. Bakken retired from Medtronic at the age of 65 and from the company's board of directors at age 70. He had instituted this retirement policy, and he regretted it later when he missed his company on the beautiful beaches of Hawaii. But he continues to make his presence felt and maintains his legacy with each new generation of Medtronic employees. During his visits to headquarters for the annual meetings, he meets with each new employee, discusses Medtronic's history, shares with them the mission of Medtronic and gives them tokens of their joint endeavor. These tokens include a medallion with the company's mission, "Alleviating Pain, Restoring Health, Extending Life" to link all the employees toward their goal of improving people's lives while earning a profit. Upon retirement in 1989, he wrote his "Reflections on Leadership" which were based on the beliefs and principles he used to guide Medtronic over the years. They included the following tenets:

- The customer always comes first.
- Everyone is an "integral part of the crucial event" called the sale.
- "Effective leadership neither buries brilliant mavericks nor lets them venture too far on their own."
- Streamline the policy manual to encourage "creative people to make the most of their on-the-job opportunities and thus better serve the customer."
- Communicate the good and the bad to help employees do a better job.
- Become a more effective leader, not just a more effective manager.
- Have few meetings. When you do have them, make them more effective.
- Develop a mission statement to clearly communicate why the company exists. Bakken cannot sufficiently emphasize the importance of a written mission statement that adds focus to the company, direction for the use of its resources, and meaning to employees lives.

Lesson: John Hammergren, CEO of McKesson, said in a commencement address at the University of Minnesota, *"People will work hard for money, but they will give* *their lives for meaning."* Medtronic was able to attract good employees because Bakken believed in adding meaning.

Rules for Entrepreneurs from Earl Bakken of Medtronic

- **The primary commandment for business is "customer first."** Customers transcend management meetings or planning sessions or anything else the business does.
- **Link each employee to the sale.** Every employee should know how their efforts help to make the sale. Without the sale, there is no company. Help employees to connect the dots between their efforts and the sale.
- **Learn to handle abrasive brilliance.** Brilliant employees can be abrasive. A great leader learns to use this brilliance to help the company fulfill its mission.
- **Understand the personal price you could pay.** Building a highly successful venture may mean that you spend a lot of time away from your family. Understand the sacrifice they are making.
- **Learn from your failures.** Success often results in self-congratulatory pride. Failures can help you to improve and grow (and successes should too).
- **Learn to develop technological winners.** Employees who are technological winners want to develop products to help people and not simply to produce a business winner. They have a strong missionary zeal and thrive on openness and freedom.
- **It is tough to forecast the market size for revolutionary products.** There may not be an obvious market when a product is developed, but if a product can help even a few, others may follow.
- **To grow, first learn to manage. Then learn to lead.** Leaders see farther than managers who are focused on nearer-term issues. Leaders have a broader vision to see other areas of problems or opportunities than managers. Leaders develop the mission and values to help all employees contribute.
- **Visualize your goal.** And don't stop till you succeed.
- **Ready, Fire, Aim (again).** Favor action over analysis. Don't stop what you are doing to be perfect. It is O.K. to fail so long as you correct your aim in the next round. Don't overanalyze. Just do it.
- **Develop a clear mission, write it down and share it with all employees consistently and repeatedly.** Doing so will help you expand from an entrepreneurial venture to a mission-driven corporation and add meaning to employees' lives. You can attract the "best and the brightest" when you do offer this, and they will stay even when times are tough.

Harold Roitenberg
Modern Merchandising

MINNEAPOLIS, MINN

Building the world's biggest catalog-showroom merchandiser

Summary: After graduating from the University of Minnesota with a degree in journalism, Harold Roitenberg started his business career working in the advertising department of Northwestern Auto Parts in Minneapolis. He found the job boring, so he left and joined Minnesota Wholesalers, which his father-in-law owned. He stayed there for 10 years. When he joined the business, the product line was focused on horse supplies and related hardware. Due to his initiatives, when he left it 10 years later in 1960, the business was a thriving catalog showroom selling name-brand small appliances, housewares, electronics, and jewelry. When his father-in-law died, his brother would not sell Roitenberg an equal share in the business, so Roitenberg decided to go his own separate way. Since he had little money, he could not open his own showroom. Instead he used his expertise and experience to found Creative Merchandising & Publishing. Creative M&P merchandised and published a catalog to be used by businesses wanting to get into the catalog-showroom business. He earned money through the sale of catalogs to these businesses. Creative M&P negotiated prices, ad allowances, terms, etc. A small merchant could buy like a giant through the volume produced by joining together. The Creative group grew into the largest catalog-showroom merchandisers in the world, with combined sales over 6 billion dollars. This is how he did it.

Before the Startup

1. The first job. Roitenberg joined the University of Minnesota Business School to major in accounting before he realized that he did not have the aptitude for the details of accounting. So he switched to journalism. After graduating from the University of Minnesota's School of Journalism, Roitenberg joined the advertising department of Northwestern Auto Parts, but soon found out that he was not cut out for a career in advertising. So in 1950 he went to work at Minnesota Wholesalers (MW), which his father-in-law and his father-in-law's brother owned. The company sold horse supplies and related surplus hardware through a retail store and a small catalog. Roitenberg helped expand the business into other consumer products. The sales rep who was selling horse-related equipment also carried other consumer products, such as blenders and toasters. He suggested that MW carry these consumer products in their catalog to increase sales. So MW added a new section to the horse-supplies catalog. Since they had printed a few hundred extra catalogs, Roitenberg sent them to businesses in the area, in addition to sending them to their regular saddlery customers. People started coming into the store to buy the products from the catalog. Based on this initial success, the next year Roitenberg went to the housewares show and added other consumer products such as small appliances, giftware, and jewelry. During the Christmas shopping season, they cleared up a little space in the store and added a consumer-products section. Roitenberg agreed to add diamonds in an advertising insert in the catalog but without carrying any diamonds in the store. If a customer ordered diamonds, the manufacturer would drop-ship the products to the consumer. Roitenberg did not even keep any samples in the store, only pictures. The first order was for $600 worth of diamonds, and the payment was in cash. His father-in-law was amazed. That was the beginning of a concerted effort to sell high-margin jewelry. It evolved into not only stocking all the merchandise, but also manufacturing and assembling in their New York diamond office. His competitors were department stores and mail order catalog houses in Milwaukee and Chicago that sent out thousands of catalogs with branded products. Roitenberg used discount prices on the name-brand products and allowed customers to shop in the store as well as mail order. Discounting name-brand products gave them the credibility that allowed them to sell more high-margin jewelry.

Lesson: When considering new products and sales strategies, be prepared to experiment with alternative products, and be creative in how to sell. *However, make the tests small so you can pull back if they do not work.* Normally, it is not smart for entrepreneurs to get into a price war against established competitors. In this case, however, the competing upscale retailers in the area could not cut their prices without destroying their cachet, and they were slow to catch on, giving Roitenberg a head start. While there were a few discount retailers or catalog retailers in the United States, Roitenberg was in the forefront of a new type of business, the discount-catalog store.

From Startup to Profits

2. **Starting his own business**. Roitenberg spent 10 years at MW building the company's catalog-showroom business when his father-in-law died, and his brother was only willing to sell Roitenberg a third of the business, rather than half. Roitenberg decided that he did not want to remain a minority partner, so he decided to quit and start his own business called Creative Merchandising & Publishing, which later became Modern Merchandising (MM), in 1960. The plan was to publish

a catalog selling name-brand consumer products, such as cameras and electronics, and also carry high-margin items such as diamonds and jewelry. He planned to discount prices for name-branded merchandise, such as appliances, housewares, cameras, and electronics, to attract customers. And he planned to sell jewelry with an attractive margin to make a profit. He met with manufacturers, selected and priced the items, included them in the catalog, and got into his own business.

Lesson: The problem with any new business concept is the uncertainty of whether it will work, and how to merchandise, market, and price the products or services. Roitenberg was fortunate that he could test the idea of a discount catalog-showroom when he worked for his father-in-law. When you know a concept works, and you have the skills to make it happen or can get the skills, go for it. But have a tested plan to attract customers and to make money.

3. **Developing the business model for large volumes when you don't have capital**. Instead of opening catalog-showrooms and stocking inventory (which needed capital he did not have) to sell merchandise, Roitenberg decided to make his profits by publishing the catalog. He decided to sell the catalog to small merchants, such as jobbers and retailers. Roitenberg got these merchants into the catalog-showroom business based on a loose-knit, annually renewable agreement. He offered each an exclusive area and respected their territory. He recruited six customers in the first year. Roitenberg negotiated for the best prices with the manufacturers who sold directly to his customers. The customers were able to expand rapidly due to the fact that they received terms on paying for their catalogs, and also many manufacturers offered terms (buy in September/ October and pay for it in December/ January). This credit enabled the customers to expand without too much additional capital. Roitenberg did not ask for a commission or a markup. His entire pricing was transparent to his customers. Why did Roitenberg choose this route rather than opening showrooms himself? To offer an attractive value proposition to his customers, he needed low prices for the name-brand consumer goods. To get low prices from the large consumer-goods manufacturers, he needed to buy in volume. Since he did not have the money to open multiple stores and send millions of catalogs, he shared the profits with those who opened and ran the stores. ***Roitenberg used other people's money in a unique way to make the business happen, and made his profits with the media and the merchandising***.

Lesson: ***Understand the value proposition of the business and its requirements***. The key to the business was the ability to negotiate prices, merchandise the products and publish the catalog. In this case, Roitenberg had to have a proposal that was attractive to the consumer-product manufacturers, who would offer him low prices only if he had high volumes. The only way Roitenberg could expect these volumes was by bringing others into the business. The others had to trust him, so he was very open about how he made his money, and did not ask for any commissions on the actual sale. The customers knew they were getting a good deal. They signed on.

4. **Know how you add value and your competitive advantage**. Roitenberg realized that he had a knack for merchandising because he understood his customers, their needs, and his competitive advantage. His customers wanted top-of-the-line name brands, such as Nikon cameras, at lower prices. Often he would price the top name-brand cameras at below-market prices as sales leaders, because customers would also buy expensive jewelry, which had high margins. It was easy for the customers to check prices of name-brand items, such as appliances, cameras and electronics. So lower prices in this area helped create the perception of a low-priced catalog and helped sell jewelry at higher margins. He avoided health and beauty aids, and clothing, because they "had a different aura" and they seemed to negatively affect jewelry sales. Fair Trade laws were in force, but some manufacturers made a secondary line of consumer-electronics goods for the discounters, since they could see that it was a growing segment of their business.

Lesson: *Know how you will make money.* In retail, allow consumers to compare prices where you can be competitive. This practice is prevalent in all of the so-called "discount" retailers. Lower prices in one area draw customers who are then encouraged to spend more money elsewhere.

From Profits to the Moon

5. **Internal financing for unlimited growth**. The "brand discounting" trend became hot, and discount catalog sales took off. Roitenberg sold the catalog to the customers and also negotiated an advertising fee from the manufacturer who gave ad allowances to his customers. The printer in Waseca, Minn., printed millions of catalogs and shipped them directly to his customers and billed them. The printer took his share of the payment and then gave the balance to Roitenberg. In essence, *the printer, manufacturers, and retailers financed the entire operation for Roitenberg. He did not have to invest, or risk, any money.* Not needing any money for fixed assets, including leasehold improvements or real estate, equipment, inventory, marketing, or working capital allowed Roitenberg to grow without the limits imposed by financiers.

Lesson: ***Design an internally funded system and financiers are unlikely to restrain your growth or take a giant share of it or sell it to someone else to get their return***. If you can design a financial structure that does not need external financing to fund your growth, lenders and investors will not control your growth. Your only limits will then be based on your market, your competition, and your leadership.

6. **Customer expansion**. The whole industry was new, emerging, and growing. As the business grew, Roitenberg's customers kept pace and started spreading out to cover the entire country. Competition thought that Roitenberg was vulnerable because the customers had not signed a franchise agreement and paid a franchise

fee, or signed a long-term agreement. Roitenberg had only asked for one-year agreements with his customers. His business philosophy was that the arrangement should be fair for both parties; otherwise, they should be free to leave. As he puts it, "if you treat them right, they will keep coming back." His annual revenues from the sales of catalogs reached over $20 million. The annual fall catalog sold for about $1 and weighed more than two pounds. Roitenberg was the largest publisher in the industry.

> **Lesson:** ***People like to do business with people they trust and like.*** Often people seek protection with long-term contracts. While contracts are necessary, Roitenberg relied on offering a fair, attractive, and transparent deal to his customers, and they stayed with him. ***His secret ingredient was the openness and fairness of his arrangement, and the trust and goodwill of his customers.*** Agreements may cause compliance, but they are also what make lawyers rich. Agreements are very helpful when you are ready to sell the business, because that could encourage buyers, who demand compliance rather than offering fairness, to pay a higher price.

7. Getting into showrooms. As his client entrepreneurs became older, they started coming to Roitenberg to see if they could sell their business. Since the price was fair, Roitenberg started buying them. His first two acquisitions were Great Western in Lewiston, Idaho, and Anchor Distributing in St. Louis, Mo. Roitenberg purchased Great Western using cash from the company's line of credit (Roitenberg thinks he overpaid for the company). Both of these entrepreneurs continued to work for Roitenberg, and they each did better under the new arrangement because Roitenberg was able to improve the financing structure of these companies. At the same time, Roitenberg's brother, Irwin, and a good friend, Leonard LaBelle, decided to open a catalog-showroom, but they did not have sufficient funding. So Roitenberg invested $50,000 and acquired 50 percent of the business. They went to a local bank (which was their first encounter with the banking world) and asked for a $50,000 line of credit with a pro-forma financial statement showing $1 million in sales in the first year. They opened a small store in downtown Minneapolis with 5,000 square feet of showroom on the main floor, and storage in the basement and on the second floor. The showroom was across the street from the bank. It was far from a perfect location. Being downtown, there were no weekend sales and there was no parking. Their actual revenue in the first year was $2 million. The banker was surprised and commented that "very few of our customers showed actual sales that were twice the projections in the first year of business."

> **Lesson:** If you want to develop a good reputation with your lender, be conservative in your sales projections, and make sure your expenses are below revenues. *Most entrepreneurs claim to have conservative projections when seeking funding from venture capitalists. The projections are usually anything but conservative. But for banks, project low and perform high.*

8. The next stage. The stock markets were hot, and one of Roitenberg's customers, Best Products of Richmond, Va., went public. Their stock soared. Since investors seemed to be interested in catalog-showroom companies as the next wave in retailing, Roitenberg was approached by investment bankers interested in taking his company public. LaBelle's had two stores at the time in the Twin Cities metro area. MM owned 50 percent of the Minneapolis stores and 100 percent of the Idaho and Missouri businesses. Each business continued to operate under its own brand name. Due to the attractiveness of the stock markets, Roitenberg took MM public by buying a public shell with $600,000 in cash, merged MM (including the catalog-showrooms and catalog publishing) into the new shell, and became a publicly traded company. He then had many secondary offerings to raise additional cash. Roitenberg now had stock that he could use to acquire more companies. Many of Roitenberg's other customers wanted to sell, so he bought more stores all over the country, and as Roitenberg puts it, he overpaid for all of them because he was paying for them in overvalued stock. MM's stock had a price-earnings multiple of 60. He would have paid a significantly lower price if he had been required to pay for the companies in cash. MM ended up with about 85 catalog-showrooms across the country. Roitenberg was still merchandising the products and publishing the catalog for his customers. He was now doing it more as a "cooperative" model with all of the customers now sharing in the merchandising. At its peak, the group ended up doing over $6 billion in sales.

Lesson: When the time is right, strike. *When the markets overvalue your stock, use it to bulk up.* But if you are an investor, watch out. As some wise sage (I think it was Warren Buffett) once said, when companies pay cash for an acquisition, they think their stock is undervalued. When they pay in stock, they know that it is overvalued.

9. Store expansion. Roitenberg's stores were destinations. People did not come to them as they were passing by, but came specifically to buy based on examining the catalog. So he rented space off the beaten path and paid "warehouse" rents of around $2 per square foot. His selling tool was the catalog, and he designed each catalog to have a shelf life of one year. They had seasonal special catalogs with three- to four-day specials. Initially, when they only had one or two a year, the special catalogs worked very well. As Roitenberg puts it, "one was good, and two was better." But pretty soon, there were too many special catalogs and then consumers did not use the main catalog as frequently because they bought from the special catalogs.

Lesson: Even discounters need to use "specials" wisely. Don't debase your primary product. Know why your customers buy from you. Use this knowledge wisely in developing your strategy.

10. Management for growth. As the company started getting bigger, Roitenberg was told to get professional management. So Roitenberg hired a professional manager who had built another company and sold it to a larger corporation. Roitenberg told this manager that after two years, he could run the company. But there were some misunderstandings and, according to Roitenberg, the manager went to the board and requested that Roitenberg be asked to step out of the way, sell him the company, or fire him and pay the severance. Roitenberg decided to sell the company to a third party for an attractive price.

Lesson: Not all arrangements work. Hire with care. Develop contracts that protect both parties and prevent abuses from either.

11. The sale of MM. Roitenberg sold MM to a good friend of his who ran Best Products on the East Coast. There were about 10 million shares outstanding and Best Products bought the company for $21 per share. Roitenberg could not sell his shares for six months, since the buyer was going to have another stock offering. The stock moved up to $33 and Roitenberg sold his shares. Best Products did well also. They sold the company to a leveraged–buyout (LBO) company that paid $1 billion for Best Products. The highest level of profits made by Best Products was $40 million. Roitenberg wondered how the LBO fund expected to service debt of $1 billion with $40 million in profits.

Lesson: *There is a time to enter and a time to exit.* Exit when the stock is priced to perfection, and none of the analysts or investors can see any flaw in the company. Why did the LBO fund pay an outrageous price? First, the trends seemed to be advantageous, and they must have been unaware of the threat from a new kind of store – the discount store. Perhaps mainly, LBO managers are paid very well when there are profits, but don't pay the consequences (yeah, I know they may not get another fund) when they lose money.

12. Listen to your customers. Even after the sale of MM, Roitenberg had an interest in the catalog. Best Products sold it to a large Minnesota company. At the first meeting, the new buyers told the other catalog-showroom owners that the company would operate under new policies. The price would be set by the new buyer, and there would be no accommodation or flexibility for each individual showroom chain. Previously, Roitenberg would adjust prices in the catalog for each showroom owner to account for differences in regional tastes. He would charge them for the change orders so these customizations were lucrative. The new policies would not accommodate such changes. All except one of the showroom owners walked out of the room and out of the arrangement.

Lesson: *Arrogance kills. The world does not dance to your tune, but to its own.* The key is to make your tune theirs. Listen to your customers. They will listen to your dictates only if they have no other choice.

Post Script

13. The unraveling. Everything has its time and place under the sun. Soon the industry started to lose favor. Kmart, Wal-Mart and Target started to open discount stores at an increasing pace and changed the retail landscape. Previously, these companies had not been selling the top-of-the-line name brands, so the threat to MM was low. However, when they started selling name-brand merchandise at competitive prices with immediate availability, the end of the catalog-showroom concept was near.

Lesson: Roitenberg had been discounting the top brands. From a competitive perspective, it was not too difficult for the retail chains to carry these lines. The concept had a long-term competitive disadvantage, and the large retail discounters exploited it.

Rules for Entrepreneurs from Harold Roitenberg of Modern Merchandising

- **Structure the deal for profitability.** Roitenberg points out that venture capitalists often talk about burn rates, which is the level of monthly net cash outflow. He prefers to structure a business to be profitable. This is why he decided to sell catalogs rather than opening stores.
- **Control the cash burn**. Resist the temptation to spend money even if you have it. Hoard it and make sure you get a good return on all your expenses.
- **Start slow, test, learn, and grow**. Roitenberg points to one company that went into the "dollar store" business. Instead of starting with one or two, the entrepreneur started 10 with accompanying administrative overhead. He went out of business.
- **Don't grow too fast. Test. Test. Test**. Expand within your comfort zone. Grow as you reduce your uncertainties and risks.
- **Hire team members to complement your skills**. Hire those who are strong in areas where you are weak. Roitenberg had no patience for details, so he found teammates who liked details.
- **Price for customers. Price for margins**. Roitenberg knew that consumers could compare prices of name-brand items, so he discounted them to draw customers. He also knew that it was more difficult to compare prices of jewelry. So that's where he made better margins.

- **Time your entrance and exit**. Know the trends and time your actions accordingly.
- **Worry about your customers. Constantly.** If his customers did well, so did Roitenberg. So he made sure that the catalog and merchandising would succeed for them. Otherwise, he would be out of business. With a one-year agreement, he had to continuously worry, and not add unsustainable overhead.
- **Look higher as you grow higher**. Initially Roitenberg would have been happy with an income of $100,000. As the business grew, so did his goals.

Eric Paulson
Navarre Corporation

MINNEAPOLIS, MINN

Building the seventh largest software publisher & largest importer of Japanese anime

Summary: Eric Paulson was a football star at his Catholic high school in South Bend, Indiana. His father played football for Knute Rockne and after graduating from college, he became a pro wrestler called Horrible Howard. So it was only natural that Paulson would take up football. Paulson followed in his father's footsteps and started playing competitive football in the fifth grade. To earn extra money, he started selling shoes and became very good at it. After high school, he kept trying to excel at college football, but injuries soon put an end to those hopes. He started selling tires, and his sales skill so impressed one of his customers that he referred Paulson to a friend who was starting a company to distribute a new way of listening to music: 8-track tapes. This started a meteoric rise for Paulson in the music business. In 1983, he started Navarre to distribute music and software. It is now the seventh-largest software publisher and the largest importer and 're-purposer' of Japanese anime in North America with annual sales of around $700 million at its peak. This is how he did it.

Before the Startup

1. **Selling shoes.** When Paulson was in high school, he needed a job to earn extra money and started searching for a job on Michigan Street, the main street in South Bend, Ind. The owner of a store selling women's shoes was looking for a stock boy to organize the inventory and keep the store clean. Paulson started as a stock boy and soon got promoted to shoe sales, which was the "best job for a high school guy." Paulson started to market to the girls in his high school, giving all of them his card. He offered to tint their shoes to match their dresses, and the service was free if they bought the shoes from him. According to Paulson, meeting girls was the best part of the job. But the money was very attractive (as a teenager, it is tough to keep your priorities straight). Paulson would stay late at the store tinting shoes. With his

commissions, he bought a Chevy Impala with a $40 per month payment. As Paulson puts it, "the car was hot and gas was cheap (at 23 cents per gallon)." This job helped Paulson develop his personality in selling and taught him many things about it. He studied people, including their strengths and weaknesses, and translated these to needs and presentation skills. His biggest lesson was to listen to customers and their needs, and to sell the product benefits without highlighting the price. Paulson learned that those who were just looking at the price tended to buy elsewhere. This was the foundation of his sales skills that would enable him to sell music to nearly every retailer in the industry.

> **Lesson**: Paulson learned a number of lessons from his job selling shoes. *By studying people's needs, he was able to customize his presentation, and emphasize how his products could fit their needs.* He learned how to be engaging and open, so that people would trust him. *And he learned the importance of offering the added touch of service to differentiate himself* from all the others selling shoes. Focus on the benefits, rather than emphasizing the price.

2. **Growing up too fast**. Paulson kept his shoe store job through high school. His dad lost his job in Indiana and took one in Wisconsin. Since Paulson's mother was in the hospital with multiple sclerosis, his dad moved her to Wisconsin to be near him. Paulson was left in charge of himself and his two younger brothers. With this freedom, and an undeveloped sense of responsibility in his sophomore and junior years of high school, Paulson went out and got in trouble. So, in the summer between his junior and senior years, his father moved the whole family to Wisconsin. Paulson had to start all over again at a high school in Waukesha. He realized that if he was going to make the football team, he needed more discipline than he had displayed to date. At Waukesha High School, he made the team as a starting end and defensive cornerback. Based on his performance he got a college scholarship, but he hurt his knee, missed the last few games, and lost the scholarship. After finishing school, he returned to South Bend to sell shoes and apply to other schools for football scholarships. He ended up at the University of Wisconsin (Whitewater) and hurt his knee again. This time, he quit college, got married and joined the Marines. When he rejoined civilian life after 18 months in Vietnam, he ended up selling tires for General Tire. He sold a pair of expensive tires to a customer who was so impressed with Paulson's sales skills that he wanted to know whether Paulson had thought of changing careers. A friend of his named Jim Tiedjens was looking for a salesperson in the music industry to sell music on tape. Although Paulson was still hoping to go back to school to play football, the offer of $600 per month was too good to pass up compared with the $450 he was earning selling tires. Paulson also liked the prospects for 8-track tapes and thought that it would expand the music industry. He decided to follow his instinct and signed on. College and football were history.

> **Lesson**: Paulson had two skills. One was football and the other was selling. To play football, your body needs to co-operate. Paulson's knees would not co-operate with his goal of football fame. So he followed his natural skills in sales.

3. **Music in the blood**. Jim Tiedjens, who hired Paulson, owned Midwestern Tape Distributors. Both Tiedjens and Paulson believed that tapes would change the way people reacted to music and that the music industry was ready to take off. Previously, people could only listen to the radio when they were in the car, while being able to listen to large tape recorders or record players at home. Immediately after joining Midwestern, Tiedjens asked Paulson to meet with Uniroyal Merchandising to sell the company 8-track tapes. This was Paulson's first business trip. Uniroyal was the automotive lessee of K-Mart, which was the hot retailer at the time. Paulson made the presentation to Uniroyal and captured the account in one visit. Both Paulson and Uniroyal knew that the people who managed the stores did not believe in tapes. Paulson had heard this from Uniroyal executives. Paulson sold Uniroyal on Midwestern's commitment to tapes, and that they could do a better job of managing this business than Uniroyal could do on its own. They leased a 'store within the store' to satisfy consumer demand for taped music in their cars. This new trend in the music industry was called rack jobbing. Paulson designed the fixtures, planned the inventory, set the prices and merchandised the music. Uniroyal only had to provide the space. Paulson followed this with stores within the auto departments of Sears and Penney's. The concept was Tiedjens' but Paulson made it happen. He got so excited about music that he forgot about college. A year later, in 1968, Midwestern went public with its headquarters in Milwaukee and Paulson owned 1 percent of the company.

Lesson: *Solve the customers' problem.* No one in the auto department of Uniroyal stores had sold music or knew how to sell it. Uniroyal had thought of the opportunity but had no solution within its corporate hierarchy. They wanted to satisfy consumer demand for taped music, but realized that they were not experts in the area and did not expect to be anytime soon. Paulson offered to solve Uniroyal's problem and got the sale.

4. **Expanding within Midwestern**. After the company went public, Midwestern bought 13 other companies in the music-distribution business and Paulson moved to New Orleans to build a Southern division and incorporate the five companies that they had purchased in the South. He was 23 years old. His major skill was sales. Midwestern had bought the businesses from the previous owners for stock, and the stock was going up. These newly rich partners could not be told by a 23-year-old how to manage their business, so Paulson had to learn how to do it through finesse. Essentially, he did what he had to do to combine their operations and expand sales, but he made sure he asked for their permission and got their support and involvement.

Lesson: Learn human relations skills. Paulson learned that he could get more cooperation from the sellers by getting them involved in the decisions.

5. **Failure in Southern California**. Based on his success in New Orleans, Paulson was promoted to fix the struggling operation in Southern California. The

parent company had grown too fast, and there were too many disagreements with all the previous owners whose operations it had purchased. They were now shareholders and they did not agree with the changes. Southern California was one of the regions with the most problems. Paulson thought he could fix the problems single-handedly. Even though he worked long hours, he could not. The company sought refuge in Chapter 11 bankruptcy. In addition, Paulson had acquired a house 90 minutes away from his office and was away from home for extended periods. His marriage failed. Paulson was not yet 25. Having experienced great success early in life, he was now experiencing failure. He realized that he had to understand the reasons for the earlier success and to know why they had failed, and he realized that most of the reasons had to do with fast growth, lax controls, and changing trends. In this case, the trends were within the company. Whereas it had once been tightly run, the company had suffered from too high a growth rate with lax controls and had paid the price.

> **Lesson**: *Grow at the edge of comfort, but not much faster. Growth without controls leads to chaos.* The company had grown too fast and did not have controls. ***Watch out for hubris***. Often the same habits that lead you to success, when done to excess can lead to failure. Rather than taking a deep breath and digesting its acquisitions, Midwestern had bought too many companies in its bid to dominate the taped-music market in the United States. They paid the price.

6. Taking time off. After the failure in Southern California, Paulson took a year off and travelled. He had never had any time off since high school when he was single and carefree, due to his family obligations, work, football, and school. He had some money saved, so he went around the country, stayed with friends and made new ones.

> **Lesson**: Sometimes it helps to know what you want to do. Take time off to replenish the soul, if you can afford it. If not, rejuvenate yourself in small doses regularly. Balance your life and don't burn out.

7. Media attention. During the year of "doing nothing," Paulson got an idea to do a live rock-and-roll show on TV similar to the Dick Clark show. He connected with Sam Riddle, who was a very popular DJ in Los Angeles, and formed a partnership with him called SRO Productions. Sam Riddle had another TV show and had TV production expertise and credibility, but he did not have a show in rock and roll. This became one of the first rock-and-roll shows on TV, and some of the invited acts had never performed on TV. Paulson was the minority shareholder and Riddle the majority owner. When they started producing this show, the timing was perfect, and the show took off. The ABC-TV network aired the show, (there were 3 series "An Evening of Solid Gold", "In Concert" and "In Session") and this was the start of ABC-in-concert series. Riddle had connections with the record companies and lined up the record labels that wanted to promote their artists. Paulson had connections with retailers and asked them to finance the show to sell their products to consumers.

Retailers had no direct contacts at the record labels, and they also did not know how to produce TV shows. That is where Paulson and Riddle came in and filled a need. The retailers financed many different series of shows. Paulson used his L.A. contacts and connected them with his retailer network from his old company, which had since changed its name to National Tape. The company succeeded, reaching about $9 million in sales. This success attracted other competitors. When other national conglomerates came calling, Paulson and his partner sold SRO to them. In the meantime, Trans Continental Music (TCM) called and asked Paulson to manage the Dallas, Texas, operation and become national sales manager for the company. Paulson moved to Dallas.

> **Lesson**: Track trends. Understand your strengths. Fill needs. Take advantage. Bring in the key ingredients you don't have with the right partner who has integrity, and can add the missing pieces to your idea to develop a successful venture. Paulson notes that the key lesson he learned from this venture is to keep looking for opportunities, and to find people who are smarter and wealthier to put together the pieces.

8. National sales manager of a turnaround. TCM was a music retailer and distributor and had a number of struggling divisions, with Dallas being the largest one in trouble. Paulson realized that this was his opportunity to learn the operational side of the record business. So he got an apartment in Dallas, kept his boat in California, and commuted back and forth. He soon realized that the operations had become bloated and inefficient because the previous branch manager in Dallas had lost interest in the business. In his previous jobs, Paulson had thought that sales personnel were the crucial ingredient in a record-distribution business because they brought in the sales. Now he realized that sales personnel would be totally ineffective if the operations were inefficient because ***competitors dictate the selling price, and vendors (customers) dictate the buying price***. In a distribution business like TC Music, operations and costs defined profits. At Dallas, he found that customers were screaming due to poor service and threatening to move their business to their competitors. Efficiency was poor, morale was poorer still, and monitoring was non-existent. He cut costs, found managers who cared about operations, improved effectiveness, morale, and efficiency, and started to make money.

> **Lesson**: Many entrepreneurs focus on their core skills. To succeed, you need to become a complete entrepreneur or have a complete, competent team, which can be expensive. To become a complete entrepreneur, appreciate and gain experience in all facets of the business and not just the one where you excel. This means that you need to know to identify and eliminate any weaknesses in yourself. Neglect key areas at your peril.

9. A new owner. A new move. When Pickwick International (PI) of Minneapolis bought TC Music, the owners asked Paulson to stay on in Dallas for six months to merge the two companies. At the end of this stint, he was asked to come to Minneapolis to learn about PI, and to enable PI's owners to learn about Paulson. In three months, Paulson spent time at each of PI's divisions. At the end of this time, he was asked to take over the Detroit operation for PI, after which he was transferred to St. Louis, which was the only one of PI's operations that was unionized. Paulson had to learn to deal with unions. He had to understand their mutual goals and to achieve them with diplomacy. American Can (a publicly traded company) bought PI, and Paulson was offered the position of senior V.P. To consolidate operations, American Can decided to have Paulson close down a division and fire 320 employees. Paulson reexamined his motivations, and whether he wanted to stay with a large company, or take advantage of the opportunity that the shutdown presented by creating a vacuum in the marketplace. He decided to start his own company. Paulson was 38 years old.

Lesson: Large companies offer a great learning experience, but you still have to do the bidding of your superiors. To reach your own goals and implement your own vision, you need to be in your own business.

From Startup to Profits

10. The sole music distribution company in Minnesota. Paulson's goal was to build an independent company in the music- and software-distribution businesses. His core belief was that there would be a convergence of technologies in the music industry, and that one technology would become the dominant force in music and computers. He also believed that technology would bring music and computers together. He took six months to write his business plan for Navarre, and obtained a working capital line of credit from his bank. To get the line, he gave as collateral his car, boat, and all personal assets. He also invested $100,000 in cash, which was every penny he had, and obtained $100,000 in cash from a partner. His partner wanted 18 percent of the equity and after two weeks of discussions, they settled on 16 percent. Later, he also gave stock to his key employees, with the understanding that they had to sell the stock back if they left the company. He opened his business in 1983 with a warehouse, nothing to sell and no one to sell to. He and his assistant were the only persons in the company. The key to getting started was to be able to convince record labels that he could be a better distributor than the current ones, and to convince retailers that he could give them great service. He positioned himself as the only independent distributor in Minnesota since PI had closed its Minnesota operations and the closest warehouse was in Chicago. He started approaching retailers and asked for their willingness to buy lines from his company. Being the only local distributor, they could get immediate access to products so as to replenish their shelves. This meant more turns and better inventory control. This was his niche. He signed up all the local retailers, including Musicland, Target, and Dart Records. And with his connections to the music industry from his past experience, he signed up a dozen labels. He was in business. He made a profit in the first year.

Lesson: *Find your niche.* When PI closed its Minnesota operations, Paulson realized that he could become the local distributor and help retailers better manage their operations. And the fact that some of the nation's large retailers were in Minneapolis did not hurt Paulson. The bigger question is why a company like American Can did not see the need to keep a Minnesota presence. With these customers, he could convince record labels who wanted to make sure that they had distribution through these retailers to sign on

11. Gaining credibility. To get accurate financial statements, Paulson decided to end his fiscal year in March so he could account for Christmas returns in the same fiscal year so as to have accurate year-end statements. Even though he was a small, private company, he hired Coopers & Lybrand, a Big 8 (at that time there were eight big accounting firms) firm, as his CPA because they were PI's auditors. Most private companies sought a smaller accounting firm due to their lower cost. C&L helped Paulson with his business plan, financial projections, and bank presentations because they were convinced that he would succeed.

Lesson: *Prepare. Plan. Get the right team. Execute to the plan. Sounds simple. It is, if you have the right niche, have developed the right plan, and have the experience to implement your plan.*

12. What is good customer service? Paulson had just changed banks when the buyer at one of his largest retail customers made an error. Paulson was a distributor for Software, Etc., a software maker, and his retail customer's buyer bought $1 million of inventory that he should not have. The buyer wanted to return it, but Paulson knew that accepting it back meant that he would be in default on his bank covenants. He did it anyway as a favor to the buyer because he did not want the buyer to lose his job, and also wanted to keep the retailer as a customer. But the bank did not take as lenient a view as Paulson took and threw Navarre into a workout situation by demanding that the loan be repaid. The bank took control of all the incoming cash, gave 35 percent to Paulson for expenses, and kept the balance to pay the loan. Paulson could not make payroll with the amount the bank gave him. He told his workers and management that he was broke and could not make payroll. Two managers left, but the rest of his team stayed. Paulson visited with 72 different suppliers and made separate arrangements with them to keep carrying their inventory. Those deals kept the company alive. He then tried to make a deal with the bank, but the bank did not want to make any alternate arrangement. After days of never-ending negotiations, Paulson got frustrated, gave the bank keys to the company, and told them "if you won't forgive the $1 million of the loan by Tuesday, you can have the company." The bank reminded Paulson of his personal guarantee. Paulson responded by saying that he did not have much anyway and was not afraid to start again after declaring bankruptcy if he had to do so. The bank kept trying to reach Paulson on Monday, but Paulson would not answer the phone. On

Tuesday morning, the bank told Paulson that it would take the $1-million "haircut" that Paulson had requested if Paulson would pay them $600,000 by Wednesday. Paulson asked two investors to invest $266,000 in the form of a loan and to guarantee a working capital line of credit for $3 million with another bank in return for 20 percent of the company. He then went to two key customers and asked for a $300,000 advance from each. He gave the bank this $600,000 and got forgiveness for $1 million. With the cash and the line of credit, he kept all the vendors current and rebuilt the business. As Paulson puts it, "the bank cannot put you out of business if the vendors and customers want you and need you."

> **Lesson**: ***Don't play brinkmanship with financiers, or give deadlines that you cannot live with. Sometimes it backfires.*** Paulson was willing to live with the consequences. And learn to work with vendors and get them to believe in you. If you are doing a good job for them, and they have faith that you will work with them and pay them on time, they can be your lifeline when all others have given up on you. Most importantly, understand that true customer service has a cost. Anyone can advertise that they go the extra mile for customer service, but few will pay a cost for it. Paulson did it for his customer even though he knew that the bank might foreclose. The bank, which used customer service as one of its key marketing slogans, did not know the meaning of the phrase. There is also a lesson here for bankers: There is a time to be tough and get your workout people involved, and a time to negotiate. *You cannot be hard-nosed all the time.*

From Profits to the Moon

13. Growth. After his near-death experience with the bank, Paulson realized that he needed to get more experience in finance. To get the right training, he attended executive-training classes at the Carlson School of Management at the University of Minnesota and at Harvard Business School. In six years, he built one of the top independent music and software distributors in the country with $100 million in revenues. But he realized that if he was to keep growing to capture the opportunity available, he would need more equity. So in 1990 he sold the business to Live Entertainment based on an arrangement that paid him partly in cash and partly as an earn-out, i.e., he got paid more if the company performed as expected.

> **Lesson**: If the right offer comes along and provides a brighter future for all the stakeholders, you may want to sell and choose the next path.

14. Tragedy and a change in plans. Paulson sold Navarre to Live Entertainment and merged the software side with Lieberman Enterprises, which was also part of Live Entertainment. Paulson became EVP and COO of Lieberman Enterprises and had responsibility for the Lieberman Organization and Navarre. The CFO of Navarre became its CEO. Just after the sale to Live Entertainment, its chairman and his wife were killed by their sons. The CEO sent a letter to Paulson reaffirming the first earn-out payment due to Paulson in six months. However, the company hired a new chairman and within 48 hours Paulson received a letter stating that the numbers were not audited, so payment would be withheld. Three months later, Paulson received another letter from the chairman that no amount was due to Paulson. Paulson sued the company, its board and the new chairman. Live Entertainment had its own problems with customers filing bankruptcy and employees suing the company. So Paulson called the new chairman of Live Entertainment and asked for the company back. Paulson paid for the accounts receivable and assumed the payables. The company's sales had fallen to an annual rate of under $20 million, but Navarre was his again. He gave shares to his key managers to make sure that he had their interest, hearts, and wallets, and could only pay them reduced salaries.

> **Lesson**: Any agreement can unravel. Make sure that you prepare for this, especially when selling a company with an earn-out provision. Buyers like earn-outs to delay payments, make them contingent on future performance, and to have this amount that they use to offset any unaccounted-for liabilities. Sellers do not like it but accept it to get a higher price. Earn-outs can become a problem when the selling entrepreneur is no longer managing the company because the buyer may mismanage the company after purchase.

15. Changing distribution. From a $20 million sales level when he bought the company back, Paulson grew it to about a $700 million level. In addition to expanding nationally in music (the company was already a national distributor in software), one of the key changes Paulson made in the music-distribution business, and subsequently in software distribution, was the concept of consigned inventory. Due to the benefits and size of the company, he was able to negotiate long-term, national exclusive distributorships with many of the record labels and software producers. He did everything but make the music, i.e., Navarre produced the media, packaged it, stored it, sold it to retailers, and controlled the logistics. Navarre became the outsourcing company for music and software firms so they could focus on the content. However, Navarre expected the record labels and software companies to pay for the cost of production, storage, etc., so that Navarre did not have to fund any inventory and accept that risk. He just handled the inventory, which allowed Navarre to grow significantly without massive doses of cash. In software, retailers did not want to stock inventory with the high cost of some of the software packages. With consigned inventory, they were able to stock the shelves and get the best distribution space in the country. The cost of inventory for the retailers and for Navarre was $0. This allowed Navarre to work with national retailers such as Best Buy and Target.

> **Lesson**: Push the true cost of stocking inventory to the party with the highest margin, i.e., the software publisher in this case. Find the problem and solve it. Look at all sides of the equation. The record labels were not experts at the non-music side of the business. The retailers did not want to pay to stock expensive inventory, so Navarre negotiated a financing arrangement with the producers.

Navarre did the work and collected the fee.

16. Going public. Paulson bought the company back from Live Entertainment in 1991-92. In December of 1993, he took the company public when it had annual sales of $70 million. The key reason for going public was that the music business, and especially retailing, was becoming very sophisticated and national in nature because of the merger of retailers. This meant that Navarre needed to invest in automating the warehouse to bring to it the state-of-the-art and offering new services to all. With this investment from the public, Navarre did so. As a publicly held corporation, Navarre's financial statements were more credible with vendors and the company got more credit lines from vendors, which is "the best kind of financing," according to Paulson.

Lesson: When there is an opportunity for a public offering, and you need the cash, you may want to take advantage. Consider the ramifications for all stakeholders. Remember, though, that you are now living in a fish bowl where everyone second-guesses your decisions.

17. Sale of the music division. In 2007, Navarre sold off the music division due to problems in both the supply-side and the demand-side. On the supply side, the industry faced the risks of artists and labels not being able to adjust to the new music industry realities and the short life span of most artists. On the demand side, the Internet and large retailers were taking market share from the specialty retailers who were the core market for Navarre. The industry was in serious decline. With both sides of the industry in trouble, Navarre did not see a future in this aspect of the business. So it exited.

Lesson: Know the trends and act accordingly. You will get more favorable pricing if you act before the trends become obvious.

Rules for Entrepreneurs from Eric Paulson of Navarre

- **Get excited and lead with positive energy**. People want to follow someone who excites them and they can believe in.
- **Control inventory and all other aspects of your business, and understand their interdependence**. Know where everything is and know what you have – in real time.
- **Know the meaning of customer service**. True customer service always has a cost.

- **Understand all facets of the business**. The aspect you don't know may haunt you.
- **Sometimes, walk.** When the arrangement gets too painful, as with the bank for Paulson, your only reasonable choice may be to leave.
- **Set a standard of ethics that everyone believes in and understands**. This buys more loyalty than anything else you can do.

Don Kotula
Northern Tool & Equipment

MINNEAPOLIS, MINN

Building an $800 million giant in tools: "He-men" served here.

Summary: What do you do for a career if your dad owns a salvage yard in Hibbing, Minn., (former home of Bob Dylan) and does not believe in sales or marketing, but you happen to like machines, tools, and selling to customers to make them happy? You build an $800 million (sales) giant in the tool and equipment industry. Leonard Kotula, Don's dad, owned a small salvage yard in Hibbing. Leonard Kotula's philosophy was that if you could walk, you could work. Don Kotula started working in the family business "since he was born." They would buy cars and equipment from a variety of sources, including area mines that were changing from mining iron ore in underground mines to open-pit taconite mines, and resell them as parts or steel. From this humble beginning, Kotula created a tool and equipment retail giant and manufacturing company with over $800 million in sales. This is how he did it.

Preparing for Success

1. **Start a business within a business**. Leonard Kotula's business was to buy cars, equipment, trucks, and tracks from various sources such as individuals, mining companies, the armed forces, and others. The company would buy and sell lots of army trucks and tracks, along with the attached hydraulics. They usually ran out of the hydraulics. Don Kotula contacted the vendors of the hydraulics parts and obtained distributorships for the high-demand parts for his area. He sold these primarily to customers in a 50-mile radius. According to Kotula, he "loved to sell stuff, especially equipment and machinery." He liked to sell because he wanted to have pleased customers. Kotula did not tell the manufacturers that he was only 15 years old. When he started to become successful, some of them sent their sales people to the yard. When they showed up and saw a 15-year-old kid, they asked for his dad. At that time, Kotula informed them that he was the distributor. They were quite surprised that a 15-year-old was achieving the level of sales he was in the

area, but none of them cancelled the agreement because of his success in generating sales.

Lesson: ***Fill an unmet need*** – you will have happy customers and you will be more successful. Don't let your age or other limitations be barriers.

2. **Cash is king.** Kotula had the responsibility to track the level of cash to make sure that it was enough for payroll and to pay vendors. This responsibility taught him the importance of tracking cash flow to have enough cash on hand to pay current bills and cash flow to pay future bills. One event particularly influenced Kotula's thinking. The government owed his father a significant sum of money for his role in building a key road in northern Minnesota. U.S. Senators Hubert Humphrey and Walter Mondale were scheduled to come and open the road on a Monday. Leonard Kotula wanted to be paid as soon as the work was done. To make his point, and collect his cash, Leonard Kotula took some of his vehicles, blocked the road, and stood guard with a gun. The sheriff was asked to remove him but Kotula's dad and the sheriff knew each other. The government opened the bank on a Sunday to pay Kotula – in cash since he did not want a check.

Lesson: ***Cash is king. Cash flow is emperor.*** When you have payroll to meet, you need cash to meet it. However, I would not recommend the tactics used by Leonard Kotula.

3. **Promote your business but test your ads.** Don Kotula realized that the company's sales were limited to the local area due to lack of advertising, and they could only display and promote new products when customers were already in the store. Although Leonard Kotula did not believe in advertising and marketing, since he thought that it would not pay for itself and that customers would show up anyway, Don Kotula had taken some business classes and believed that advertising could be profitable. When he was 14, Kotula got his dad's permission to try advertising to expand his territory and to get additional sales. However, his dad wanted Kotula to show that each dollar spent on advertising paid for itself, produced additional marginal sales and was profitable. Kotula advertised in the local and regional shoppers (newspapers that were very popular before the days of Craigslist) and other media, such as national construction magazines, to see what worked and what did not. He tracked each ad to see how it did because he had to prove to his dad that he was not wasting money. The company's market, sales, and profits expanded significantly. To sell some materials that they had bought from the army, the younger Kotula placed an ad in a national construction-machinery magazine and sold some of the equipment to a man named Fidel Castro in Cuba. At that time, Fidel was not considered to be an enemy of the United States. After seeing the additional sales, Leonard Kotula was convinced of the value of targeted advertising.

Lesson: ***To expand, know your customers, how to reach them, and how to sell to them.*** Kotula learned early that he had to prove to his father that he could earn a positive return from his investment in advertising. Many entrepreneurs never learn this lesson and hope that their ad investments will pay off (because they too often trust their ad agencies) and don't test it before risking significant sums. Test. Test. Test.

4. **Pricing your products to show value**. Don Kotula also experimented with pricing to see how much he could charge (before he lost sales). His father would guess at what he could charge, sometimes would ask friends, and would often base it on cost. Kotula wanted to know the value to see what people would pay. He compared the prices for similar new equipment from the vendors, checked the Sears and Wards catalogs, and called competitors to know their prices and to see if they were willing to mark it down. He found that he had to be in a range that was about 30 to 40 percent below the price of new equipment, but he could be at the high end of the range for equipment that was in demand. This detailed price knowledge helped him to increase his margins.

Lesson: Pricing is one of the most difficult tasks you will do, and one of the most important. The right price can mean the difference between success and failure. ***Learn the value of the product or service to the customer so you can price it to value, not just base it on cost.***

5. **Learn the basics of business**. When Kotula finished high school, he enrolled at the University of Minnesota in Duluth. He liked his father but knew that he could not work with him. So he trained his younger brother to take over his position. Since Don Kotula had a good head for numbers, he majored in business and finance. He went to school till 1 p.m. and worked from 1 till 7 p.m. buying, fixing, and selling used cars. He made enough money selling cars that he was able to drive around campus in a Jaguar XKE.

Lesson: Pursue your passion. You will have fun and maybe make money.

6. **Outside experience in the corporate world**. When he was done with school, he received offers from a number of corporations; he chose Montgomery Ward and the catalog business. Kotula had studied computers in school, and he put this to use at Ward's. Ward's was automating its catalog business and during his two years at Ward's, Kotula learned how to manage a catalog business and how to sell products using a catalog, including list management, tracking, merchandising, and so on. From Ward's, Kotula moved on to Northwest Airlines. This was when the airline business was exciting and growing fast. Kotula supervised the budget department and another 30-some people in interline billing. He learned how to improve efficiency and productivity by talking to people and asking them for feedback and suggestions. He changed and improved operations and learned cost control under the legendary CEO of Northwest, Don Nyrop. Nyrop had become famous as the CEO who removed the doors from the toilets – he did not want his employees to spend too much time there. There were many older managers at Northwest and his upward mobility was limited so Kotula moved on. His next stop was Caterpillar because he

always liked machinery and equipment such as tractors and other big-ticket items, and he loved selling. At Caterpillar he was buying heavy equipment from dealers, buying excess equipment back from contractors and selling it to large contractors around the country and the world. Due to heavy demand, contractors had to wait two years for new equipment. So they were ready for used equipment and Kotula developed a network to find it. At Caterpillar, he was always the most aggressive salesperson, and he would call contractors both to find out their needs and get lists of their excess equipment, while the other sales people waited for the phone to ring. He quickly became the top Caterpillar salesperson. He would continuously check new markets and the progress of projects. When contractors completed major projects, they often sold excess equipment that they did not have immediate use for. Many of them wanted cash, which Kotula provided, but only if he got a better price. By keeping in touch with the construction network, Kotula knew who wanted equipment and the type of equipment that was hot. This led him to sell equipment in Mexico and other countries. He bought equipment from the Alaska pipeline and sold graders to Jordan. When interest rates began to exceed 20 percent, sales of equipment slowed down considerably, and Kotula decided to move on. He was now ready to start his own business.

> **Lesson**: Get a well-rounded experience so you have no weaknesses. At Ward's, Kotula learned the skills needed to manage a mail-order catalog. At Northwest Airlines, Kotula learned how to operate efficiently and with high productivity. He also learned from Nyrop the power of positive thinking and getting the job done. Who needs someone who cannot solve the problem? At Caterpillar, he learned the market for heavy equipment, and the value of a network and information about excess supply and demand, which allowed him to provide value.

From Startup to Growth

7. **The start of Northern Tool & Equipment**. Kotula started Northern Tool & Equipment (at that time called Northern Hydraulics) in the summer of 1980 while he was at Caterpillar. He reintroduced himself to the hydraulics manufacturers whose products he was selling at his father's business. He put together a catalog to sell log splitters and the parts to make them, including the hydraulics, valves, and other parts that he bought from the manufacturers. Initially, Kotula relied on his customers (mainly farmers, loggers, and people who were handy with tools) to make their own frame, but in six months he found a local welding shop with excess capacity that made the frames for him. The customer had to assemble the equipment, and Kotula wrote a 20-page book called "How to Build Your Log Splitter" that his wife typed and he had copied at a local copy shop, retailing the book for $10. He started his business with his life savings of about $20,000. The buyers sent $2 for each catalog and then used credit cards to buy the log splitters. He got terms

of 30 days from his vendors, while he was paid immediately (via credit cards) by his customers. He stocked some of the parts, but monitored their sales closely to make sure that he did not carry excess inventory. He added new products to his catalog but only after carefully testing their potential and sales. He would move to pallet sizes only when his sales levels justified it, notwithstanding the fact that he got discounts for the larger orders. He opened Northern Hydraulics as a mail-order business, but he also had a retail store so he could display his products. Customers in the region would stop by to pick up their order, and this gave Kotula a chance to talk to them. Kotula got feedback from his customers, who gave him suggestions for improvement, and ideas for new products that they would like to buy. His monthly sales reached $100,000 by January (in about six months) with a gross margin of 35 to 40 percent and a net income margin of 5 to 7 percent. He outgrew his initial space and moved to a 1,300-square-foot shop. By March, his monthly sales were $250,000 and by May, $566,000. He expanded to 4,000 square feet. The reason for his rapid growth was that hardly anyone was selling industrial products by mail, and Kotula had identified a hungry market with unmet needs.

Lesson: Kotula knew that there was a market for log splitters from his previous work with his father. Note that he did not give anything away. ***Everything (catalog, book, and product) had a price***. He found out that customers were more likely to buy the parts or the product if they bought the book, so he promoted the book very heavily. He also kept a tight grip on inventory and got terms from his vendors to maintain a positive cash flow.

8. Have a competitive edge. Other catalogs in the market sold industrial products and machinery, but none of them sold log splitters. One of them could become a potential competitor for Kotula after he identified the market for log splitters. To make sure that he had a competitive edge, he bought all the valves in the country so his competitors did not have valves even if they wanted to introduce a similar product.

Lesson: One of the most frequently asked questions by skeptics is "if the idea is so good, why isn't someone else doing it?" This is sometimes a good question and sometimes not so good. This is where you need to know your market and test it. But having proved it, protect yourself and maintain your competitive edge unless you want someone else to get the benefits.

9. Know where to find your customers. Kotula placed small ads in various magazines that he knew his core market read. These magazines included Popular Mechanics, Popular Science, Farm World (and other ag magazines), and a variety of other magazines for the construction industry. He tracked the orders and placed ads only in the magazines that produced results, such as Popular Mechanics and Popular Science. He also found that there was seasonality to his sales so he adjusted his marketing accordingly and did not waste money in the low months. He developed his own mailing lists from his ads and got customers' addresses from their checks.

He would encourage his customers to refer their friends to receive a catalog, and most of them were happy to do so. This helped Kotula to expand his mailing list without a high cost.

Lesson: ***If you spend too much money to find customers— or worse, you spend too much time and money to find the right customers – you could be broke before you have a chance at success.*** The key is to know who your customers are and how to reach them most effectively and efficiently.

10. Make or buy. As noted earlier, Kotula did not build his own steel frames for the log splitters because he did not want to invest money in a welding shop. There were many welding shops with excess capacity, and he used one of them to get the best price and service, and without his having to make a fixed investment.

Lesson: Many entrepreneurs do not think carefully about their business. Kotula knew that he could buy the frames from a number of shops. His competitive edge was not in making the frames but in finding customers and giving them good value. Getting a good price for the frames allowed him to attain high margins without an investment in the plant and equipment. Evaluate the make-or-buy decision carefully because it can affect your financing needs and your break-even levels. The faster you show a profit, the happier you, and your financiers, will be.

11. Know what sells. Know who buys. Kotula codes every ad and every catalog, and he tracks the resulting prospects and customers and their lifetime sales by the ad and magazine that first attracted them. He knows what they buy, how much they buy and how profitable they are for his company. This showed him that catalogs are much more productive than ads, that ads in July don't work, and that there is high degree of connection between those who like tools, those who fish, and those who buy cabins. Many companies expect 3 to 7 percent returns on their mailings. Kotula finds returns of 10 percent on lots of catalogs due to the company's knowledge of customer profiles.

Lesson: ***Track everything.*** Know where you have been and where you are going. *If you are driving without vision, sooner or later you will crash.*

12. Price as a competitive edge. Kotula found that some products were not available from his competitors while others were more common. He charged more for products that had no direct competition. The other products were 2 to 3 percent lower. When customers compared prices, they would compare the products that were widely available and got the impression that Kotula was cheaper. Other major retailers do this also. That's how they promise low prices, but keep their margins high.

Lesson: Price is key. *Higher prices with high sales are a great formula for high profits and high valuation. Learn how to get it,* which is by solving customers' unmet needs better than your competitors.

From Profits to Home Run

13. Repeat business = sales growth. Because Kotula focused on customer satisfaction, he got repeat business, and the customers recommended his company to their friends because they were so happy with the catalog, the products and the service. He also added more products recommended by his customers and by vendors, such as tires for log splitters. Kotula continues to ask his vendors to give him the best ideas and the best deals first. That keeps his competitive edge. One of his tire vendors observed that the tire used in log splitters is also used for boat trailers. So Kotula added parts for boat trailers and started targeting marinas and boat owners. Sales soared because nobody was selling parts to boat trailer parks, such as tires, springs, and so on. Kotula also found that anyone who buys a cabin is a good customer because cabins seem to need constant maintenance.

Lesson: It is easier to grow when you get repeat business from your customers than when you don't. It is easier to grow when your customers tell you what else they want to buy, so get their feedback. It is easier to grow when you find other groups of customers who can use the same products you are selling because nobody has made it easy for them to buy. It is easier to grow when you find many segments of "customers from heaven."

14. More staff and controls. As sales grew, Kotula found that he needed more staff. So nine months after he started his business, he hired his first assistant. Soon, he fired his first assistant for stealing his lists. He also hired someone to watch inventory for ordering, and he started a phone room to take calls (Kotula did not add 800 numbers until much later – he let his customers pay for their own calls). He showed all his staff how to build the log splitter and the other items they sold because he wanted them to be product-line experts. Kotula developed his own rules for hiring employees. He looked for hard workers characterized by punctuality, courtesy, and mechanical ability. He also wanted them to be clean cut and not drunk (isn't it amazing that people showed up for job interviews in a state of intoxication?).

Lesson: Some people have great work habits and attitudes. And then there are the others. Find the former.

15. More stores. Kotula found that his customers came from a wide region, so he decided to add more stores with about 7,000 to 8,000 items per store. He preferred selling through the mail since he could test and experiment before making larger bets on products and marketing strategies. In the stores, he had to have displays, larger levels of inventory and expensive sales personnel, which added to costs. But many customers liked to pick up the equipment, kick the tires and talk to the sales personnel. With his mailing lists, he knew where his customers lived, and he could open stores near the hot markets. Kotula opened bigger stores in large metro areas and smaller stores in rural and semi-urban areas. The smaller stores don't stock the big items. He developed a hot catalog for new products with its own hotline. This allowed him to track sales of new products and reject unsuccessful ones. The only catalog that he developed without first testing it was the first one. He based all the products after that on testing.

Lesson: There is a role for instinct, and that is to identify the opportunity. ***But those who succeed test their instincts.***

16. Hiring at the right level. As the business continued to grow, Kotula got a 65,000-square-foot warehouse. But he outgrew that space within a year. He hired a professional warehouse manager and started hiring more seasoned people and managers. In retrospect, Kotula thinks he could have gone up a notch in some areas of hiring, such as in purchasing, where he had two buyers, but could have had better decisions with a vice-president of merchandising who could make decisions independently. He hired vice-presidents in his fifth year. One of his goals in hiring managers was to do less fire fighting, and have more time to think about how to increase the company's competitive advantage. One area where he thinks he could have done better was in developing more co-op advertising with his vendors, in which they absorb some of the cost and offer better terms and more exclusivity due to Northern Tool's increasing clout. As vendors became more interested in promoting their products, Kotula hired a more aggressive executive to strike better deals, such as exclusivity on the company's hottest products. He also hired professional mail-list analysts to sift through the customers to find out more about them and their interests and to increase cross-selling.

Lesson: Understand the types and skill levels of the people you need to hire. If you hire relatively inexperienced managers rather than high-level vice-presidents who have the experience to make better decisions more independently, you will spend more time on the details and less on the important strategic decisions that help growth and profits.

17. Know your numbers and financial statements. Kotula is a fanatic about numbers. He learned from the best, Don Nyrop, who ran Northwest Airlines with an iron fist. He tracks sales performance of each store on a daily basis and compares it to previous periods and the same day in previous years. He also ranks the stores to see which are doing well and which are not. Consistent poor performance gets his attention. He tracks his income statement, inventory, and cash flow on a weekly basis, again ranks the stores and devotes more attention to the ones at the bottom. The statements are widely circulated among key decision makers so that all of them are fully aware of how the company is doing. He likes to get his key staff together each week to discuss the finances and to improve coordination between sales, marketing, inventory control, and cash flow.

Lesson: Good numbers and face-to-face discussion among respectful colleagues improve coordination. *Become an information-driven company.*

18. Northern Tool & Equipment University. Kotula believes in training his staff when they join, as they grow into new jobs, and as the company adds new products. This keeps the staff motivated, since they see a long-term future with the company. The university also trains the staff to sell "one more thing" to customers and to up-sell.

Lesson: *Help others achieve their own goals, and they will be motivated to achieve your common goals.*

19. The hardcover catalog. One of the ideas Kotula received from his printer was to try hard-cover catalogs. Initially, Kotula reprinted his paperback catalog as a hardcover. That strategy failed. When they improved the paper, the hardcover catalog succeeded. These looked much better and lasted much longer than the paperback catalogs. The hardcover catalog's shelf life is "forever," i.e., the customers seldom throw it out. The hardcover catalogs improved the average ticket, the percentage of repeat business, the perceived value, and the profits. Kotula has increased the hardcover mailing from 50,000 in the first year to about 700,000 now. He sends them to his best customers, the larger farms and large construction firms. Kotula has found that smaller catalogs are very good for selling products, while larger ones can also help promote the company's image.

Lesson: Test, read, and react. Then expand when everything works. That is Kotula's rule.

20. Global business expansion. Northern Tool plans to be a global company, selling in every viable international market and buying from partners around the world. The company already sells in Europe and Canada, and plans to move into South America soon. In addition, Northern Tool recently started buying tractors and other products from China. He informed the executive who visited China to buy something on his first trip. This was his method of seeing how well the vendor did. Kotula wanted to see the difference between the vendor's promises and performance.

Lesson: Test new strategies, but try it with a small sample.

Rules for Entrepreneurs from Don Kotula of Northern Tool & Equipment

- **Find a market waiting with unmet needs.** Know the customers and their needs.
- **Hire the most talented staff you can attract.** Kotula looks for people with a bounce to their step, not necessarily years on their résumé. *He would rather hire attitude with the right aptitude rather than years of experience combined with lack of enthusiasm.*

- **Keep good records.** Kotula believes in extremely timely (practically instantaneous) reports and information. He keeps a very close watch on the numbers of the business, including sales, profits, inventory, and cash flow.
- **Track performance**. Kotula also tracked performance so he knew his best performers and the worst ones. No one wanted to be at the bottom for four weeks in a row.
- **Travel and examine**. Kotula believes in examining the various operations in person, especially the ones that are showing subpar results.
- **Change your vision and job description as the business grows**. Having grown Northern Tool from a startup to over $800 million in sales, Kotula's advice is to find good managers who can handle the operations, monitor them constantly so you know what is going on, and then spend the time on the big picture and on your competitive advantage. ***Always look at the next step***.
- **Mostly promote from within**. Kotula always keeps a list of those who are good and performing well. He likes to promote from within, but occasionally goes outside. "A little fresh blood does not hurt" is his motto.
- **Motivation**. Kotula believes in giving high incentives for great performance. His sales staff can make an additional 50 to 75 percent more than the base.
- **To motivate customers, learn what works**. Kotula offers gift cards to his best customers, who love equipment and tools. He has found that a $20 gift card can result in a $150 sale of an item that would not have otherwise sold.
- **Eliminate weaknesses**. Kotula has always liked numbers and had an accounting background. He also was good at sales by learning at his dad's salvage yard. His first job taught him catalog marketing. His second, at Northwest Airlines, taught him how to operate efficiently and effectively. His third job took him back to equipment sales. By the time he started his business, he was very well prepared. He continued to learn, test, and improve.
- **Enjoy your venture and find people who enjoy their job**. "If you like what you do, it is not work."

Ed Flaherty
Rapid Oil Change

MINNEAPOLIS, MINN

Jump on a trend to change oil and build a $200 million+ chain

Summary: At the age of 11, Ed Flaherty started mowing lawns. His dad saw that Flaherty was starting to make money and told him, "Congratulations, you are now grown up and can buy your own clothes." He was only half-joking. Flaherty continued to work at his dad's auto body shop and his dad's friend's auto junk yard, learning more and more about cars. When he finished high school and college, he set out to be a school teacher. But before that came the Army. Flaherty worked at the Pentagon and got an MBA in the evening. Then he joined a consulting firm that worked with the Pentagon, where he drummed up so much business that he was offered a partnership. But he did not want to stay in the East Coast, and went back to his native Montana to teach. After a year of teaching, the entrepreneurial bug bit him and he started a company that sold software to high school coaches. The software helped coaches to analyze team tendencies. To expand and get more resources, he moved the company to Minneapolis from Montana. As he was selling his software and franchises around the country, he was introduced to a computer service bureau that was unloading its assets. He bought the assets for $1 plus assumed $15,000 of debt, and grew the company from $0 in sales to $1.25 million. In the meantime, he found that service stations expected him to leave his car there all day to get his oil changed, and he had seen a different model where they did it faster and more conveniently. So he leased a gas station close to his house and started his first Rapid Oil Change. While the name said Rapid, Flaherty knew that he was not that fast. One day, the chief mechanic of an Indy-car racing team (whose name Flaherty never found) came to his store and gave him detailed suggestions to become faster at oil changes. This is when Rapid truly became rapid. The chain grew and Flaherty soon found himself courted by the major oil companies. He sold to one of them, took the proceeds and bought the rights to grow Applebee's restaurants and developed a chain with sales in the hundreds of millions. It helps to be at the right place at the right time with the right smarts. This is how he dit it.

Before the Startup

1. **Cars, cars and more cars**. Ed Flaherty's dad was in the auto body shop business, where Flaherty used to hang out and see what cars were all about. Around the age of 13, he started to work at one of his dad's friend's junkyards, where he learned even more about cars. Flaherty wanted to own a car, and his dad suggested that Flaherty buy a wrecked car and fix it. So Flaherty bought a two-door 1955 Chevy hardtop that had been in an accident. Its left front was wrecked and it was sitting in his dad's shop. Flaherty bought it for $140, spent $200 for parts and fixed it with the help of his dad and his team. Flaherty did not have a driver's license yet so he could not drive the car. When it was fixed, his dad mentioned that there was a new guy in town who wanted to buy a car, and suggested that Flaherty sell the car. So he agreed and asked his dad to sell the car for $750. His dad came home the next day with $700 and told Flaherty, "I think the price is pretty good." By 20, Flaherty had fixed about 18 more cars. His goal was to buy them cheap, fix them to "make them look good" and sell them. In the summer he worked at his dad's shop for $1 an hour and fixed cars on weekends and evenings. He saved his money so he could invest in a business.

   Lesson: When you see an opportunity, grab it. When you see a hurdle, overcome it. When you expect to need money to start your business, save it.

2. **The college years**. Flaherty was also an athlete. The summer before his senior year of high school, Flaherty decided that he wanted to be All-State, All-American and the captain of the football team. Setting these goals, *and writing them down*, helped him set his priorities, and according to Flaherty, it helped with his maturity. He was going to school, working forty hours a week at his father's shop, fixing cars and lifting weights to get into shape. As he puts it, he enjoyed every minute of it and none of it seemed like "work." He achieved all his goals. He became the captain of his high school football team. It won the state football championship and he was named All-State and All-American (1962). As Flaherty puts it, "setting goals and working toward them is a gift you can give yourself. Money is only a barometer. Achievement is not about money." When he graduated, he went to college on a football scholarship. There, he got hurt and that ended his football career. He graduated from college with a degree in math and education. He was planning on becoming a teacher and coach.

   Lesson: Set achievable goals and work hard to reach them (sounds like a cliché, but unless you are incredibly lucky, it isn't).

3. **Pentagon whiz kid**. When Flaherty graduated, the Vietnam war was raging and he was drafted. After eight months of training, he was assigned to the Pentagon to help one of Secretary of Defense Robert McNamara's whiz kids. This individual had been planning on becoming an astronaut, but he got hurt and became a whiz

kid. Flaherty learned the value of thoroughness from this job. Previously, as he puts it, he tended to be a "short-cut artist" and got to "80 percent of the answer." At the Pentagon, he had to get to "110 percent of the answer"; otherwise, he would have the honor of redoing his work. He had to examine under every stone and defend every assertion. His bosses were demanding and threw back bad work. Flaherty found that he was capable of doing good work, although he had never challenged himself in the past. Now he had to.

Lesson: Your returns depend on your investment. *Talent without dedication is a waste of resources.*

4. **Part-time MBA**. When Flaherty went to the Army, he had two choices. He could see it as a waste of time and act accordingly, or he could make full use of it and take advantage of the resources available to him. Since he was based in Washington, D.C., he decided to get something out of it. In addition to his full-time job, he went to school four nights a week and studied on the weekends. He got his MBA degree from George Washington University in two years.

Lesson: Time is precious. Don't waste it.

5. **Consulting sales.** When Flaherty got out of the Army, he joined a small management-consulting company that worked with the military. There were about forty very smart people in this consulting company, with about half of them having Ph.D.s. The owner was the only rainmaker in the firm, getting all the contracts. Flaherty knew he could get sales contracts because he knew the Department of Defense, he knew the contract process, he knew the analysts, he knew their problems, and he knew they had the budgets for consultants. He started calling on the analysts and talking to them about their problems, which they would freely tell him when asked. He would then regurgitate their problems back to them in the form of a proposal that his firm and the high-IQ people could solve, and get the contracts. Flaherty found the pain and solved it. According to Flaherty, the high-IQ people were mostly introverts and could not find clients, but could solve problems. Soon Flaherty grew tired of the East Coast, so he decided to go back to his native Montana and become a coach and teacher. When he gave his notice of resignation to the owner of the firm, he was offered 10 percent of the firm if he stayed. Flaherty told him, "I want 90 percent. Ten percent does not work for me." He exited, stage left.

Lesson: ***Hunt. Kill. Eat. In business, nothing happens until you get the sale***. If you can sell, you have a valuable talent. To sell, know the pain that your potential customers have, and understand how you can solve it. When you know the terrain, you become a better hunter. So hunt in the terrain you know, or get to know the terrain you want to hunt in.

From Startup to Profits

6. **The first business.** After returning to Montana, Flaherty found that he did not like teaching and coaching. So he started his first business while he was a teacher, with his savings and a $15,000 loan from his family. He developed a product that offered a computerized scouting system to football coaches. He developed and wrote the software with some help and started to sell it, along with the service, to high school and college football coaches in his area. This is when he began to realize as many other young men and women before him that Montana was a "desert for opportunity." So he moved his business to Minneapolis. He needed a place to process the data and found two men who had a computer service business. He bought their assets (hardware and software) because they wanted to upgrade, but he could not buy the customers. He did not have the cash to make a down payment but offered them a five-year note that he would pay out of cash flow. He then found other teachers like him around the country and licensed them to sell the software and service in a franchise agreement. Why did he franchise? He did not have the funding to expand himself, and he wanted to cover a wider territory. He knew that teachers did not make much money, so many of them also became entrepreneurs and had a part-time business. The key was finding them. He went to a new town, got dimes and started calling people involved in football, including coaches, athletes, directors, state football association members, etc. He was looking for people who were enterprising and liked sports. He occupied the phone booths in the lobby for hours because the phones in the room were very expensive. The athletic business started to grow, but it was very travel intensive and he was gone for two to three months at a time. He found that he could not spend enough time on the athletic business and his service bureau and do justice to both. Flaherty was newly married, and he and his wife had a new son, so he did not want to travel as much. He was also living on Diet Cokes and popcorn for a few weeks at a time when money was tight, and the diet was getting tiresome. So he sold off the athletic business. The athletic segment, however, had helped the growth of the computer service bureau, and Flaherty had added regular business processing, such as accounts payable and accounts receivable processing, and built it to annual sales of over $1 million.

> **Lesson**: Although Flaherty attributes this early success to his flexibility (in moving to Minneapolis), hard work, and perseverance, he did not fully assess the potential before entering the business. If he had, he would have learned how complex a business it was. But if this had stopped him from starting his business, he may not have moved to his next phase, which was a gold mine in the guise of used oil.

7. **Side business in real estate.** Flaherty majored in architecture for the first two of years of college before he switched to math. He was always interested in real estate, so every year he would design one home in the winter, build it in the

spring, and sell it in the summer or fall. They were all speculative homes, and at first Flaherty borrowed their entire cost. Later, he would take all his profits and reinvest in the next new home and continuously increased the size of the home and its cost. This worked very well, until interest rates soared to 18 percent. The last home after that rate jump ate up all the profits in his real estate projects.

Lesson: Buy right and you can make a fortune. Buy in a bubble and it can cost you one.

8. **Future of the service business.** Flaherty built the service business to an annual sales level of $1.25 million, and he was always monitoring technology and trends, so he could decide his future direction. This future became limited when the first Altair was introduced. The Altair was the first personal computer. Previously, with the dominance of the mainframes, most small businesses could not afford to buy a computer, so they used a service bureau that could allocate the time of a mainframe among a variety of users. With the introduction of the PC, everyone could afford to buy a computer. Flaherty became one of the first dealers of the Altair in the Twin Cities. When he installed the first PC at a client's office, the client laid off five people in the back office. Flaherty knew that the days of the service bureau were numbered. He sold it.

Lesson: Track trends. *When trends are favorable, take advantage before others do, i.e. before the others.* When unfavorable, jump off before others.

9. **The oil-change business**. To get his car's oil changed, Flaherty used a gas station that was near his office. The station's customers had to leave their cars all day for an oil change. On one of his trips, Flaherty had seen a 10-minute oil change store in Southern California and thought that the concept was ripe for Minnesota. So he decided to exit the computer-service industry and enter the oil-change industry. For his first location, Flaherty selected an empty gas station in one of the Twin Cities' suburbs. He leased this store, which had two bays, from a private school on a three-to-five-year lease term, the renewal of which he would have to negotiate with a member of the school board. He cleaned up the store, put up signs, bought inventory, and hired a manager. He had just entered his new business, which was amazingly like his first business in the auto-repair industry. The key reason for his selection of this particular location was that it was close to his home. As he puts it, "Divine providence was looking after me." This turned out to be his best store due to the large number of homes, businesses and heavy traffic in the area. His initial success with it helped him rapidly expand to more stores in the metro area, and his next six were among the best in his portfolio.

Lesson: Keep your eyes open. When you see an attractive business opportunity, see how you can benefit in other markets. Flaherty realized that quick oil changes were the new thing to help people save time and add convenience. He moved out of the shrinking service bureau business and entered the new, hot thing.

10. Make the operation efficient and live up to its name. Although he was advertising a 10-minute oil change, each one was actually taking him 30 minutes. One afternoon, in his store in the Minneapolis suburb of Bloomington, a customer came in and began studying his operation intently. Being the friendly sort, Flaherty started chatting with the man, who turned out to be an employee of Andy Granatelli, the owner of a famous race-car team. This man knew how to change oil and how to do it fast. It turned out that his wife was from Bloomington, he was in town to visit her parents and he was bored stiff. His first comment to Flaherty was, "You don't know what you're doing, do you?" When Flaherty agreed, the gentleman reorganized the store's layout and helped Flaherty reduce the time to change oil from 30 minutes to 5 to 7. This man gave a tremendous gift to Flaherty, but he never gave his name.

Lesson: You need to be smart and hard working. But it helps to be lucky. What's interesting is that the ones who become lucky are among the ones who are smart and hardworking.

11. Cash flow and profits. Rapid Oil Change had positive cash flow from month one. Each store had positive cash flow, and Flaherty made sure that he only went into locations where he knew he could develop cash flow immediately. To achieve this, Flaherty first analyzed his competitors' prices without accounting for any temporary promotions and loss leaders. He realized that many customers were willing to pay up to twice as much as the "loss leader" prices that his competitors sometimes promoted. He segmented his customers and used loss-leader pricing only to get the marginal customer who could come in during slow periods when the store was not busy and be willing to wait for three to four hours. Flaherty calculated his fixed and variable costs, estimated his sales, and determined that he needed 50 percent gross margins (after accounting for direct labor and direct materials) to be competitive and profitable and reach 20 percent operating-income margins (operating income divided by revenues), which was his goal. Some of his stores reached operating-income margins of 40 percent. He estimated his corporate overhead at 5 percent of sales.

Lesson: *Test your pricing to the find the right level.* Pricing is often the most important decision, especially for revolutionary products or services. Since quick oil changes were new in his markets, Flaherty had to truly understand the amount of premium his customers were willing to pay to avoid the long waits. He found through market testing that he did not need to discount that price. However, he offered a program for his price-sensitive customers who could wait, thus allowing him to show a marked differentiation between his two price levels. In addition to knowing the competitive value of your product or service, you need to know your costs and be able to project revenues with a reasonable level of confidence to achieve the desired level of profits.

12. Promotion. Initially, Flaherty did not know the right way to promote the quick oil-change services to attract the type of customer he wanted. So he tested a variety of media to see what worked and what did not. He realized that he needed two kinds of promotion. He needed to build his brand throughout the metro area so that customers would learn of his business and feel comfortable using his services. Brand building also attracted the higher-margin customer. He achieved this objective through mass media such as TV and radio. However, to attract traffic to each store, he needed to conduct neighborhood-targeted marketing, and this he did with direct mail, door-to-door coupons, and advertising in the local newspaper. He measured his investment, and the sales and margin returns from each media investment, eliminating ones that did not work and enhancing those that did.

> **Lesson**: ***New businesses usually fail to project accurately in two key areas: The first is the level and timing of revenues, where entreprenerus are too optimistic. The second is the cost, and the right way, to get sales, i.e. your sales drivers***. There is an old cliché in advertising that "half your advertising works and the other half does not. The problem is knowing which half works." Actually, if you don't know which half, you also don't know if it is only half that is a waste. Test, test, test to know what works and what does not.

From Profits to the Moon

13. Rapid's growth. As the business started to grow, leases became a problem. If a lease ended, the profits ended. This meant that Flaherty needed to own the real estate. However, two other trends were coming together in his favor. The savings and loan associations had been deregulated; they were flush with cash and had developed loose lending practices. In addition, due to the Arab oil embargo of the early 1970s, there were numerous gas stations that had closed, and the owners were ready to unload them at fire-sale prices. Flaherty found that this was an ideal situation for him. He could buy the stations with 20 percent down, fix them up, get them reappraised at 120 percent of his total cost, borrow to recoup his investment, and reuse the funds in a new site. The prices when he purchased were attractive because oil companies wanted to unload the stations. His repairs and reuse as a Rapid Oil Change station added value due to his attractive business model, and allowed him to borrow his entire investment. This was the virtuous circle for Flaherty, and he rode it all the way to the late1980s when all the best sites had been taken, resulting in higher prices for the stations. And the savings and loan industry's poor lending practices had destroyed the industry and resulted in the end of a cheap source of expansion capital.

> **Lesson**: One of the key ingredients you need when you grow is the right financing. Normally, high growth and high levels of debt are not compatible with each other because debt comes with debt service, which means you need cash flow to make the payments. However, *because Flaherty bought stations at attractive locations at good prices, and was able to increase their value and increase cash flow, he was able to borrow against his property and reuse his equity*

for more growth. The key to this strategy was that each store started to show a positive cash flow immediately to repay the debt.

14. Find excellent store managers. As the chain grew, Flaherty needed to find excellent managers for the stores so he could minimize any operational problems and focus on growth. At first, he looked for people from the auto industry, but they did not last because the pace of his operations were fast and Flaherty expected a high level of customer service. He studied the job requirements for his store managers and realized that he needed people who liked fast-paced work. When he tried a few from the convenience store industry, he found that they only liked to collect money behind the cash register and liked a slower pace. However, one of his early successful managerial hires was from the fast-food industry. Flaherty found that the fast-food industry trained its managers to manage people, equipment and operations to provide a high quality of product (as much quality as fast food can deliver) and service. And they needed to know "time compression," i.e., how to deliver this high-level of service in a fast-paced environment. Also, the fast-food industry paid its store managers well, but the industry was not as generous with its assistant managers. Since the fast-food industry was starting to slow down from its torrid rate of growth, the assistant store managers were no longer finding as many challenging opportunities for growth and promotion – and were facing a dead end. Flaherty's new store manager, who had been an assistant manager at a fast-food store, pointed out to him that the pace at his new job was just as fast, challenging and fun as his old job in fast food. But that it was more profitable. This manager also knew many fast-food assistant managers who were anxious to make their mark and eager to jump into a hot new company that valued their skills more. Flaherty started recruiting from the fast-food industry.

Lesson: First of all, know what you want. Otherwise, how will you know when you are not reaching your goals? Flaherty claims he "lucked out" when he started finding fast-food assistant managers, but he had developed standards and was measuring his managers against this standard. He was analyzing the problem, constantly measuring to identify the best managers, and then seeking more like them. That is why good luck seems to favor smart, hard-working people.

15. Motivate employees to offer great customer service. To make sure that everyone was working toward the same goal, Flaherty set up an incentive system at Rapid. Everyone in the store received a percentage of store profits. He split his operating income with managers, assistants and employees and structured it so that they made more if Flaherty made more. Flaherty found that some managers turned customers away before closing time to clean the store, so they could finish at the closing time. So Flaherty added a $1 incentive per car after a certain number of cars were serviced during the day. He also offered a share of sales from parts. However, to prevent his employees from selling parts that customers did not need, the employees did not receive any percentage if the parts sales exceeded a certain percent of store sales. He did not want greed to affect customer satisfaction. Flaherty also believed in giving his existing employees first shot at any managerial positions, if they were outstanding employees and had the right attitudes. This motivated them to work harder.

Lesson: Structure incentive packages intelligently. ***People work for themselves.*** If you are fair with them and offer them a fair share of the profits, they will work harder for you. But make sure you develop a fair system and don't offer incentives that could short-change your customer.

16. Control the operation. Flaherty is a huge believer in controls and security. At the time that Flaherty was building Rapid, there were no point-of-sale cash registers. So Flaherty used numerically sequenced invoices to minimize the temptation and threat of employee theft. He had lots of internal auditors, and managers needed to complete a variety of control sheets at the end of each day. He also had an area manager for every six to eight stores. Half of the area manager's time was devoted to relieving his store managers so that the area manager could audit the store. Early in the morning, on a random basis, the area manager would inform the store manager that he was going to that store and that the store manager could take the day off. This allowed the area manager to track all the variables at the store and compare performance with other days to check for any discrepancies. Flaherty developed a system of checks and balances. He got an accounting of physical inventory, such as oil and oil filters, every day. Flaherty believed that a few will steal no matter how controlled the system, but he wanted a system that kept the marginal person honest. He also wanted the employees to know that if they stole, they were only putting a great job and benefits, including their career growth, in jeopardy.

Lesson: ***Companies grow to the limits of the entrepreneur's capacity to delegate effectively.*** This is especially true in a cash business.

17. Find great locations. In addition to seeking low-cost real estate and experienced store managers for growth, Flaherty also attempted to understand what made a store's location successful. He tried to build a mathematical model of his store's sales and profits as a function of the location, including variables such as traffic counts, demographics, speed, competition, corners, turn lanes, signage, etc. He came to the conclusion that site selection was half art and half science. One could never completely predict how well the store would do, but he realized that performance was distributed along the normal (or bell-shaped) curve. So he developed an average and standard deviation (which measures how much the sales could vary from the mean according to a probabilistic distribution). If the proposed store location was likely to be profitable at a 3-sigma (about 99 percent probability) level, Flaherty would buy. If not, he would not buy it, unless the underlying real estate was much more valuable than the asking price. In such marginal locations, he would buy the site and build a store for its marginal contribution toward overhead. He never failed due to a location. But he could never find the perfect predictor.

Lesson: In retail, location is key. There may be no such thing as a perfect predictor, and Flaherty found that out. Formulas are not perfect and the key is to develop human judgment (if only the geniuses of Wall Street had figured that out). However, he did his best to analyze locations and to understand the range of possibilities. And he never built on a site unless it was a "sure" winner or if the price was too good to pass up. Where there is any doubt, negotiate a lower price to reduce your risk, negotiate clauses that allow you to terminate the lease if the site does not do as well as you would like, or take a walk. At the beginning of your operation it is far better to risk losing a good site than sign unfavorable terms on a poor site. Even later, you can only afford so many lousy sites.

18. The right growth rate. Flaherty expanded Rapid Oil Change at the rate of six to eight stores per year, with the highest being about 10 per year. His goal was not to grow at any random rate but to grow with control and to be profitable from month one. This meant that he needed to spend the time to find and select the right location and financing, find the best manager and use his scarce resources to promote the store to reach immediate cash flows. Control was more important to him than just a rate of growth, but he also wanted to grow fast enough to be able to capture the best sites that were available.

Lesson: ***Control your greed and the fear.*** There is no magic number for a growth rate. The key is the market need and your resources — financial and managerial. Always ***expand under control*** and build your infrastructure as you grow.

19. Grow organically or via franchising. In 10 years, Flaherty had reached annual sales levels of about $37 million in 83 stores. All of the stores were company owned. Flaherty did not want to franchise the concept, since the stores were very profitable, paid for themselves from the first month, and he could take his money out and invest in a new store. He wanted to control his risk by allocating his scarce resources to his own stores than to a franchising infrastructure in which he would have to give away a lot of the profits to franchisees.

Lesson: If profits per store and return on investment are very high, grow organically. If they are moderate, consider franchising.

20. The exit. There were three giants in the oil-supply industry, Pennzoil, Quaker, and Valvoline. Valvoline did not have an alliance with a retail chain, unlike Pennzoil and Quaker, and it was eager to establish one to enhance its brand at the retail level. So Valvoline ardently courted Flaherty to sell to it. Flaherty was also experiencing a tightening of the real estate market and a reduction in attractive locations, which drove prices higher. He was also facing a restriction in financing that made it tougher to secure attractive financing, and knew that his net worth was tied up in this one business. So when Valvoline expressed its interest and willingness to buy, Flaherty did his homework. He found that one of Ashland's (Valvoline's parent company) board members had sold his own company to Valvoline and did not object to Ashland enriching entrepreneurs. He also got positive feedback about his firm at a Valvoline reception. So when Valvoline made an initial low-ball offer, Flaherty countered with $50 million, which was an attractive price for him ("like a medical company" according to Flaherty), and pointed out to Ashland why it was still a bargain due to its expansion potential. In addition to his price, he also got a very nice package to stay on and manage the business for the buyer. Over the next two years, Valvoline invested $100 million to expand the chain to 240 stores with annual sales of nearly $200 million. At the end of two years, he had his annual meeting with the CEO of Valvoline. Flaherty opened by saying that he wanted more authority to run the division. Valvoline's CEO opened by saying that he wanted to tighten control. Obviously, they did not agree. Flaherty left the company. They parted amicably, and Flaherty admired Valvoline's integrity.

Lesson: Do your homework to get the right price. But realize that oil and water don't mix just as entrepreneurs and corporations usually don't mix.

Post Sale

21. Building new businesses. After selling Rapid Oil Change and building it to nearly $200 million in sales, Flaherty had no business but plenty of cash. He invested in three businesses and land:

- Miller Milling, which Flaherty and his partners built from a startup to $250 million in sales. The company produces bread flour and semolina, which is used in pasta.
- Applebee's: Flaherty and his partners were the first franchisees of Applebee's, and they built it to 170 stores in eight states and $300 million in sales at its peak.
- A sign company that Flaherty built to $35 million in sales, and
- Enough land to build 500,000 square feet of office and retail space around one of the top shopping centers in the Twin Cities.

Lesson: Once you have money, you have more options.

Rules for Entrepreneurs from Ed Flaherty of Rapid Oil Change

- **Have the right motivation**. Fear of failure was a key motivator for Flaherty. Find yours.
- **Find your passion**. Flaherty ate popcorn for dinner on many days and worked long hours before he succeeded. Don't start your business for money. You may not make much. Do what you love.

- **Never give up.** There were many days when Flaherty was tempted to quit and get a job. Why did he not do that? See "passion" above.
- **Pay attention to the details.** That is where the devil resides.
- **Don't be dependent on a few customer**s. Diversify your customer base.
- **Make sure you structure your costs and investment so that you are profitable.** Flaherty liked 10 to 20-percent operating-income margins.
- **Build barriers to entry**. Offer great service if you don't have any other barriers.
- **The golden rule matters.** Treat employees and customers the way you want to be treated.
- **Be lucky.** Working hard and smart seems to help in this regard.
- **Save**. Defer gratification so you have a nest egg to invest when the right opportunity comes.
- **Business before employees.** First take care of the business before taking care of the employees. If you don't survive, you will not be able to take care of them anyhow.
- **Produce**. In the end, we are all paid to produce.
- **Time your acts**. Flaherty sold the Applebee's stores when the segment became very competitive. Know when to enter. Know when to exit.

Glenn Hasse
Ryt-Way Industries

Lakeville, Minn

Building one of the country's largest outsourced food-packaging companies

Summary: Glenn Hasse started helping his mother and older brother manage his parents' drive-in restaurant at Excelsior, Minn., at the age of 11. His dad managed a creamery in Plainview, Minn., which was 100 miles from Excelsior. His dad's goal was to manage the best creamery in the state. After Glenn spent two summers of long days working at the drive-in and dealing with customers, he started working at the creamery for his dad. Hasse learned how to run a spotless, state-of-the-art food operation from his dad, who emphasized the need for cleanliness, sanitation, effectiveness, and efficiency. These lessons were his foundation when he started Ryt-Way before he was 24. He started packaging general products for large corporate customers, some of whom were in the food business. He found that he liked the food industry and that he could erect barriers to competition, earning a higher return. So he focused on blending, packaging, and distributing food products for large consumer food companies such as Quaker Oats and General Mills. As he grew, he continuously searched for new packaging concepts. One such concept that he developed was the coated cereal cup that could be heated for retail consumers and for hotel breakfasts. This breakthrough helped his company take off. When Hasse sold Ryt-Way, it had a throughput value of about $800 million, more than 600 full-time employees and 280 part-time in three plants that covered more than 600,000 square feet. The original investment in the business was about $3,000. This is how he did it.

Before the Startup

1. The first job. Hasse's dad managed a creamery in Plainview, Minn., and his brother and he would help out whenever they could. When Hasse was 11, his dad bought a drive-in restaurant, and Hasse and his older brother helped his mother manage it. Hasse learned the value of customer service – the friendliest carhops made the largest tips. He did this for two summers, after which he started to work for his dad at the creamery. At the creamery, Hasse learned that his father was a hard taskmaster because he wanted to run the best creamery in the state. The creamery was open seven days a week and his father expected people to put in the effort. He wanted all the food-processing equipment kept ultra-clean to avoid all bacteria. But his dad never asked anyone to do what he would not himself do, including working long hours and doing physical labor, when needed. And he would always reward those who worked hard and worked smart. None of his employees left their jobs voluntarily and he let them go only if their performance was not satisfactory. His dad worked till he was 72, and he never took a vacation.

Lesson: Average does not win when someone is willing to work harder and smarter. And hard work with friendly service beats hard work alone. Hasse also learned that he wanted to be in a business that did not have perishable food due to the problems with processing food on a 24/7 basis. It was a mission without a break.

2. **The college years**. After finishing high school, Hasse entered the Institute of Technology at the University of Minnesota. One high school teacher had noted that Hasse did not fit the profile of an engineer, but Hasse entered the program anyway. After a year of studying to be an engineer, he realized that his teacher was right and that he did not enjoy engineering as much as he thought he would. For one, he found that there were very few girls in engineering, and that the guys were intelligent but not much fun. He found that he enjoyed business administration more, so he switched his major. He also thought that business school would be a better preparing ground to develop leadership qualities. He thought that he could always hire an engineer if he had an engineering problem. He continued working in the creamery during summers, weekends and on vacations.

Lesson: Know who you are and what you want.

3. **The first corporate job**. When Hasse finished his bachelor's degree in business administration, the Vietnam war was raging, and he had a 1A draft number. This meant that he had a high probability of being drafted, so he was limited in his choice of jobs. Employers did not want to hire someone who was likely to be around for only a short time. The best job he could find was as an assistant buyer in men's clothing at a local department store. After six months in this position, he was promoted to being an assistant to an executive V.P. Hasse found that, although he was always excited about getting up and getting to work every day no matter how horrible the circumstances, many employees at the department store did not share his enthusiasm nor did they believe in doing a great job. They were mainly interested in pleasing their managers. Based on his short stint in the corporate world, Hasse decided that he was not cut out for corporate life. He wanted to do what he thought was right, rather than always trying to read his managers' minds. He lasted at the department store for 18 months, after which he joined the Minnesota Air National Guard for four months. He wanted to become a pilot, but the demand for flight

training was very high, and the Air Force had priority. So Hasse did not get into flight school. After four months of service, he left full-time duty. His father noted that one of his customers in Northfield, Minn., had a new product and was looking for someone to run with it.

Lesson: Pursue your passion and you may not notice the long hours.

From Startup to Profits

4. Starting the venture. Hasse met with the principals of the proposed venture and found out that they had developed a new packaging concept, packaging instant non-fat dry milk from his father's creamery into poly bags instead of using the traditional paper boxes with foil overwraps. They were offering a high-quality product in a better package than was generally available, and they wanted Hasse to package the product. Hasse calculated the number of bags that could be produced. He assumed that, with the capacity of the equipment, he would do very well. With a capacity of 400 cases per day, he expected to have sales of $660,000 per year. The packaging service fee was $36,000 and Hasse would have a net income of $15,000, or about twice what he could have made at an executive job working for a large corporation. Hasse would buy the equipment from the inventor, who would finance it. Hasse expected no problems in selling his entire inventory. He agreed to package the product exclusively for the inventor. Hasse bought the equipment, hired employees and started what he thought would be a new profitable enterprise. However, after selling 2,500 cases, they ran into a brick wall. They could not sell any more product. So Hasse realized that he would also have to sell the product if he wanted to survive. But even with all his efforts, he found that he could only sell an average of 10 cases a day, which translated to about $400 in sales. To increase sales, he met with Hancock-Nelson, a major food distributor in the Twin Cities. The executive at Hancock-Nelson pointed out to Hasse that food is a percentage business. If they sell some product for $20, they would make two percent, or 40 cents. If they sell if for $11 as Hasse was proposing, they would only make 22 cents. Since customers were buying the higher-priced product anyway, he asked Hasse, "Why should I buy yours?" He told Hasse that having the lowest price would not get the channels excited. Hasse had about $3,000 invested in the business, which included his entire life savings of $1,000, along with money from his family. He was stuck. He had to find a solution.

Lesson: Hasse learned a number of lessons from this stage of the business.

- Customers never beat a path to your door. No matter how good your product, you have to know what makes people buy and you have to sell your benefits.
- Do not start a business with only one prospective customer (unless of course you have a guaranteed contract assuring your profitability). Identify more prospects; i.e., do not put all your eggs in one basket. That is an old cliché but a true one.

- A lower price does not always get you business. Obviously, Hasse could have tried to increase his price to offer a higher profit to the distributor. Pricing, margins, and channel discounts are among the key decisions you will make.

5. **Financing the venture**. To start the venture, Hasse invested $1,000 that his father lent him, and his father and brother each invested an additional $1,000. After two years, they each invested an additional $3,000. Hasse, his father, and brother each started out with 33.3 percent of the venture. But, after two years, the company owed Hasse a portion of his salary, and the shareholders agreed to change Hasse's ownership to 66.7 percent of the venture in lieu of his salary, and his father and brother ended up with 16.7 percent each.

 Lesson: When you are starting out, the only ones who may finance you are your friends and family. Be nice to them.

6. **Check for alternatives**. Hasse now faced a choice – he could try to make this venture a success, or quit and try something else. His brief stint in corporate America had convinced him that he did not belong there. So he started searching for alternative customers. This time he first started with some criteria. He did not want a service with geographic limitations. He wanted to have the ability to sell in national or international markets. The higher level of competition in these larger markets did not bother him, because he was confident that he could provide value to customers and be competitively priced. He had one direct competitor in the Twin Cities and others who were scattered around the country. When he attended a trade convention, he overheard one of his competitors telling a colleague that "he was going to whip that guy" (meaning Hasse). This only made Hasse more determined, and he decided to prove to customers that he could satisfy their needs. He found that his original assumption about the level of demand in the milk business was incorrect, so he approached a customer-promotion company and offered to package any items that they could not do themselves, or products that did not fit easily into their operation. His first product was to package foreign coins in a pouch for a meat company that wanted to use them in its promotions. He added more equipment and got additional business from Malt-o-Meal, General Mills, and Hormel. Hasse agreed to package anything that he could find. Why did they select him? According to Hasse, he "was dumb enough to do it." He made enough profit to keep his doors open.

 Lesson: Without knowing it, Hasse had stumbled into outsourcing at the dawn of the outsourcing age. If Hasse had done a "business plan" before he started, he may have discovered that his original plan was infeasible and may not have entered the business. But once he was in, he did not want to admit failure. Sometimes it helps to be in the right place before the right time – and then to hang on till the wave takes off.

7. **Control costs and learn to price**. Hasse had learned that price was a very important factor in his industry and as noted earlier, he had to worry about the pricing at each level of the food-distribution chain. *Having a cheaper product did not mean that the distributors would sell it. He tested constantly to check what the market would bear.* He would try different pricing levels and margins to see what worked and what did not. To stay competitive, he made sure to keep his cost of equipment and labor low. He excelled at cost control. When he got a major contract with Hormel, he designed and built the equipment himself. His year in engineering had just paid off. He improved the automation of the equipment as he got more experience and specialized in improving its efficiency. He realized that the food business had some unique aspects that he could master. Due to Food & Drug Administration (FDA) regulations and inspections, he realized that there were barriers to entry, and his experience working with his father had given him the expertise he needed. A company could not just decide to enter the field on a whim. It had to build and design its plant to FDA specs. So he decided to specialize in food packaging. By this time, he had been in business for about four years. He had a small loss in his first and second years and a small profit in his third and fourth. By the fifth year, he reached $1 million in sales. He still could not afford to hire any staff to help him in the office, but he was big enough to move to a larger plant. In the first 10 years, he was the general manager, operations manager, and sales manager. When the plant was busy, he was managing the work. When the plant slowed down, he would solicit business. While this may not have been ideal from the perspective of balancing the work, Hasse realized that he had to do any job that was needed if he were to succeed.

Lesson: For most businesses, the early years are the toughest. Keep your overhead and administrative costs low, and you can survive even with low level of sales. This is when you can "experiment" with alternative products and services, try different markets and pricing, find your competitive edge, and erect barriers to competition to increase your profit margins. Build a strong foundation before constructing the superstructure.

8. **Competitive edge**. Most food companies had their plants in the eastern half of the nation, because that is where most consumers were located. Because Hasse's plant in Minnesota was farther away from the markets, he decided that he would not compete on price, but on his commitment to provide quality, service, and speed. The companies in the food industry worry about the quality of the product (to avoid any harm to their brand), the level of service (to them and to the supply chain), and the timeliness of deliveries (to avoid stock-outs). Not having product on the shelves, especially when a promotion was going on, would be devastating. Those were the variables that focused Hasse's attention.

Lesson: Develop your edge based on your customers' real needs. While all customers have a strong focus on price, it is not the only focus. You need to be able to offer the level of quality, service, and timeliness that customers seek, especially if you are a valuable link of the supply chain. That gets you higher margins and profits.

From Profits to the Moon

9. Growth with 3M. About 40 years ago, 3M Corporation was one of the first to understand the importance of outsourcing and made it a part of their core corporate philosophy. They were pioneers in outsourcing before outsourcing became popular. This was the trend that Hasse jumped on to grow his business. When the first copier machine was introduced, it needed a third piece of paper (the onion skin) sandwiched between the original and the copy. 3M wanted millions of packages of 20 onion sheets per package, and these packages had to be assembled in a dimly lit room so as not to spoil the onion sheets, which were light-sensitive. 3M approached Hasse and wanted him to package these onion sheets for them. They had come to the realization that they should stick to the value-added tasks of market monitoring, product development, and marketing. And they were seeking to outsource the lower-end manufacturing and packaging tasks to others who had a lower overhead structure and specialized in this area. However, to keep their vendors lean and mean, 3M was offering only a one-year agreement. This meant that the vendor had to stay competitive and not allow its costs to balloon, since 3M had the option to take its business elsewhere. This short-term agreement also kept Ryt-Way competitive since it had to stay vigilant about costs and efficiency. To keep his risks under control, Hasse amortized any equipment that he had to buy for the customer over the life of the contract, and the customer paid to buy the equipment at its market value if the contract was terminated before it expired.

Lesson: *Understand the importance of protecting your interests when working with large customers and large orders.* It is exciting to think about the growth potential, but make sure that you have protected yourself against the risk of losing the contract and bankrupting your company. Don't gamble your company and your net worth.

10. Finance as a competitive advantage. When Hasse decided to expand his building to handle the added capacity, he contacted the industrial development group in his local community to get favorable terms for his building. Due to the number and quality of jobs he was creating, Ryt-Way was (and is) considered a very attractive company to have in the community, and he got favorable offers for low-cost financing. Instead of adding huge amounts of debt to his balance sheet, Hasse decided to rent the building with an option to buy. This reduced his cash outflow and allowed the use of a larger facility, and he did not have to use his hard-earned equity to pay for real estate. Hasse learned the same lesson when it came to equipment. He knew that his core strength was to manage a very efficient packaging operation and that this business was one of "nickels and dimes." He had to watch his expenses, and more important, he had to watch his risk. So he learned that he always had to have his customers finance the equipment directly or indirectly over the life of the contract. He was not going to risk his low-margin business with high-risk, high-cost equipment that he could not use.

Lesson: *Pick the best financing sources that are available to you from among equity, debt, and development finance sources.* Development finance sources consist of local, state, and federal government sources and the intermediaries who help develop areas. For more on equity, debt and development finance sources, see *Finance Any Business* ***Intelligently***® (available at www.infinancing.com). They offer the cheapest and most attractive financing. Also look to customers and suppliers for financing, especially when they can help to reduce costs. This will reduce your risk and allow you to focus on improving your core strengths rather than lurching into bankruptcy.

11. Key requirements for success. Normally, customers selected a package when they developed a new line of products. The food companies were experts at product development and marketing, but they did not want to blend, package, and transport the product. They left this to the outsourcers. So Hasse had to obtain ingredients from around the country and the world. Ryt-Way would then blend and package the product using specialized equipment, and then issue the product in a variety of packages and quantities. Lastly, Ryt-Way was responsible for shipping the packages *in the right quantity at the right time to the right destination with the right mode of transportation for cost reduction, efficiency, and effectiveness.* This is the expertise that Ryt-Way had to possess – and did. Customers seldom moved the product to another outsourcer after the initial selection due to the potential risks to the supply chain. They only moved it to their own plant when the product became successful, and if the volumes grew to justify their own plant. But only 25 percent of the products became very successful and justified their own plant. This meant that getting the order from the customer was not easy, since the customers wanted to have long-term relationships with the outsourcer (or "blender"). So for most products, Ryt-Way blended, packaged, and distributed the products for the product's lifetime, unless it did not perform to expectations. According to Hasse, the keys were a total dedication to making sure that there were few, if any, mistakes and that the customer did not suffer if there were any. He lost customers only because of a poor fit between the customer's product and Ryt-Way and never because of a poor relationship with the customer.

Lesson: When you are a major component of the business of large corporate customers, each order is worth millions. But each mistake can also cost a significant amount both in money and reputation. Understand the key ingredients to succeed in your business, and then excel at these.

12. Be fair to your employees. Employees are a major component of a business like Ryt-Way. In the early years, as the company was growing and fully utilizing its facility, Hasse was unable to have an adequate employees' lunch room and offer other amenities. There was some grumbling, and a few disgruntled employees tried to organize a union. The effort failed. But this was a wake-up call for Hasse. Everyone talks about how important the employees are to the success of a company. But Hasse learned that he needed to "walk the talk." He started to develop programs to keep his employees happy and offered them competitive benefits and incentives. He started a profit-sharing plan, with 15 percent of any profits above $100,000 going to the employees. Even as the investment in the company increased, perhaps justifying a higher floor for the start of profits, he decided not to change this floor. Near the end of his ownership of the company, Hasse gave 25 percent of net profits to employees and managers. He also promoted people from within the company and provided them with the training to grow. There have been three unionization attempts since. None succeeded. The last one was a lopsided vote against the union.

Lesson: Employees know when the business is doing well. When they feel that management or the owners are not treating them fairly, they strike or organize. If you want to keep your employees happy, take care of them before you are forced to do it, unless of course, you find a way to run your business without employees.

13. Hiring managers. As the business grew, Hasse started to hire managers for various functions. One of the first was a person in charge of the quality-control department. Since this manager worked well with customers, he was also placed in charge of sales and marketing. Hasse also needed a person for a special project. The person whom he put in charge of the project did very well, so Hasse promoted him to operations manager. One of Hasse's chief criteria was how well the person worked with people within the firm and with customers before hiring him as a manager, and he always tried to promote from within. He did not offer stock options to his managers or employees, but he offered generous profit-sharing and bonuses. His goal and philosophy was to treat people as he would want to be treated. He expected that they would put their families first, the business second. This was his father's philosophy. It became his also.

Lesson: Achieving the desired results and having favorable relationships with customers and with others in the company should be important criteria in the selection of your managers. Hiring from the outside for key positions can negatively affect your existing employees.

14. The second stage. When the business was about 30 years old, Hasse grew concerned about his competitive advantage. Competitors were consolidating their business to offer more benefits to customers. Hasse had five plants in five different locations, and efficiencies were becoming more important to customers. So he moved all his plants from the Northfield area to Lakeville, which was closer to the metro area, but still within commuting distance from Northfield for existing employees. Being closer to the metro area allowed Hasse to recruit from a larger employee pool, especially for technical employees. Since Lakeville still was partly rural, he was able to meld the urban choice and rural ethic together due to the strong core group of employees and management, and the culture that he had been able to build. However, he did sacrifice a little of the small-town work ethic.

> **Lesson**: Your location can have a major impact on your workforce and efficiency. Urban locations offer a larger selection of employees, but experience has shown that rural workforces are often more productive.

15. When trends favor you. As noted before, food companies would outsource their blending and packaging for new products in the early stages of a product's life cycle. But when products matured, the companies would build their own production plants and distribution networks. However, as more corporations decided to "buy" rather than "make," many of Ryt-Way's customers chose to keep the projects with Ryt-Way rather than taking them in-house. This gave Ryt-Way a huge base of sales, and they could now add new projects without losing successful ones. This resulted in the second growth phase of the business.

> **Lesson**: Trends change. Some are favorable and some not so. When the trends are favorable, and the Gods are smiling on you, look up, say "thank you," and enjoy.

16. Other trends. To continue his company's growth, Hasse kept monitoring all types of trends, including marketing and technology, to see which ones would be the next major vehicle for growth. One of the first trends he noticed was the growth of microwaveable foods. He was the first to take advantage of this trend with a microwaveable cup for individual servings of cereal. Quaker Oats, which was a customer, was selling oats in pouches, and they asked if Ryt-Way could put oats into microwaveable cups. Initially, the cups became too hot to handle when heated, and they needed a barrier material to shield the hand from the heat. A California company had developed the technology to coat the barrier on bottles and cans, but not on cups. Hasse looked at various types of equipment and personally engineered this technology to coat cups with this barrier using a circular conveyor. Using this new technology and equipment, Ryt-Way started to package oats in individual servings for breakfasts at hotels and restaurants. Quaker Oats introduced this product and it was extremely successful. So he followed this entry with cups for other kinds of cereals and other kinds of foods, such as macaroni and cheese for Kraft. This became one of the most successful launches of any product in Kraft's history. Ryt-Way became one of the largest suppliers of such individual serving cups in the country. Food retailers also started sending real-time sales data to the food companies, who offered this data to the blending and packaging companies such as Ryt-Way. This provided a seamless data link from the market to the supply source, making the food chain more efficient and putting companies like Ryt-Way in the middle of the flow. Ryt-Way used this information to increase efficiency.

> **Lesson**: Monitor trends, including trends in technology, markets, and needs. When you find something new, such as a new technology, that can be adapted for your company, jump aboard. But, as Hasse did in this case, do it with a customer so that there is a real market when you develop your product.

17. The biggest mistake. Every business makes mistakes. When Hasse's business was about two years old, he was doing blister-skin packaging, and using this technology for packaging signs. He commented to an associate that the technology would be great for forming snap-shut insulated trays and boxes for foods, such as pizza. Two years later, someone else came up with the same technology for McDonald's hamburgers and made a fortune. Hasse could have patented the technology and enjoyed a piece of the profits. From this episode, Hasse learned that he needs to take the time to look at alternative applications and technologies, which is how he developed the cereal packaging (noted above) for Quaker Oats. As he puts it, "if I had known this earlier, I would not have had to spend 35 years in packaging."

Lesson: "Could have, should have, would have" are among the most poignant words in the English language. When you get new ideas, make sure you evaluate them and decide carefully what to do with them.

18. Bleeding edge of competitiveness. Hasse's goal for Ryt-Way was to lead the pack in all key competitive benchmarks, especially sanitation, cleanliness, and quality. This came from the lessons he learned about food safety from his father. He knew that his company's value could be destroyed if it had even one quality problem. In addition to emphasizing this with his employees and making this a part of the company culture, Hasse incorporated an inventory-control system that was at the leading edge of the industry. It was better than any competitor's and exceeded the expectations of the customers. In addition, he invested in research and development to find new products and technologies, and developed and invested in more state-of-the-art equipment so as to offer the most competitive prices and service to his customers. When customers were deciding who should manufacture a new product, Hasse wanted to be at the top of the list. He always wanted to be financially sound so that customers would not worry about his company's financial health. He insisted on great working relationships with his suppliers and vendors, and made sure that he listened to all of their suggestions and ideas for improvement. As Hasse notes, "It is a small world, and your equipment and material vendors can be on your side or they can be against you." *Surprisingly, Hasse claims never to worry about what competitors are doing*. As he puts it, "it may sound conceited and it is not meant to be, but we looked at how we can improve all the facets of our operation for our customers consistently and continuously, and did not worry about what our competitors were doing."

Lesson: *Take care of the three-legged stool, as Hasse calls it — this includes customers, vendors, and employees—and they will take care of you*. Not benchmarking competitors is unique, but some other leading-edge entrepreneurs have shown the same trait. Once they found out that they were leading the pack, they stopped going to trade association meetings and sharing their data because they found that they were not getting anything of value back from their competitors (see also the profile of Robert Kierlin of Fastenal).

19. Financing the growth. Hasse was always good with numbers, and since his company was in a low-margin business, he monitored all aspects of his business daily, weekly, and monthly. Production efficiency, inventory, and turns were the core of the business. To make sure he controlled costs, he calculated the revenue per production person as well as cost of the inventory, the carrying costs, insurance, and other related costs and added them to the price charged to the customers. Hasse controlled accounts receivables, and expected his customers to pay on time if they wanted the most attractive prices. Over 43 years, he only had two bad debts, and both were from small companies. His large customers always paid on time. All his customers knew that they would have to pay on time to keep their supply chain full. All equipment was hedged with customer-contracts, and completely paid for during the term of the contract. When he borrowed to buy equipment, the depreciation and cash flow was more than enough to pay for the rest of the overhead and provide profits. To finance the company's growth, Hasse reinvested all of the profits back into the company. He used a line of credit from a bank as needed, and used the cash flow generated by the business for growth. Hasse also depended on vendors for favorable terms. He made sure he always paid them on time so that they did not cut his credit. Hasse knew all the relevant numbers on a timely basis, especially incoming and outgoing cash. By using financing that was non-dilutive (no equity), Hasse did not have to share the value created with investors or sell the company before he was ready – just to give investors an exit.

Lesson: There are many ways to finance growth. Equity financing has a high cost, which is a share of the company and the need to find an exit for investors. *Internal financing can mean that you need to reinvest profits, manage your numbers so you don't have excess inventory, receivables, equipment, or real estate; use non-equity sources and hedge your debt with customer contracts.*

20. Bringing family into the business and/or the exit strategy. As Hasse was getting into his 60's, he and his Board knew that they had to address the inevitable, i.e. Ryt-way without Hasse as the CEO. They had three options, hire a CEO, turn the business over to the next generation or sell the company. Being a typical owner who started the company and knew how fine the line was between success and failure, Hasse was reluctant to hire a CEO. Turning over the business to the next generation was an option since Hasse's son had been with the company since he graduated from college ten years earlier. The difficulty was that he joined the company when it was over 30 years old, the company's revenues were in excess of $100 million and the management team was firmly in place. Change in leadership is always difficult especially when the next generation is expected to step right in where the founder left off. Hasse's belief was that children work elsewhere in a similar business for 10 years to gain management experience and to build a reputation outside of the company, and then purchase the company if they are qualified. This was not an option for Hasse for other personal reasons. The third option of selling the company became a very viable option when a competitor in Chicago was purchased at a

favorable price and heightened interest among private equity institutions to acquire Ryt-way. When a suitable private equity firm that met Hasse's criteria was found, Hasse sold the business.

Lesson: Combining family and business is tough. Unlike the founder, the children have to join an existing enterprise, and existing managers look at them skeptically . They have to learn fast, and they have to be gifted. This is not always easy.

Rules for Entrepreneurs from Glenn Hasse of Ryt-Way Industries

- **Business should be fun**. Hasse developed close relationships with his customers, which made business fun. He notes that, nowadays, all relationships have degenerated to e-mails and impersonal connections.
- **Get a good board of directors**. Every company should have a competent board of directors with whom you can discuss items that you could not share internally.
- **Mentoring is critical**. Hasse benefitted significantly from being mentored and has been a mentor himself.
- **Be prepared to do everything**. When Hasse started his business, he would do whatever was needed, including fixing the forklift, sweeping the floors, and managing inventory. Even as the company grew, he knew all aspects of the company.
- **Failure is OK**. People do make mistakes. Expect them. Keep them small. Don't repeat them.
- **Share the good times**. *If you share the good times with your team, the team will help you during the bad.*
- **Don't do it just for the money**. Enjoy the journey. *You get old way too soon.*

Brett Shockley
Spanlink Communications

MINNEAPOLIS, MINN

Building a high-growth venture in call center technology

Summary: Brett Shockley's parents were entrepreneurs. His mother taught dance and baton twirling. His father owned a foreign car and repair shop and Shockley started working on car engines at the age of 10. It was only natural for Brett to create products and services, and sell them, and he got into entrepreneurial activities in junior high school. That is when he learned to ride unicycles in gym class – in fact he became so focused on learning to ride that he skipped other classes to learn and then built his own unicycle because he couldn't afford to buy one. When he was 16 he dropped out of high school and started at the University of Minnesota on an early entrance program where he got his B.S. degree in mechanical engineering, and his MBA. He joined ADC Telecommunications following graduate school and he got an introduction to the fast-changing telecommunications industry. He then spent some time at a manufacturer of products for recreational vehicles. But the entrepreneurial bug was still around, so at the ripe old age of 28, he joined three friends to start Spanlink Communication, Inc. with $3,000 of invested capital. This was the only equity invested in the venture till its initial public offering. When Cisco wanted to invest in the company, Spanlink went private at a valuation of $80 million. Subsequent financings and transactions over the next few years established a company value in excess of $130 million. This is how he did it.

Before the Startup

1. The unicycle king. Long before Shockley built a mini-giant in telecommunications, he became a world-record holder in unicycle riding. Since his dad owned a car repair shop, Shockley gravitated to repairing and rebuilding engines at the age of 10 by helping out in his dad's shop. In junior high school, he was hooked on unicycles and, since he could not afford to buy one, he built his own six-foot unicycle with a regular bicycle chain. He found it was easier to build taller than smaller unicycles and he would weld them in his dad's shop. Others wanted to buy his unicycles so a business was born. He started building unicycles for his friends and schoolmates, and after he had performed a few shows with his unicycle, he got requests from audience members to build unicycles for them—all by the age of 14. He got a tax identification number and vendors extended him credit. He sold a few hundred unicycles at prices ranging from $100 to $300. He would build them in his dad's shop and sell them to other enthusiasts and professional entertainers across the United States.

Lesson: Find your passion and get involved. It may not make you an instant millionaire, but it will give you the confidence that you need for bigger pursuits.

2. **Promoting your business**. To promote unicycle riding, Shockley started a club of enthusiasts called the Twin Cities Unicycle Club (which still has more than 200 members today) and became president of the Unicycling Society of America at age 16. This got him more business, and he started building ever taller unicycles. About this time he discovered that people were also willing to pay him to perform on his unicycles. He went from building six-foot unicycles to performing on unicycles of all shapes and sizes as high as 16 feet. He had an opportunity to learn the entertainment business while performing at Valleyfair, a theme park in Shakopee, Minnesota. He then decided to set the world's record by building and riding a 50-foot unicycle. When his agent went looking for the appropriate venue to set the record, it turned out that Southdale, the world's first indoor shopping mall in a suburb of Minneapolis, was looking for an attention-getting promotion for its annual summer sale event. They agreed to pay Shockley to set the record as part of their event, but he only had two weeks until the event. In that two weeks Shockley built the unicycle, and found a crane company that could place him on top of it. Like most things Shockley sets out to do, he had done his homework and was confident in his ability to build it and ride it; he had an adviser named Red Stevens, a friend of his father's, who was one of the country's top assembly-automation engineers. () Stevens told him that "anyone who says that anything is impossible is an idiot, and they are to be ignored." Shockley could not practice the event, since his contract with Southdale was to make the world record attempt for the first time in the mall's parking lot. When the crane lifted Shockley to the top of the cycle, a strong wind started blowing, but Shockley was still able to ride successfully. When measured, the unicycle turned out to be 51 feet, not 50. Shockley had set a new world's record and written his name into the Guinness record books. Why did Shockley want to do this? He wanted to be one of the world's best. Shockley finished high school and entered college at the University of Minnesota at the age of 16, paying for college with money earned from his unicycle sales and entertainment business.

Lesson: What do you want to achieve? The first step is the hardest. Shockley set his sights on being the best and always enjoyed a challenge. As he puts it, "you will never achieve great things if you don't set your sights high."

3. **Learn to make presentations.** Shockley also found that riding tall unicycles was entertaining to many, and he got requests to ride unicycles at fairs, amusement parks, and parades, for which he was paid. He discovered that he could make more money entertaining than building unicycles, so he focused on performing. When he visited Valleyfair in its first season, he saw professional entertainers juggling on unicycles. He asked them how he could break into the business and they pointed to the president of Valleyfair. Shockley went to meet him and tried to sell him on unicycle performances. He referred Shockley to the entertainment director, who hired him after an audition. The Valleyfair paycheck helped him pay his expenses at the university. When Shockley started doing tricks on the unicycle, he learned that there was a wide chasm between doing tricks and entertaining. An old vaudeville professional named John Shirley who had been around the world with Ed Sullivan taught him the difference. Shockley was cramming a whole bunch of tricks into his seven-minute act. The audience was overwhelmed, but not necessarily entertained. Shirley taught Shockley to make his unicycle act tell a story and keep his audience engaged. The whole performance now took 30 minutes and Shockley's audience numbers soared. Shockley tried new ways to draw audiences and keep them entertained. Valleyfair provided a great learning environment: Shockley was doing five shows per day, six days per week and would have to gather his audience from people on their way to the next ride. Eventually he was able to gather and hold an audience as big as several hundred people for the entire performance. Although it did not hit him at that time, these lessons from entertainment taught Shockley a lot about how to make complex business presentations by bringing the audience along and showing them the benefit of each feature.

> **Lesson**: In life, timing is everything. Shockley used this lesson in timing to become a better presenter. Learn how to make what you are doing fun, exciting and relevant. He learned that when you present one feature after another, you overwhelm the audience. Instead present a feature and note the benefit and return on investment for the customers – and bring the audience along. Show what's in it for them – the benefits – along with the features.

4. **Price right.** Shockley found that pricing for his bikes and performances was far from simple. He checked the market prices for regular bikes and unicycles. He tried different price levels to see what the market would bear for his customized unicycles. He wanted it to be a profitable enterprise for himself, and in retrospect he thinks he could have charged more. When he started performing as a unicycle showman, Shockley worked with an agent in Chicago who spread the word, and he also obtained referrals from other performers. He performed the same routine every time but he was paid $200 when he did it for the Boy Scouts and $2,000 when he performed at McDonald's headquarters. Shockley learned that his cost was irrelevant in determining what a customer was willing to pay. Instead, Shockley found that people pay for value – they don't tell you what they will pay, but will ask you for your price. If he offered too low a price, they often assume that he was not very good and was hungry for work. If he offered too high a price, he could price

himself out of the market. So he needed to know the right level. Perceived value, not cost, was the key factor in determining what customers were willing to pay.

Lesson: Pricing is always uncertain for innovative products and setting the right price is complicated. Just because you are willing to charge less does not mean that you will get sales. Customers often equate price to value, especially for unique or revolutionary products or services. The best way to find the right price is to understand your customer's business and the value of the product or service you are providing. Then try to set your price to get fairly compensated for the value you are adding. Ultimately, the lowest price you will charge is the one that allows you to make whatever your threshold for profit is – don't make the mistake of setting your price by starting with cost and adding a margin because in most cases you will leave a lot of value on the table.

5. **Motivation and the college years**. After high school, Shockley joined the mechanical engineering program at the University of Minnesota. When he was about 75 percent of the way through the program, and his entrepreneurial business was doing well, he decided that getting a business administration degree was going to be important to his future. So he started taking more business courses rather than engineering courses. Shockley found out that a large university offers many opportunities but is very complex to work your way through. The red tape can be daunting and it can be a giant bureaucracy (no different from a large corporation, as he soon found out). He started taking classes that were offered by both the engineering school and the business school. He petitioned to have the business courses fulfill similar operations courses for the engineering school to get his undergrad degree, so when he enrolled for his MBA, he had already finished his prerequisite courses. But the business school told him that, even though he got a 98 percent on the GMAT exam, his grade-point average wasn't high enough. (Shockley was spending every weekend driving around the country performing his unicycle act.). So he went back and did extra work to improve his undergrad grades, and got all As on the remaining 24 credits that he had to complete. The business school accepted him for the accelerated MBA program.

Lesson: Learn to navigate bureaucracies. Don't take no for an answer and solve the problem.

6. **Manage the fraternity**. He got involved with managing his fraternity and found that it was fascinating. It was like a business incubation lab and it taught him how to run a very dynamic, small business with its own employees (cook, etc.), budget, and tenants. He went through various positions in the organization and found how much fun it was to organize and work with a group than to do solitary tasks like riding the unicycle. He also found that managing volunteers is supremely challenging because none of the volunteers are are compelled to contribute just because you ask them to, but because they think it is the right thing to do and enjoy doing it. As Shockley puts it, "It's all about motivation. In the corporate world you

don't get the best from people due to your level in the organization structure but because they want to do well and are motivated by the team that has been created." When he was managing the fraternity, Shockley found that the students became enthusiastic about getting involved when it was fun. And he noticed that the best ideas and greatest progress often came not from the most charismatic or most intelligent people, but from the quiet ones. He started to appreciate diversity in teams.

> **Lesson**: Create an environment in which your employees enjoy what they are doing and give them a reason to contribute fully. They may do the job grudgingly if you are the "boss" but they will do it better if they enjoy what they are doing, believe in the mission and feel like they are a successful part of the company's success. Employees can get totally involved or they can do just enough to get by. If your employees are doing the latter, you may want to seek a government bailout.

7. The first job. In his final quarter before finishing his MBA degree, Shockley joined ADC Telecommunications. At ADC, he became an assistant product manager, in which job he managed a telecommunications product line. This meant that he had responsibility for profits or losses, but like a product-management job, he did not have control over everything needed to deliver his P&L. He learned what it was like to be inside a growing company. ADC grew from $25 million in sales when he started to $150 million in five years, when he left. And he learned to work with diverse groups in a corporation in which he had to build broad support across engineering, manufacturing, and sales to be successful. Due to his background in engineering, he was able to think of alternate technological solutions to customer problems and offer these to engineering when they were stumped. In one case, after working with the engineering team to solve a technology problem for New York Telephone, the engineering team added Shockley's name to the patent that resulted.

> **Lesson**: Joining a major corporation is always helpful when you graduate since it shows you how large companies operate. If you operate as an intrapreneur in a large company you will learn about a lot of the challenges that will face you in the start-up world as you try to attract capital, answer to investors, build a new product and create a market for your innovation. For some entrepreneurs, it is also a reminder about the bureaucratic hell that awaits them if they don't succeed in their venture, and it spurs them on to succeed. But even in large corporations and even with limited authority, it is possible to grow by being creative and solving customer problems.

8. International experience. After several years, Shockley was promoted to international product manager, a position that taught him how to market internationally. He learned that time spent on the ground in your markets is a critical success factor. When he first approached potential customers in new international markets, he found he was often asked to "invest in building the relationship."

Customers would always ask him to offer his products at large discounts to help "build the relationship" and accelerate entry into the market. To Shockley, this was another way to get taken to the cleaners. He refused these "generous" offers, and started to sell the prospects on their benefits from the use of the product. When the product had a competitive advantage and benefits, people bought. As Shockley puts it, "Good business is good business everywhere, and working for free only proves that you are willing to work for free." Shockley also found the risks of corporate life and international business. He wanted to sell one of ADC's products in the United Kingdom, but the corporate attorney thought there was a risk that the product violated a competitor's copyright. The attorney tried to get the CEO to stop the sale, and also to keep Shockley from attending the meeting between himself and the CEO to discuss the topic. Fortunately for Shockley, the CEO agreed to hear his side and agreed with Shockley that the business opportunity was much greater than the potential cost of copyright litigation. Ultimately it was a business decision, not a legal decision. This episode did nothing to entice Shockley to live in the bureaucracy of a mid-level job in a large corporation, and he realized that with his entrepreneurial spirit, he should perhaps start thinking about his next business. But before he did that, he decided to take a detour to another corporation.

> **Lesson**: Don't think that you need to give away your products or services as a price of entry. By doing this, you are tacitly admitting that your services or products are not worth what you are asking. Sell the benefits, and if there are none, you may want to reconsider your business.

9. **From ADC to Onan**. After five years of being a bit of a "controversial" figure at ADC, Shockley began thinking of starting something new but got recruited by Onan to run a large recreational vehicle (RV) product line. This was the largest product line at Onan, and Shockley wanted to take advantage of this opportunity. It was a new type of business for Shockley, i.e., non-high technology, but he found it interesting. Japanese manufacturer Honda was entering the market, with the next-generation water-cooled, ultra-quiet generator. This was a major threat for Onan, which dominated its market. Shockley worked with the Onan engineering team to find a response that would be faster than developing an entirely new generator from scratch. The solution was to develop a high-tech box as a sound dampener around the existing air-cooled generator. This was quieter and simpler than Honda's water-cooled product. Simultaneously, Onan started an ad campaign featuring simplicity that was based on the company's history and heritage to appeal to older generations of Americans. Honda backed out of the market for a number of years.

> **Lesson**: Find new ways to compete that rely on your company's strengths and don't blindly emulate your competitors. If you compete on their turf, they may be stronger. Honda was selling quiet, reliability and high-tech. Shockley and Onan knew their markets, and countered with a quieter product, but they added the history of the company and the shared heritage with the customers. Recognize threats and then find the most appropriate solution that you can.

From Startup to Profits

10. From Onan to high-tech. While Shockley was with Onan, his heart was still in high-technology and he wanted to start his own company. The seed was planted a few years earlier at a conference in Washington, DC at which many suppliers and interconnect companies were discussing the future of telecommunications after the 1984 breakup of AT&T. The market was transitioning from the Bell System to an entrepreneurial world with a plethora of new ventures all angling for a piece of the huge pie. Shockley started putting a few ideas on paper and talking with friends – one was a colleague and the other a classmate from sixth grade. This was the genesis of Spanlink. They started it with $3,000 of their own money and a lot of family support, and did not need any more equity or debt till the initial public offering (IPO).

Lesson: Keep looking for ideas in your area of interest. The best opportunities are in emerging industries or industries thrown into turmoil by a new technology, or regulatory changes (such as the AT&T breakup). Many new potentially high-growth ventures are started at such times. When starting your venture, make sure your family is up for the adventure. Starting a new business is likely to be a 24x7 roller-coaster ride. Shockley noted that the spouse of an entrepreneur typically falls into one of two camps, the painfully aware spouse or the blissfully unaware spouse. Regardless of which one your spouse is, you are going to need more support from them than you can possibly imagine.

11. The opportunity. Shockley had been around the telecom market during his days at ADC Telecommunications. He knew the trends and identified an opportunity for interactive voice response applications. An interactive voice response system is used to automate or route incoming calls to corporate sales or service departments and provide a recorded voice application to conduct business, such as checking your account balance, transfer funds or stop your newspaper while you go on vacation. The technology was becoming more accessible and corporations were starting to buy these systems. Shockley and his co-founders started Spanlink to capitalize on this opportunity with AT&T's products as their foundation. They knew that AT&T had great products, but thought that AT&T did not know how to sell them, and that Bell Labs (the research arm of AT&T) was not efficient at customizing the products for individual customers. So Spanlink became a value-added reseller (VAR) of these solutions. They planned to buy the hardware, write the software and sell the systems for interactive voice-response systems. To prove the opportunity, however, Shockley notes that they did not do "all the things they should have done." Their business plan was an informal one and they were relying on their knowledge of what customers wanted based on their experience in the industry.

Lesson: Many entrepreneurs have started new businesses without a formal plan and succeeded. Having a written plan can help to coordinate the team, to monitor the business, and to obtain resources, if needed. In this case, Shockley and his partners were in constant communication and did not need external resources, so they forged ahead with a limited plan and made rapid adjustments to their strategy as they learned from their interaction with customers.

12. The alliance with AT&T. Although Shockley and his partners wanted to work with AT&T, AT&T was not sure it wanted VARs or partners, and the AT&T product manager would not return Shockley's phone calls. Finally, after numerous calls, Shockley got a hold of the product manager and found out that he was coming to Minnesota for a class reunion but he did not share his schedule with Shockley. Shockley called every hotel in the Twin Cities to find the hotel where the class was having its reunion, and sent flowers to the product manager's room. The product manager's wife made him feel guilty and asked him to call Shockley. They subsequently became good friends and AT&T agreed to have Shockley represent them. Spanlink soon became one of the largest resellers of interactive voice response solutions for AT&T.

Lesson: We have all heard about the difficulty of getting potential customers to return calls. Large companies can be equally difficult to reach even when you want to sell their products because they do not always want small companies, especially startups, representing them. You may have to be just as persistent to sell for them as with customers.

13. Selling to large customers. When Shockley started the business, one of the first large customers they pursued was the StarTribune, the major newspaper in the Twin Cities. Shockley met with the executive in charge of the buying decision and explained to him the great things Spanlink could do for his company. They had a need so Spanlink offered a proposal. Although their proposal was the most competitive and offered the greatest benefits, StarTribune's committee in charge of making the decision recommended a much larger and better-established competitor. Their preference was the "safe" decision - Wang Laboratories (which was liquidated a few years later). The executive who had ultimate decision-making authority asked Shockley to convince him why Spanlink was still going to be in business in a year. The executive ultimately overruled the committee and hired Spanlink. Shockley was determined to do a great job for the StarTribune. He hired a market researcher to understand the customers' needs and how to reduce and eliminate negative issues such as customers' anger when they did not get the newspaper in the morning. They built prototypes, held focus groups, videotaped the sessions and watched what happened. They attended agent-training classes and learned how the agents were trained to handle customers and what they did. This attention to detail got them great feedback about the human factors of interactive voice response systems. They learned that customers would accept an automated apology for inadequate newspaper delivery from a machine about 35 percent of the time, and this was a huge gain for the publisher since it saved a lot of human time and maintained customer relationships. The videotape of the focus groups also helped the newspaper's publisher to realize that a properly designed automated voice response system would increase customer satisfaction as well as significantly decrease costs. In designing the system, Shockley went beyond the obvious interactive systems that ask customers to push a variety of buttons to solve their problems. He studied how customers reacted to the machine and adjusted to make sure that each customer was served in the way in which they felt most comfortable.

Lesson: Pay close attention to your customers and their customers. Learn why you are doing what you are doing. Understand and adjust for the human factor. If your customers' customers react favorably, your customers will too.

14. Solving Toro's problems. Spanlink's second large project was for Toro, the lawn equipment manufacturing company. Toro wanted to improve the way its agents handled customer complaints and make the process more efficient. They had encountered technology-related problems because Toro had purchased a number of companies, and each had a different part numbering system for its inventory. Until this point, the variety of alpha-numeric numbering schemes had prevented Toro from implementing a touch-tone parts ordering system because of the challenges of identifying a unique part number on a touch-tone keypad. All of Spanlink's competitors told Toro they needed to develop a new comprehensive part numbering plan for all products. This was a problem for Toro since all of its distributors already knew the existing part numbers. Spanlink developed a new "dial-by-name" algorithm that allowed customers to press the touch tone that corresponded to the letter or number and then was able to find the part number desired statistically. This new system was able to offer the right product, and also suggest alternate products that would meet the need if the part was out of stock. Spanlink also helped Toro roll out the system to its dealers and repair shops. The benefit was that the company could now offer a guarantee that any part that was ordered by 3 p.m. would be shipped the same day. They also offered equivalent products that were available in different warehouses for even faster deliveries, and sold people on faster delivery times, more convenience and better options. Toro was a happy customer. Within six months of startup, the company reached profitability with these first two customers.

Lesson: Make life easier for your customers. Solve the underlying problem rather than just selling them technology and treating a symptom. Shockley learned that customers were much happier if he and his team were able to understand the problem, reengineer the business to solve the problem more efficiently and end with higher customer satisfaction, rather than just automating the existing business model. Solve problems and add value. Customers will pay you more.

15. Bootstrap the startup. Shockley and his partners had decided to bootstrap the company's growth rather than seek external financing. This meant that they were not going to seek equity, but to provide the needed financing by carefully managing expenses and generating cash from operations. They got cash before they spent it, convinced customers to pay down a portion of the contract to buy the equipment, and asked for milestone payments as the system was developed. They were fixated on cash flow. This helped them grow by using the customer's cash rather than having to obtain it from the outside, which would dilute their ownership interests. They also aligned incentives and terms to get the business to develop positive cash flow. They paid sales personnel when the customers paid, and the level of commissions was based on the profit margins of the business they sold. Shockley found that large corporations become suspicious about the venture's financial stability when he asked for down payments. J. P. Morgan (the bank) told Shockley that they never paid vendors until after the work was done. Shockley responded that Ford had paid a deposit, and that Times Mirror had paid a deposit (implying that Spanlink was in demand and there was something wrong with J.P. Morgan if they did not pay a deposit). J.P. Morgan paid a deposit.

Lesson: Don't be intimidated by large corporations. Get the cash. Don't be bashful. Start with what you want. You might get what you need. If you don't ask, you will not get it.

From Profits to the Moon

16. From job-shop to a packaged product. After Spanlink was established and profitable as a job-shop developing customized solutions for larger companies, Shockley started to look at the viability of developing a proprietary product to take the company from a job shop to the next level of packaged solutions. He realized that the growth potential with an attractive proprietary product was higher than from developing customized solutions. He noticed that AT&T's competitors had features in the voice sub-system of their PBX products that could be added to AT&T's products to make them more attractive. AT&T could have developed these features but their priorities were elsewhere. Spanlink developed the solution and sold it via AT&T's global sales force. The product took off and AT&T sold thousands. Spanlink did not ask for any prior volume commitment from AT&T because Shockley was able to bootstrap the development costs, and Shockley's belief was that large companies would demand the rights to the intellectual property if you ask for a substantial financial commitment up front. Shockley believed in developing the solution and selling the product, but not disclosing the technology. That was the start of Spanlink's rapid-growth phase, which came because Shockley profited from higher-value packaged solutions that could be sold in larger markets than custom solutions.

Lesson: Many might find it surprising that a company with AT&T's resources had not identified the problem and developed a solution. This is not uncommon – disruptive innovation most often comes from entrepreneurial startup companies. Sometimes entrepreneurial ventures are closer to the market and faster at execution. The key is to find unmet needs, be agile, solve problems and find a way to profit from the development.

17. Developing expertise at developing products. To succeed in this new strategy, Shockley needed to have internal expertise at developing and designing products, to configure the product to solve customers' specific problems, and write documentation for a smooth transition to the customers' staff. To do this, he realized that Spanlink needed to become more disciplined. So Spanlink shifted its focus to process and consistency, spent more time understanding customer needs and "made sure that they were not writing code in a loft" but in the real world. This led Shockley and his team to focus on the features that really mattered to customers. Many things are possible with technology, but you need to stay focused on the features that add business value. Shockley believed that the key was not throwing technology at a problem, but first understanding problems that affected large numbers of customers and then finding the right technology solution. Following this philosophy, Spanlink created the world's first Web-enabled call center called WebCall in 1995. This leading-edge product combined Voice over Internet Protocol (VoIP) and databases to improve customer service.

Lesson: Don't make your solutions too complex. Include only those that are needed and valued. To develop the best solutions, know the technology and its (and your) capabilities, but first analyze customers' unmet needs and develop a better solution. Then combine the two. The key is to know how the product will be used, and having the discipline to include only those features that are needed. Having too many unneeded features is usually not the best solution.

18. Customer acceptance – a problem with leading-edge products. As Spanlink developed products, sometimes they were too far ahead of the market. An example was WebCall, the application that let consumers click a button on the Web site to reach a call centre agent. The problem was that incorporating this solution required several corporate departments to work together, and one of them was IT. These departments had usually never worked together before. One memorable presentation was to Merrill Lynch. Twenty-five people crowded the room at the first meeting, all introducing themselves to each other. Shockley quickly realized that this did not bode well for a quick sale.

Lesson: Make sure that your solution can be operationalized by your customers. Pushing large corporations to work together in new ways takes time, marketing muscle and a solution that is very compelling from both a financial and a business perspective.

19. Helping W.W. Grainger. One of Spanlink's largest and most successful customers was W.W. Grainger. Grainger had 500 stores around the country but they all acted autonomously. Shockley and his team worked closely with the company to understand their business goals, challenges and opportunities. They developed a system that allowed Grainger to connect all its stores so that a customer who called a local branch would always get their call answered by a knowledgeable person within 20 seconds. If no one was going to be able to answer your call in the branch you called within 20 seconds, the call would be answered by a representative of a branch that might be nearby. That representative could provide the same experience, including product information and availability, and he could even discuss the weather or sports scores. A pick ticket for the customer's order could be printed in the appropriate branch, and the part would be waiting when the customer showed up at the branch they had called 20 minutes earlier. Spanlink improved Grainger's business by linking all 500 stores as one for the customer, which helped Grainger add tens of millions of dollars in new sales the next year. The CEO gave credit to this new system as one of the company's key success factors for that year at subsequent analyst and earnings calls.

Lesson: Technology is a tool. Leverage it to solve the customer's problems. This means you need to ask questions until you understand the problems and then develop ways to solve these problems for added growth. Creating technology is great, but the reward is in increasing customers' benefits.

20. Everyone sells. According to Shockley, sales is the most important job in the company. To build a company with long-term sustainability, everyone in the company needs to understand customer needs, spend some time in front of the customer to sell, and develop direct knowledge about how their actions help in the sale. Shockley believes that entrepreneurs are always selling themselves to investors, customers, suppliers and employees. Some of his suggestions to improve sales include:

- Start high. It's easy to go down. This applies to prices and where you start prospecting in the company.
- Sell yourself first. Then the company. Then the product.
- Know the customer, including the business and the people.
- Know your product and understand the value you bring to your customer.
- Take the high-road and build a long-term relationship.
- Be willing to walk if the people or the deal stinks.
- Get the compensation right. Don't place caps on sales commissions. But align commission levels and timing of payment to profit margins and receipt of cash.
- Have fun when you sell.

Lesson: Everyone sells. Whether you are selling to customers, investors, analysts or employees, selling is the key success factor for an entrepreneur. If you still don't want to sell, you may want to consider an alternate type of vocation, or find a partner who can sell.

21. The IPO. When the public stock markets became hot in the mid-1990s, Spanlink decided to take advantage of the market and go public. It had about $9 million in sales. The company did an initial public offering in 1996 through Summit Investments, a local investment bank and picked up a largely Midwest based group of investors. Knowing what he knows today, and given the nature of the market at the time, Shockley believes that they should have raised significantly more than the $8 million they did raise and could have done it at a much higher valuation due to the nature of their internet call center based market story. As a publicly-held company, Spanlink now had the expenses of a public company but needed scale.

To help achieve this scale, Spanlink bought another company called Aurora Systems that was(original equipment) manufacturing a complementary product to AT&T's successor Lucent Technologies as well as Nortel and Siemens. The company was a startup and it was a good fit, and formed the basis for growth to $12 million. That is when Shockley got a phone call from an executive at Cisco who reported to John Chambers, the CEO of Cisco. Shockley knew this executive from his days at AT&T Bell Labs. Even before this phone call, Shockley had invested the time to become familiar with Cisco's leading-edge products and was very impressed with them. But all of Spanlink's revenues came from their alliance with Lucent Technologies. To resolve this dilemma, Cisco agreed to invest $40 million in Spanlink for a 49 percent stake in the company and fund a transaction to take the company private, valuing Spanlink at a valuation of $80 million. Subsequent fundraising, and transactions over the next few years established a company value in excess of $130mm. After the transaction, Spanlink refocused their entire product line on VoIP and Cisco. Shockley moved to Cisco as an executive at that company to run their contact center business.

Lesson: When someone wants to buy you at an attractive valuation, sell.

Post Script

22. Cisco culture. Spanlink did very well with Cisco becoming their partner of the year and leading Contact Center VoIP vendor. Shockley calls his time at Cisco an "amazing" experience. He compares it to a sports team, where they believe that anything is possible. People took risks, and small doses of failurewere commonplace and expected. Since all the employees were rich from stock options, they were unafraid to challenge anyone. The key was performance, and you were expected to defend your assertions and take risks. Or exit. At Cisco, Shockley learned a successful technique for keeping executives close to customers and sales. All of the executives, including CEO John Chambers, made presentations to customers in executive briefings, and they were rated by their customers. These ratings impacted their bonuses. This was Chambers' way of keeping the company's executives and staff connected to customers. After the stock market crashed, Shockley returned from Cisco and grew revenues to an $80 million annual run rate. In 2005 he secured venture capital to grow the company, and subsequently Spanlink split into two companies because one company was selling to the other company's customers. This freed both to seek their own destiny. Shockley also exited from his creation to seek his own destiny elsewhere.

Lesson: You define your company's culture. Understand what you want. With a performance-based culture, you can unleash the entrepreneurial spirit of the employees and let people succeed or fail based on their abilities. Give people the authority to take small degrees of risk, reward success disproportionately, expect some failure, but seek overall growth and success. Hold them accountable for results. Better yet, let the group hold them accountable. The group will often do a better job of it than you ever could.

Rules for Entrepreneurs from Brett Shockley of Spanlink

- **Develop stretch goals**. Reaching higher leads to greater achievements.
- **Get the order, get the cash, and satisfy the customer's needs – in that order**. Getting some of the cash from the customers before doing the work helps you to grow without expensive financing.
- **Convince through example**. Shockley believes that the best way to convince your team to do something is to be willing to do it yourself. If you can get it done, they will follow. If you develop or recognize good ideas, they will do it.
- **Seek diversity in teams**. The best ideas often come not from charismatic types or A+ students but from quiet ones. Get diversity in teams to get different skills, experiences and backgrounds.
- **Get urgency**. Know the value of time. Shockley has always been eager to make the most of his time. That is how you accomplish a lot in a limited time period.
- **Be clear about goals and adjust to change**. Organize for efficiency and effectiveness. The organization structure matters, but experiment with different options to find the right one for each situation. Each market, including global ones, may need a uniquely designed structure.
- **Eliminate poor employees quickly**. Shockley believes that one of the biggest mistakes is not moving a poor performer out fast enough. Such employees poison the well.
- **Build a business. Not a job**. Increase the value of the company. Make yourself irrelevant.
- **Hire A+ people without experience before B people with experience.** You may not able to afford experienced A+ people.

- **Shockley's favorite books:**
    - The E-Myth by Michael E. Gerber.
    - Going the Distance by Kevin Kennedy and Mary Moore.
    - Only the Paranoid Survive by Andy Grove.
    - Good to Great by Jim Collins.
    - Strategic Selling by Stephen E. Heiman and Robert B. Miller.

JILL BLASHACK STRAHAN
TASTEFULLY SIMPLE

ALEXANDRIA, MINN

A passion for gifts to build a $140 million-plus easy-to-prepare food business

Summary: Jill Blashack Strahan dropped out of college because she wanted to "connect the dots" of what she was learning. She worked at a department store and a gift store, and then co-owned and managed her father's restaurant before starting her own gift basket business. Though these efforts were not huge financial successes, they were very rewarding in providing some of life's greatest lessons.

When her son, Zach, was born, Blashack Strahan realized that the scarcest ingredient in life is time. To make every hour count, she closed her gift basket business, which required long hours but resulted in earnings less than $6,000 per year. And then another door opened. She was invited to sell foods from her gift basket line on the Holiday Crafter's tour in Alexandria. She decided to offer taste-testing, and to her surprise, her easy-to-prepare foods sold out. But there was no big "aha." A year went by and the search for her mission continued. She repeated the tour the next year, and again sold out. One week later, after reading an article about the success of home parties, Blashack Strahan says something suddenly went, "Ding-ding!" She got the inspiration to sell exceptional convenient foods through home parties. She shared the idea with Joani Nielson, who loved the idea and offered to invest as soon as she heard it.

With humble beginnings and big dreams, Blashack Strahan bootstrapped the business with a total of $36,000 – personal savings, an investment from founding partner Joani Nielson and a $20,000 Small Business Administration loan. She discovered that people were interested in hosting parties, buying and selling delicious products, and she was off to the races. She had a clear vision, set goals, did taste-testing parties, and one by one recruited a sales team. But it was a slow start, causing Blashack Strahan to lose confidence and get frustrated. Realizing that she had begun to lose faith and that she needed to believe before others would, she renewed her determination and expanded beyond her wildest dreams. When she finished her five-year business plan Blashack Strahan was not sure she could ever run a company with sales exceeding $11 million. In 2008, Tastefully Simple's sales were in excess of $140 million, the company was debt-free, and Blashack Strahan continued to hold 70 percent of the company. Until 1998, Blashack Strahan had never earned more than $14,000 in any year. *Dreams don't just come true. You make them happen*. This is how she did it.

Before the Startup

1. Find meaning. After finishing high school in a small farming town, Jill Blashack Strahan decided to major in English at the University of Minnesota (Morris), where her stay was short. She soon bade farewell to the U because she did not find any inspiration there, and the learning was not "hands on." She started attending the local technical college because her brother Mike had attended the same college. Her advisers suggested Fashion Merchandising as a major, but because she wanted a broader base of study, Blashack Strahan decided to enter the Sales Associate Program and then the Marketing and Sales program. While there she created a business plan as a class assignment. She decided to write a business plan on a gift shop called Rainbow's End (where you can find your pot of gold). Blashack Strahan dedicated herself to this project and was pleasantly astonished when she won second prize at a state business-plan competition and became a finalist at the national competition. This success boosted her confidence and became one of the key steppingstones in her life. The first lessons she learned were the importance of branding a business, as well as the numbers in a business plan. But perhaps most importantly, she realized that she did well when she dedicated herself, invested the effort, and was passionate about what she was doing. To Blashack Strahan, this meant 100 percent passionate, not 15 percent. She decided that she was not going to do anything that did not fulfill her purpose.

> **Lesson**: Jill Blashack Strahan learned that meaning and purpose, as evidenced by passion, were her key motivators – not money or security. Unlike many entrepreneurs who try to avoid the numbers, Blashack Strahan learned why entrepreneurs need to make the numbers work. This knowledge can save you a lot of grief, and later on it helped Blashack Strahan structure Tastefully Simple and make sure that it was profitable.

2. The first job(s). After graduating from college, Blashack Strahan got a job doing advertising and displays at the local JCPenney store. After one year she quit and accepted a job at a local gift shop for less money and no benefits. Her grandmother wanted to know why she was quitting her job at JCPenney, especially since it had pension benefits. Well, Blashack Strahan wanted to learn more about the gift business, apply her business plan and expand her skills rather than just dust displays. To her immense surprise, the manager at JCPenney encouraged her to pursue the opportunity, even though a new employee would have to be trained. The manager knew that the new job would give Blashack Strahan a broader set of skills and experiences and help her growth.

> **Lesson:** The experience at JCPenney taught Blashack Strahan that "if we believe there's more than enough to go around, there will be," which she has termed the Law of "Abundancy," and is one of her fundamental principles. Develop arrangements where everyone can maximize their gifts to increase the size of the pie and share in the growth. Some call it "win-win."

3. Get real. Be humble. About this time, Blashack Strahan's dad bought a café in her hometown near Alexandria and asked her if she would manage it if he matched her salary at the gift shop. Blashack Strahan was 21 years old and clueless about the restaurant industry. But she accepted the offer and learned a number of details about the restaurant industry and about herself.

- When she was placing her first order for hamburger patties, her food vendor asked her whether she wanted 4:1, 6:1 or 8:1. Blashack Strahan was confused since she thought she was being asked about the odds on hamburger gambling! Actually she was being asked how many beef patties she wanted in a pound. She knew that most of the people with whom she worked knew much more about the restaurant industry and that she needed to be humble and *accept the limits of her knowledge* (rather than bluffing) and ask questions. Acting as if she knew everything could lead to disastrous consequences, rather than just saying "I don't know."
- On her first day as the café's manager, she found delinquent bills galore – sales taxes, unemployment taxes and workers compensation withholdings. She wondered how she was going to "eat this elephant." The answer was one bite at a time. She eventually paid all the back taxes and brought the café to a sustainable position. This taught her the importance of organization and structure.
- She had an employee who decided to leave Jill's Grill in order to take a job across the street that offered higher pay. Blashack Strahan objected to the employee getting unemployment benefits, and the employee was enraged. Blashack Strahan learned to handle conflict, be calm and simply accept that sometimes one is not liked by everybody.
- Blashack Strahan also learned the power of the right mentor to handle tough situations. A local businessman, who owned an implement dealership and was a regular customer at her restaurant, gave her encouragement and guidance when she needed it most. This helped teach Blashack Strahan how to encourage others to reach their own full potential.

Overall, Blashack Strahan managed the restaurant for three years. What she learned there was that good teammates help, especially when you are a leader who is out of your depth. And she also learned that sometimes you need to get out of your comfort zone if you want to grow.

Lesson: Step out of your comfort zone. But be humble, know what you don't know and admit it. Acting as if you know it all could be hazardous to your business. It also helps others who work with you to ask for assistance when they need it. And surround yourself with good mentors and become a good mentor to others.

4. **New start in Alexandria**. Blashack Strahan then moved 20 miles away to the slightly larger town of Alexandria. When she moved, Blashack Strahan had less than $200 and no job. She tried to borrow money from the local bank, but it denied her the loan. One day she got a call from Jan Strauss, her high school teacher and adviser, who was opening a tanning salon. Strauss's father had been Blashack Strahan's mentor in her restaurant. Strauss offered her a job, and after thinking it over, Blashack Strahan accepted. Now she had the job of managing the salon, which they opened in two months. Part of their marketing strategy was to rely on a grassroots, word-of-mouth marketing campaign to build the salon's sales. This meant that Blashack Strahan had to make sure that all the customers had a great experience at the salon and would spread the word. To encourage it, they developed a referral program and offered customers a free tan if they brought a friend. There was another tanning studio in Alexandria, and Strauss's strategy was to offer a newer facility with better equipment, an excellent brand and higher standards of customer service, and charge a higher price – $6 vs. $5 per tan. This was new to Blashack Strahan, who was used to seeing businesses compete with lower prices. Strauss installed timers so that the tanning session would end at a pre-arranged time rather than relying on someone pounding on the wall. They offered fresh towels, headsets, bigger tanning beds and cooler rooms in a new building. They became so popular that they had more than 100 clients in a day and started to show a profit in less than one year. Blashack Strahan learned about excellence and the value of a great partnership from Strauss. Even though Blashack Strahan was not a financial partner in the business, she was the operations manager, and she and Strauss ran the business as a partnership. They made a good team and offset each other emotionally. When one was down, the other was up. Blashack Strahan left Sun Studio when she was offered a sales position at First American Bank to cross-sell services. After that, she and her husband went to live in Sweden for one year.

Lesson: Do **not** settle for lower standards and do **not** necessarily compete on price. There is nearly always someone bigger and cheaper than you. You may get sales but not profits, and you may end up in a price war where the strongest win. Learn how to compete with higher standards of quality and service, and you are more likely to succeed. And never underestimate the importance of a good partner.

From Startup to Profits

5. **Back to gifts**. When Blashack Strahan returned from Sweden, a friend suggested they get into the gift-basket business. Blashack Strahan took a class at the technical college on business plans (*many entrepreneurs proudly point out that they started their businesses without a business plan, but it is noteworthy that Blashack Strahan insisted on doing one for every business before she started and now encourages her sales consultants to create a "dream map"*). When she finished the class, Blashack Strahan decided to get into the business on a full-time basis. Her friend, who wanted the business as a part-time hobby, started another business. At first Blashack Strahan sold baskets out of her home. Then she rented a kiosk at the local mall during the holidays. As her business grew and she could afford it, she graduated to a storefront and lived in the back of the store with her husband. There were other gift-basket businesses in the state, so she examined what they did and learned from them. Blashack Strahan not only experimented with the contents of the basket, but also with gift occasions and themes. She found that creativity in names, themes and designs had a strong influence on sales, and she added unique gourmet foods. Because Alexandria is part of the lake country of Minnesota, she started a fisherman's bait cooler called "Bait & Bobber." It included pretzels, nuts, snacks, chocolate fish and other candies, a fish-shaped pencil and soda pop. It was practical and innovative. To save labor and money, Blashack Strahan planned to build just one basket of each kind and try to sell via special order. But her first employee, a woman named Glenda, convinced her that "You can't sell out of an empty basket!" She needed to have multiple baskets of each style to fill the store. People like to see, touch, feel and pick up the products they are buying, and want the "experience." Blashack Strahan found that Glenda was right. Sales increased, and she built the business to more than 3,000 clients.

Lesson: Creativity is a huge part of standing apart from the crowd. Blashack Strahan learned that when she had little money, she had to get the maximum bang for each buck. To get that, she had to develop products for occasions that no one had thought of, and do it with flair and creativity. And she needed a plan. A plan tells you whether you are going in the right direction to reach your goals. Think before you act.

6. **Know the time value of money and the money value of time**. Although the gift-basket business grew, it did not reach Blashack Strahan's expectations. She was netting about $6,000 per year and "putting in unreal hours." Her son, Zach, was born and now she wanted to spend time with him. She realized the importance of being effective and efficient and wanted each business hour to show a reasonable return. She had never earned more than $14,000 per year, and she had to open her mind to greater potential and higher value. So she closed the store.

Lesson: *Learn the scarcity of time*. Blashack Strahan learned that it sometimes takes a child to help set priorities and goals. All of us have a limited amount of time. Those who accomplish much know the value and scarcity of it.

7. **New direction in gifts**. After she closed her store, Blashack Strahan was invited to join the local Holiday Crafter's tour. She accepted. This was an annual event in Alexandria where shoppers would go on a tour of various houses, and five or six artisans would sell their products in each home. The event was held during hunting season, when Blashack Strahan often said "the men kill animals and the women spend money." She offered six gift basket themes and also decided to sell seven of her best, easy-to-prepare food products from her gift basket business. The second year she included her very popular Reindeer Chips (flat pretzel chips dipped in almond bark with colored swirls) and offered those in the Holiday Crafter's tour along with samples. When she began selling specialty foods at Care with Flair Gifts & Gift Baskets, she had been skeptical whether people in a small town like Alexandria would buy them. But she had found that they sold very well when combined with food tasting "experiences." As Blashack Strahan puts it, "There are no new ideas, just tweaks on old ideas." The results? She nearly sold out her inventory. But the idea for Tastefully Simple did not strike Blashack Strahan just yet. She repeated the Holiday Crafter's Tour for a second year and sold out again. And she was still trying to find her mission.

She attended a personal-development retreat for four days in September, and at the retreat she participated in an activity to build a prayer arrow – a stick wrapped with various bright colored yarns and adorned with leaves, feathers, and other objects she found while walking in the woods. As she created her prayer arrow, she repeated this affirmation over and over: "I'll know what I want by November 15." The final step: Blashack Strahan planted her prayer arrow in the ground at Brophy Park.

She had the big "aha" for Tastefully Simple at 3 a.m. November 14 following her second year at the Holiday Crafter's Tour.

Based on the two Holiday Crafter's tours, she knew **what** she wanted to sell. But she did not know **how** to sell these products and build a great business—until she saw her solution in a magazine article about a company that had become very successful selling household décor items through home parties. She connected the dots between the products, the sales strategy, her skills, and her passion. She knew that everything about the concept fit.

- She believed that if her affordable indulgences sold in Alexandria, they would sell anywhere. Her products had sold out at the Holiday Crafter's Tour and everyone was raving about them. Most importantly, the feedback was real. Customers had proved it by buying them.
- People loved to taste new foods and got hooked when something connected. And they loved to chat with friends, old and new. The home parties were

ideal venues for tasting, sharing and having fun. They were fun experiences for everyone.

- She knew that more and more women were working outside the home and did not have time to make elaborate meals, but they wanted to pamper themselves and their families with foods that were simple and affordable. So she developed the concept of "small indulgences for busy lives." This has since evolved into "The food you love, the time you deserve."
- *The idea appealed to her because she could sell directly to consumers and it did not require marketing money she did not have, or distribution channels she could not access.* The home party was the ideal fit. It was scalable and she had read of others who had built very successful companies using home parties. She had attended a few home parties and people (particularly women) seemed to enjoy them. They bought products and some even chose to start their own business to sell Tastefully Simple products.
- Blashack Strahan knew she was the right person for the task. She had hit on a trend that wasn't going away — busy people and great food.

Blashack Strahan knew her direction. She committed to it with her prayer arrow, and planted the seed to build a mighty oak.

Lesson: To grow, you need to seek the *"abundancy" of potential*. In other words, think big. Expand the pie so others can share, and together you can achieve great goals. To build a great business, you need high-potential business opportunities – the right products, right customer segments, and the right strategy that grows on the wave of underlying trends. Most importantly, it needs the special gifts and passion that you bring, and the meaning you give to those who join you. When you do find your mission, make a commitment and go into it with full passion. Few entrepreneurs succeed at this level with half a heart. But test, test, test. Make sure that the market is right for your products, and ready for you. ***Success requires one foot in your vision and the other in reality***.

8. Find the right partner. Blashack Strahan got the initial inspiration for Tastefully Simple on November 14. The next morning she shared the idea with an acquaintance and local hair-salon owner named Joani Nielson, who immediately agreed to invest in the plan. Blashack Strahan respected Nielson's vision and smarts, and this was the validation that she was hoping for, which gave her the confidence to move forward.

Blashack Strahan and Nielson were aligned in their vision to grow Tastefully Simple into a large company. After running her initial projections, Blashack Strahan was fearful that she would not be capable of running an $11 million company. She called Nielson, whose response was, "If you can *grow* an $11 million company, you can *run* an $11 million company." This was comforting to Blashack Strahan.

But she was not totally sold on the concept of having a partner. Over the years she'd heard horror story after horror story about the disadvantages of having partners. So Blashack Strahan spent hours talking to various businesspeople about the pros and cons of partnerships. Every person but one suggested she do it on her own and without a partner. But Blashack Strahan's intuition told her something different. Good partners who have complementary skills and temperaments can help to build a bigger business than one person alone. Blashack Strahan respected Nielson and knew she was an astute, savvy businesswoman. She offered Nielson 30 percent of the company. Blashack Strahan retained 70 percent.

> **Lesson:** As Blashack Strahan puts it, "Surround yourself with motors, not anchors." The right partnership can lead you to greater heights. Look at Jobs and Wozniak (Apple), Gates and Allen (Microsoft) and Brin and Page (Google). Get a partner who is emotionally and psychologically balanced with you, and get feedback from others.

9. Why 70-30? It took Blashack Strahan about three months to make this decision. She wanted to make the number meaningful for Nielson since she had agreed to invest $10,000 – a significant chunk of the investment in the business vs. $6,000 from Blashack Strahan. But because Nielson would not be working as an employee in the company and would not have any sweat equity in building the business, they agreed to an unequal split. Clearly this partnership has been rewarding for both of them as well as for the company. Blashack Strahan is the leader and the outside spark of Tastefully Simple. And in 2000 Nielson came on board as COO, managing operations and ensuring the company delivered.

> **Lesson**: As Blashack Strahan puts it, "Surround yourself with motors, not anchors." The right partnership can lead you to greater heights. Look at Jobs and Wozniak (Apple), Gates and Allen (Microsoft) and Brin and Page (Google). Get a partner who is emotionally and psychologically balanced with you, and get feedback from others.

10. Understand the impact of the numbers. When Blashack Strahan decided to start Tastefully Simple, one of the first things she did was to develop a business plan and *run the numbers* to see what she could pay her sales consultants. She concluded they would receive up to 36 percent commission on the sale of the products, and they would also be paid as they sponsored other people into the business. She originally planned to pay out 6/4/2, which meant that when the sales consultant sponsored someone and trained them, they would receive 6 percent of first-line sales, 4 percent on second-line sales and 2 percent on third-line sales. When she did her projections with these commissions, Blashack Strahan found out that she would be out of business within four years. So she changed the compensation plan to a 5/3/1 payout.

> **Lesson**: Become a "numbers person." Everything about your business (including your enthusiasm) is ultimately reflected in the numbers. Don't let accountants

and others intimidate you about how complicated the numbers are. Calculating taxes may be complex due to the never-ending changes and deductions in the tax laws, so make sure you hire an expert. But the rest is quite straightforward, so understand it. Otherwise, you are driving without clear vision, and sooner or later, you may crash.

11. Goals and assumptions. When Blashack Strahan was developing her business plan, she knew the importance of establishing good goals – goals that were simultaneously realistic, achievable and challenging. So she needed to know what to expect from herself and her team.

Initially she started by speaking with salespeople from other companies in the home-party industry, such as Creative Memories, Discovery Toys, Longaberger Baskets and Pampered Chef, to see what they were able to achieve. This gave her the range of possibilities and allowed her to benchmark her goals against the reality of the industry. Then she made educated guesses, writing down her goals, such as the number of parties per month, the amount of sales from the party and the number of people who would become consultants each year. And she monitored against her projections.

Lesson: Goal-setting is one of the most important attributes of a leader. Goals need to be in writing so you commit to them. They need to be realistic and achievable so you and your team don't get disheartened. And they need to be challenging so you don't get sandbagged, and your team knows that exceptional rewards are truly reserved for outstanding performance. Blashack Strahan has been a fanatic about quantifiable goals – for herself and for her team. She publicizes the goals and shares their actual performance in comparison. There is no hiding. The goals are the first thing you see when you enter Tastefully Simple's headquarters. She challenges everyone, including herself, which is perhaps the key reason why she is able to inspire thousands and thousands of Tastefully Simple sales consultants across the nation.

12. Bootstrap and avoid investors. Blashack Strahan started her business with no fixed costs, no rent, no salary, and no overhead, and all her expenses were variable. Nielson offered the free use of a shed on her property for Tastefully Simple's first headquarters – the building had a concrete floor and no running water. Blashack Strahan was able to spend money on inventory and minimal marketing materials, such as catalogs, brochures and order forms, to generate home parties and sales. Her husband had an income, so Blashack Strahan did not take a salary. Blashack Strahan was the only employee for several months, and at the end of three years had fewer than 10 team members. Blashack Strahan did not draw a salary for the first three years of the business. She had taste-testing parties at night and on the weekends, and ran the company during the day. She lost $6,000 in the first year. In addition to the $10,000 investment from Nielson and her own $6,000, Blashack Strahan had also secured a bank loan with an SBA guarantee in the amount of $20,000. In the second year, she obtained a $15,000 loan from her mother as insurance. By the end of the second year, Tastefully Simple was profitable. By bootstrapping, Blashack Strahan has essentially built a $140 million-plus business with $16,000 of equity and $20,000 of bank debt.

> **Lesson**: Bootstrapping is a great way to minimize your financial needs and avoid having to raise equity from investors. Know when to bootstrap (when you have not created value in your venture, when it is tough to obtain external financing or when the cost is high) and when you need to seek financing (for competitive reasons, if you can build exceptional value, or the money is available at reasonable cost).

13. Initial sales. Tastefully Simple's initial product line included 22 products, with an average price of $5.95, in a simple, well-designed brochure with line illustrations of the products. All of the products were specially chosen to fit Blashack Strahan's goal of being either "open and enjoy" or not requiring more than two ingredients to prepare. Several products were privately labeled for Tastefully Simple, but due to minimum quantity restrictions, she was forced to offer some products that were not branded with Tastefully Simple labels.

Once her inventory was in hand, she was ready to have her first home taste-testing party. Her original goal was to have 12 people at each party and sell $300 worth of products, for an average sale of $25. She was also expecting one or two people at each party to offer to host additional parties. She also planned to have five sales people by the end of the first year. At her first party, she sold about $200 worth of products to five people (for an average of $40). The attendance was smaller, but the average sale was higher. Most importantly, four wanted to host parties. From this start, ***Tastefully Simple has grown to 28,000 sales consultants nationwide***.

How did she get hosts to hold parties? Blashack Strahan started out with people she knew in the community as well as her friends who would have fun socializing and eating. They invited their friends, and her business snowballed. As new sales consultants joined her, she offered basic training, which mainly consisted of shadowing her at her parties. All of the marketing was based on word of mouth at the grassroots level. She packed all the orders on a pool table. Nielson installed software and entered orders at night after working all day in her hair salon. Eventually they graduated to Quickbooks, the accounting software package. All sales were for cash up front, and she had to pay for her inventory in 30-45 days, so if she watched her inventory and overhead, she could have a positive cash flow relatively quickly, even with a low sales level. Her business started to generate positive cash flow.

> **Lesson**: Sales usually are slow in the beginning because potential customers may not have heard of you and may not want to buy from a new company. That is why in high-growth companies, sales grow in the shape of a hockey stick – slow

at the start and rapidly after you understand how to sell and after the market has accepted your product. This is what happened at Tastefully Simple. But the smart move was to keep costs low and inventory under control so the company would have a positive cash flow even with low levels of sales. *Don't spend what you don't make.* And make sure you have a positive cash flow to pay your bills. Otherwise, your vendors will cut you off.

From Profits to the Moon

14. Faith and enthusiasm. Blashack Strahan's goal for 1995 was to have between ***six and 18 parties each month*** and recruit five sales consultants by the end of the year. She ended the year with seven sales consultants. She wanted to end 1996 with 30 sales people. She had 33. For 1997, her goal was 100 – about eight new consultants per month. By August, the number of sales consultants was at 31. Tastefully Simple's growth had started to sputter and Blashack Strahan was becoming increasingly frustrated and desperate. What brought her back to reality was a radio story about Patty Wetterling's continuing quest to find her son, who had been missing for a number of years. Blashack Strahan realized that her problems were only related to business and that setbacks do happen. She decided to accept the problem rather than hide her head in the sand, changed her business plan to reflect the new reality, redefined her goals and renewed her efforts. She then went as a corporate guest to Creative Memories national conference, a nearby direct sales company that was a pioneer in scrapbooking and growing at an astounding pace. Blashack Strahan listened to the spark plugs at Creative Memories and started to get infused with a new sense of optimism. She learned new skills as well as the value of having faith in her journey and the importance of setting goals. When she returned, she was rejuvenated and set a goal of signing eight new consultants in the next four months. She signed them up in six weeks, and by the end of the year had a total of 55 consultants.

She knew that the company had great products and *they only sold it to people who eat.* As Tanya Roufs, her second consultant, said, "It isn't like we have a trunk full of toothbrushes. *It's food*!" And there happened to be plenty of people who liked to eat and liked to eat her products. All she needed was faith and enthusiasm.

Lesson: ***Entrepreneurs need faith***. Faith is about how you can shape the future. ***To succeed, you need challenging goals based on faith, and faith based on the reality of the market's potential and your competitive edge***. The reality was that Tastefully Simple had barely scratched the surface of the market's potential, and could continue growing for many years. But to do so, Blashack Strahan had to believe in her company and the mission, and then act with that belief.

15. Hang on to the right partner. Within three and a half years Tastefully Simple grew to $1.4 million in sales. During this time, Nielson offered to sell her shares back to Blashack Strahan. She felt guilty because she didn't have the time to devote to the company due to her own thriving business. Blashack Strahan pointed out to her that 30 percent of $0 was still $0, and even if Nielson wanted to sell back her shares, Blashack Strahan would insist she keep 5-10 percent because she had believed in the possibilities. Nielson stayed with her investment, and today that investment is worth millions. She is currently the Founding Partner & Chief Operations Officer of Tastefully Simple.

> **Lesson**: Nearly all companies struggle in the early years. Sometimes the confidence is justified. Sometimes it is not. So why stay in? Because it is your passion and you alone know whether continued passion is justified.

16. Stop chasing three rabbits. As she was building the business, Blashack Strahan was doing three jobs. She was organizing parties and selling products. She was managing her team of sales consultants and helping them to sell more. And she was leading the business. As she notes, "You can't chase two rabbits and catch them both." In this case, Blashack Strahan was chasing three. Blashack Strahan ***realized that she needed to focus her efforts on growing the business by recruiting and training more consultants, and help them sell more products so that everyone could prosper***. They needed to know how to manage and grow their own businesses, including setting and achieving goals, having parties, recruiting sales consultants and selling products. If they were facing problems, they needed to know that others, including Blashack Strahan, had faced similar hurdles and overcome them. If they were doing well, they needed to be congratulated and given the tools and encouragement to do even better, if that is what they wanted. And that is what they wanted. They had the advantage of knowing the history of sales results at Tastefully Simple, and the range of results from other consultants. They could benchmark their own performance. They could set goals in a supportive group setting and help each other grow. Since Tastefully Simple pays its sales consultants on commission, it's important for their work to be exciting, entertaining, fun, and financially rewarding. This is not always easy. That is why it takes leaders who are focused and committed to one task–helping their sales force. Blashack Strahan stopped chasing three rabbits and propelled the exponential growth of Tastefully Simple.

> **Lesson**: If you are a team leader, lead. It is often difficult to be a team member and a team leader unless the business is very small and simple, such as a two-person carpentry operation (and even this can be complex). Leaders need to help team members define and achieve their own goals. Their success is your success. Their struggles become your struggles. Help them and help yourself.

17. Growth phase. Blashack Strahan found that there was plenty of growth left in the company, and her faith in its mission and belief in its products brought enthusiastic new people to the company who could feed further growth. Now that the growth had come back, she had to manage the company prudently. Growth brought its own needs. She started developing regular goals in all areas of the company along with her team, promoting them and monitoring them. She built the infrastructure needed by the company and asked Nielson to join to manage the operations as the COO (while Blashack Strahan handled the sales and marketing). Today the product line includes more than 50 stock-keeping units and Nielson has expanded the warehouse several times to better serve their clients. Rather than just hiring for present needs, the company had to start hiring for future needs and move employees to the jobs that were best suited to them.

In 2000 Blashack Strahan joined a group of CEO peers to learn how others worked through the challenges of growing a business. She also decided to hire an executive coach to help her better define her role in the ever-changing company — because her role had changed. Previously, the "hands on" value that Blashack Strahan brought to the company was clear. Now most of the victories were those of the team. This is an issue she continues to face as the company reaches ***over $140 million-plus in sales with more than 28,000 sales consultants*** across the United States.

Lesson: Uncontrolled growth can be dangerous. So build the infrastructure to control it. And expand your skills so you grow as the company grows. Otherwise, you could be headed for problems.

18. The match made in heaven. It seems as if Blashack Strahan and Tastefully Simple are a match made in heaven - and everyone can learn from her skills. Her values and motivations match the needs of an organization that relies on thousands of part-time commission-based consultants around the country for its sales. She leads them by motivating and encouraging them, and helping them through periods of doubt that she knows they face since she has overcome them herself. She creates a positive atmosphere and celebrates successes led by "motors, and not anchors." She realizes that to be a leader, she has to know herself, which means being candid and humble about admitting what she does not know. She needs to have the vision to shape what she wants to create, develop the plan with goals and timelines to make the vision real and measure progress, and have the toughness to accept the challenge to improve the business. As Blashack Strahan puts it, leaders need the "skin of a rhino, the heart of a lion and the soul of an angel" (from the *Priorities for Life: Leadership* video).

Lesson: We all have unique skills and passions. ***The first rule of success is to "know thyself." The second rule is to design your company to follow the first rule***.

Rules for Entrepreneurs from Jill Blashack Strahan of Tastefully Simple

- **Dream it. Believe it. Work it.** Everything and anything starts with a dream. What transforms dreaming and believing into success is the willingness to make it happen through *action.*
- **Set goals.** Create a plan, build your business with intent, and write down goals that will stretch you a little further every time. It will keep you moving in the direction of your focus, and it works – *the mind is a magnet.*
- **Define your principles – and your expectations.** Decide what you do – or don't – want to be known for as a company. That clarity is foundational, so as your company grows, there will be no confusion about your expectations. Remember, *great things happen through teams, not individuals.* We don't do it alone.
- **Reserve the right to get smarter.** When you're willing to admit your mistakes and embrace change, it frees you from trying to be perfect. And it helps you discover that there's often more than one right answer.
- **Be willing to build from least to most.** "Least-to-most" means you can start small and grow incrementally. A company needs to grow at the right pace based on market needs and company resources. You don't have to do it all at once, so try to find that sweet spot.
- **Know where you're going.** Be clear about your products and your brand. The important thing is to stay true to the heart of your concept, whatever it might be.
- **Enjoy the journey. Be patient with yourself.** There's no pixie dust or magic bullet for success. We build a business one by one by one. One decision at a time, one sale at a time, one relationship at a time. *So start where you are, don't stop and the rest will follow.*

Glen Taylor
Taylor Corporation

MANKATO, MINN

From the farm to the Forbes 400
"Printers like presses. I like customers" ... Glen Taylor

Summary: When Glen Taylor was 16, he was a father, husband, manager of a farm, and a 4.0 GPA (if you don't count typing) high-school student. When he finished high school, his teachers persuaded him to enter college rather than go into farming. With scholarships, loans, and a part-time (32 hours a week) job in a printing company, Taylor pursued a degree in math, which he completed in three years. At the printing company, he implemented so many profitable, "common-sense" improvements, that, upon graduation, the owner asked him to join the company as the #2 guy for an annual salary of under $5,000. Taylor listened to his advisers at the college and agreed to join the printing company, even though he would have made more as a teacher and would have had his summers off. His professors told him that challenging opportunities in business do not show up every day, and he could always go into teaching later. Within a few years, he had made so many improvements to the company (and asked for a piece of the larger pie) that he was making in excess of $35,000, and had bought 13 percent of the company with his savings (he could live on the original $5,000 salary). That is when the owner of the printing company announced that he was ready to sell and gave Taylor a year to put together an offer. Initially, Taylor planned to buy the company with two of his colleagues. However, he soon found that they had differing goals. Taylor wanted to expand, and expand, and expand. The others did not. So Taylor bought the company on his own. Today his company is a colossus in the printing industry with operations throughout the world, putting Taylor on the Forbes 400 list of richest Americans. On the side, he owns the Minnesota Timberwolves NBA franchise and was the Minority Leader of the Minnesota State Senate. Who knows, one day he might even become one of the best schoolteachers on the planet. This is how he did it.

Before the Startup

1. **Connect the dots between results and rewards**. Glen Taylor was raised

on a farm. His parents did not have much money. Each year they borrowed money to farm and then paid off the loan from the results of their efforts. They did not get too far ahead, but life was good. They had a large garden, an orchard, chickens, cows, and pigs, and they sold the produce, eggs, milk, etc., to buy other items. This gave Taylor a basic understanding of business: the more you produced, the more money you made. Although his dad was a farmer, he did not like farming. His father liked people and sports, and so did Taylor. The rules of his house were fairly simple. Taylor could play sports, which he enjoyed, if he got good grades; treated others, including his siblings, well; and did his chores. He learned the direct connection between results and rewards (or lack of same).

Lesson: ***Build a very clear connection between effort, values, results, and rewards***. This lesson helped Taylor join the Forbes 400.

2. **How you see affects what you do**. When Taylor was a junior in high school, his girlfriend became pregnant, and they got married. Taylor was 16. At this time, his dad had another job and his older brother started college. So Taylor had to manage the farm. His routine started at 6 A.M. with his chores. Then he went to school, after which he had more chores, and then field work until midnight (except in the winter). He learned time management and to set priorities. He found out that he had to get his school work done at school. While the teacher was explaining problems to the class, Taylor was doing his homework. The hard work and long hours could have encouraged Taylor to drop out of school like many others had. But he stayed. In his senior year, his family decided to sell the farm and Taylor ended up working at another farm to earn money. When he finished high school with all A's except a B+ in typing, his teachers strongly suggested that he should go to college and not into farming. Taylor saw how difficult it was for his father to get a promotion in his job because he did not have a college degree, even when he was qualified for the job. This convinced Taylor. He went to Mankato State University (MSU).

Lesson: Your lens affects your vision and your vision affects your behavior. ***If you focus on problems, you will see hurdles. If you focus on opportunities, problems become stepping stones to growth***. It's your choice.

3. **Multi-tasking before the term was invented**. Taylor was awarded an academic scholarship to attend MSU and he obtained a National Defense Loan that he did not have to repay if he became a teacher. And to support his family, he also got a part-time job working 30-32 hours a week at Bill Carlson's company, Carlson Letter Service (subsequently Carlson Craft), where his wife also worked. In addition, his brother moved back to MSU and they worked together as laborers doing anything from mopping floors to handyman jobs. He never had to use the money from the National Defense Loan program. He majored in math, and minored in physics and social sciences. He was sharp enough to excel at all of them. His goal was to become a math teacher since that would give him the flexibility to teach anywhere in the country, and he also found that he liked to work with people and motivate kids. Even

with the job and family responsibilities, Taylor got his degree in three years due to the "setup in high school" where he had to develop good habits, value time, and prioritize his life to survive and excel.

Lesson: ***Brains help. What's important is what you do with it.*** Mix good habits, a strong work ethic, and clear direction, and you can do wonders. To quote an old cliché, Taylor excelled at making lemonade from lemons.

4. How many jobs can one man have? As a student at MSU, Taylor joined Carlson Craft (at that time called Carlson Letter Service). The company's owner, Bill Carlson, hired a number of college students, and there were about 20 others from MSU who worked there alongside Taylor. Taylor's first job was running a press, which was considered to be an entry-level position. When another student who was in charge of inventory took a summer vacation (amazing the other students, since summers were for working), Taylor offered to do his own job and also that of the vacationing student. Carlson agreed. Taylor did both jobs and offered a variety of suggestions to change inventory practices to save money, such as reusing cartons and envelopes. Carlson appreciated the additional savings and offered the job to Taylor on a permanent basis. When the other student returned from his vacation, he learned that he had been assigned to the press and quit. Taylor then asked if he could help in ordering and saw how they could save money there. He noticed that he could get better prices by combining orders and he negotiated for them. He also examined freight bills and noticed that they could qualify for lower freight charges by combining freight. When Taylor graduated from college at the age of 21, Carlson asked him to stay on with the company as the #2 person.

Lesson: *If you have a summer job and a "Glen Taylor" wants it, don't go on vacation.* When bureaucratic corporations ask you to think outside the box, they do not tell you that they want you to stay inside a larger box that is outside your inner box. Entrepreneurial firms place no such limits. They want to save money and make money. Take advantage of your opportunities. Great ones are rare and they come in disguise.

5. Could have, would have, should have... decisions that alter your life. When Carlson asked Taylor to join the company on a full-time basis after graduation, Taylor asked him about his salary. Carlson suggested that Taylor check out his other options to see what he was offered. Taylor was planning on becoming a math teacher. This is when "modern math" was being introduced into schools. As part of his undergrad education, his professor had asked Taylor to evaluate an eighth-grade class in the local district, which wanted to test this new concept. Taylor was asked to be the student teacher, and teach modern math to the top eighth-grade students and the bottom ninth-grade students in the school. His report's conclusion was that the top students got it easily, but that the schools should teach the bottom students more basic math skills, such as percentages, that they would need in life. This experience and report made Taylor a hot commodity as a teacher recruit. When he graduated, top schools in the country, such as Edina in Minnesota and schools in California, called to have him teach modern math in their schools. Taylor asked his professors for advice, fully expecting them to suggest the teaching career. Instead they suggested that he join Carlson, pointing out that he could always go back to teaching (and be a better teacher with the practical experience), but that an opportunity like the one at Carlson did not come along every day, and it could reflect Taylor's special talents. Taylor accepted Carlson's offer.

> **Lesson**: *When making life-altering decisions, select mentors wisely* and know your passion. Some options expand your horizons and help you reach your goal. Others restrict your choices, as Cortez did when he scuttled his ships and forced his conquistadors to win or die. Key is what you do after you make your choice.

6. **Your word.** Taylor still had to arrive at a mutually agreeable pay-scale arrangement with Carlson. Since Carlson had never had a #2 guy, he was unsure what he should pay. Taylor knew what he could get from the school districts who were trying to recruit him. But he was not sure what to ask for (especially since he wanted the job and did not want to blow it by asking for too much), and so he went and told Carlson, "whatever you decide, I will take." Carlson offered $4,250, which was below the market (compared with salaries of $5,000–6,000 that Taylor was offered as a teacher and that, too, with free summers). While Taylor thought that perhaps he should have asked for more, he agreed to the pay offered by Carlson. As he puts it, "I said I would, so I did."

> **Lesson**: *Don't give your word casually.* When you do, live up to it. Years later Taylor found out that Carlson offered him $4,250 because he was paying himself only $4,500. If he had asked for $6,000, he might not have been offered the job.

From Entry to Ownership

7. **Why are you in business?** Carlson Craft was primarily a printer of wedding invitations. The company offered its products as pamphlets in a catalog with a hard cover. These catalogs were distributed without charge to drug stores in the region, and customers examined catalogs from various printers to select the printer and type of invitation. After he joined the firm on a full-time basis, one of the first things Taylor did was to compare the company's catalog with those of the leaders in the wedding-invitation printing industry, which were primarily from New York and Chicago. He believed that if they were to succeed, he had to "go against the best and be better than them." Their catalogs were big, well-done, attractive, and looked very professional. Taylor laid these catalogs next to his firm's own to compare them, and to understand customers and competitors by looking for similar products, features, and strategies in each of the catalogs. And he asked himself a simple, billion-dollar question: "Why would people buy from Carlson?" He could not see an obvious advantage, and concluded that many of their customers were buying from them because they were local and slightly lower-priced. He came up with a new strategy

that included the following:

- Develop a fancy, rich-looking catalog that copied (also called "fast follower" in business school-speak) the competitors' designs.
- Include all the products that were most commonly featured in the various catalogs, assuming that the more frequent the occurrence of a product, the higher its popularity.
- On items that were easy to compare, set prices slightly below (around $1) the competitors, giving customers a reason to buy from him rather than from his competitors. But have higher prices on accompanying items and customized options. As an example, the standard wedding invitation price was at 11 lines with a higher price for more lines (but the cost to add more lines was minimal). The invitation shown in the catalog had more than 11 lines, with the hope that customers would choose to add more lines and increase the package price. His total package was comparable to that of his competitors, but he was thought of as very competitively priced.

He printed 500 catalogs compared with the previous run of 300 and widened the distribution. Sales started to increase.

Lesson: ***The fundamental question in business should be "why would anyone buy from me rather than from my competitors?"*** Taylor calls this common sense, which is actually not very common. To answer this question, know your customers and their choices.

8. Customize to satisfy customers' unique needs. The new catalog got Carlson noticed. Customers and retailers started paying more attention to the company. Brides were impressed with the catalog, which placed Carlson in the same league as the leading companies in Chicago and New York. But Taylor found that, very frequently, they were not ordering the products in the catalog but calling in because they wanted custom designs, wording, and colors. They wanted their wedding invitations to reflect their personalities on their special day. Previously, when this happened, the company's (and industry's) response had been to tell them that "you can get what we have." Taylor, however, noticed that the brides were not asking about price when they wanted to satisfy their unique wishes. He decided to try to satisfy these customers. Whereas previously, Carlson was the low-price vendor, now they started selling customized products at a higher price. Taylor realized that this could be a unique competitive advantage for Carlson and started to focus on answering the broader question, "what does the bride want?" He hired a designer to design new types of invitations. The innovations and new designs were taken to groups of local female college students, employees, and young women for feedback. Taylor specially organized these groups to make sure that his company's innovations were in sync with the market. Although these initial groups were very homogenous, and did not include many ethnic and religious groups, he appealed to a large segment of the country. In later years, he broadened the scope and composition of the test groups.

When he noticed that these groups and customers wanted unique colors beyond the ones in the catalog, he asked the mills to make his paper in those colors. Since he had to buy minimum orders, he had to make sure that he offered colors that were in demand. To know which colors would be in demand, he started going to the New York bridal shows to examine the latest fashions and colors. He pointed out to his customers that they could coordinate all the colors in their wedding, including the paper products, invitations, bridal dresses, etc. He could not keep up with demand. Bill Carlson was looking for minimum of 5 percent gross margins. By differentiating his company's offerings to satisfy the unique needs of his customers, Taylor could increase the size of his typical order by 5 percent and increase his profits by over 60 percent. The company started to take off.

> **Lesson**: Henry Ford said that customers could get "any color – so long as it's black." That's why GM overtook Ford. ***Companies that satisfy customers' needs better than their competitors nearly always do better than those that satisfy their own needs***. Taylor developed a structure for getting good ideas and for testing them. Ego or the "not-invented-here" syndrome was not a factor in his selection. The result showed up in company sales and profits. Why did Taylor test and not use his own instincts like many do? As he puts it, "what did I know?" When customers ask you for something, listen.

9. Innovate for more customers. About the same time, Taylor helped an entrepreneur start a business to supply school proms. His concept was to offer products based on the hit songs and movies of the day to replace his competitors' tired themes, such as Hawaiian hula proms. He needed a variety of paper-based items for his business, and Taylor offered to supply him. When this business took off, Taylor used the concept in wedding invitations. The industry had been built on standard themes and wording based on religious affiliations, such as a Catholic wording and a Protestant wording. Taylor noted that brides were not much older than the high school graduates who attended proms, and that they would be listening to the same songs. Taylor and his team came up with new wording and themes based on hit songs and movies. Brides liked these themes, and they further customized their invitations with their own words at a slightly higher cost.

> **Lesson**: Innovation often means applying an idea that works in one place to others. Ideas can come from competitors, customers, and vendors. Keep your eyes and ears open to catch the latest trends and capitalize on them.

10. Who/what comes first... customers or machinery? Since machinery is the most expensive investment in a printing business, Taylor knew that if he did not worry about press utilization, efficiency, and cost, his company would not be in business for long. They needed to modify operations, improve press utilization, and reduce initial setup costs to be profitable. They did so by modifying machinery and adjusting business practices. Most of Carlson's competitors were printers and emphasized operations and machinery utilization (due to the investment), and

asked customers to adjust by not offering smaller order quantities. Taylor looked at business from his customers' perspectives and adjusted his operations to make a profit. With a printer's perspective, machinery issues ran the business. With Taylor, customer needs ran the business. This was a key difference. His competitors liked large orders due to the savings in press utilization. Taylor liked small orders because there was less competition and offered higher margins, and the huge number of customers with smaller orders meant potentially large markets and volumes.

Lesson: ***You can manage your business to make your machinery efficient or your customers happy. Put customers first. They will make you rich***. Why didn't the other printers do it? As Taylor notes, "They liked machinery. I liked customers."

11. But cut costs to become competitive and make money. Lower prices on standard, easily comparable items, and customization for higher margins, were only part of Taylor's strategy. He knew that this would grow the top line, i.e., revenues. Taylor wanted to grow the bottom line, i.e., profits and cash flow. This meant that he had to make the operation more efficient and effective to cut costs while satisfying customers. In addition to charging more for smaller orders, Taylor started looking at every aspect of the business. As examples:

- Carlson was buying raw materials for envelopes and invitations in packages, which were then unpackaged, printed, repackaged, and sold. He streamlined this process and bought in bulk to reduce raw-material costs and the cost of labor to open the packages.
- They scheduled all orders of a certain color at the same time to minimize press-setup time.
- He started to develop standards for labor and machinery so as to be able to measure and improve individual and company productivity and drive down costs.
- He developed stronger controls to know the cost and proportion of raw materials that were wasted, and then he cut the waste.

Lesson: It is easy to cut prices – until you fail. Taylor cut prices selectively on easily comparable products. To succeed with lower prices, cut costs. And offer other products and services, such as customized products, that have higher margins.

12. Expanding with UPS. As Carlson started to grow, Taylor started to expand the distribution network. In addition to drug stores, Taylor started expanding geographically and also adding florists, printing shops, and dress shops. At the time, UPS was expanding into rural America. Previously, Carlson could only ship via the Postal Service, which resulted in a high level of damage. He had always been happy with UPS, so he decided to expand his geography based on UPS expansion plans. He obtained free Yellow Page directories for cities and towns with more than 1,000 residents in the states where UPS was expanding its reach to get the names of retailers who advertised wedding services. He then calculated the number of dealers he wanted to have based on the population of the town and the estimated number of weddings they were likely to have. If there was more than one advertiser in the Yellow Pages, he first selected the one with the bigger advertisement. He sent the selected retailers a card inviting them to order the catalog for free. When he did receive a card back, he checked their Dun's profile to make sure that they would be a strong customer. He also started offering faster service. Chicago and New York printers normally shipped in 14 days. In contrast, Carlson shipped products on the same day for rush orders (at a slightly higher price, of course). On others, the order was shipped within one to four days. No one was faster. With customization and speed, sales shot up and so did margins. As UPS expanded its geographic reach one state at a time, so did Taylor.

Lesson: ***Grow with the trends (also known as "go with the flow")***. The expansion of UPS to rural areas allowed Carlson to expand its territory, offer faster service, and increase the number of distributors. Customization, speed, and efficiency allowed Carlson and the retailers to earn higher revenues and profits. Give customers what they want, and price becomes secondary.

From Ownership to the Moon

13. Get the means to acquire the company. Carlson Craft had never made over $50,000 in annual profits. Taylor's customization program had the potential to increase profits, and Taylor wanted a piece of this increased pie. So he asked Carlson if the managers could have a bonus based on profits over $50,000. Since the company had never made profits above that in any year, Bill Carlson was skeptical about the potential to make this meaningful to the managers. Taylor added that this may end up being a theoretical discussion, but it would be a great incentive. So Carlson agreed. The company made $150,000 in net income the next year and Taylor was convinced that they could sell more invitations at even higher markups. At the end of the year, Bill Carlson had the books audited and then invited the three managers to dinner at a fancy restaurant (Taylor's salary was still $5,000 so this was special) and gave them their bonus checks. He also informed them that he wanted to change the agreement with the three managers. He increased their base salaries, with Taylor's salary growing from $5,000 to $26,000. Taylor and his family could live on $5,000. He saved the rest.

Lesson: Negotiate for bonuses to build your nest-egg based on growth. Offer the same to your employees. They will work harder. Taylor noted that he would not have done what Carlson did by increasing the base and eliminating the bonuses. His philosophy was to increase the base salaries by a small amount, but increase the level at which bonuses were calculated so that managers always got rewarded for increasing profits. After the first year, future years' profits at that level belonged to Taylor. Managers had to keep the business growing and raising profits.

14. Bulls make money. Bears make money. Hogs don't. Taylor's success had not gone unnoticed outside the walls of Carlson and he had other options. He had been approached by investors who offered to invest in a new company at which he would receive a handsome salary of $100,000 – but no stock. Taylor did not trust the offer because he thought that he may be out of a job after he had set up the investors in the new business.

> **Lesson**: If you want to recruit superstars with a proven track record, make it worth their while but make them share the risk. One assumes that these superstars are not stupid. Why should they accept an offer where the gains can be temporary but the losses permanent?

15. Become a shareholder. When Taylor started with Bill Carlson in 1959, Carlson Craft's sales were in the neighborhood of $180,000. By 1974, sales had reached $7 million, and the company had no bank debt. Taylor had started "pestering" Carlson about buying stock in the company by 1965 and continued to ask him about the possibility of becoming a partner. Ultimately, Carlson had relented and sold Taylor and two of his colleagues in the company's management team one share each out of the 100 shares he owned. As soon as Carlson agreed to sell one share, (the proverbial "camel's nose in the tent") Taylor asked for more. He used his savings to buy more shares in the company. Soon Taylor and the other two managers had accumulated 13 percent each, with Carlson owning 61 percent. Taylor asked Carlson not to sell any more shares to others.

> **Lesson**: Once you sell shares to others, even if it is one share, remember that they are your partners. Make sure you want them as partners. So think about whom you want to own equity in your business and offer it for results or cash. In this case, obviously, it was a very profitable arrangement for both Bill Carlson and Glen Taylor.

16. Partners with the same vision. In January of 1974, Carlson approached his partners, the three managers, and told them that he wanted to sell his shares by December. Taylor negotiated the price on behalf of the team (he was the #2 guy in the company) and went to the bank and asked for a loan in excess of $1 million to buy Bill Carlson's shares. His assumption was that the three managers would each own a third. While Taylor was arranging the package, his friends and advisers suggested that Taylor buy the company on his own because partnerships do not always work, especially if the partners have different visions of how the company should operate. Taylor's response was that he knew his partners and had worked with them. After he had lined up the financing, he informed his partners and suggested that Taylor and the others would have salaries in the same ratio as in the past (Taylor's was higher), and that Taylor would be CEO while the others would be vice-presidents (their titles at the time). He also wanted to give a few shares to up-and-coming hires he had made: five to six MSU graduates who had joined the company at Taylor's invitation to make their fortune. He wanted to offer them, and other future employees, the opportunities to grow that Taylor had enjoyed. To Taylor's surprise, his potential partners rejected the structure because they did not agree with Taylor on his growth plans and sharing of equity. While both perspectives are justifiable (people and their goals can differ), this is not what Taylor wanted. He wanted to grow the company to make it a giant in the industry and to bring in new shareholders who could help him to reach this goal. The others did not agree. Since they had differing goals, they decided to alter the arrangement. Taylor agreed to buy all the shares and own the company by himself. The other two managers wanted to be treated fairly and to maintain their salaries, titles, responsibilities, and perks, which was fine with Taylor. One of the two managers decided to leave the company within a couple of years, and the other stayed on and had a very productive ongoing relationship with Taylor.

> **Lesson**: ***Aim high to achieve much. But make sure that your partners agree on the vision before you get on the ship***. Otherwise, you will end up having many internal fights and business divorce can be as painful as the other kind.

17. Structure the right deal. Taylor bought the company on January of 1975. He went to all three sellers and asked them if he could borrow the acquisition financing that he needed from them rather than from the bank. He structured the loan with a 10-year term, with the option of extending it to 12 years if he needed to do so due to unforeseen adverse situations. He paid off the loan in less than 10 years.

> **Lesson**: When buying a company, seller financing is usually the most flexible and lowest-cost financing you can get. It is highly recommended, especially for your initial acquisitions. Structure the terms realistically, and give yourself a cushion in case there is a hiccup and your projections are overly optimistic.

18. Track the numbers. Taylor hired his first accountant in 1975 as soon as he bought the company. He hired someone he already knew, and according to Taylor, "his accountant was surprised at the amount of information I was collecting." Taylor recorded everything he needed to know to keep track of the company and to know "what was out of whack." He knew all his raw material costs, labor costs, labor productivity, raw-material waste (even some of what was not being reported to him), overhead, equipment usage, etc. His accounting team added to that base knowledge and implemented systems to allow Taylor to be able to control costs and predict performance as he continued to grow.

> **Lesson**: *Know your numbers. You cannot drive your company if you don't know where you are going*. If you cannot predict your performance, and are unable to adjust your costs as your sales change, you are not running a tight ship. You are living on hopes. Sometimes this works. Usually it does not.

19. Grow or be left behind. After acquiring Carlson Craft, and before he started to acquire companies around the country, Taylor attended an executive workshop at Harvard's Graduate School of Business. He wanted to answer the question, **"Why**

should I succeed when others don't?" According to Taylor, what he learned was that there were a number of key reasons for failure. In addition to poor financing, they included the following:

- *Business grows but managers do not*. Poor managers want to run every detail of the company and do not learn how to delegate responsibly. Taylor realized that he would reach the limits of his company quickly if he ran everything himself. This meant that Taylor had to develop great managers, and direct them according to each manager's unique personality, needs, and skills
- *Trends change but managers do not*. Taylor realized that computers were becoming an increasingly important part of business, and he did not know enough about them. So he went to IBM's school for executives to know more about computers and learned how to apply them to his business.
- *Scope grows but controls do not*. As the business grew, Taylor needed to track all the important numbers of his business, which included the accounting and financial numbers, and the operations and marketing numbers, on a regular basis so he and his managers could identify problems before they became threatening. Taylor was a math major, so using numbers came naturally. He developed control systems to monitor performance by identifying key numbers and tracking them before they became major issues.
- *Managers win but workers do not*. When Taylor first heard of "win-win" at the session, he wondered "what kind of pinkie idea is this?" But he realized that when he worked with his managers, employees, customers, and vendors as teams, all did well when compared with deals where one did well and the others did not. Taylor realized that he could be more successful by getting a smaller share of a larger pie than hogging a larger share of a smaller pie. People work for their self-interest. The key is to blend yours with theirs.

Lesson: Answer the question: *Why should you succeed when others don't?* Become a better manager. Find the right people, train them and "incentivize" them. Share the profits and develop control mechanisms to delegate responsibly. Help people reach their goals, add meaning to their lives, and they will help you reach yours.

20. Expand beyond the footprint. Now that Taylor had a company that was selling in the Midwest, he put out the word in the industry that he was in the market to buy other companies and asked his industry peers to call him if they were planning to sell. One day, Taylor heard from a competitor in Indiana who was in trouble. He knew this entrepreneur from industry conferences and had even helped him in the past. Taylor immediately took off to see the potential seller and knocked on his door at 2 A.M. Taylor already knew enough about the company to make an offer. He knew that the company was smaller and the catalog was not up to Taylor's standards. He knew that the company was not making a profit because it had too many employees, poor productivity, high levels of waste, and poor employee morale. The company could also suffer if there were a paper shortage, as feared (see next paragraph). He knew he could fix these problems. The seller wanted $1 million for the business (so his wife would be taken care of if he died). Although Taylor thought that the price for the business was a little high, when he quizzed the man, the man replied that "that's the figure I want." Taylor figured out that he could pay $900,000 for the business with seller financing, but that he could pay an additional $200,000 for the building because he could have it financed at a lower rate with amortization over a longer-term. Both parties got what they wanted and the deal was done.

> **Lesson**: *Understand the seller's real needs when structuring an acquisition. Make sure you know the company's problems, how to value the company, and how to structure the deal so it does not put you under.* Taylor had made it a point to know other, similar companies in the industry and their problems. He knew he was ahead of all of them in the improvements he was making and the results he was achieving. When they started to show up on his doorstep, he started buying them out.

21. Distance management. Since the Indiana acquisition was Taylor's first business outside his home base, he wanted to make sure that he did not make any mistakes. He selected a manager who had worked for him while going to college, and then had gone to work for an insurance company after graduation. Taylor had recruited him back, and he picked this young manager to run the new Indiana business. They went over the business plan and laid out the formula based on what had worked at Mankato. Taylor had trained this manager and had high expectations. He also offered him a share of the new company to reward him if he performed. He never worried. Taylor knew that he could quickly increase the company's sales and pay off the debt in about three years. He ended up paying off the $900,000 loan to the seller in two years.

> **Lesson**: Managing at a "distance" is a very important step if you want to grow, and it is a difficult one. At a distance, you cannot do everything or keep on eye on everything. You need to be able to track progress, monitor problems, and assist without being there to observe the situation. You need to know how to train managers, set expectations, and monitor for results. Many entrepreneurs never make it to, or past, this stage.

22. Increase delegation with growing trust. Taylor realized that he would have to develop great managers and delegate effectively to manage his growing business. He decided to run each company as its own profit center, and he told his managers that they should run the company as if they owned it. However, before he gave them this authority, he developed some rules. He would only hire people from within his company or people he knew. He found them in his college classmates who had joined large companies and had developed corporate discipline from these companies. He recruited them and gave them an opportunity to grow with him. Initially, he would delegate in small steps and make sure that they developed the plan together, and he would monitor it very closely. Taylor always heard, "Don't you trust me?" from every one of his managers because he checked everything in the early stages of the manager's tenure. Taylor's response was, "Yes, I trust you, but I want to check for the first few years because I want you running this business for a lifetime." He believed in "over-managing for the first few years and under-managing later." After he developed a degree of comfort with the managers, he would 'under-manage' and would receive monthly financial statements, a report of whatever they wanted to tell him, and an annual budget. He got the background before the budget, so he was aware of the situation before he saw the numbers. Taylor called them only if there were surprises.

> **Lesson**: ***Your own limits become your business's limits***. If you want to grow beyond your own capacity, learn to find good managers, train them well, and delegate effectively. Practice variable delegation to keep control at the optimum level, more at first and less later.

23. "We" screwed up, not "you" screwed up. On major decisions, Taylor would go over all the details involving the situation with his managers. Once they made a decision, he would tell them, "I back you and support you. We are in this together." If something went wrong, he would tell them that "we made this decision together, so I am equally responsible. Now let's find a solution." He wanted his managers to know that he would never say, "I told you so." This gave them the comfort to admit any mistakes fast and find a solution before the mistake became a cancer.

> **Lesson**: ***Everyone makes mistakes. The insecure don't admit it***. "I told you so" can be four very destructive words in a business relationship. People will try to find ways to avoid hearing it because they think they will be blamed, and they will not tell you when problems arise. You need to decide whether you want to score political points or make money.

24. Plan for the downside. Soon after Taylor bought Carlson and the Indiana operation, there was a scare about a potential paper shortage. The expectation was that all printers would get a reduced but proportionate share of paper. This would mean that his core invitation-printing business would have to shrink. To prevent this, Taylor found an envelope company that was in trouble and purchased it at a very reasonable price. His plan was to shut it down and use its paper quota to protect his core invitation-printing business. But the shortage never materialized, and the scare was unfounded. Taylor had obtained seller financing for the envelope-company purchase with a small down payment, and he found that he had another profitable business.

> **Lesson**: Understand the risks and protect yourself. Rather than just accept the potential for a shortage of raw materials, Taylor bought a company at a reasonable price to protect his overall business. Know the risks and develop a strategy to overcome them.

25. Be loyal to build loyalty. When Taylor bought the envelope company, he had to find the right manager for the company. One of his key employees had an autistic baby, and Taylor knew that the baby could get more resources in the larger Twin Cities metro area, where the plant was located, than in Mankato. So Taylor offered the employee the opportunity to move to the Twin Cities suburbs to manage this company, so he and his wife could find more resources and greater opportunities for their child. This employee was not the most experienced manager among Taylor's options, but because Taylor had helped him, he turned out to be one of the best managers in the company.

Lesson: *Loyalty is a two-way street. Don't expect it if you don't practice it.*

26. Raise productivity. To increase productivity, Taylor set about developing standards for employees and machines, and then set about increasing it, as Andrew Carnegie did when he was developing U.S. Steel in the mid-19th century (Carnegie and his operations chief listed the level of production of each shift as an indication to the others and created an internal competition among the various shifts). He analyzed all his operations and then simplified them to gain efficiencies. He monitored all his divisions and their key components every day. This included orders, shipments, and production. He instituted information systems even before the prevalence of computers by developing a card system to keep track of the key data he needed. All supervisors had to know the productivity for each of the people they managed at the end of each day. There were four pay scales (A/B/C/D) based on production. Employees started at the lowest scale, and were promoted to higher pay scales as their productivity improved. In essence, Taylor was basing pay scales on productivity, rather than on time served. This was the result of his farm upbringing, where he learned to connect the dots between production and results. If employees could not maintain their productivity, the supervisor would assist them. If they needed a slower pace, they were moved to another job at a lower scale. Production employees were also offered a profit-sharing system tied to their individual companies (not to the parent Taylor Corporation), along with a pension fund and a 401(k).

Lesson: To improve productivity, you need to know what to expect, and then organize to make your operations more efficient. Take action when your standards are not met and reward employees based on their productivity and contribution to the company. Make sure you are fair. The word gets around.

27. Reward managers. Managers are paid bonuses based on their performance on a variety of criteria such as cash flow, net income, productivity, etc. Taylor believes that "you get what you incent" and so makes sure that there are systems to motivate and also to prevent abuse. He provides motivation for generating new profits by offering a giant share of first- year profits to the managers. Taylor's philosophy is that managers significantly benefit from an increase in profits in the first year, but he gets to keep a large share of the profits from subsequent years at that level.

Managers get a percentage of their salary as bonuses, and this percentage can go as high as 200 percent of salary. The normal range is between 50-75 percent. They get 100 percent of the goal if they meet their budget, and can get up to 200 percent if they find a really unique way to make money. This offers a huge incentive to meet budget and do better. The next year they get a base bonus based on the higher platform. Each company's bonuses are based on their own reality. If company A is in a bad economy, the base is reduced. If company B can get a competitor's business, then the managers are paid a higher bonus. Taylor finds that some do try to "sandbag" (seek lower performance targets because they claim that "business conditions are worse this year" and then try to get bonuses based on this lowered base), and his observation is that the same people try it year after year. He believes that you have to know the people with whom you work. If he knows someone is sandbagging, Taylor raises the stakes – they need to reach a higher proportion of the budget before they qualify for bonuses. In addition, if at the end of the year, the managers have done "non-normal" things to meet their thresholds for bonuses, Taylor reserves the right to adjust. As an example, if they cut advertising budgets to get bonuses, then their threshold is adjusted, since the following year could suffer. Taylor also has found that some employees (the "dreamers") set goals higher than they should. Taylor lets them set dream goals since he does not want to de-motivate them. In this case, he sets the bonus at under 100 percent of budget.

Lesson: As a leader, your goal is to get the best possible performance from your team. To do this, standards and measurement are necessary. But you need to have experienced judgment to implement these standards and measurements to be fair and realistic and adjust for each individual's unique perspectives. *Incentive systems need to be customized with judgment.* This was one of the key areas of Taylor's attention.

28. Use the proven formula to grow. As Taylor's company grew, more opportunities came his way. Now he could add size to his customer-focused, operationally-efficient business. The result was a super-competitive juggernaut. He kept buying competitors, placing strong managers from his team at the helm of the new business, making their marketing more customer-focused, improving their operations and repeating the formula that made him successful. This became the virtuous spiral. He managed by exception, i.e., those managers who needed extra help, or were not performing well, or had not built a successful track record with Taylor, got his attention.

Lesson: When something works, repeat it. Keep an eye out for the exceptions and for changes in the trends.

29. Cross the seas and the borders... there are always issues. Taylor owns a number of operations in foreign countries. He has found that the foreign operations, and even those on the East and West coasts, are not as profitable as those in the Midwest. His first expansion to the coast was to a community in New Jersey that had a 13 percent unemployment rate, compared with 4 percent in Minnesota. Taylor needed young, part-time students for employees, and he assumed that he would have no problems with their skill levels and productivity. However, he found that the quality of the workforce was lower and that fewer people had the educational levels to fill the positions demanding high skills. So he moved his operations to another school district, where he was told that the district would be responsible for the hiring of part-time students, and that it would only offer students who were disciplined and maintained good grades. If their grades suffered, the school district would ask them to drop out of the program. He did much better in this school district, but it was still not as good as Minnesota.

Lesson: Different areas have different cultures. Understand the culture of the place where you plan to expand. Try it out if you can before putting down roots. Site selection is not as easy as it sounds, and local economic-development officials will not always give you the true facts – after all, their job is to sell the area.

30. When should subsidiaries compete with each other? When Taylor started buying up companies around the country, consumers did not always know that the different companies they were comparing for the best products and prices were owned by the same parent. And Taylor let the companies compete against each other. The presidents of each of the companies ran their companies as their own, and Taylor let them keep their share of the profits without having to disclose unique strategies and advances. As an example, he bought a company in California that was competing in a slightly lower niche than the Minnesota parent. The company had the benefit of the parent's resources and expertise, but it maintained its unique niche in the marketplace. Taylor supported this uniqueness in his companies until he dominated the competition, after which he did not have to maintain the differentiation. They all made money and dominated their specific markets, and it also allowed more creativity. Taylor found that when headquarters came up with new strategies and ideas, they tended to go to the same, favorite people rather than to people who could make best use of it, and these people were not as successful due to their distance from the customer. This prompted him to encourage innovations from the bottom up, rather than imposing them from the top down. He also kept the information-technology department local to serve customers' needs and dominate the market. The corporate IT department focused on long-term corporate needs.

Lesson: Understand what it takes to win, and don't think that corporate control is always the best strategy. Often the people closer to the customer may have a better perspective. Push decision making to the appropriate level and don't discourage bottom-up innovation. All the brains don't reside at headquarters, even if you hire MBAs.

31. Enjoy the potential, but watch the risks, with large customers. As Taylor's companies grew, they were able to satisfy the needs of corporate customers who were seeking larger vendors with total capabilities. Taylor's goal with these large customers was to "do everything for the customer" to make it difficult for customers to switch vendors due to the huge array of benefits Taylor's companies offered. As an example, Taylor's services include design, manufacturing, warehousing, marketing, and fulfillment, so that he can control how to market products and how orders are handled. Taylor also is open to take the upfront risk of starting these companies' programs, so long as he sees a way of recouping his investment from the customer or by adding other customers, and he offers total confidentiality so that customer information is never shared with anyone else, which enhances trust. He keeps his prices competitive while simultaneously driving efficiencies in his operations so as to increase profitability. In addition, a key Taylor advantage is that he can offer management stability and continuity, while larger companies have high turnover of staff and management. This allows him to minimize the risks of change and discontinuity in the customer's program, obtain increased efficiencies from experience, and to make long-term commitments. However, Taylor is always prepared to walk if the customer demands become unprofitable. He hedges his risks by having backup strategies for his major investments. On occasion, Taylor has found himself facing a lower bid from a competitor with lower margins to take away a key Taylor account. When this happens, Taylor has not hesitated to approach some of the competitor's key customers and offer rock-bottom prices to take away the competitor's cushion. The competitor gets the message in a hurry.

Lesson: Large customers can mean large orders, but large orders with huge investments also mean giant risks. That's why elephants dance with other elephants.

PostScript: The Timberwolves

32. Buying the Timberwolves. Taylor owns the Minnesota Timberwolves, the NBA franchise in Minneapolis. He believes that it was his "win-win" philosophy that helped him buy the team. Because Taylor had been the Minority Leader of the Minnesota State Senate, Minnesota Governor Arne Carlson asked him to meet with the two partners of the team to see what could be done to keep them in Minnesota. These meetings with the owners of the team had given Taylor a deep understanding of their needs and goals. When the opportunity came to buy the team, he drafted a contract that satisfied their needs and was a good arrangement for both. They were concerned about a number of issues, including the types of payments, the amounts, and how public relations was handled. Taylor was able to satisfy them.

Lesson: Understand the other party's needs and structure your offer creatively so that all parties win.

Rules for Entrepreneurs from Glen Taylor of Taylor Corporation

- **Risk is a part of entrepreneurial life**. But to minimize risk, you need an experienced, trained, and motivated team.
- **Customers are more important than machinery**. Machinery exists to serve people, not the other way around.
- **Everyone makes mistakes**. Good leaders recognize mistakes fast; bad leaders justify them. Acknowledge mistakes fast, cut losses, learn, don't repeat them, and advance.
- **Don't say "I told you so."** Support your employees. Get in the boat with them and row in the same direction. Tell them, "We made a mistake, so what are we going to do to fix it?"
- **Remember the Golden Rule**. Treat your employees the way you want to be treated.
- **Ask your managers about what motivates them**. To develop the best incentive system, ask your managers. They will tell you what motivates them. If it is sales, base it on sales, but have control systems to deliver profits. Everyone is different. Customize your plan.
- **Never stop learning**. *Maintain the humility to know that you don't know everything and keep learning*. This will help you improve yourself, your business, and also to see the world and your customers as they are rather than through your ego-filled filter.

Richard Copeland
Thor Construction

MINNEAPOLIS, MINN

Building one of the U.S.'s largest minority construction companies

"You don't get a job at GE based on how much you know. You get it based on how fast you can learn" ... GE CEO Jeff Immelt on the Charlie Rose show; October 20, 2008

Summary: Ask Richard Copeland why he succeeded, and his answer is that it is because he is "always a hustler." When he was growing up in Minneapolis, Copeland saw that the hustlers had the cars and the clothes. Obviously, one does not build a $100 million+ business by being only a "hustler." Copeland saw business opportunities, went after them aggressively, learned on-the-job at breakneck speed and had the character to persevere. If there is a prototypical entrepreneur as envisioned in the movies, Richard Copeland would fit the mold (in fact, he would even say that the mold was created with him in mind). He combined street smarts, leadership abilities, an opportunistic perspective, unlimited ambition, and the courage to enter new fields where he was a novice, with the willingness to learn and work endless hours. He started his business with one pickup truck and built a national construction company with annual revenues exceeding $170 million and projects in Minneapolis, Las Vegas, Atlanta and Los Angeles. This is how he did it.

From Startup to Profits

1. As a youth. As a youth he upheld the traditional activities (for all entrepreneurial success stories) of newspaper routes and shoveling sidewalks. However, what he found was that he could be the person who brought in the contracts, kept the customers happy and collected the money. But he did not have to do all the work himself. He "leveraged" himself by getting his sisters and neighborhood kids to do the work alongside him. This allowed him to build his business beyond a "one-man" (even if a very young man) business. Some of his "employees" tried to do an end run around him and take the customers. Copeland prevailed because he developed a bond with his customers, and they were eager to see a young entrepreneur grow, especially one who was enthusiastic and willing to offer good service, and so most customers did not switch.

Lesson: Learn how to leverage with controllable risk. ***Leverage can take many forms.*** *Financial* leverage (borrowing money) can mean high risk if you cannot repay the loan due to unforeseen problems (and there will always be unforeseen problems). *Staff* leverage, especially if firing your staff is easy, may mean profits without much risk. And it is very important to understand the *power of incumbency and the reluctance of many customers to switch*. Most people will not switch to new customers if they are happy with the work done by current vendors and the difference from switching is minimal. This is why new entrepreneurs should not seek to dislodge existing vendors if the new businesses are only offering small benefits from switching. ***The benefits of switching have to significantly exceed the costs.***

2. **Devil in the details.** When Minneapolis erupted in the race riots of 1967, Copeland's father moved the family to the suburbs where the family bought a small farm. Copeland and his dad bought five cows, of which one was Richard's. One cow died and his dad decided that that was Richard's cow. Richard lost his investment.

Lesson: The devil is in the details. You may not be able to spell out every detail – although in this case, a fair partner would have allocated the losses among all parties. Get a fair partner, and spell out the details of the agreement.

3. **Get involved.** As a young man, Copeland moved with his family from the inner city, where all the residents were African-American, to the distant suburbs, where he was the only African-American student in the school. As the only black kid, he was initially teased and ostracized. Despite this, due to his outgoing personality, he made friends in the new school. He was the class president in grades seven and eight (in the old school) and in 11th grade (in the new school) and homecoming king. He also ended up with a monopoly on candy sales in his new school. How did he do this? When he joined his new school, he was assigned someone who was supposed to show him around the new school. It turned out that this person ran the "underworld" in the school and was the "worst of the worst." So Copeland could get a monopoly on candy sales in the school.

Lesson: Network, network, network. Be friendly and get along. Copeland was not an introspective person (and claims that he still is not). He just took advantage of the situation as it was presented to him. As the cliché goes, when life gives you lemons, make lemonade.

4. **Switching colleges.** After finishing his first year of college in a community college in the Minneapolis suburbs, Copeland found out that an all-girls college in Duluth was becoming co-educational. Copeland immediately switched his enrollment. According to him, there were 100 boys and 900 girls. Given that ratio, he did not do too well in his studies (wonder why) and he lasted two quarters.

Lesson: Young men will sometimes let their libido control their brains. This can lead to undesirable (at least in the short run) consequences. This taught Copeland that not focusing on his career can hurt it. Another lesson: You might get what you want, which might not be what you need.

5. Growth of the family trucking business. Copeland's dad worked for the post office as a full-time employee. As a side business, he owned a trucking firm that he had started with one truck. When Copeland did poorly in his college studies, his dad invited him to join the trucking business, which had grown to six trucks and had Ford Motor Company as one of its accounts. This was 1975. Within six months, Copeland sought new business aggressively by making calls and selling new accounts. One day, Copeland and his dad had a disagreement. The same day, Copeland found himself no longer welcome at his father's firm. Copeland bummed around for 12 months until his mom got him and his dad back together. Between 1976 and 1980, he grew the business from six to 12 trucks. He got many new customers in residential moving by aggressively advertising in the Yellow Pages and flyers, and offering lower rates. He got lots of new customers by word of mouth. He had great workers. He hired his friends and they worked, played (on softball teams) and lived as a team. He kept overhead low by sleeping at the office. As the business grew, he made his trucks do double duty by carrying freight during the day and doing commercial moving on nights and weekends. He reduced his dependence on residential moving to focus on steady, big-ticket jobs for major accounts. He increased volume by being aggressive on pricing and was surprised that competitors did not reduce prices to compete with him. He kept track of his cash flow on a regular basis (daily, weekly, monthly) although he did it with a basic cash "input-output" statement, i.e., cash coming in and going out. Copeland used the monthly payments for equipment, so it was possible for him to keep things simple and understandable. Then he got into another fight with his dad, who again banned him from the firm – this time at the point of a gun. That's when he became an entrepreneur and started building his $100 million+ business. His dad's trucking business fell from 12 trucks to two, when Ford Motor Company threatened to switch truckers unless Copeland took over the business. Copeland and his partner (who had the money) bought the business from his dad.

Lesson: *Monitor and track your finances.* Understand your costs and know how to use your resources (assets and employees) for maximum productivity and efficiency. If you are more efficient and productive, you can gain market share by cutting prices if your competitors are inattentive and don't notice their loss of market share. But make sure that your competitors have less staying power than you do before starting a price war. In a price war, the weakest company loses. If your competitors are good managers and have deep pockets, they could bankrupt you. If you do lose your job, it is not always the end of the world. Capitalize on your strengths to pursue your goals.

6. **Hear it on the grapevine.** One day, a contact in Copeland's network told him that a minority subcontractor for NSP (the local power utility) was not doing a good job of fixing the landscape after the power company had laid the lines. Copeland immediately went to the offices of the power company and asked about the potential of becoming a subcontractor. He was told that the current subcontractor was slow and was asked to come back when he got an insurance bond. Using his last $200, Copeland got the bond and went back to NSP the next day. He was given a stack of orders for landscaping lots after the utility crews had finished laying or fixing the cables. He started working by himself. Initially, NSP was not happy with his work and asked him to improve his quality and bring the site to the same condition as it was before they started and they showed him how to do it. Although he had told NSP that he was a landscaper, he had never done any complicated work such as planting a tree. He read a book to learn how to do this right. Copeland did this from "sunrise to sundown, seven days a week" and he found that he was making about $200 per day. However, this was in the fall and since the days were getting shorter, Copeland decided to leverage his organization. So he recruited about six friends, many of whom had pickup trucks, and subcontracted with them to do the work under his supervision. It was a warm fall and Copeland was able to landscape till December. He did so well at this that the next year his revenues grew to $80,000. He expanded and started working for all the utilities (gas and phone) in Minneapolis. This was the start of the business. One of his friends suggested the name Thor Construction (after Thor, a Norse god). The friend thought clients would be expecting an owner of Scandinavian heritage, and that it would be fun to see their faces when an African-American showed up.

Lesson: Keep your ears to the ground and learn about opportunities. The information could be extremely valuable. If you contracted to do more than your capabilities, get new skills or else you will fail. Copeland learned all the details of the business. He trained his new recruits to do it right and fired those who did not learn or had the wrong attitude. He wrote a book on how to do utility work. He worked with the crew to show what he expected from them. He motivated from the ground up.

7. **Eliminating seasonality.** Since landscaping was a seasonal business, Copeland started a snowplowing business to even out his revenues over the year. He had done some snowplowing when he was with his dad. He added snowplows to his trucks and got contracts from some of the largest companies in the Twin Cities, such as NSP, Medtronic and Honeywell. He had 60 snowplows clearing business parking lots in the winter. These counter-cyclical revenues balanced his business and raised his annual revenues to over $2 million.

Lesson: Copeland took advantage of the minority purchasing contracts that are available to minority businesses. But even in this segment, competition can be stiff. Within a few years, even lower cost competition had undercut Copeland's business with the utilities and snowplowing. By then, he had moved on to more complicated construction projects and higher value-added revenues.

From Profits to Construction Giant

8. The start of construction. When he started in construction, Copeland began as a truck broker and in demolition. He started hauling aggregates, since that seemed to be the next step for expanding his business. He had two dump trucks and six trailers. He leveraged this equipment to become a dump-truck broker using his own equipment and working with independent trucks. To do this, he needed a system to know how many trucks were available with proper insurance and how many were in use at all times so he could keep everyone busy. Truckers like to stay occupied on a consistent basis or else their huge investment in the trucks can cause a major drain on their finances. However, a major trucking company in town that was also doing brokering in demolition started blacklisting Copeland among truck owners since he was taking the company's business. The company sent a letter to other trucking businesses advising them not to work with Copeland. The result was that contractors would call asking for 20 trucks and promising payment within two weeks. Then the next day they would either cancel their order for the trucks or change the terms of the payment to six weeks. Some even spread rumors that Copeland had been paid, but was not paying the truckers. Without steady work, the demolition truckers went elsewhere. Copeland tried to keep them by hauling aggregates, but that was a very volatile business, so he lost most of the independents. In two months, his revenues went from an annual rate of $2 million to $400,000. He got out of aggregates, demolition and hauling.

Lesson: *Don't underestimate your competitors, especially when you take on large ones with a frontal assault on their main business.* Stay below the radar. When threatened with a loss of market share in their main businesses, large companies could strike back and drive you out of business. Understand the level of competitive actions large competitors have taken and are likely to take. Be nimble and stay one step ahead of competitors. Diversify so that you are not too dependent on one industry, especially one with vicious competitors.

9. Expansion. When Copeland was involved in hauling aggregates and in demolition, he noticed that he was pretty low on the food chain. To go up the food chain, he started looked at some simple construction jobs, especially those that involved landscaping. He noticed that there were general construction jobs in small landscaping projects, such as small parks that involved aggregates, landscaping and demolition. But these projects also involved construction of small buildings, which he had not done before. That did not stop him. He learned to read blueprints and started bidding on such jobs. He taught himself construction of these small buildings. He found that the small buildings were easy and that being a general contractor gave him power over the project and control of the other subcontractors.

He could now use his leveraging skills to greater effect. This was the start of the construction phase of Thor, which led them to their current size.

Lesson: Learn how to add value and learn in small steps. Copeland added one new area as he grew, which led him to higher-value projects and greater power, control and profits. He focused on his core strengths and businesses, and "threw a lot of mud at the wall" to see what stuck. (See Jeff Immelt's comment at the start of this profile.)

10. Pride and showing off. As his business grew, Copeland wanted to enjoy the fruits and bought himself a Cadillac. Immediately, his profits fell. His customers thought he had become too big and did not need them, and that he might charge them higher prices to pay for his more expensive overhead and toys. People also don't want you succeeding at their expense. He sold the Cadillac and bought a Pontiac. Business went up again.

Lesson: *Humility is always in fashion.* The most important time to be humble is when you first become successful. Don't show off. Don't buy expensive toys. Don't accumulate trophy houses, trophy boats, trophy planes and trophy spouses. You are likely to pay the price, and the bank could take the houses, boats and planes. The trophy spouses leave on their own.

11. Financial difficulties. Construction is a cyclical business, and Copeland has had to struggle when times were tough. His rule when the business was struggling and cash was short was that he would be the first to cut his pay. He has gone for up to two years without a paycheck and he has done this three times. What he finds is that going without a paycheck is a huge motivator for him. It brings the fire back. Copeland becomes more aggressive and focuses on immediate performance. It also makes a strong statement to his staff. They get his sense of urgency and focus on getting the business back to profitability. Obviously, it works for him.

Lesson: ***Find ways to keep the urgency immediate, the fire hot and the motivation high before your business is threatened.*** How can you do this? Keep setting goals that are higher and get the fire when you fall short. This will prevent you from having to go for months without a paycheck. Your spouse and kids will also appreciate it.

12. Dealing with a partner. When Minneapolis elected an African-American mayor, the Public Housing Authority wanted more minority firms involved in the construction of buildings. Ten projects were put up for bid and the city said that majority-minority alliances would be given priority. Copeland noted this and formed an alliance with M.A. Mortenson & Co., the largest construction company in Minnesota. Copeland was serving on a board with one of the vice-presidents of Mortenson. While other firms bid on a few projects, Copeland and Mortenson bid on all – and won six out of 10. This became a very profitable partnership for Copeland. Together they built a number of landmark buildings in the Twin Cities, including the

Minneapolis Library, the hockey arena in St. Paul, the Twins stadium in Minneapolis, and the new University of Minnesota Gophers football stadium. Mortenson expected Copeland to become big enough to start competing with it, and he has. Copeland has also used partnerships as he has expanded to other cities, including with some of the largest construction firms in the country such as Perini and Clark. To succeed in these partnerships, Copeland had to sell his new partners the value he was bringing to increase his margins. Otherwise, the majority partners would have been perfectly content to give Copeland a small token portion of the business, with little profits.

Lesson: Copeland has learned that he needs to sell new partners on his value to make profits. The partner is likely to keep the giant portion of the profits unless they truly understand your value and you can bring negotiating clout to get your fair share. Secondly, understand the factors that can affect your business. Whereas he got 49 percent of jobs (although they were smaller) when the mayor was African-American, he got a much smaller proportion when Minneapolis elected a white mayor.

13. Challenge to hire good people. As Thor grew, Copeland needed to hire an increasingly qualified team to make sure that the business was efficient and effective. However, he found it tough to recruit highly qualified staff as a minority entrepreneur because they did not perceive his business to be the most desirable place to work. Copeland was also not a traditional manager. He was not always methodical and did not know business school lingo and etiquette. He went to classes to learn these techniques. Now that he is a big company, that perception has changed and he has been able to hire a competent and capable team. However, to keep key people motivated, Copeland has sold a minority interest in his company to key staff members. This way, he wants to make sure that these key staff members have the same goals that he does.

Lesson: Even if you are a minority company and are able to get preference on contracts, you are unlikely to get preference on hiring. The best people will still go to the 'best' places for them. Adapt and learn how to make your company a great place for the most desirable employees and managers to join. To continue growing, you will need a team that is more capable than you are by yourself.

14. Expansion to other cities. To continue growing, Copeland had to expand his markets. He was already getting a large share of the construction business in Minneapolis-St. Paul. Since he was one of the largest minority contractors in the country, he thought that he could gain a significant share in other cities. He could expand into other markets and use his experience to get additional business. However, he learned that he had to find the right markets. The first two markets he selected were Atlanta and Las Vegas. However, Copeland found that Atlanta was a mature market with a number of existing contractors, making it difficult for him to expand. Las Vegas was a new market that was easier to penetrate. However, even in Las Vegas, Copeland found that the first year was frustrating, with many bids and no success. What he found is that many contractors had come to Vegas but left after the first year when they did not get any business. So developers were reluctant to use newly arrived contractors to see if they had staying power. Business improved significantly after the first year.

Lesson: Nothing is easy or quick. Success has a price. Check the market before jumping in.

15. Know your key strengths. Copeland knows his strengths – the ability to get the big deals. He uses his sales skills and networking ability to find the deals and negotiate good profits. However, he has also realized that he needs good managers to implement the construction jobs. This means that he needs to improve his monitoring skills. According to him, he delegates more by letting managers do the job, and gets involved when key events happen. This could also create surprises.

Lesson: Focus on your strengths but also strengthen your weaknesses. Delegation is not abdication. So monitor closely to avoid painful surprises.

16. Management team. Recently Copeland was facing problems within his management team, with some members expressing dissatisfaction. They recommended that Copeland hire a "medium" (a facilitator by another name) who tried weird practices to bring the team together, such as turning the lights down at a meeting and tugging at Copeland's moustache to make sure he was grounded. Copeland was. He got disgusted, fired the medium and the ones who recommended the expert. Performance improved.

Lesson: *Poor managers often disguise their inadequacies by shifting attention to other made-up problems. Don't get distracted.*

17. Strong balance sheet. Currently, Copeland maintains lot of "dry powder" (cash) to take advantage of opportunities as they show up. He is using this strength to add new cities such as Los Angeles and New Orleans to expand access to business. He is also adding interior remodeling as a new source of business.

Lesson: Always seek new business aggressively. No one comes and offers it to you.

Rules for Entrepreneurs from Richard Copeland of Thor Construction

- **Leverage yourself.** Do good work and get others with complementary skills, especially in areas where you may be weak. This will leverage your talents exponentially.
- **Stick to it**. Copeland emphasizes the importance of perseverance and the courage to try new things and learn new skills. He tries. If he fails, he tries again until he bounces back.

- **Be candid**. When Copeland fails, he candidly admits it, tries to find how to fix it and tries again. (Author's note: However, in construction, admitting too many faults gets you to the poorhouse. So don't screw up too much).
- **Seek access to opportunities**. Copeland is always aggressively seeking opportunities. Currently, in the economic downturn of 2008-09, he is expanding into new cities and beating the bushes vigorously to get new contracts. Copeland knows the value of networks and relationships, so he joins many organizations and serves on lots of committees. Get involved.
- **Don't be afraid to make decisions**. You will always be a little uncertain when making decisions that take you to the next level. However, monitor closely so you can make adjustments. Don't bet it all on one roll of the dice and persevere – nothing great happens easily. But when faced with overwhelming odds, as in the truck-brokering business, rethink your decision.
- **Growth changes your needs**. Copeland has found that running a business becomes easier as it grows and reaches a critical mass of exposure, reputation and size: you can attract better people. However, note that you will face new challenges as you grow. You need to grow with the growth of the company. Understand the needs of the business and make sure everyone is concentrating on the goals. Hire good executives and focus their attention on the job and not on office politics or each other.
- **Hire slowly and fire quickly**. Copeland has found that poor hires don't change. They stay bad. So he has made it a rule to fire them quickly. He has found that good people don't waste endless time parsing the details of job descriptions. They understand their responsibility and get it done.

Richard Burke
UnitedHealth Group

MINNEAPOLIS, MINN

Building one of the world's largest health-care companies

Summary: Richard Burke grew up in Marietta, Ga., graduated from a local high school and enrolled in the engineering program at Georgia Tech. Three years into the program, he realized that he liked business better (a lot better than chemistry, math, physics, biology, and mechanical drawing), and switched to business school. While in undergraduate school, Burke worked full-time at the local office of two insurance companies processing health insurance claims and learning about managing people. After finishing his undergraduate degree, he enrolled in the MBA program at Georgia State University, working full-time during the day in the office of the Governor of Georgia while he went to school at night. He then decided to pursue his doctorate in business administration, but before acceptance of his dissertation, he took a job with a leading-edge Minneapolis healthcare think-tank called InterStudy (IS) that was interested in his healthcare/insurance and state government credentials. IS had a federal government contract to develop a new kind of healthcare organization called a health-maintenance organization (HMO), what today is the foundation of the "managed-care" industry in the United States. While at IS Burke developed three managed-care organizations that were models for the later growth of the industry. After three years at IS, Burke wanted to expand this "HMO management" business further, but couldn't reach a meeting of the minds with his superiors over the scope and management of the proposed new business venture. So Burke left IS and formed his own firm to organize and manage HMOs for physician groups around the country. From this start, he built the company, took it public, and acquired other, similar organizations around the country, before later giving up the CEO role. At this writing, Burke is chairman of the board of UnitedHealth Group, a company in the Fortune 100, and the largest private health insurer in America, with annual revenues exceeding $84 billion and covering approximately 70 million American citizens through one or more of the company's products. This is how he did it.

Before the Startup

1. The early years. Richard Burke grew up in Marietta, Ga., mowing lawns and performing other odd jobs to earn spending money. His parents were not wealthy, but neither was anyone else in his neighborhood or within his community of friends. The family valued education, however, so he knew he was going to college; it was only a question of where. When he graduated from high school, Burke enrolled as a full-time engineering student at Georgia Tech, because, he said, "his father was an engineer, so he thought that he should become one also." This educational experience lasted approximately three years, at which point Burke found that he could no longer afford it; instead of dropping out of school, he found a full-time job and remained a full-time student. He also switched his major to business, realizing that his real interest was in finance and economics. His first "during school" job was in a department of a local bank collecting delinquent loans, followed by work as a claims adjuster for two health insurance companies. This was Burke's first introduction to health insurance and to managing people. It was to lead to his fortune.

> **Lesson**: It would have been easy to quit, but his parents had instilled in him the value of education, finishing what one starts and achieving the goals one sets. Burke then chose a profession that built off skills he had developed while growing up and in his early jobs, learning the lesson that employers are most likely to pay for what prospective employees have shown they know how to do; less so for what they can only speculate someone might be able to accomplish.

2. The first healthcare job. After getting his undergraduate degree, Burke enrolled in the evening MBA program at Georgia State University, continuing to work during the day processing and paying health insurance claims. He finished his MBA in two years, working and studying long days and weekends. He had to pay for his own tuition, room, board, food, and books, so finishing as quickly as possible was a priority. Burke graduated with a double major in economics and finance; he liked economics, but found that he had a knack for finance, and concluded that the business marketplace would likely value financial skills more highly than economics skills. Burke took a job with the Governor of Georgia's Office of Planning, Programming and Budgeting, a new state department intended initially to address state program and budget issues. After approximately 18 months in the governor's office, Burke applied for a new doctoral program at the University of Virginia to pursue a DBA degree, at the time finding the prospect of consulting and teaching at the college level to be an attractive long-term vocation. Though the academic world continued to look interesting, after a few years in the doctoral program, Burke realized that he was a 'what' person rather than a 'why' person. He had advanced to the dissertation stage of the degree, but decided to leave academia before completing the process and go back to work. He got a job with Amtrak analyzing the economics of, and closing down, train stations around the country—and conveying the bad news to local politicians. As he puts it, the job was "ridiculously confrontational." This was when he was asked to come and interview for a new job with a health care think-tank in Minneapolis, Minn. Burke arrived on a Friday in November for his interview with Dr. Paul Ellwood, the chief executive of InterStudy (IS), who had secured a large government grant to implement a new kind of health "insurance" company. Burke's background in health insurance claims and state government was right for the job, and Ellwood offered him a position as the person responsible for the new government contract—plus a $5,000 bonus if he agreed to join by the next Tuesday. The weather was unusually gorgeous for a November day in Minneapolis, and the money was appealing. Burke agreed.

> **Lesson**: Study yourself and know your abilities and limitations. Look for opportunities that play to your strengths. Burke had developed great work-study habits, and self-discipline. He had a curious and analytical mind, but was interested in execution rather than study and process. The variety of jobs he had held had given him a range of experiences, and importantly for him, some that prospective employers were willing to pay for. This showed him where his passion lay, and a direction for where the marketplace would likely reward his talents. That led him to the job that would change his life.

3. Starting HMOs. IS was a think tank that specialized in generating new government policy initiatives. One of these initiatives involved helping pass a federal law in 1973 (PL93-222) that was designed to promote a new kind of health insurance (managed care) organization in the United States. Following passage of this new "enabling" legislation, IS had received a consulting contract from the federal government to promote this new concept, and Dr. Ellwood needed someone with the skills to help sell and implement the new concept among private practice physicians. There were already a few so-called "health-management organizations (HMOs)" around the country, staff model plans like Kaiser and Group Health that offered limited physician access and, as a consequence, had limited marketplace appeal. The new concept envisioned by Ellwood involved building off private-practice doctors to provide the medical care in his new managed-care entities, or HMOs. Two key features of the new federal law were that it overrode the state laws that had historically inhibited organizations of this type from operating, and required employers with 26 or more employees to offer at least one HMO option in addition to their traditional indemnity insurance plan. The contract funded IS to help physicians, hospital organizations, and doctor groups around the country to design and set up a new type of entity that would offer a complete array of medical services through the private sector for a fixed fee.

Burke discovered three organizations in Minnesota that were interested in implementing the concept, conducted the necessary business-feasibility studies, and established a new state-regulated entity (that was really an insurance company), but which was to be called an HMO. Each of these three organizations had unique features. One was a large multi-specialty group practice with a number of clinic locations. The second was an organization that was a spin-off from an old railroad-employee medical clinic trying to re-make itself to serve a wider insurance and medical marketplace. The third group was the local county medical society, acting on behalf of the majority of local private-practice doctors: a disparate group of more than 2,000 local physicians of various specialties and sub-specialties. Through IS, Burke became at one time the contract CEO for two of the managed-care entities he helped organize around these groups, the beginnings of UnitedHealth Group as an "HMO-management company."

Lesson: *In the forefront of a new industry, the "rules" often are being written along the way, and the "wisdom of experience" is lacking.* Burke pursued this challenge because he felt (based on personal experience) that the business concept was a good one, and that the idea of "contract development and management" of these new healthcare entities could be very successful and profitable.

4. Organizing the managed entities. There was no template for Burke and Ellwood to follow with the new HMO/managed-care ventures. There were few templates to work from or emulate, meaning virtually everything was new. The first six to 12 months of each new health plan were taken up with incorporating the organization, defining its legal structure, negotiating and drafting the contracts with physicians, hospitals, pharmacies, and other necessary health-care professionals, and obtaining approvals from inexperienced regulators. Without a template, Burke and his staff typically made things up as they went along, and the learning curve was steep. Every employee, contractor, physician, and organization needed a contract, and state regulators had to approve all such agreements, as well as those with the employers to whom Burke and his staff sold the new products, before they could be used. One saving grace was that, if the HMO agreed to abide by the terms of the new federal HMO-enabling statute, the regulatory rules were consistent across state lines, and (theoretically) the federal law overrode the various state regulations if there was a conflict. At the end of three years, Burke had three health plans up and running and profitable. IS was getting a percentage of the revenues from the managed-care organizations for contract-management services, and also doing well. At this point, Burke went to the CEO of IS suggesting that the company make a business out of organizing and managing HMOs, since in Burke's opinion the potential for such a venture was high. IS was amenable to the concept, but Burke was told that he was too young for the job running the new business. He disagreed with this position, especially since he felt he was already the de facto CEO, and he knew the industry, the issues and the intricacies of managing these organizations as well as anyone else. When an understanding on the management issue couldn't be reached, Burke resigned his position with IS to organize his own company, which would develop and manage HMOs. The parting with IS was an amicable one.

Lesson: Timing and experience are very important to successfully start a business. Having organized three new companies in an attractive, emerging industry, and knowing how to manage them successfully, reduced for Burke the potential risks of starting a new business. Most people are lucky to get one great opportunity in a lifetime; recognizing it when it comes and executing on the opportunity when it presents itself are fundamental keys to success.

From Startup to Profits

5. Focus on your market segment. Burke concluded that he would select from among the three types of HMOs and focus his new company's energies on one model to the exclusion of the others. One type of HMO (the group practice model) was built around a fairly self-contained multi-specialty clinic where the physicians were employees of an existing organization and had virtually all the medical capabilities in house that were necessary to serve customers. The second model involved smaller, primary-care clinics, which would require contracting with numerous medical specialties not available through the clinics. The third model would be built around a large loose-knit group of physicians, an approach that would be tougher to manage and control, but which offered greater marketing appeal to the consumer because of the large number of physicians and clinic locations to select from. Burke concluded that the multi-specialty group practices would most likely try to manage the HMO themselves, which meant that Burke and his company could add less value. The second kind of HMO was, he felt, too specialized to serve a mass market. The large physician-network segment model had the strength of numbers (of physicians and hospitals) and could offer all the specialties that a successful HMO would need to serve the most customers in a large metropolitan region. More members/consumers meant more potential revenue and profits for the management company, but this model had all the noise and potential chaos of a democracy. It also would require the installation of medical cost and utilization controls far beyond anything then in common practice. Burke thought that it was nonetheless possible for his new company to add more value at the large physician-owned organizations, like the PHP/Medica model that had been developed through IS, than at the others. And he felt he knew how to bring order to them, knew where to find the computer software to operate them, and had a record of success with this model that made him the front runner to start prospective physician groups. While others might promise success, Burke felt he could give the physician-owners the most confidence that their venture would succeed. So thereafter, he focused his efforts on new health plans to be developed through local physician/medical societies.

Lesson: *Find the market segment where you can add the most value and try to be the best and dominant player in it.* If this is also the segment that is the most profitable, you have found the nexus to build a great company.

6. Negotiate a great deal. If possible, make it win-win. After leaving IS, Burke formed a holding ownership entity called Ryan-Taylor, Inc. (RTI), which he named after his two sons (at the time). This firm later morphed into UnitedHealth Care

Corp., and today UnitedHealth Group. To fund this new venture, Burke sought approximately $250,000 in investment capital and an initial customer to serve as his new company's prototype HMO. Once the prototype was up, going, and successful, the focus would then be on finding similar opportunities around the country to replicate the prototype. Burke found the initial seed capital for his company from Charter Medical Corporation, a psychiatric hospital chain in Macon, Ga. But just in case, he took out a $40,000 bank loan with a second mortgage on his house, which he "banked" for future contingency purposes. Burke then formed an operating company that he called Charter Med, Inc. (CMI) as a subsidiary of Ryan-Taylor. According to the business plan, CMI's employees would staff and manage HMOs for a percentage of the HMO's gross revenues and pay the associated expenses from these proceeds. When the HMO's revenues were small, CMI would lose money; as the HMO grew, profits would follow from the significant economies of scale. Since CMI did not take the "insurance risk" in the HMOs it managed, it needed less capital to start. The insurance risk (the risk that the premiums paid by client companies were inadequate to pay claims) was assumed by the physicians within each of the new managed HMOs. The doctors were often skeptical, but knew they needed to do something different because of the potential loss of their patients to group-practice or staff-model HMOs under the new federal HMO-enabling legislation. The doctors typically did not want to invest in an uncertain enterprise, or often even invest money up front to develop a business plan, organize the HMO and/or obtain the needed approvals to operate. So Burke's new company performed these tasks for them, thus minimizing the upfront investment required of the sponsoring physicians to start their new ventures. Since Burke was absorbing all the upfront cost/risk, he was able to insist on very long-term management contracts to recoup his investment and earn attractive rates of return. Why long-term? According to Burke, it didn't make sense for his company to take the upfront risks of organizing and developing the HMO for a short-term contractual relationship. With a long-term contract, he could build a significant business with a modest investment and minimize/control the risk of failure for the enterprise. What if the physicians weren't willing to sign on to a long-term commitment? Burke walked. He knew there were attractive prospects elsewhere that would be willing to meet what he considered the minimum terms for his new business to grow into something sustainable over the long term. Otherwise the business would become a short-term consulting venture with minimal long-term promise and sustainability.

Lesson: *Emphasize the value you add to your customers, know what you require to be successful, and be willing to stand by your convictions.* Try to develop a "win-win" scenario that addresses the critical needs of your customers and earns a solid profit for yourself. Don't take short cuts you don't have to; if you do, understand the consequences.

7. A rule for survival. Once CMI was profitable, Burke bought out his investor Charter Medical Corporation. The parting again was amicable. It was then that he needed his "backup capital" because, without this key investor, he needed the capital to build the business. The new HMO startups required capital. What was available was limited, and needs always exceeded what was there. The company frequently had to look for revenue sources outside its primary business to keep the company alive until the core business matured. For example: his data-processing staff found medical-transcription customers, which helped the company meet payroll for almost a year.

> **Lesson:** ***A business plan is what one starts the day with. One should anticipate changing and refining it daily to meet critical needs, in particular cash-flow requirements.*** The key is whether the diversion from one's business plan meets a core short-term need and doesn't unnecessarily compromise the long-term objectives of the business.

8. The financial arrangement. The key to an "open access" HMO functioning profitably is getting the physicians to co-operate in controlling medical costs and utilization of standard procedures. The beginning step in obtaining this co-operation is making it in their financial interest to do so. The key performance metric that had to be accomplished in each new HMO was assuring that the fixed amount paid by the patients/corporate customers for healthcare coverage was enough to pay the physicians, hospitals, and the other medical providers, and still make a profit. Reimbursement to the physician providers was adjusted to assure that there weren't financial shortfalls by holding back 20 percent of the amount owed to each doctor until the end of the year. This reasonably assured that the HMO would meet its financial obligations during the year and earn a reasonable profit at the end. Burke's management company received a percentage of the HMO's gross revenues (the top line), out of which it paid its employees, overhead, and profit. He owned the management company and its cash flow, and while capital was in short supply, he did so without assuming the potentially catastrophic medical-insurance risk. That risk was the physicians'.

> **Lesson:** A key success factor in any new business venture is minimizing the risk of business failure. Burke successfully managed the financial risk of his new enterprise within his available capital by transferring the potentially catastrophic (business) risk to others who could more reasonably afford it. He balanced the interests of his client HMOs, the physicians, and his management company. If the HMO did well financially, all parties prospered; if it did not, there was no prosperity, but Burke's company survived nonetheless.

9. Direct vs. indirect competitors. Ellwood had authored the federal HMO-enabling legislation very intelligently. The statute included a clause that required all companies with at least 26 or more employees to include at least one so-called HMO option among those they offered their employees. This requirement opened up a huge market in corporate America and overnight legitimized a new industry. Now the HMOs had to sell themselves to these "willing" corporate clients and perform/

execute once they did. By working with a large amalgamation of physicians in each metropolitan area and organizing them into HMOs, Burke positioned his company and its client HMOs to be the most attractive HMO option available, the one likely to be the most appealing to corporate employees and their families. The federal enabling legislation offered a way for the newcomers (the so-called HMOs) to successfully market their products against entrenched competitors; Burke found a way to offer the most attractive, competitive option within this new market framework.

Lesson. When you have a competitive advantage, pursue it aggressively. Most new ventures compete against stronger, entrenched competitors that benefit from customer inertia, greater size, resources and economies of scale, credibility, and established business relationships. New ventures often have to offer significantly greater value to make inroads, to get customers to change products. Burke's client HMOs capitalized on the federal legislation's requirements to gain marketplace credibility and entry, and took advantage of their competitive advantage to earn and retain market share.

From Profits to the Moon

10. Taking over PHP/Medica again. When IS decided that it did not want to joint-venture the HMO/management business with Burke, there was a period of uncertainty among the original IS HMO clients while Burke rebuilt the business as a free-standing operation. In the interim, PHP/Medica, one of the original three IS client HMOs, had taken over its own management and the business was failing. Burke and his new firm were invited back in and his company took over the complete management of PHP/Medica. Burke had earlier designed the structure of PHP/Medica so he felt it could work if managed properly. The condition for his firm taking over the plan was that Burke had to be CEO of the HMO, in addition to being the CEO of the management company. He maintained these dual roles for the next decade, managing the operations of the company's prototype HMO, and the company contracted to manage it as well.

Lesson: One's business and operating model must be flexible and driven by available capital and cash-flow considerations, not the other way around. ***Success in any new venture is in no small part a function of management/ ownership's willingness and ability to adjust to changing circumstances and unexpected results, both good and bad.***

11. Board of directors. Each new HMO required its own separate local board of physicians (mostly) and some corporate community representatives. Typically the board representatives from the medical community had a very difficult job. They had to "front" for difficult financial decisions involving reimbursement and medical-cost controls that were necessary to keep their HMO solvent, and then go back to their constituents (a frequently skeptical audience of the same physicians), listen to their complaints, and explain/justify their actions. It took a lot of courage, and those who did it were typically not even paid for their time and trouble. It was a thankless job. Burke realized early on that one of the key requirements for a successful "open access" HMO was finding the right people to serve on these HMO boards of directors, doctors who would be willing to make thankless decisions for the good of the overall physician community. They had to be physicians who understood that the status quo was not sustainable, that they and their peers had to change to keep their patients, had to practice differently, and that they had to allow Burke's company to control medical costs aggressively. Burke focused his organization on finding and nurturing these people, encouraged them to sit on the boards and helped them make the hard decisions. When an HMO board wanted to forgo or delay difficult actions, it was the management company's job to show them that the consequence of inaction was failure.

> **Lesson**: A good board of directors is critical to success. It is a resource for providing quality input and ideas to senior management, improved decision-making, and helping develop and sustain good corporate culture.

12. Price to your competitive advantage. Burke and his company sought and found a product niche that offered an opportunity to charge a premium price compared to the competition. The product selected offered the advantages (over competing HMOs) of greater medical-provider access, and an enhanced opportunity for consumers to keep their relationships with their existing physicians. The product likewise offered significant benefits over traditional indemnity insurance products: significantly improved coverage for routine medical services, the absence of claim forms and other administrative headaches. The trick was to find where the most advantageous price points were. The higher revenue this strategy generated for the HMO became another of those rare "win-win" situations. The HMOs Burke's firm managed became financially stronger as a result; there was more money available to pay the doctors, which made them happier and ambassadors for the services of Burke's firm elsewhere. Burke's firm became more profitable and successful as a result. The improved pricing model turned around the fortunes of PHP-Medica almost overnight so that Burke's firm had its successful prototype to exhibit to similar physician groups elsewhere in the country.

> **Lesson**: Product pricing is a key performance metric for any company, new or mature. ***Burke and his staff turned the seeming disadvantage (the organizational chaos of thousands of otherwise unrelated physicians) into a competitive advantage***, then sought and solidified a significant price premium. It is always easier to visualize selling successfully at lower prices, the entrepreneur's first instinct, as it is the frequent advice of marketing professionals who can more easily succeed when they have both the best product and the lowest price. The right way to price is based on perceived value to the customer. Understand what your customers want, know your competition and the competitive value you offer. Then ***have the courage to price to value***. What

do your customers want? What do they value? Find the right answers and grab the gold ring.

13. Expanding the focused marketing. Having decided to focus his corporate strategy on physician-owned, open-access health plans, which his new company proposed to develop and manage, Burke sought the most productive, affordable strategy to market his company's services to prospective new clients throughout the country. He and his staff focused in particular on state and local medical societies, initially with no geographic boundaries. They sent out targeted mailings, always highlighting PHP/Medica and its success, the company "laboratory" for successfully managing this new type of health plan. Few physician groups wanted to start an HMO of this type on their own, or risk their financial well-being with a company that was untested. Burke and his staff carefully selected prospects based on their degree of interest and apparent willingness to do what was necessary to make the HMO succeed. He looked at the potential market size, the number of available physicians, and the number and strength of local competitors.

Lesson: When you are the lowest–risk, most-attractive option, you have a competitive advantage of significance. Push your advantage while it is there; what may be a barrier to entry for potential competitors today probably won't be tomorrow.

14. The right exit. Two other CMI employees besides Burke were key to the company's early success and growth. One was an information technology expert who was in charge of CMI's IT department, and the other a person who performed a variety of critical management roles. Early on, Burke gave each of them a significant amount of stock in RTI, which had always been close to financial break-even or profitable. By approximately its seventh year of operations, the company was managing a significant number of HMOs, profitable, and growing rapidly. Separately, these two key individuals approached Burke to "cash out" their stock and retire. Burke pointed out to them that the company anticipated a public offering in the near future and that their shares could increase dramatically in value if this occurred; they insisted on selling nonetheless. Burke bought their stock back and became the sole shareholder of a company about to initiate a successful public offering.

Lesson: Looking in the rear-view mirror at our decisions, no matter how tempting it may be, is not fruitful. We have our own personal priorities, and make the best decisions based on available facts when we make them.

15. Growing to the moon. These were the good days. Burke had changed the name of the company from Ryan-Taylor, Inc. to United Healthcare and still privately owned it. Another similar organization in Pennsylvania successfully completed a public offering and its initial stock price soared. Previously, Burke had been told by investment bankers that UHC was not a good candidate for an initial public offering (IPO) because it was an "HMO management" company that did not own its health plans. The accounting consequence of this was that the company could only book the fees it received for management services and not count the HMO's revenues or profits as its own. Another perceived negative of the company in the minds of the investment bankers was that UHC "only" had management contracts (albeit very long ones), but not actual ownership of its HMOs. The bankers were worried that UHC's HMO customers would/could cancel the management contracts even though all were very long-term, UHC owned the infrastructure and computer systems of the HMO operations, and all of the employees of the HMO were on UHC's payroll and under its control. This conclusion by the bankers overlooked the fact that, offsetting these perceived shortcomings, was the fact that UHC had no insurance risk. It could grow faster, with less capital and wasn't susceptible to the historical financial ups and downs of the industry business cycle. After the successful IPO by the Pennsylvania firm, however, the investment bankers changed their mind and were eager to talk. In early 1984, UHC successfully completed its initial public offering.

> **Lesson**: Stay at the table and be persistent. Being first isn't always best. When an industry is hot, investment bankers and venture capitalists often cannot get enough. As an entrepreneur, take advantage when the opportunity is there. As an investor, however, watch your wallet. Typically the early stages of a new industry produce some big winners and a lot of losers.

16. Growing via acquisitions—develop the culture you want. Burke admits that initially he "could not spell corporate culture," and that he simply "hired people like himself." He rewarded what he thought was superior performance and results, and let go those people who didn't or couldn't fit in. But when he started buying other companies with the "currency" from the public offering, he realized the importance of not only diligence on the company itself but on its key personnel; that companies operated much differently, didn't do things the same way or emphasize or reward the same outcomes. This was particularly obvious with UHC's first significant acquisition, which was motivated by a perceived need to address the "management company" image of UHC: The acquisition of firms that owned their HMOs rather than managing them. One of the acquired company's CEOs told Burke that "they celebrated their failures" as a way of learning. Burke realized by contrast that his "corporate culture" only celebrated their successes, although it didn't punish risk-taking. There were other signs of important cultural differences between the two companies. At meetings, Burke and his staff expected a clear agenda, time lines, and decisions at the end of the meeting. At the acquired company, he found that staff often would meet for an entire day, with the only decision being to meet again until they could turn a majority consensus into unanimity. Burke realized then that thereafter he needed to consciously define and promote the corporate culture he thought was the right one, one in which success and results were rewarded. He realized this required recruiting, training, and promoting good people into the right jobs where they could and would be successful; but it also necessitated separating those people who did not perform or fit in with the company as soon as performance problems or cultural issues were identified. Additionally, the cultural lessons suggested that, in future acquisitions, the compatibility of the cultures of the companies would become a significant determinant of feasibility.

Lesson: Know what you want and need. Put it in writing. Promote it. Monitor to see that your company does it.

17. Private and public CEO. After his company went public, Burke realized that he now had three jobs. One was running the public company; the second involved managing PHP, its largest client HMO; the third job was the equally important obligation to investors and analysts. Analysts who followed the company and the industry expected to be kept up-to-date so they would feel comfortable and informed in promoting UHC to their customers. Burke also learned that unlike privately held companies, which are typically managed with cash flow as a primary metric for success, public companies are managed for earnings-per-share; that he had to make sure his company delivered on its earnings and growth promises each quarter. As a private-company CEO, he had managed for cash flow and his own personally determined performance metrics, with little or no perceived obligation to others outside the company.

Burke stayed as CEO of United for about six more years, during which time UHC bought a number of companies with its new public stock "currency." They bought some from the industry and others that they had managed in partnership with physician groups. This further increased revenues and profits, but with intent added "insurance risk" to the business model. United bought a company that had developed a strong niche in Medicare, a new growth platform in the public sector market, and over time UHC bought almost all the HMOs it had started in partnership with the physicians and medical societies (not an unexpected outcome in the original strategic plan). As Burke puts it "we had been living so long together that getting married was relatively easy for both sides."

Lesson: Understand both the benefits and the obligations before you take your company public. Public shareholders expect certain things from management, and the operating and financial focus of management is not the same for public and private companies. As a public company CEO, you need to be even more disciplined, and understand/accept that you work not for yourself but for a board of directors and shareholders.

Rules for Entrepreneurs from Richard Burke of UnitedHealth Group

- **Your business plan is a guide, not gospel**. It is what you start your day with and modify with changing circumstances. The front end of one's operating/management plan is the company's critical financial metrics, not the other way around. One's business plan is at the end of the day driven by what is affordable.

- **Value cash.** Businesses succeed or fail based on the availability of cash to operate. If you have cash you can operate and hopefully afford to do so properly; if you don't you can't. For cash-short businesses, the most important financial tool is the cash forecast, which of necessity will and should guide decision-making.
- **Price for value.** Create value and price accordingly. Identify where you add value, and price both for this value and to build an enduring enterprise.
- **Raise money when you can.** When money is available at an attractive cost and terms, take it. When you need it, it either won't be there, or you won't like the terms. Cash provides the means to take advantage of opportunities.
- **Learn to delegate.** Burke promoted from within until the jobs outgrew the people he started with (more than once); then he went outside to recruit. This meant that he had to learn to train and delegate. His rules of delegation:
  - Give responsibility to someone who can do it.
  - Give clear directions on what is expected and when.
  - Check in along the way to see how matters are progressing.
  - At the end, provide feedback (good and bad) and reward success. The feedback helps the individual grow from the process, as do the outcomes, good and bad, and the reward system.
- **Control appropriately.** If something matters, pay attention. If it matters a lot, pay a lot of attention.
- **Monitor to know reality quickly and accurately.** Burke demanded strong controls, regular reporting and monitoring of results. He emphasized accurate and detailed financial statements both for internal control and management purposes, and for satisfying external reporting requirements. He expected every aspect of the organization to have a top-notch budgeting and financial/operational monitoring capability.
- **Place people in jobs at which they can succeed.** If someone fails in their job, there are two potential culprits: the company, for placing them in a position in which they couldn't/didn't succeed, and the individual, for not performing.
- **Emphasize integrity.** The organization has a reputation for excellence and doing the right thing only one time. Once it is lost, it rarely can be recovered. "Do it right; do it quickly; do it well."

MARK KNUDSON
VENTURI GROUP

MINNEAPOLIS, MINN

Building three medical ventures with combined valuation of about $250 million

Summary: After getting his doctorate in physiology from Washington State University, Mark Knudson got a National Institute of Health post-doctoral fellowship and joined the faculty of the University of Washington, where he spent four years. This is when he realized that his patience with the pace of academic life was growing thin. Faculty meetings seemed to go on forever, including one to decide whether the department head should get the corner office. And Knudson realized that he wanted to do more interesting things than teach or conduct research, and to do it at a faster pace. So when he got an inquiry about a job with a division of Eli Lilly Company in St. Paul, he packed his bags and moved with his young family. Subsequently, when Eli Lilly moved this division to Indianapolis, Knudson decided to strike out on his own and started his first venture in medical devices called Sentech Medical Corporation. He subsequently sold this venture to Johnson & Johnson. To explore the other side of venture development, he joined a venture capital firm and saw many of the mistakes made by entrepreneurs. One of the major mistakes he saw was that entrepreneurs developed and fell in love with technology before knowing whether there were paying customers for them. Instead he decided to start with large attractive markets that were being served "barbarically," and then to find the best global solution with strong intellectual property (IP). Using this reverse venture-development process, Knudson started a venture incubator and has built three companies with cumulative market valuations in excess of $250 million. This is how he did it.

Before the Startup

1. Blissful academia—not. After receiving his doctorate in physiology, Knudson joined the faculty of the University of Washington and realized that life in academia can sometimes be slow. Faculty meetings discussing whether the head of the department should receive the corner office went on for hours, and he realized that he could become old if he did not get out soon. He also realized that while academic research was rewarding for some, he wanted to do more than research and teach. So when he received an inquiry about a job in physiology research with a division of Eli Lilly Company, he resigned from the university, packed up his bags and moved to St. Paul to head Lilly's division to start a clinical physiology-focused research organization.

Lesson: The seemingly leisured pace of academia may be fine for some but not for others. *What is your passion*?

The First Startup

2. **From corporation to venture**. Eli Lilly soon moved the division that Knudson had joined in St. Paul to Indianapolis, Ind. Rather than moving with his family to Indiana, Knudson decided to explore the option of starting his own venture in Minnesota. So he approached the person who had developed and sold him his home (who had become his friend), and they discussed the pros and cons of starting a venture together in the medical industry. Minnesota was a hotbed of new medical ventures at the time, so the time and place were right. The venture they wanted to start was to develop a product to do a number of tests with a single disposable test card. The customers would be the professionals at the "point of care," i.e., the physicians in emergency rooms and operating rooms who wanted quick results from multiple tests. They started the company as Sentech Medical on March 1983, and subsequently changed the name to Arden Medical Systems. He and his partner raised the money, and Knudson did the new-product research.

Lesson: All jobs have their pros and cons. A corporate job often comes with golden handcuffs and a requirement to move with corporate reorganizations. If you have identified a market need that you believe in, know how to serve customer needs better than the others and can get it financed, you may want to consider letting go of the golden handcuffs. However, be sure before you leave the corporate womb. Often you cannot, or do not want to, go back.

3. **Where can you find security?** When he was starting Sentech, Knudson asked one of his engineer friends whether he wanted to leave the big company he was working for and join him. The engineer talked to his wife and told Knudson that he had decided to stay with the company since he would qualify for retirement in three years. He was laid off in 18 months.

Lesson: *Security may not be where you think it is*. Great opportunities do not show up like a Swiss train on a schedule.

4. **Touch reality with the *Critical Experiment***. In Sentech, Knudson and his team had to build tiny electrodes to make the test product. They would test these electrodes individually in a beaker with blood substitutes rather than real blood. Instead, they should have built a prototype and tested it using the blood that they would use in working conditions, i.e., with real blood, and test them all together.

They did not do this. So they ended up doing all of their work and then repeating it again under real conditions. The net result was that it took them much longer to develop a commercially viable product, and cost them more because they did small "nibble" tests rather than developing a complete critical test to prove that the product worked under actual conditions.

Lesson: This episode led to perhaps the ***most important lesson in Knudson's growth*** as a venture developer that he has carried over to all of his subsequent ventures, and that is to ***devise the real world critical experiment for the entire prototype and to do it as soon as possible. Don't nibble at the edges.*** Entrepreneurs often nibble because they often don't want to know that their solution may not work, and postponement lessens the anxiety they feel. In reality, they only manage to postpone facing reality. The critical experiment should determine without any ambiguity whether the product will work under real working conditions, meet the unmet needs of the customer and confirm the existence of the market. At the end of the experiment, entrepreneurs should know whether the product works and solves the problem, and whether customers will buy. ***It is much better to manage your anxiety, and know reality, when you have money and credibility to try new alternatives.*** Do not delay the inevitable until you run out of money, cannot raise any more, complain that financiers are not sympathetic, and have to close the venture. So devise and implement the critical experiment as soon as possible to know if your product works in real situations – and offers value to customers to get them to switch.

5. Customer feedback for product development. As many successful product developers recommend, Knudson and his Sentech team talked to potential customers about their product and solicited their feedback on what should be included or not included. When customers made a suggestion, the team's reaction was, "yes, we can do that," without checking the cost and time needed to make the change, and ascertaining the impact on their business plan and finances, including cash reserves. They did not talk to investors to keep them informed about needed adjustments to the cash forecast. They thought they could implement these suggestions because they could make that one component work, without evaluating its impact on the entire system. This was one of the key reasons for Knudson and his team needing more cash than originally planned. If the public markets had not been favorable, allowing them to raise money from an initial public offering, their venture could have failed.

Lesson: Get feedback from a wide variety of potential customers to understand their needs and their requirements for buying. Then categorize the suggestions into broad categories based on time and cost, prioritize the top needs for the next product, and move others to future generations. Then check the impact of adopting these suggestions on your business plan, and re-challenge your initial assumptions to make sure that you have used your new learning to improve your plan. You don't have to develop the perfect solution. Bill Gates did not become the richest guy in the world by selling a perfect product.

6. **Sentech's structure.** Sentech was started with three other partners, two of whom were in the Eli Lilly group with Knudson. The three were responsible for research and development, finance, and product management. Knudson was the CEO of the venture, and the others reported to him. However, these four members were also on the board of directors, and Knudson reported to them as the board. This made for many awkward situations and a confusing organizational structure. Knudson resolved never to structure a circular arrangement again.

   Lesson: *It is not efficient or effective to have a circular (or 360-degree in current business speak) reporting arrangement where you report to the persons who report to you.* Be careful before placing your employees on your board of directors.

7. ***Barbarism Index*** **to determine whether customers will switch.** Before deciding to develop a new revolutionary product, determine whether customers will switch. If they don't, you may have a great product, but no customers and no revenues. To make this tough decision well, Knudson developed a "Barbarism Index" to determine the minimum requirements of early adopters. He examines the state of the art, i.e., what they are currently doing, how barbaric it is to the patient, and the time requirements and costs to the practitioner. The higher this level and the more barbaric the current practice, especially when compared with his own potential product, the more likely he thinks customers will be to switch to his new product. The second order costs and benefits he considers are the source of the money to pay for his product, and who benefits and who loses. He also does not consider developing a product that can cause losses to anyone who is responsible for the payment.

   Lesson: Have clear rules and decision-making structures to decide whether to move forward with a revolutionary new product. ***Customers do not switch from established practices for small benefits – they want major benefits before they give up long-established customs and habits.***

8. **Early adopters.** Any new business selling a revolutionary product can benefit immensely if it can identify its early adopters, i.e., the segment of the market that is likely to buy it immediately upon introduction because the benefits to them far outweigh the costs. These are customers who are willing to be the buying vanguard, and do not need others to buy and validate the product before venturing on their own to buy it. Knudson is a strong believer in identifying early adopters for his product. He did this by looking at medical specialties that are ***"traditionally aggressive because the practitioners don't have sufficient products to support their lifestyle."*** Professionals whose time is fully utilized and at attractive income levels are not as aggressive and interested in being early adopters – another way of saying that those with a full stomach are not very hungry. Knudson would check the starting salary for the various specialties and especially for new persons entering the field. He would talk to people in the field and read the literature. He would seek to identify those who are trying to establish themselves as up-and-comers. He would

talk to a representative sample to assess their personalities. He would then pick the hungriest ones to be the early adopters.

Lesson: Most ventures fail because they don't get the sales they expect when they want them, and at an affordable cost where they can make a profit. To succeed, be especially clear on the psychographics (what your customers think) and demographics (who they are) of the early adopters. By knowing this group, you can pinpoint your marketing and sales to this group, reduce your cost of getting customers, improve your revenues, and speed up your sales growth. Make sure you adjust your strategy for the next segment after you have penetrated the early-adopter segment.

9. Financing Sentech. This was the first time that Knudson had raised money. He and his partner used an attorney who had minimal experience in private-placement memorandums (PPM) and they ended up taking longer than expected. They were able to raise $250,000 in equity and $1 million in a Research & Development Limited Partnership (R&D LP). R&D LPs were in vogue at the time and were a strategy to take advantage of tax benefits to develop products. Subsequently, they folded the R&DLP into the parent company. The second round of financing was from local venture capital funds that invested $5 million. If the company achieved certain pre-defined milestones, they could demand that the VCs invest an additional $5 million. With the natural optimism of entrepreneurs, Knudson had underestimated the time and cost needed for development and so the venture did not qualify for this second piece of the second financing.

Lesson: R&D LPs were in vogue in the 1980s, but subsequently fell out of favor due to tax law changes and because investment bankers oversold the concept. It originally was an attractive concept that took advantage of the tax laws before they were changed. Know and consider all your financing alternatives. Most importantly, entrepreneurs are an optimistic bunch and usually find it very difficult to meet the demanding milestones of VCs. So obtain as much money as you can up front if the valuations are reasonable, and raise more than you think you need. Everything costs more than you expect in the early stages of venture development, and takes more time.

10. Sale to Johnson & Johnson. It took Knudson three years to develop the technology, test it and get it into the market. The company needed additional funds for expansion, but venture capital funding was expensive. However, the public markets were favorable, so Knudson and his team decided to take Arden Medical public. Unfortunately, the day they picked turned out to be the day of the 1986 market crash (in Septemberof 1986), so they were not able to raise as much money as they wanted. They had been discussing the option to sell Arden to Johnson & Johnson (J&J). Two months later in December of 1986, J&J offered a premium to the market price and bought the company. Knudson's understanding at the time of the sale was that he would be managing the operation. However, three months after the sale, J&J decided that the St. Paul facility would only be a manufacturing operation, and that other divisions would do the sales. A year later, sales had fallen by about 13 percent and J&J agreed to have Arden do its own sales. This meant that Knudson was doing two things he did not like – spending a lot of time on planes and working for a large company. He decided that ***big corporations and big universities have some big things in common – big bureaucracies, big politicians and big pontificators***. He quit.

Lesson: Do not agree to an earn-out (where you get paid more if the venture meets specific targets) when you sell your venture to a corporation unless you have the authority to manage the operation. That way, if the corporation interferes or changes the original strategy that worked, you can trigger your earn-out. If you do not have this authority, get all your money up front. Large corporations do well with venture acquisitions when they add money and resources but do not change key aspects. When they do make changes, it is often to make the venture fit into the structure of the larger corporation. Often these changes cause the venture to fail. So take cash if you don't have the authority. Fortunately, for Knudson, he did not have an earn-out clause. He had received cash for his stock.

The Second Venture

11. After the exit – venture capital. After exiting from J&J, Knudson joined a small seed-venture-capital company as a special limited partner. Knudson was well off from the sale to J&J so he did not have to work, but wanted to see what being a VC was like. He looked at many start-ups, but ultimately realized that this was not the path for him. He read thousands of business plans and realized that most new ventures were new technologies in search of a market. In a few cases, there may have been a market, but unfortunately the technology was not well aligned with it, and the cost to align the technology would be too high.

Lesson: Some of the lessons he learned from his brief stint in venture capital were:

- Small companies have to perfectly align the product to the market when designing the product. This means that ***the product's benefits have to vastly outweigh the costs of the switch for the market to shift to the new product***.
- There are too many boards to sit on and not enough time to serve them well. Remember this as an entrepreneur. If you get your money from a VC firm because you have been convinced by a senior partner that the firm will assist you, and then an inexperienced junior partner shows up to sit on your board, you have been had. If you are looking for the senior partner's experience, seek to put it in the contract. See if they agree.
- As a board member, Knudson saw many management mistakes. But as a board member, he could not demand change by himself. The board could

fire management, but that would be drastic and a step that is not taken lightly. Another trigger to get management to change its strategy was when the company needed cash. This is one of the reasons why VCs usually fund a venture in stages, so that management will hear them and adjust.

- Knudson also thought that small VC funds are more likely to fail. When the few successful ventures in their portfolio need more cash, the small, early-stage funds are likely to be diluted by later, larger funds. And smaller funds do not have the resources to assist troubled companies.
- Knudson believes that not enough is known about board governance of small companies. These boards often rely on hiring the "perfect" CEO, which leads VCs to the "white knight syndrome." When things are not going well, they try to find a new white knight, which is the aspect they can control. At every board meeting, the VCs are testing the CEO and the CFO against their perception of "the white knight."

12. Importance of timing. After his stint at the VC fund, Knudson started his second venture, a heart-stent company. Stents were hot at the time and the industry was a favorite with investors. Knudson was able to raise three rounds of financing. After he got his third round of institutional VC funding, he and the board decided to hire a president to start sales and marketing, before the venture had finished a thorough clinical proof-of-concept. The president did not know what he was supposed to sell because the product was still not proven or ready. The venture was sold to another stent manufacturer for a loss.

Lesson: As is true with many ventures that do not meet expectations, Knudson learned some valuable lessons from this one. ***He "married" a technology rather than a real need***. This was his first mistake. He also recruited a president who was great at sales and marketing, but not in technology or clinical trials before those key issues were off the table. This episode ***proved the need for the Critical Experiment*** and the importance of timing.

The Third Venture: Developing the Venturi Group

13. The first venture under the new model: Restore Medical. Simultaneously with developing the concept of the critical experiment, Knudson started talking with venture capitalists about the Venturi Group (VG). VG was to be an incubator that would design and develop ventures in serial. It would first identify an attractive and large ($1 billion+) market with strong unmet needs, find the best technology solution with strong intellectual property, license the best one that fit the need, and develop the product based on this technology. He was able to convince two venture capital funds to invest $6 million in the Venturi Group Search Incubator. The first new venture to be developed under this system was Restore Medical. To decide Restore's mission, Knudson examined a variety of market needs including plaque detection, pulmonary disease, and snoring. He used his criteria for ranking the markets, which included a high "barbarism index" (see earlier), the market size ($1 billion and up), and whether the physicians would use "technology-agnostic" products. This meant that the physicians would buy the product if the problem were solved, regardless of the technology that was used. Based on the above criteria, Knudson and his team selected snoring as the top-ranked problem to pursue. It was a huge market, and the "*barbarism index*" for the currently popular solution was high – it involves throat surgery to fix the problem. The key to solving this problem was to understand how air flows over the soft palate (back of the mouth) and to minimize the flutter it caused. Knudson and his team talked to experts around the world to find the best solutions with strong intellectual properties (patents). They found out that this was an aeronautical problem, and that large commercial jets had the same issue, Knudson found a doctoral student at Stanford University's aeronautical engineering department who had just finished his dissertation and had developed software programs to design damping pads to reduce flutter on airliner wings. He hired a recent Ph.D. from the department, raised an additional $14 million from venture capitalists, and developed the product after three years of development and trials. They focused on selling to "soft-pay" snoring centers, where the patients would foot the bill. The product worked on a large number of snoring patients with mild sleep apnea. Based on these successes, Restore Medical went public at a market valuation of $180 million. However, instead of focusing on this market, Restore tried to expand its market and get approval for reimbursement from health insurance for treating sleep apnea. But the insurers would not approve sleep apnea for reimbursement. This secondary focus drained funds from Restore, and the company thought that it would be better off under a corporate umbrella. So Knudson and his team sold Restore to Medtronic.

Lesson: There are a number of lessons here:

- ***Find the best technology to solve the problem***. If your solution is not the best, or cannot be defended, your odds of success are small. Knudson sought to find the best solution from global experts and research centers. He had resolved that he would not enter the market if he could not find the best technology and develop the best product.
- ***Focus***. As Knudson notes, after you have developed a product for a market, stay focused on the market. Don't fall in love with the product and waste your resources seeking to conquer the world before you have dominated the first market. Focus on the one best market.
- Raising venture capital is one of the most difficult tasks in business, since VCs are very selective. Knudson was able to raise VC funding because of his personal track record and network.

14. Ride the trends. After selling Restore to Medtronic, Knudson and his team searched for new medical problems to solve. They decided that a very attractive, expanding market was obesity, or gastro-intestinal (GI) therapy. In their surveys of medical experts, GI was the one problem that was mentioned as the new major trend. The market was huge and growing. Most of the research money in the United States was going toward obesity. He realized that this was a hot field. But drugs to treat GI issues were being pulled off the market due to their side effects and ineffectiveness. Knudson and his team thought that the market was wide open for devices because few drugs were expected to be introduced in the near future to solve the problem. Knudson thought that GI was the "last great frontier for medical devices."

> **Lesson**: Ride the trends. *It is far easier to grow when the market is growing and not adequately served, than trying to grow in a flat market or without a major competitive advantage.* Examine all types of competitors, including direct competitors, such as those selling the same types of products, and indirect competitors. Customers are likely to select the most advantageous product for them.

15. Finding a solution. To understand the problem, Knudson studied all the diseases related to GI, such as pancreatitis, irritable bowel syndrome, eating disorders, etc. People became obese when they ate too much and ate too often. His research determined that for decades, doctors treated ulcers by cutting the vagus nerve, which controls acid secretion in the stomach. When the nerve was cut, patients lost their appetite. However, after two months, people went back to eating because the body adjusted to this surgery. In his literature search, he found a paper that told him that he needed a technology that controlled the vagus nerve intermittently to offer a long-term benefit. So Knudson followed his five-step process to develop Enteromedics:

- ***Prove the clinical need. Make sure that the patients, physicians, and payers have a problem and that they will pay for it.*** Knudson likes to emphasize the Willie Sutton principle. When Sutton, a famous bank robber, was asked why he robbed banks, he replied, "That's where the money is." Knudson found that obesity is an attractive market because payers and people will pay for obesity treatment because it causes a variety of other health issues.
- *Understand all the issues related to the problem before attempting to design the product to minimize changes to your specs, your cost, and time.* This was one of the key principles that helped Knudson to meet his milestones. As Knudson puts it, understand the "therapeutic paradigm." By understanding all the issues, he was able to design a product that was able to control the nerve without any damage, and developed broad intellectual property (IP) protection to add value to the venture.
- Find the best technology. Knudson found a developer in Europe who had designed a similar circuit for a different need that could be used to control the vagus nerve. He contracted with the manufacturer to build the product from its technology base with Knudson's company's modified circuit and

software, saving 90 percent of the cost of having to design and manufacture from scratch. He found another company that made the electrodes, modified them to suit his needs, got intellectual property protection and incorporated it into his product.

- Develop the critical experiment to test the market and test the above three issues.
- Buy rather than make, especially when it does not compromise your IP. As Knudson puts it, ***"Never use your equity to make something if others can make it or have made it." Your money is far too expensive.***

Lesson: ***Find a market. Solve a need effectively and efficiently. Add value to the venture.*** Most entrepreneurs develop a product and then seek a market, but one may not exist. That is why most ventures fail. Knudson finds a market and then seeks a product. And his search for technology is global, and he does not pursue a product unless it can be the dominant solution. The initial market-research phase is often more time consuming, but at least you know a market exists when you are ready to sell the product.

16. Financing Enteromedics. Based on the growing need to treat obesity, and the limited competition from drugs (which are usually preferred over devices), Knudson was able to raise about $3 million from venture capitalists in the first round, $6 million in the second, $45 million in the third and $48 million from an IPO with a market valuation of $145 million. Knudson has found it easier to raise the next round of financing when he meets the milestones from the previous round. He and his team have finished the prototype, and have treated 30 patients at three different world-class treatment centers, with additional international trials at two centers. The product worked in tests and Knudson was able to design the product and conduct the critical experiment with cash in the bank. According to Knudson, some of the biggest mistakes entrepreneurs make when raising money, which can cause excessive dilution and "cram downs" are:

- Running out of money before meeting milestones, or reaching milestones with under six months of cash in the bank
- Seeking more than three – four rounds of venture capital funding
- Seeking a perfect product rather than a product that serves customer needs. As he puts it, ***"seeking perfection in product development is the enemy of entrepreneurial success."***

Lesson: It is easier to raise money when you have a track record (get team members who have one if you don't), when you are able to set reasonable milestones and achieve them, and when you are seeking additional funding with money in the bank. ***Desperation is not a great financing strategy.***

Rules for Entrepreneurs from Mark Knudson of Venturi Group

- **You have to succeed in two markets.** Never lose sight of the fact that you need to sell customers and financiers. In health care, you also have payers.
- **Focus, focus, focus.** Knudson's earlier business plans listed many options, which confused investors and affected their perceptions of him. He then focused on one market and product, and succeeded in raising money.
- **Understand financiers.** Know their criteria and how they think.
- **Be open to options about your vocation and don't be afraid to reach for it.** Uprooting his family to St. Paul was tough, but Knudson realized that he had to listen to his passion.
- **Get good teammates.** Surround yourself with people who are smarter than you on your team and your board, and then listen to them. Getting different perspectives before making decisions is key. ***You cannot know everything.***
- **Make the smart decision. *Being smart is a whole lot more than being intelligent.***
- **Manage your emotions.** Panic and arrogance are contagious.
- **Make venture capital investors think you are the white knight who will lead the company to glory.** Be a little more humble when you are managing.
- **Watch for dilution in (VC) rounds B and E.** A, C and D are not as bad as you think. (Note: A is the first round, B is the second, C is the third and so on).
- **Buy, not make.** If you can buy a product without risking your intellectual property, do so. Don't waste precious venture capital.
- Listen to the **NEED, NOT** to the **TECHNOLOGY.**

Bonnie Baskin
ViroMed & AppTec

MINNEAPOLIS, MINN

Building two microbiology businesses worth over $200 million by enjoying the journey

Summary: In her early years in Chicago, Bonnie Baskin was not sure of her direction. She was interested in science. When she read Rachel Carson's Silent Spring, she decided to become a marine biologist. So she attended the University of Miami where she joined the marine biology program. One boat ride, and seasickness, convinced her that marine biology was not her destiny. She chose to remain on land, and graduated with a degree in microbiology. During her summer vacations, she would work at her father's chemical company where she learned from her father the value of treating employees, customers and vendors with respect. After finishing her graduate degree, she worked as a post-doctoral researcher at the National Institutes of Health, and then came to Minnesota with her husband. She joined the University of Minnesota, but left after a year to start her own business called ViroMed. ViroMed would focus on testing human samples for viruses. Baskin built and sold this business 18 years later for $40 million. She then ran and built a spinoff from ViroMed, called AppTec, and 6 years later sold it for $163 million. This is how she did it.

Before the Startup

1. **The early years**. Baskin's dad owned a mid-sized chemical company in Chicago. When she came home for the summers during her college years, she worked for her father and interacted with his customers. Some of the customers were food companies like Kraft, and Baskin ended up gaining experience by working for some of them also. Her interests were not always focused on a clear goal, but she knew she liked to try new things even if they were risky. Her parents wanted her to be a teacher, but that was not what Baskin wanted. Someone suggested grad school, so Baskin went back to the University of Miami for her Masters' in microbiology and worked as a teaching assistant. After one year and some tests later, she transferred to the Ph.D. program and got her doctorate in 1975. Then she did a two-year post-

doctoral fellowship at the National Institutes of Health, got married, had two children and started looking for a job. Her husband, an ophthalmologist got a job in a practice in Minneapolis so they moved to Minnesota. Baskin also got a job at the UM medical school. But within a year, she found that the rules were stifling and the job "did not work out." She realized that she was not good at being managed, and control was the issue. So she started talking about starting a business with her family and friends in the summer of 1981. She had learned how to run a business from her father who had great empathy with his customers and connection with employees. Baskin knew that the FDA was planning on approving the first anti-viral drug for herpes simplex. The whole viral world was changing, and the industry was just emerging. New business opportunities were being created. The existence of viruses was well known but the treatment was still in its infancy. Viruses infect the body, get into human cells and then change the cells for their own growth. The industry was expected to create many opportunities, and Baskin decided to start her first business, ViroMed, to get into viral diagnostics. There was only one other company in the field that Baskin knew of, and she thought that the market would expand dramatically and create more opportunities for new ventures.

Lesson: As Baskin puts it, *"entrepreneurs can be unbearable" as employees* because they want to do their own thing. If you are one, find opportunities in your area of expertise. And if you are lucky enough to be at the leading edge of an emerging, dynamically growing industry, you may want to get in with both feet.

From Startup to Profits

2. **Starting the venture**. Baskin got the idea for the business during a walk with her father in the summer of 1981. Her father was a smart businessman and a good mentor. She had two ideas for her new business. One was to open a discount store for children's clothing. The other was to open a viral diagnostics company. Baskin understood the science of the field and the direction of the technology because she had been working in the area. She liked to be in the service side of the business *because it would let her get started immediately*, rather than spend time and money on product research. Based on her background, interest, and potential competitive advantage, Baskin decided to open a viral diagnostics lab. She estimated her needs for rent, salaries and equipment at $50,000 and borrowed the money from her father. She did not do a formal business plan, but estimated that the $50,000 would last for 9-12 months even if she had no revenues.

Lesson: Pick an area that you like, where you have expertise and an edge over others, and an area with strong potential growth. *If you find all three, you may want to get started.*

3. **Due diligence.** To verify whether her business concept made any sense, Baskin decided to talk to some pathologists who were her potential customers. She went to six pathologists who represented 80% of her market. And she asked them if they would work with her if she started a lab, and if so, how much business they could send her way. One of her potential customers, who was concerned about her success, said "don't do it because viruses are not that important." This customer admitted his poor forecast years later. The overall feedback was that the business could barely make it. Even with this disheartening news, Baskin decided to move forward and two of her co-workers from the University left their jobs and joined her. They were suffocating in their jobs, and thought that working for Baskin would be challenging. They also believed that Baskin would succeed and they could profit from equity in the firm that she promised them. She rented 800 SF of space in a Minneapolis suburb, bought equipment and started ViroMed in March 1982.

Lesson: Faith is essential. It is always wise to do your homework and contact potential customers to see if they are likely to buy from you. But if the industry is emerging, don't expect the answers to be very encouraging. Market research in emerging industries or for breakthrough technologies is usually wrong because the respondents don't know the benefits from the product or service being evaluated.

4. **The angle.** To generate sales, Baskin thought that she needed an "angle" so that customers would work with her. So she offered a special courier service for her Twin Cities customers to pick up samples for testing from the hospital. And since the virus often dies between the time of pickup at the hospital and delivery to the lab, Baskin equipped a van as a lab to keep the virus alive. Baskin herself became the first courier so that she could meet more customers, know their needs, offer great customer service, make sure the samples were handled with care, and to save money. This strategy succeeded and customers started working with her. However, she later found that she did not have to use the van as a lab because they found other means to keep the virus alive.

Lesson: Get close to your customers and know how to offer superior service to obtain a competitive advantage, and increase sales.

5. **Co-operate rather than compete, if you can and if both can benefit.** To do the diagnostic work with viruses, Baskin had to have living cells for the viruses to thrive. There were two companies on the East Coast that provided the cells. They provided fresh monkey kidney cells each week. This was very expensive because of the minimum purchase level that Baskin had to satisfy. For Baskin, the minimum order was way more than she would need and she would have to throw away a lot of cells, wasting money. So she found the manager at a hospital in St. Paul who was going to start an in-house lab at the hospital. Baskin called him and offered to sell him a part of her purchase of the monkey cells. He agreed to let Baskin buy the cells, process them and sell the final product to him. This cell product division grew to

include over 25 types of cells and became a multimillion dollar national business. So, the strategy evolved for ViroMed to be both a clinical testing laboratory for hospitals and also a supplier of the raw materials to similar and competing testing labs throughout the country.

> **Lesson**: Sometimes your competitors can become your customers if you know how both can benefit. Find their pain and solve it. In this case, Baskin used her pain-point to check with others, including potential customers, to see if they would co-operate.

6. **Pricing**. To determine her prices, Baskin first analyzed her costs, both direct and indirect, including depreciation and amortization. Then she did the "intuitive" thing and marked this cost 100% to arrive at her prices. From this level, she negotiated volume discounts.

> **Lesson**: Costs should only be one factor in determining prices. The key one, especially when you have no direct competitors against whom to benchmark, is value to your customers. It is difficult to determine value. Asking customers does not help because they will usually "low-ball" this number. Test various price levels with different customers in the same segment, and then select the best price that satisfies your goals.

7. **Selecting advisors**. Baskin did not have a board of directors. She was it. However, she did rely on her attorney and accountant for advice. They knew of things that she did not, especially in their fields of expertise. They were both referred by people she knew and trusted. She lasted with her first accountant for a while, but decided to move to a larger firm when her firm grew and her needs became more complex.

> **Lesson**: *Know your strengths and your weaknesses*. Baskin had learned about business by working for, and observing, her father. She learned everything she needed to know about viruses from her education. She completed her needs by working with professional advisors to prevent her from making mistakes.

8. **Picking samples and making sales calls**. In addition to managing the fledgling enterprise, Baskin was also the sales person. She started using various routines to get the courage to make sales calls. One was to see if she could make six calls before lunch. Although Baskin claims not to be a good sales person, she knew the technology and her services, and as the CEO was also the best spokesperson for the company. She also knew that she had a good service that offered real value. Lastly, she had no choice. She would not have taken a sales job, but being the sales person for her own company was different. As she stated, "if she did not sell, who would?" But, as noted earlier, Baskin did a very smart thing by becoming the company courier. Being the courier helped Baskin to build relationships with her customers, including the physicians, hospital administrators, and managers. But as the company started growing, Baskin no longer had the time to be the courier. She

had to lead the company's growth and ensure quality service. After 18 months, she moved to a larger 2000 SF space.

Lesson: Initially, as an entrepreneur, you may have to do a variety of jobs – actually anything that needs to be done. That is one reason why CEOs of new companies are also the "chief cook and bottle washer."

9. **Hire the right people**. As Baskin puts it, she was lucky and "got wonderful people" to work with her. Her recruiting job was made tougher at the time because larger companies had not yet started laying people off. Baskin found that people liked to work where they feel comfortable with the leaders and the potential for success. To leave the security and fringe benefits of jobs with larger, stronger companies, Baskin realized that the employees wanted to have confidence in the business and the leaders, to feel that the work would add meaning, to have the potential to create wealth for themselves (via equity), to feel that they are part of the team. Baskin offered stock to her employees via an employee stock ownership plan (ESOP) that she started in the first six months – even before the company had shown a profit. Her initial employees did very well following the sale of the company. She had 250 employees. All of them were part of the ESOP. 12 became millionaires (or close with net worth exceeding $800,000).

Lesson: *To recruit really good people to emerging ventures, offer them a path to the brass ring.* And treat them as you would want to be treated. Studies have shown that the initial employees of many successful entrepreneurs worked with them in a previous job. They had been a team, and so did not have to waste time and effort getting to know each other and each other's strengths and weaknesses. This means that they evaluate your skills and abilities as an entrepreneur and are likely to join if they perceive favorable odds on the business success, and the potential to become wealthy.

10. **Sales, value and pricing**. Early on, Baskin had decided that she was not going to sell her service as a mass-volume commodity. This meant that she had to learn how to truly offer value, and show the value to the client so that she could get higher prices and margins. And when it came time to hire additional sales people, Baskin had to make sure that she needed to hire those who could also point out the value to ViroMed's customers and sell on the basis of value rather than price. Her initial thought was that she was essential for sales due to her technical expertise, but she soon found that others, especially professional sales people, could do better. In sales, Baskin found that she did better with technically-savvy sales persons. She tested whether it was easier to teach sales to technical people or technology to sales people. She hired a V.P. of sales and found out that in high-end technical sales, it was better to hire sales professionals who had a technology background or who could understand technology easily.

Lesson: As you grow, make sure you hire those who are better at their specific job than you are. That is one of the ingredients to build a great team.

11. Right timing. The timing was right since it coincided with the spread of sexually transmitted diseases (STD). After six months, Baskin changed the company from a Sub S to a C corporation (Sub S can be initially helpful if you expect to lose money since the losses can be deducted from the personal tax returns of the shareholders). Baskin did not draw a salary from the company for one year. With the cash flow of the company, she could have done so, but she did not want to take a salary. Instead that money was used to reinvest in the growth of the company. Additionally she paid her dad back within a year.

Lesson: Good timing can be based on luck or knowledge. In this case, Baskin knew that the field of virology was emerging, and would create the demand for new services, and she took advantage of it before others. That would qualify as knowledge. The initial financing for your venture, especially when no institutional financier believes in you, can be extremely valuable. Be grateful, especially when it is offered without cost. Have a long term view of your company and reinvest the profits for growth. This can payoff in multiples of the base amount.

From Profits to the Moon

12. With a detour towards trouble. As ViroMed grew, Baskin looked for new opportunities and markets. The federal government put out a request for proposal (RFP) for HIV testing for the Navy and the Marines, and Baskin decided to "go for it." There were two major components to the proposal. One was to test samples from around the country on a large scale, which ViroMed could be scaled up to do. The other was to develop a computer program to interface the results of the tests with the other databases of the military. For the latter, Baskin decided to partner with an IT firm from Washington, DC. They got the contract, which was worth in the millions. However, they had to be ready to accept samples within 90 days. Given the tight time schedules, Baskin had started organizing the testing aspect even before she got the contract. The IT firm also sent screen shots of the program to show that they were making progress. But at the end of 90 days, there was no program – only screen shots. The Navy buyer had taken a risk in giving the contract to a small vendor, and Navy brass would call at all hours of the day or night to call and complain. Baskin came close to giving up on the contract and incurring any penalties. However, when she called the Navy officer, she got great advice –utilize whatever resources that are available, be creative and most importantly finish the project. Baskin and her staff found another company to complete the program and worked around the clock seven days a week to manually enter the data to complete the contract. Baskin worked with her staff to do the work and solve the problem. Her employees appreciated that she was personally willing to put in the effort.

Lesson: You don't build a great company without going through adversity. If it were simple, everyone would be great achievers and rich. So the first lesson is not to give up. Most importantly, don't think you are above the fray and just give orders. Get in there and work with your team when needed. Under adverse conditions, harness the power of working together to solve the problem. But if you have not hired good, hardworking people, built the right culture, and been fair to them, they are unlikely to put in the effort for you.

13. Growth of ViroMed and sale. The market kept growing and so did ViroMed. With overnight delivery becoming more common, customers could be anywhere in the U.S. Having been one of the pioneers in molecular diagnostics and genetic analysis, by the fall of 2000, ViroMed had grown to annual sales of $25 million and was highly profitable. Baskin also realized that creating and building the business was a "high" for her personally, but managing was not as interesting. When building, she could not wait for the weekend to end. However, when it grew and became more stable, daily operations became more predictable and boring. So she was constantly searching for new products or services. When she went to a store to buy items for her son who was going to college, she saw a line of anti-microbial mattresses and decided to develop a line of anti-viral, anti-microbial tests which she marketed to disinfectant companies. She got a grant from the Environmental Protection Agency and became the national expert in this area. Her expertise in clinical virus testing gave her a unique perspective to take a leadership position in anti-viral properties of household cleaning products. She also found that no one was testing medical devices (for microbiological safety) in Minnesota, which is one of the hubs of the medical device industry. They were being tested in California and Ohio. So Baskin started a division that did this in Minnesota and ultimately bought a company in Atlanta that was in the same field. The woman who owned the business did not want to continue the business side, such as working with the bank, but was interested in the technical side. It was a good fit. Baskin was interested in creating a complete testing company from devices to clinical to cover all types of industries at the high-end. Baskin also bought another business in Camden, NJ, which was a unique service focused on the medical, clinical and pharmaceutical industries. The business was financed by venture capitalists and it was not doing well, so Baskin bought it for "pennies on the dollar." Since the business had done poor testing in the past, it had some liabilities. Baskin bought the assets and not the stock, leaving the liabilities behind. By 2000, the high-end clinical testing portion of the business had reached maturity, while the industrial testing part was still emerging and growing. So Baskin decided to sell the clinical portion of ViroMed, and spun off the industrial testing into a new business called AppTec.

Lesson: If your core business is maturing, you may want to consider other growth opportunities in related areas where you can apply your core competence. And you may also want to capitalize on the business you have built and sell it (if that is your goal) when the market still values it highly.

14. The sale of ViroMed. Companies with good basic businesses with high margins in high-tech areas had good valuations in 2000. The CEOs of the large labs knew that they needed to enter the high-end area, which was ViroMed's niche. ViroMed had no proprietary technology and the large labs could enter and cut prices to drive sales. ViroMed was considered to be the national leader in the field and got a reputation as a high-quality, high-end, esoteric lab. The larger companies had not yet entered the high-end, low-volume "esoteric" niche and preferred the large market of the basic high-volume tests, and based their pricing on the number of patients per hospital rather than price per test. This meant that ViroMed would be a good business for one of these larger companies to buy. So she thought that this would be a good time to sell. She contacted an investment bank and put a package together. She did not want an auction for the company, but wanted to sell it at the right price to a strategic buyer. The company was sold in June of 2001 to one of the largest labs in the U.S. for $40 million.

Lesson: *There is a time to enter and a time to exit.* Baskin got out when she had built value and when she was ready to move on to new challenges.

15. The growth of AppTec. When Baskin sold ViroMed, AppTec, the spin-off of the industrial testing division had sales of $10 million, 130 employees and two buildings. After the sale, Baskin had agreed to manage ViroMed for one year. So the CFO of ViroMed took over the management of AppTec. At the end of the year, Baskin rejoined AppTec. Their goal was to have a larger impact on the medical industry, by being horizontally integrated with different kinds of products, and vertically integrated at the high-end of biologics (therapeutics). This means that the company needed to be at the leading edge of testing and manufacturing of high-end therapeutics and needed a new state-of-the-art facility. The company was using its existing facilities totally and had no room for expansion. In the summer of 2002, Baskin wrote the business plan and thought that she should "hire a CEO better than me." She showed the business plan to a few venture capitalists who told her that they would fund the venture if Baskin became the CEO due to her track record of success at building and selling ViroMed, and building AppTec. She raised $14 million, which was the largest biotech deal in Minnesota until that time. The company was breaking even. She cut expenses, laid off some employees, increased productivity and became more efficient and profitable.

Lesson: Venture capitalists like to fund entrepreneurs with a track record of success, or an attractive, proprietary technology in a high-growth, emerging industry. Before spending a lot of time seeking venture capital, study their criteria and talk to people who can make introductions.

16. New building and exit. Baskin did not expect to raise any more money, but ended up receiving a package of loans, grants and tax concessions to locate her 75,000 SF facility in Camden, NJ, across the river from Philadelphia. Baskin had not built a building of that size before, and it became difficult to coordinate the construction of the building half-way across the country. Everything cost more and took more time. They ran out of money. Baskin obtained a bridge investment of $4 million at the same terms as her earlier "A" round of investment and got an additional $6 million from B round investors. All salaries were cut. The valuation of the stock got cut, which is called a "down round" and is never pleasant. There were stipulations regarding revenues, valuations, and milestones (which means you give up more stock if you don't hit milestones). Then the building was finished and the company started to grow, fulfilling its promise. Revenue grew at a 40% annual rate, even during tough economic times. But costs were a problem and were increasing at a rapid rate. The company was just starting to show a profit. Baskin had signed on for two years, and she was ready to leave in 2006 when the contract ended. But the venture capitalists did not want to take a chance with a new CEO. The IPO market was terrible. So they decided to sell the company. However, they waited until the company started to meet its projections so that the credibility of the company and its valuation would increase. When the sales of the second quarter of 2007 was on target (for an annual rate of $70 million), they decided to sell. J.P. Morgan Chase had taken a Chinese company public in the U.S. and this company wanted an American footprint in biologics. They signed a letter of intent in September of 2007, and then went through "incredibly long due diligence" by the Chinese company, who hired 16 consultants. In November, Baskin told the bankers that she was "done." The bankers told the Chinese who asked "what's the problem? This is the way we do things." They closed the sales in January 2008 for $163 million.

> **Lesson**: When the time is right, sell. If you lose enthusiasm for the company, sell. If you get a good price and you don't want to run the company for a long time, sell.

Rules for Entrepreneurs from Bonnie Baskin of ViroMed & AppTec

- **Have impeccable timing.** This is the key lesson from Baskin's profile. She was not personally attached to the business. It was always a business, not her baby. It "defined a part of me but not all of me."
- **There is a learning curve.** Especially in manufacturing. Keep improving your productivity because others are.
- **Control may require short distances.** It is tough to control new endeavors at a distance. Hire experience.
- **Learn how VCs operate.** They have their modus operandi. If you don't like it, don't take their money. When you take VC, you "work for the man."

- **Know your business.** If you are a high-margin business, don't go for low-margin customers. Baskin tried to apply her high-margin service to grocery stores, which is a low-margin industry. She did not succeed.
- **It is a journey, not a grand vision.** Baskin enjoyed the journey and excelled at it. She built the company to great value one step at a time, i.e. "event after event after event."
- **Banks have no mercy.** When Baskin's company was in trouble, the bank cut her line of credit. Banks do not like to lend to companies in trouble.

Rod Burwell
Xerxes Group

MINNEAPOLIS, MINN

Building the largest manufacturer of underground gasoline tanks in the U.S.

Summary: Rod Burwell graduated from high school in Grafton, N.D., which is 40 miles from Grand Forks, where he went to college at the University of North Dakota. He had an aptitude for sales and wanted to be a sales engineer. So he earned a degree in industrial engineering and a second degree in business administration, while starting and managing a janitorial service. After a stint in the Army, where he tried and failed to incorporate efficient business practices, Burwell moved to Minneapolis and soon started a company, called Proform Inc., to manufacture his own patented product, which was a patented river-barge cover. He then started Xerxes Corporation to build underground gasoline tanks and other fiberglass equipment. When Burwell sold Xerxes, he used the Burwell Enterprises umbrella for his other companies. Over the years, Burwell has built a business empire with over $400 million in annual sales. This is how he did it.

Before the Startup

1. **The college years**. Burwell had an aptitude for sales and wanted to become a sales engineer. While attending the University of North Dakota (Grand Forks) for a degree in industrial engineering, he realized that he could also get a degree in business administration without investing much more time. So Burwell decided to get two degrees, one in industrial engineering and the second in business administration. To put himself through school, Burwell worked at many jobs. Since his dad was a partner in a janitorial company in Minneapolis, Burwell knew the industry, and he decided to start one in Grand Forks with a loan of $350 from the bank for equipment. Essentially, the bank was making a "character" loan. To drum up business, he canvassed the owners and managers of all the major office buildings in Grand Forks. Most had their own janitor, but Burwell convinced them to outsource the function. He was charging $5 per hour while the internal cost was $1 per hour. But by working smarter and not just harder, and using his industrial

engineering education, Burwell was able to do the job faster and save the company money. Around examination time, customers were a little more lenient with quality issues because they saw that Burwell was working hard, saving them money, and that his company would go back and redo the job at no extra cost if the customers were not satisfied. His profit grew to $900 per month and, when he graduated, Burwell sold the business to a statistics professor at the university for $2,000. In a few months, the professor lost two major customers and had to shut it down. Why did the new owner lose the business? He thought that since a student was managing it and making a profit, the business had to be a "no-brainer." What he did not realize is that Burwell was working and studying about 18 hours per day. Burwell wanted to make money and he worked hard to satisfy his customers. He knew the business from working with his dad.

> **Lesson**: *Balance brains with action. Brains are not enough. Hard work is also essential.* Actually, brains may be a hindrance in some instances if you analyze excessively instead of acting.

2. **Bringing business practices into the Army.** After graduating from college, Burwell joined the Army Corps of Engineers for seven years. Having managed his own business, he tried to run his platoon with the same sound management principles that he had used in his firm. They did not work. The Army had its own way. In his defense, he was 21 years old. He did not succeed. Either his sales skills were not persuasive enough, or the Army had other priorities. He learned that "in a football field, you play football and not baseball." He learned to play by the rules of the game. The Army was a bureaucracy with its chain of command, and everyone had to work within the system. He had to do things the "Army way, not the business way." He learned that, in the Army, if you thought outside the box, there was a second box outside the first one. This stint taught him how to fit into a large bureaucratic organization – and that his future was not going to be in such an organization.

> **Lesson**: Innovation needs a willing receptacle. Some organizations do not want to change, and it often takes great disasters for them to consider alternatives – notice the disasters of the auto industry. The key is to know whether you fit. If you don't fit, balance the benefits of the system, such as security, against the disadvantages, such as wasting your potential. You decide.

3. **The family business.** When Burwell left the Army and came home, he became a partner in his dad's janitorial business and started to expand the business rapidly. His dad got concerned about overextension, and whether Burwell could control the business and keep customers satisfied. He and his dad got into an argument about who was in charge. To restore family harmony, Burwell ended up selling his interest in the company back to his dad for $4,000. Now years later, Burwell has three sons who are 20, 17, and 15 years old. He does not know what they will do, but his expectation is that he will give them a certain amount of money and tell them to "do your thing." His brother works for his company, and his brother-in-

law is a partner in some of his businesses. Each is good for the position he has. The CEO of each company that Burwell owns can fire them at will.

Lesson: There is a right time and place for family in the business. Don't allow family members into your business just because they are family. It often creates more problems. Make them earn their position.

4. A real job. After his stints with the Army and with his dad's business, Burwell tried to find a job with a private company. He wanted a senior level job since he had managed 200 people in the Army and had entrepreneurial experience. Employers said no. The job that he did find that fit his interests was in a company that made structural fiberglass plastic panels for buildings. He was the general manager, and his analysis showed that the company was bidding jobs below cost. He asked the board to fire the CEO (who was a major shareholder in the company) to save the company. The board fired him instead. The company ended up going out of business.

Lesson: If you go along with decisions that you know are wrong, perhaps to take advantage of other benefits, you may pay elsewhere. If you speak up, you may lose the job. So there is a price. This is where your conscience comes in.

From Startup to Profits

5. The call from Cargill. Due to Burwell's connection with the fiberglass company, Cargill, the giant food company, asked him whether he could build a fiberglass cover for its river barges. The covers needed to be 30 feet wide and about 20 feet long. Cargill used the barges to haul fertilizer and salt to the north and grain to the south. Fiberglass was a lot more expensive than steel, but steel rusted and could spoil the grain. The tensile strength of fiberglass was the same as steel, but it was a lot more flexible. The problem was the size. No one had built a cover this big before. Actually, no one had built a fiberglass panel larger than 5 feet by 20 feet before. The covers also had to absorb a lot of abuse from barge operators. Burwell decided to meet this challenge and set up an operation to develop such a cover. With the help of a good molder, he came up with three designs. One design was flimsy, one was expensive, and the third was strong enough and within the price targets. The key to the design was that the cover used the structure of the barge for its strength. It was in the design of an arch and pushed against the barge, and it was affordable. Burwell patented the idea and offered the covers to Cargill for $18,000. Burwell had compared the value of his covers to that of the steel covers. Steel covers were selling for $13,000 and had a life of about 9-10 years. Burwell was confident that his fiberglass covers would have a longer life. Cargill decided to try the covers and ordered one set. Burwell was in business.

Lesson: Find a problem. Solve the problem. Develop a competitive advantage. *Get a contract to reduce the risk.*

6. **Financing the venture.** Burwell invested $4,000 and $15,000 in intangibles, including a 25 percent interest in an airplane. The CFO of the company where Burwell had worked invested $10,000, and Burwell's brother, family, and friends invested some additional money. Burwell did not own a majority 51 percent interest, but he was the only one who knew how to manage the operation and build the product, so his minority shareholder status did not matter to him. According to Burwell, not having much money helped because he could not hire a lot of workers and experts to develop the product. He had to experiment with many options before he hit the right design.

Lesson: *You can make not having money into an advantage, if you bootstrap wisely.* You can try to keep control in many ways, but good performance is often the best way to keep it.

7. **Getting started**. Burwell found a building in Minneapolis that fit his needs. In August 1969, he rented half of the building. The owner of the building, who repaired fiberglass boats, occupied the other half. Burwell had already built the prototype in his home garage. For the next few weeks, Burwell worked on setting up his manufacturing plant with the help of one assistant, solved all the problems that came up, and did all that needed to be done, including driving a semi-truck for the first time to take the finished product to the dock. The key to successfully developing the cover was that all the barges in the United States had the same, standard width (to be able to move through the locks). In Europe, there were no such standards, so getting started there would have been much more difficult. The product needed to be 19 feet, but he could not ship a 19-footwide cover down the road. So he built it in two pieces and bolted it at the dock. He had to have the product done by Thanksgiving, which gave him about 10 weeks, because that is when the last barge left the Twin Cities before the river froze. This meant he had to work about 16 hours a day for many straight days. When Burwell finished the first product, he took it to the river and found that the fit was not perfect. He adjusted it and made it fit. The barge went on its way.

Lesson: One of the luxuries of being a CEO of a large company is that you can order others around. *As an entrepreneur, you get to order yourself around.* Understand deadlines, and know that you may have to wear all the hats to save money and get the job done.

8. **The second sale**. After delivering the first product, there was no activity from any customers for about six months. Burwell kept trying to figure out how to sell the second set of covers, and had resolved that if he was not going to sell barge covers, he would make and sell something else. So he started making and selling fiberglass parts, molds, and patterns for snowmobile and boat companies. He was flexible in his business plan because his first rule was to pay his bills and stay in business. He checked with Cargill. The barge cover was working well, but it had only been in operation a few months. He did not take a salary, and the family

lived on the money from his wife's piano lessons. Yet, he lost $49,000 the first year. In the meantime, Burwell had been going to trade shows to promote his fiberglass barge cover. One day, six months after his first cover sale, he received a call from a barge owner in Ladysmith, Wis., who had seen the covers and wanted to buy some. Burwell had his second customer.

Lesson: Introducing a new product into a cynical market (and new markets are always cynical) can be daunting. That is why you need perseverance.

9. **Solving the cash flow problem**. Due to his initial cash-flow problems, Burwell was slow on his rent payments. When he started getting orders, he went to his landlord and explained the situation about the influx of orders but lack of working capital. He was trying to get some leniency from his landlord. He got more than leniency. He also got excellent advice. The landlord explained to him that when his customers came to order boats, they would have to pay a 50 percent deposit with the order, another 40 percent when it was finished and 10 percent upon delivery. He suggested that Burwell try the same. So Burwell called the customer back and asked for a 35 percent deposit with 55 percent to be paid upon completion and the balance upon delivery. The customer agreed and sent his check. Burwell had cash and he had orders. He dropped some of the ancillary fill-in work he was doing and started to fill this order.

Lesson: Cash flow is the biggest problem for most companies. Learn how others manage cash flow. Some smart entrepreneurs get the customers to pay them in advance. *If customers really finds your product unique and with high value, they may pay a portion in advance.*

10. **Lead by example.** After Burwell had started his business, which he ultimately named the Xerxes Group, he was aggressively seeking sales wherever he could find them. One of the orders he received was for a custom product that had an attractive profit margin, and more important, could offer Burwell cash to pay his bills. When he talked about it with some of his employees, one of them noted that it could take up to six weeks to make the right patterns and molds for the product. Burwell had only one week to do it. So he went on the floor himself, worked with two aides and worked 20-hour days. He finished the mold in two days. This experience formed one of Burwell's fundamental philosophies about his management team. He wanted managers who were leaders, i.e., who were not afraid to get into the arena and take up the challenge. He required all of his leaders, including the CFO, to work in the plant for two weeks. This not only helped them understand what the business did, but it also introduced them to those who did it. They understood both the employees and the business.

Lesson: You never know if you can do something until you try. And it's not enough to be a "manager." You need to lead, and usually this means that you need to show your team that you can do what you ask them to do. This helps them understand that they can also do whatever you ask them to do.

11. Financing growth. About six months after they ordered the first barge cover, Cargill called again. They needed 30 covers and they were calling before a major trade convention because they wanted to be sure to get the covers first. Their analysis was that other barge operators would see the benefits of the covers and order substantial numbers of them, which would mean that Cargill would not get its needs filled in a timely fashion. With his new policy of 35 percent down, Burwell had no cash problems satisfying the order. This is when the bank walked in and offered to lend him some money with a Small Business Administration (SBA) guarantee. Burwell did not need the money, but he borrowed $50,000 anyway. He never drew the loan down, but it was nice to know it was available. He then called his suppliers, told them that he had a bank line and asked them for a $350,000 line of credit and 60-day payment terms. Previously, they were reluctant to give him extended terms, but with his new line, they readily offered him longer credit. It took Burwell about 1-2 weeks to build a cover. So within two weeks, he got 90 percent of the selling price. He paid his vendors in 60 days, which made them happy. Burwell was able to grow the company without cash-flow problems, and never had to raise equity again. The company grew and grew.

Lesson: It is true. *Everyone wants to finance you when you don't need it.* What they are looking for is strength. No one wants to finance weak companies that could fail. Banks like to lend money when you are strong enough to pay it back – so if they think you really don't need them, they will want to work with you. And if you can avoid investors, you get to keep all your profits, and not be diluted or lose control of the business.

From Profits to the Moon

12. A second plant. The initial plant was in rented space and did not have room for expansion. To handle increased volumes, Burwell started looking for a permanent plant. His markets were in the heartland of the country, and the State of Kentucky and a local banker there made him an offer he could not refuse. They offered significant financial benefits and found an attractive lot in Paducah that was adjacent to the river. There was a huge gulley between the road and the lot that was conducive to a plant. The state filled the gulley and made a railroad crossing. There were numerous construction problems in the first year, and on many days the trucks could not get into or out of the plant. Finally, after a long delay, the road was in and he started Xerxes' operations in a 10,000 square-foot plant, with offices in a trailer. His plan was to hire 30 people. However, he got so many orders that he was forced to hire 350 people in a few weeks. His original plan was to hire only well-trained and highly productive employees. However, the increased demand forced him to recruit some who were not totally trained for their jobs. So he made sure that he had great managers who could train the new employees. The expansion went off smoothly.

Lesson: Efficiency, effectiveness, and productivity are key. To get these, you have to hire good people and pay them fair wages with incentives. Paying lower than market wages may get you warm bodies but not the best results. But note that just paying market wages does not guarantee productivity. You still have to organize the work and manage for productivity. For this, you need a qualified management team.

13. Growth and pricing. With the expanded capacity at the new plant, the company kept growing. Sales grew from $2 million in 1972 to over $55 million in 1980. He built plants in Louisville, Ky., and in South St. Paul, Minn. The Louisville plant was across the street from the largest barge builder, and customers could send their barges across the river for covers. This helped them become more efficient and save money. Burwell believed in pricing for value, not cost. How did he determine value? He would raise prices until the customers said no. Simultaneously, he wanted to keep his plants operating efficiently and to constantly reduce costs. His pre-tax operating margins were around 38 percent.

Lesson: Cost should be the floor. Value should be the ceiling. ***Price to value***. It is easier to charge more if you are adding value to your customers. If you are a "me-too" vendor, you will have low margins.

14. New competition. Having observed Burwell's growth, a major barge builder started making fiberglass barge covers with Owens-Corning, a Fortune 500 corporation as a major consultant. Burwell was confident they would fail. Why? Because they thought they were experts and did not have to consult anyone to understand the special issues Burwell had faced and overcome. According to Burwell, they were corporate bureaucrats who believed that they had all the answers. Burwell had solved the problem of developing the barge covers by knowing he did not have all the answers. He experimented with many types of materials and structures when developing the covers. He talked to all the barge operators, the CEOs and the maintenance people. He knew the decision-influencing factors of the buying executives and the operational problems of the barge operators. He had solved their problems. He did not assume that he knew what his potential customers were thinking. He asked them. He built in the solutions to all the problems in his cover. His competitors did not. They failed.

Lesson: Be humble. ***If you think you know it all, you will screw up. If you assume that all the world's brains are in your corporation, you will screw it up, but it may not be immediately apparent: In large corporations it takes time for the results to be evident***. Find the customers' problems. Solve the customers' problems, and don't make assumptions.

15. Real boom or tax-based boom. Burwell had tracked the growth of the barge industry, and found that, based on demand, the number of barges was expected to grow at an annual rate of about six percent. However, in the late 1970s and early 1980s, the federal government offered lots of tax incentives for investing, and this brought the investment banks and tax-shelter promoters into barge leasing. They bought barges more for the tax incentives than to satisfy any unmet demand. Production went way up to satisfy the tax-based demand for barges, but the operators' demand did not go grow. Burwell knew this could not last, and that the demand for barges was artificial. Since he expected sales to fall, he had two choices – sell or diversify. He sold the barge-cover operations, but kept the rest of the business.

> **Lesson**: Understand the real demand and business cycles. There are often temporary spurs that spark demand. If this demand is based on artificial incentives, such booms may not last. Expanding to satisfy pseudo-booms could be a disaster. Sell and/or diversify.

16. Diversification. Since Burwell expected sales in the barge industry to fall, he decided to diversify. He started building fiberglass covers for railroad cars and domes for sewer plants. He bought the fiberglass division of a large company. They made underground fiberglass tanks for gas stations, and the company had about $15 million in sales. He expanded into other types of fiberglass tanks and started building pollution-control equipment to sell to his current markets. He started making fiberglass covers for truck trailers. In short, he looked at all the different markets where his covers could be used, especially in the transportation industry, and expanded to those markets. He bought other businesses that used the raw materials where he had expertise, so he could add them to his current product line. What was his reward for all these mergers, acquisitions, and new product development? Annual sales fell from about $70 million to around $40 million while barge-cover sales fell off the precipice from $55 million in sales to under $2 million. However, Burwell was expecting the drop and had cut expenses. The barge cover business continued to make money at the $2 million rate. Burwell sold off the barge cover business in 1984 and got a reasonable price for it.

> **Lesson**: When you see a hurricane coming, take action. Others may be expanding to meet demand. If you know that it is artificial demand, you may want to seek other pastures. In a cyclical business, there are ups and downs. Develop early-warning signals and be prepared.

17. Acquiring volume to dominate on price. During the downturn in the barge-cover industry, Burwell sold his barge-cover business and concentrated on underground tanks. Due to new environmental regulations in the oil and gas industry, sales of underground tanks started to take off in the 1980s. Burwell knew he had no proprietary competitive advantage in the product, so he focused on reducing costs of materials and increasing productivity. To reduce his costs, he bought a business that made fiberglass panels. The benefit of this acquisition was that it increased the amount of fiberglass and resins that Burwell bought, and it helped him control his raw material costs. He was able to price more competitively, which gave him more volume, which, in turn, gave him better prices, and on and on.

He was in a virtuous cycle. The fiberglass-panel business only broke even. But that was acceptable to Burwell because it gave him the initial push to reduce his costs. Burwell's competition in this industry was a large corporation. Burwell's analysis was that the only way a big company can beat a small one is due to more resources. But larger companies are also less flexible and locked into existing methods of operations, and can't change as fast as a small company. As a small company, Burwell continuously improved his molding processes to offer better products, stayed close to his customers to offer better service and satisfy their specific needs, and to offer more value. His larger competitor never kept up. Burwell became the largest supplier of underground tanks in the country.

Lesson: Large companies talk about synergies, especially when making acquisitions. Some are real. Most are not. It you cannot document on paper how you will add value to any purchase, stay out.

18. Selling Xerxes – twice. In 1987, Burwell crashed a boat at 105 miles per hour and ended up in the hospital. So he decided to sell his business. His brother-in-law, an investment banker, put together the selling "book" and had an auction for the company. Burwell was offered a great price and sold. In the second year after the sale, the market was down and the company was not earning enough to pay the interest on the huge debt used in the acquisition. The buyers offered the business back to Burwell if he would assume the outstanding debt, along with a conditional earn-out payment of $2 million. Burwell did not want the business but had emotional ties to it, so he bought it back. In time, the market turned around and a Canadian company, which had enjoyed a huge growth in valuation due to exchange-rate fluctuations and Canadian stock-market conditions, came down and offered $42 million for the company. Burwell sold again. The company is still doing well.

Lesson: Buy low. Sell high. This is easier said than done. Be lucky.

19. Investing in new businesses. After selling Xerxes for the second time, Burwell invested in businesses that include environmental testing, John Deere dealerships, hotels, and a private aquarium company. Combined revenues of all of these companies exceed $400 million. When he bought the John Deere dealerships, the business's market share was below expectations. Burwell built up sales and the spare-parts business, along with service. He also diversified into new regions of the country so that he was not dependent on one geographic area and one crop. When he bought a convention hotel from bankruptcy, he noted that the location was near the state capitol. He knew that state governments never go out of business. The developer was running the hotel for the banks, and the banks were glad to get rid of the hotel to anyone who would repay their loan. When he bought the environmental-testing business, the industry was in a recession. Burwell bought it and invested to improve quality. When the economy improved, the business did very well. In all of these companies, he wanted to find good businesses that were in trouble, but had more value in hard assets than the purchase price. For each dollar he paid, he wanted $2 value in hard, tangible assets. Then he added experienced executives to run the business, developed a strong financial structure, delegated authority to them, and motivated them with high rewards for great performance.

Lesson: Know what's wrong with the business. Give lenders the confidence that you can solve the problems (you need to be credible). Fix the problems.

Rules for Entrepreneurs from Rod Burwell of Burwell Enterprises (& Xerxes Group)

- **Hire and promote good people**. Look for those who perform. One of his employees did not seem to have the qualifications to be a plant manager, but he always came in with better than expected results. Burwell promoted him. He made an excellent manager.
- **Delegate completely**. After he develops confidence in his managers, Burwell discusses the goals and strategy of the business, and then lets them do the job without second-guessing their strategies.
- **Build leaders**. Burwell advises managers when they seek feedback, but he advises them to use their capabilities and authority.
- **Overpay for great performance**. Burwell pays more for great managers who show great results. Overpay but get the best people.
- **Eliminate poor performers**. Burwell gives managers six months to a year to show performance. If they don't, he changes leadership.
- **Get good information regularly**. Burwell believes in getting up-to-date information on the status of each business. His CFO watches the performance of each company. They regularly compare the actual results to the plan, and they expect the operating managers to achieve the goals.
- **Build talent**. Help people grow. Offer education, expertise, and experience. Assist them in their weak areas and find complementary advisers as needed.
- **Share and compare performance**. Highlight the performance of each business so that the managers benchmark against each other. Compare the productivity of similar departments and publicize results. Let people see how all their peers are doing. Have top ones share their innovations and reward them for it. The poor ones often strive to do better.
- **Have an open book philosophy**. Share all company information with company employees. Burwell shares all data at least once a year with all employees.

They understand what they need to do for the company to make money. Not all understand the strategy immediately.

- **Develop a culture based on hard work, integrity and customer service.** Make employees proud of the company.

THE FINAL WORD

Contrary to popular entrepreneurial belief, this book shows that entrepreneurs **can** bootstrap to success. You don't have to raise venture capital and lose control of your one great idea, unless, of course, you don't want to pay the initial price. But bootstrapping may not be a sound strategy for you if money is the only competitive advantage, and you don't have it.

I wrote these profiles and lessons based on my discussions with the entrepreneurs, and on my experience in managing and financing ventures, and advising entrepreneurs. You may have noted that some of the entrepreneurial strategies and lessons conflict with each other. As an example, some raised venture capital, while others did not. The entrepreneurs did what they thought was right for their businesses. New-business development is not like science or engineering where you can repeat the experiment and get the same results. In business, you never stand in the same stream twice (since the water has moved on). In business, time moves on. Customers change, competitors adapt, and you have to keep on improving if you want to lead. There is risk in standing still, and there is risk in not standing still. That is why you have to know your current and potential customers' unmet needs, and satisfy them better than your competitors.

That is also why you need to develop good judgment. Although I believe that there are fewer ways to succeed than to fail, there is no one formula for success. You have to pick the strategy that is right for your times, your industry, your customers, your resources, and, most importantly, for you.

But even the best have setbacks and moments of doubt. The successful entrepreneurs profiled in this book did not quit. They worked harder and smarter to better serve their customers. So you, dear entrepreneur, are the main ingredient in your business.

I plan on adding to these profiles on my new web site (uEntrepreneurs.com), and incorporating these lessons in my next book for entrepreneurs and business developers.The book will help them evaluate new business opportunities, and design the right strategies - business, sales, marketing, operations, management and financial - to succeed. I hope these efforts help you reach your goals.

Dileep Rao, Ph.D.

Index to Lessons

INDEX BY WORD

A

D

E

F

G

H

I